Business Studies:

A CORE CURRICULUM

Business Studies:
A CORE CURRICULUM

IAN DORTON AND ALEX SMITH

Hodder & Stoughton

A MEMBER OF THE HODDER HEADLINE GROUP

ACKNOWLEDGEMENTS

The authors and publisher would like to thank the following organisations and people for the use of illustrations and information in this publication:

British Gas: Use of logo for Figure 10.16; Ford Motor Company Ltd: Use of logo for Figure 5.4; Interface Digital Library Limited: Figures 4.1 and 10.9; Life File Photo Library: Figures 5.3, 5.9 and 10.12; McDonald's Restaurants Ltd: Use of logo for Figure 5.4; PA News Photo Library: Figure 11.1; Sainsbury's PLC: Use of excerpts from their Annual Report, 1992 (p. 13, p. 14) and from their Annual Report, 1996 for Figure 5.1; Telegraph Colour Library: Figures 5.2 and 8.1; Thames Water PLC: Use of logo for Figure 10.16.

Every effort has been made to obtain permission with reference to copyright material. The publishers apologise if inadvertently any sources remain unacknowledged and will be glad to make the necessary arrangements at the earliest opportunity.

Orders: please contact Bookpoint Ltd, 39 Milton Park, Abingdon, Oxon OX14 4TD. Telephone: (44) 01235 400414, Fax: (44) 01235 400454. Lines are open from 9.00 - 6.00, Monday to Saturday, with a 24 hour message answering service. Email address: orders@bookpoint.co.uk

British Library Cataloguing in Publication Data

A catalogue record for this title is available from The British Library

ISBN 0 340 67401 6

First published 1998
Impression number   10   9   8   7   6   5   4   3
Year   2002   2001   2000   1999

Copyright © 1998 Ian Dorton and Alex Smith

Typeset by Wearset, Boldon, Tyne and Wear.
Printed in Great Britain for Hodder & Stoughton Educational, a division of Hodder Headline Plc, 338 Euston Road, London NW1 3BH by Redwood Books, Trowbridge, Wiltshire.

Table of Contents

UNIT 1

The Nature of Business

SUMMARY

1 Industry is often classified into primary, secondary and tertiary sectors.
2 The size of businesses may be measured in a number of different ways and there are a number of factors that affect the eventual size of a business.
3 Large businesses may experience internal and external economies of scale, although there may also be an element of diseconomy involved.
4 There are many stakeholders in business, both direct and indirect. These are shareholders, employees, customers, suppliers, financiers and the local community.
5 There are many different legal forms of business structure, such as sole traders, partnerships, cooperatives, franchises, limited companies [private and public], multinationals, public corporations and local government enterprises.
6 The business environment is constantly changing and the management of these changes is essential to the running of a successful business.

THE CLASSIFICATION OF BUSINESSES

Economic activity covers a whole range of processes and occupations and it is not surprising that attempts are made to place these activities and occupations into some form of classification. The most usual way is to split the productive part of the economy into three sectors:

The primary sector

This relates to extracting the natural resources, such as coal or oil, that are considered to be the gift of nature. The main components of this sector would be agriculture, fishing and the extractive industries, like mining and quarrying. Any firm that is involved in one of these activities is said to be a part of the primary sector.

Usually, as an economy becomes more developed, the relative importance of the primary sector tends to diminish and the other sectors become dominant. Indeed, it is the ability of the primary sector to produce excess food for the manufacturing workforce that enables an industrial revolution to take place. This is one of the reasons why less developed countries find it difficult to achieve manufacturing growth.

The secondary sector

This relates to the manufacture of products, i.e. tangible goods. It can be anything from toothbrushes to motor cars. Any firm that is involved in the production of tangible goods is said to be a part of the secondary, or manufacturing, sector. Developing economies would have a large secondary sector, which would be growing at a faster rate than the primary one. A developed country, such as the UK, would have gone beyond this and the fastest growing sector would be the tertiary one.

The tertiary sector

This relates to the provision of services, direct or commercial. Direct services are those that are provided directly to the consumer, such as a haircut or a visit to the theatre. Commercial services are provided as support for business, such as business insurance or the transportation of goods. Any firm that is involved in a service activity is said to be a part of the tertiary sector.

Developed countries, such as the UK, have the largest proportion of the workforce working in the tertiary sector and it is also the fastest growing. Manufacturing accounts for approximately 22 percent of output in the UK, whilst services are approximately 70 percent. Thus, the primary sector is only responsible for about eight percent of output.

Structural changes in the UK

In 1950, manufacturing output made up approximately 35 percent of total output in the UK. At the same time, the provision of services accounted for about 50 percent. As has already been said, this imbalance is now even more marked and there has been a noticeable de-industrialisation of the UK economy, not just in relative terms, but also in absolute terms. Very few manufacturing industries have grown since 1985 in absolute terms and those that have, have only grown marginally, such as food and drink, chemicals, and man-made fibres.

This change in the structure of production has, obviously, affected the pattern of employment in the UK. Almost 75 percent of the workforce is employed in the tertiary sector, whereas the secondary sector accounts for only around 20 percent. The remainder is employed in agriculture, forestry and fishing, energy and water, and construction.

■ THE SIZE OF BUSINESSES

There is no ideal size for a business. Small businesses need a relatively small amount of capital to start up operations; they often form a more friendly and intimate working unit; they are more easily adaptable and open to change and they tend to be more in tune with their market.

However, they may well lack the ability to raise finance easily; they do not have a great deal of opportunity for specialisation and the division of labour, and they cannot benefit from economies of scale.

All sizes of business unit exist in the economy and we need to consider means of measuring the size of businesses and the factors that affect their size.

Measuring the size of businesses

Before we can discuss the size of businesses, we need to be aware of the fact that business size can be measured in a number of different ways.

1 **Turnover**   This method usually measures the value of the total sales of a business over a period of one year. This is the method used when *The Times* calculates its 'Times 1000' list, which shows the 1,000 largest companies in the UK, based upon turnover.
2 **Profit before tax**   This is a method that leads to large changes in status from year to year, since businesses may have marked short-term fluctuations in profit before tax.
3 **Capital employed**   This is a

measurement of the total funds raised through equity and borrowing.

4 **Employees**   The number of employees directly employed by a business may be used as an indicator of size. This method is frequently used to define small firms, since information on turnover and capital employed is often difficult to discover.

5 **Stock market value**   If a business is quoted on the Stock Exchange, then its relative size might be measured by calculating the market value of its equity (shares).

Factors affecting the size of business

There are a number of factors that will affect the size of a business unit.

1 **The market in which the business is operating**   Some markets do not lend themselves naturally to large-scale production and thus do not have large scale business units. An example of this would be a shoe-repair shop or a specialist fishing tackle shop. Most firms will attempt to gain growth in order to benefit from economies of scale (see below), but this is not always possible. In the same way, small firms may exist in a large market, if they can fill a particular market niche. Often, larger firms in the market will allow the smaller firm to continue its operations, without interference, so long as it restricts its activities to its particular market niche. Large firms often tolerate small firms because the small firms will deal with jobs that are too small for the larger, possibly national, firm to be bothered with. An example of this might be found in the removal business. Large national removal firms will often over-quote on small jobs, so that they lose them and smaller firms can take them up. The large firm would not be able to operate efficiently with these small

jobs. They will not interfere with the small firms so long as the small firms do not attempt to move into the national, larger-scale, market.

2 **The finance available**   The expansion of businesses is often restricted by the finance available to fund the expansion. Small firms will often remain so simply because they cannot generate sufficient investment for growth.

3 **The objectives of the owners and employees**   The size of a business may well be set by the objectives and ambitions of the owners and management. In many cases, owners and managers take a business to a certain size and are then happy to exist at the level that they have achieved. This is a concept known as satisficing. The owners and managers are satisfied with what they have and would have to work much harder and, more to the point, take more risks in order to gain further growth. This concept of satisficing is now considered to be a serious factor in the determination of business size.

Economies of scale

One of the main attractions of large-scale business operation is the benefits to be gained from the economies that are enjoyed simply through the process of increasing in size. Economies of scale are any of the factors that might cause the unit costs of output for a business to decrease as the business gets larger. These economies are often split into two types, internal and external.

Internal economies of scale are those cost advantages that a business experiences as a direct result of its own growth. They have been identified by Professor E.A.G. Robinson as follows.

1 **Commercial economies**   Large businesses are able to buy and sell in bulk, thus gaining cost advantages. Distribution economies, such as a specialised

distribution system, and marketing economies, where advertising can be spread over a greater output, can also be gained. In addition to this, overheads may be spread over a greater output and more resources may be given over to market research and the development of new products.

2 **Financial economies** Large businesses are considered to be more financially secure and thus a better source for loanable funds. Banks and other financial institutions usually offer lower rates of interest to large businesses when borrowing is taking place. This is an obvious cost advantage for the larger businesses.

3 **Managerial economies** Large businesses are able to be split into a number of departments, where highly skilled workers and management can specialise in distinct areas, where their expertise can be fully utilised. Owners and employees in small businesses have to cope with a variety of tasks and, by definition, cannot achieve efficiency in any one.

4 **Technical economies** Large businesses use techniques and capital which smaller businesses cannot adopt. The larger capacity and efficiency of the capital can significantly reduce unit costs.

5 **Risk-bearing economies** Larger businesses may be able to diversify into a number of different activities and markets, thus reducing their dependence upon any one. They may be able to gain involvement in different areas of their original market, e.g. supplying raw materials and running retail outlets as well as producing. On the other hand, they might diversify into completely different markets, thus reducing their dependence upon the success of a single area.

External economies of scale are the advantages of scale that benefit the whole industry and not merely individual businesses. These might be as follows.

1 **Concentration economies** If an industry concentrates in one geographical area, a number of benefits might accrue. These could include the formation of a pool of skilled labour; the development of relevant local college courses to train labour; attracting suppliers of components and machinery, thus reducing delivery costs and, possibly, supply costs and improving services of maintenance and advice; the development of the infrastructure by the local authorities, keen to attract more industry to the area.

2 **Information economies** Large industries often set up information services that will then benefit all businesses within the industry.

Diseconomies of scale

It is argued that there are some factors that might cause unit costs to rise as the scale of a business increases. These might be as follows.

1 **Information diseconomies** Because of the size of large firms, information flows are often blocked or distorted and so decisions are either made wrongly, based upon the wrong information, or too slowly. Either way, there can be serious cost disadvantages involved.

2 **Human diseconomies** Large size in business can cause a loss of the sense of belonging for the workforce, and indeed the management, and this can lead to a lack of motivation and morale, with a subsequent cost disadvantage.

STAKEHOLDERS IN BUSINESS

A stakeholder is an individual person, or group, with a direct interest in the performance of a business or organisation. The main stakeholders are as follows.

Shareholders

These are the owners of the business who, since they own a share of the concern, are known as shareholders. They are unable to get their investment back from the business and, instead, if they wish to end their relationship with the concern, they must sell their share of the business to another person or group of people. For a public limited company, this transaction would normally take place through the Stock Exchange.

Ordinary shareholders have certain legal rights. Each of their shares carries a vote in the business and they can use their votes at the annual general meeting to, for example, elect directors or vote for the chairperson. Obviously, the size of a shareholder's holding will determine the influence that the shareholder can have upon the business. For most people, their shareholding is relatively very small and so they cannot influence the decision making of the business. Thus, if the shareholder is not happy with the dividend paid, or the activities of the firm, he or she would normally have to sell their shareholding.

Ordinary shareholders do, in effect, own the annual profits of the business, but it is up to the directors to decide how much of the profits will be paid out in dividends and how much will be used for other purposes.

It has been noticeable in the last few years that groups of shareholders in large firms have been demanding more influence, especially over environmental issues. In the light of this, it is hardly surprising that some large public limited companies are spending much more time arranging informal meetings and question and answer sessions for their ordinary shareholders in order to make them more confident of their standing within the business.

Employees

Employees have a vested interest in the business within which they work. At the simplest level, they should care about the success of the business, since their continued employment depends upon it. However, their involvement goes much deeper than this.

Employees will influence the quality of output, the levels of productivity, relations with customers and the public, and the views of management. In modern times, the role of the employee has become much more important. With the advent of modern production methods involving worker self-responsibility, the influence and effect of the employee has been magnified. The views of workers are considered to be much more important, both in terms of increasing the efficiency of the business and in terms of increasing worker participation and, thus, motivation.

Customers

Customers, obviously, have a direct interest in the performance of a business. They will wish the business to carry on so that they can continue to purchase the commodities that they like. They will also, however, have views on the way that the business is run and they have the ultimate sanction if they do not agree with it. They can cease to purchase the products. Consumer pressure groups are much more active these days and they can have great influence upon the efforts of businesses to improve their public image. Examples of this would be the work of animal rights activists to influence the research methods of cosmetic companies or the work of environmentalists to restrict demand for products that harm the atmosphere.

Suppliers

The suppliers of a business are those firms that provide the business with its raw materials and also any necessary services that it requires, such as insurance or catering. Obviously, suppliers are stakeholders in the performance of the business since, if the business fails, then the suppliers will lose a market. The importance of the efficiency of suppliers has been increased by the advent of such things as Just-in-Time production/stock control.

Financiers

Financiers have a vested interest in the performance of a business. Financiers are those people, groups of people, or institutions that invest in businesses in order to make a return on their investment. Obviously, the greater the success of a business, the greater should be the return to those who have provided the finance for the activities of the business.

The local community

The people in the area where a business is situated will have an interest in the activities and success of that business. For a start, the business may well provide employment, both direct and indirect. It may also generate positive externalities, such as an improved infrastructure, e.g. roads. However, there is also the danger of negative externalities, such as pollution, which would cause the local community to take particular interest in the activities of the business.

Many modern business theorists hold the belief that, although some groups of stakeholders do not have formal rights or authority, it is still very much in the long-term interest of a business to ensure that these stakeholders are as satisfied as possible.

THE VARYING LEGAL STRUCTURES OF BUSINESSES

There are many different legal forms of business structure. In many cases, the legal structure adopted by a firm is determined by its size and its life span. Small firms usually take the form of sole traders, partnerships, cooperatives or franchises.

Small firms have a number of advantages. They can satisfy specialist demand in small market segments, they can avoid diseconomies of scale, and they ensure that the entrepreneur keeps control of the enterprise. By definition, firms that are setting up as new concerns will almost always be small. We can look at the legal structure of small firms in more detail.

Sole traders

This is the simplest and most common form of business entity. An individual begins to trade, having set up the business using personal funds and/or through borrowing. The individual may work alone or employ a small number of workers. The business is easy to set up and there are no legal formalities that have to be completed before it begins to trade. However, the business does have to register for tax purposes and, if the business fails, then the sole trader is liable for all the debts of the firm. There is no limited liability.

There are a number of other advantages to this structure. Decision making tends to be fast, the owner has complete control of the business, and all profits belong to the owner. Against this, the capital available to the firm for expansion is limited and there is very little scope for specialisation and the division of labour.

Partnerships

These are a form of business where two or more people work together under the

Partnership Act (1890). Usually, the partners share liability for the debts of the business and so it is necessary for the partners to have a high level of trust in each other. Partnerships are most common in the professions, such as between doctors, lawyers and accountants.

Partnerships have a number of advantages over sole traders. They allow more capital to be raised for expansion and there is more scope for specialisation and the division of labour. However, the ability to raise large amounts of capital is still restricted, since an ordinary partnership has a legal limit of twenty partners.

There are a number of other advantages to this structure. Partners have more personal freedom and are able to cover for each other and to have holidays and breaks. As in sole traderships, partnerships do not have to publish their accounts or have them audited. Against this, decision making is a little slower and there is a dilution of control and a sharing of profits. There is a type of partnership, known as a **limited partnership**, where some of the partners have limited liability for the debts of the business. **Limited liability** is a legal protection where owners are only financially responsible for the debts of a business up to an amount equal to their investment in the concern. Thus, their private possessions are safe-guarded and investment is therefore encouraged because the level of risk is reduced. However, in a limited partnership, there must always be at least one of the partners who has **unlimited liability**. Partners with limited liability are often known as **sleeping partners**. These are partners who supply capital to the firm for a share of the profits, but who take no part in the running of the business.

Cooperatives

These exist where groups of people join together to run a business; working, decision making and sharing the rewards. There are a number of different forms of cooperative in existence.

Producers' cooperatives

This occurs where groups of people get together to produce goods or services. The cooperative might be an agricultural one, producing cereal crops, or a workers' cooperative, producing motor bikes or coal. Workers' cooperatives usually operate on the one member, one vote system and members receive equal pay. There has been a marked increase in the number of workers' cooperatives over the last ten years, perhaps as a reaction to the recession of the late 1980s and early 1990s.

Retail cooperatives

These exist where customers get together to buy in bulk, normally at wholesale prices, and thus to reduce prices to themselves and any other people who wish to participate. Members of retail cooperatives have to buy a £1 share in the cooperative and this entitles them to vote at meetings of the business.

Marketing cooperatives

These are more rare and tend to exist as a means of promoting the sale of agricultural goods for small-scale producers in developing nations. The cooperative buys produce and then carries out the whole marketing scheme by promoting, distributing, and selling the goods. This has been used to good effect to market hand-woven cloth from India. Producers were exploited by unscrupulous entrepreneurs and were unable to rectify the situation because they had no access to the market or business experience. The emergence of the marketing cooperatives meant that the producers could sell to them and gain a fair return for their efforts. These sort of cooperatives are often set up by charities or government bodies.

Franchises

This is where a business is started up under the name of a major organisation, such as Pizza Hut. There is a legal contract between the business and the franchising company. The contract places very strict conditions on the operations of the business. Normally, the business has to pay an initial lump sum fee and then an annual payment based on a percentage of turnover. The business has to set out the premises in a precisely stipulated manner and must buy all supplies from the franchising company. In return for this, the business gains a recognised trade name and reputation, which will guarantee immediate demand. There is also the fact that the franchising company uses part of its income to run the advertising campaign for the products, thus gaining economies of scale for the individual outlets.

Over time and in the right economic and business conditions, firms may grow. Large firms have a number of advantages, not the least of which are the ability to raise investment capital and the ability to exploit economies of scale. We can look at the legal structure of large firms in more detail.

Limited companies

A limited company is, quite simply, a company where the shareholders enjoy the protection of limited liability (see limited partnership, p. 7). The company is a legal entity in its own right and can enter into binding contracts, sue and be sued. Investors are encouraged to buy shares by the aspect of limited liability and so limited companies tend to find it easier to attract capital and thus achieve growth.

When setting up, a limited company has to present a Memorandum of Association and Articles of Association to the Registrar of Companies. The Memorandum describes the name, address, objectives and capital of the company. The objectives are kept as vague as possible in order to allow the company to follow as many directions as it wishes. The Articles describe share procedures, company meetings, accounting conventions, and the appointment, powers and responsibilities of company officers. Once the Memorandum and Articles have been approved, the company is given a Certificate of Incorporation and can begin to trade. There are two forms of limited company.

Private limited companies

These are usually medium-sized firms, although some may be quite small, run by families. They must be called 'Ltd' and have a share capital of less than £50,000. They are able to generate larger amounts of capital than the types of business looked at so far, but the owners also manage to retain a fair amount of control. They must have at least two shareholders, but they are not allowed to be quoted on the Stock Exchange. They tend to be firms that operate on a regional basis, such as the brewers Greene King, but a few private limited companies have grown to be very large indeed, such as Heron Ltd and the Virgin Group.

Public limited companies

These are usually medium- to large-sized firms. They must be called 'PLC' and have a share capital of over £50,000. They normally have a wide spread of shareholders and they are quoted on the Stock Exchange. The advantages of a PLC are that it is easier to raise capital, gain economies of scale, and employ specialisation and the division of labour. The disadvantages are set up costs, diseconomies of scale, having to issue public accounts and the danger of loss of control.

Multinationals

This is a business that has its headquarters in one country but carries out its operations, in terms of production and assembly, in a number of other countries. These businesses tend to be very large indeed and to operate on a truly global scale. Examples would be BP (UK), General Motors (USA), Royal Dutch Shell (Holland) and Mitsui (Japan). Multinationals have developed for a number of reasons. A major reason would be to circumvent foreign trade barriers. Thus, non-EU multinationals like General Motors might produce in Spain or Germany to avoid tariff barriers or quotas. Another reason is to take advantage of low-cost factors of production, especially labour, and it is for this reason that many multinationals have established production units in developing countries. It must be remembered that although the developing countries might gain in terms of employment and income, there is always the danger of exploitation of resources, excessive political influence, and the repatriation of all of the profits.

On top of these two major reasons, multinationals will also produce as they do in order to reduce transport costs of finished goods, to keep control over the quality of their products instead of licensing the production abroad, and to spread risk over a number of economies and thus markets.

Public corporations

This is the official title for a nationalised industry. It is a business that is owned by the State and produces goods or services for sale to both the public and private sectors. Examples of a public corporation would be the Bank of England or the Post Office. A number of industries were nationalised after the Second World War. The reasons for this were varied.

1 To control industries that were considered to have high strategic importance, such as steel or coal.
2 To control industries that were too dangerous to leave in the hands of the private sector, such as nuclear power.
3 To protect employment.
4 To ensure services to the whole country, even if some of them were unprofitable. In certain areas, private companies might not supply such things as a postal service or electricity, if a profit could not be made.
5 To ensure consistency and to avoid the duplication of services. It would be pointless to have three different railway lines between two cities, especially if they were different gauges and so incompatible.
6 To gain economies of scale by producing in one large concern.

The Thatcher Governments of the 1980s privatised a number of the nationalised industries, such as gas and coal. They claimed that the industries were inefficient and would improve their performance in a competitive environment.

Local government enterprises

In many local authorities, the councils run various forms of businesses, such as sports centres, car parks and theatres. These may be profit-making, thus contributing to the revenue of the councils, or loss-making and subsidised by the council in order to promote the activity.

The present trend is for councils to stop running their own organisations and to offer the services out to private firms for tender. It is argued that the private firms are more efficient and thus less costly to the councils. The councils simply have to monitor the performance of the firms to which they have contracted out.

THE MANAGEMENT OF CHANGE

The world of business is an ever changing environment and it is up to management to cope with any changes that might take place. There are a number of different aspects to this. Much depends upon whether the change can be foreseen, or not.

Foreseeable change

If changes can be anticipated, then management should be able to plan for the expected events and to implement procedures that will cope with the changes. Thus, in this case, business failure is likely to be the fault of management and an inability to plan effectively.

Unforeseeable change

Changes that cannot be predicted are obviously very problematic for businesses and it is those who cope the best with these sort of upheavals that will survive and prosper.

By definition, the **business environment** in the economy is usually beyond the control of individual businesses and so changes in the factors involved will mean that there is a need for a constant alertness and revision of policies and plans.

Factors that are usually beyond the control of the business are such things as:

- Population trends
- The financial climate
- Technological changes
- Social and cultural forces
- Legislation
- The existence of competition
- The availability of raw materials and labour
- Trade unions

Changes in any of the above can be calamitous for a business and, when one considers that they are all constantly changing, the task of business management can be seen for what it truly is, difficult! The management of change is an essential skill.

THE OUTRAGEOUS AMBITIONS OF MICROSOFT

Engineer of the electronic era: Bill Gates, chairman and cofounder of Microsoft

When Bill Gates and Paul Allen formed Microsoft in 1975, their slogan was: 'A personal computer on every desk and in every home.' At the time, it was an outrageously ambitious proposition, since the personal computer was little more than a toy for computer hobbyists. Today, however, that vision is rapidly approaching reality, with more than 45 million PCs sold worldwide this year alone. The vast majority of those PCs run Microsoft software programs such as the Windows operating system and applications like Word and Excel, the spreadsheet. This has made the company – based at Redmond, near Seattle in the north-west Pacific state of Washington – by far the largest software publisher in the world, with revenues of $4.65 billion in 1994. Microsoft's success has also made Gates the richest person in the US, with an estimated net worth of more than $9 billion (much of it tied up in Microsoft shares). These achievements alone make Gates a man whose every pronouncement is scrutinised by the computer industry and analysed by investors. But in 1994, he added further to his stature, with plans for products that will bring the Information Superhighway into every sphere of life. Microsoft's planned acquisition of the software manufacturer, Intuit, adds Quicken, the leading PC personal finance program, to the company's software portfolio. Gates recently unveiled plans to create the Microsoft Network, a global online service supplying information, bulletin boards, electronic mail and entertainment to PC users through cable and telephone lines.

Gates predicts that computer technologies will soon have an impact on every sphere of life – commerce, education, communication, medicine and entertainment. Within the next decade, Gates says, information highways will link most businesses to their customers and suppliers. Wallet or wristwatch PCs will be able electronically to transfer funds directly to shop cash registers, as well as store personal identification documents and even family photos. Doctors will have direct video links to emergency response teams. Teachers will have access to resources that enable

them to bring multimedia lessons to the classroom. Interactive television services will provide news and entertainment in the home tailored to the user's personal interests. 'We are investing way, way, way in advance to create the software platforms and tools for such services,' Gates says. Microsoft has 600 programmers dedicated to this effort and many more working indirectly on his long-term goals. 'It is a huge investment and it is based on our belief that these kind of electronic applications will catch on in a very big way before the end of the century. Our investment level is predicated on having millions of people hooked up to the broadband [high speed, multimedia] networks within the next three or four years.' The pace of computer technology change is accelerating, Gates warns. 'Every company is going to have to avoid business as usual. The only big companies that will succeed will be those that obsolete their own products before someone else does.'

In pursuit of his 'information highway' strategy, Gates is reaching beyond the computer industry to form partnerships with telephone companies such as BT and France Telecom, with cable television networks such as Tele-Communications of the US, and with publishers and Hollywood producers. A partnership with Visa, the credit card company, could allow secure online purchasing of goods and services. Making computers more user-friendly is essential to the proliferation of information highway services, Gates believes. Microsoft plans to create easy-to-use, fun 'social interfaces' for the intelligent electronic devices of the future.

QUESTIONS

1 As what type of business would you classify Microsoft? Explain your answer. [5]

2 a How has the size of Microsoft been measured? [3]

   b Would Microsoft be considered to be a smaller company if its size was measured by the number of employees? Explain your answer. [7]

3 Explain why you think that Microsoft has grown so quickly, since it was founded in 1975. [8]

4 a As Microsoft has grown, it has benefited from economies of scale. Using Microsoft as an example, explain economies that may have been experienced. [7]

   b Discuss the problems Microsoft might have experienced as the scale of its business has increased? [10]

5 How would the different stakeholders in Microsoft have benefited from the growth of the business? [7]

6 What advantages might accrue to Microsoft as a multinational company? [8]

7 Discuss the importance of 'management of change' to the success of Microsoft. [15]

Total [70]

Organisational Objectives

SUMMARY

1 Organisations begin the process of objective setting by working from an overall single objective called a mission statement.

2 Businesses can have a number of different objectives to work towards, including: profit maximisation, cost minimisation, survival and quality.

3 To achieve its overall objective, the organisation needs to work through the various stages in the hierarchy of objectives.

4 Each function within a business has its own objective. Managers need to manage these objectives to achieve an overall business mission. This involves resolving conflicts of objectives that might arise.

5 Within businesses the objectives of individual people have a crucial role in determining how successful the organisation is in achieving its own objectives.

6 Managers need to harness individual objectives, and resolve the conflicts that arise between individual objectives and the organisation's objectives.

Clearly-defined objectives are absolutely critical for the successful operation of any organisation. Objectives provide the people in organisations with the direction and purpose they need to direct their decision making. Without a framework of objectives businesses lose sight of what they are trying to achieve, reducing their effectiveness as a consequence. Clear objectives are also important as a target with which businesses can compare their actual performance with that set down in their objectives. For managers, the comparison of actual performance to that set out in their objectives is a key method of judging the organisation's success or failure.

THE MISSION STATEMENT

The mission statement set out by an organisation specifies the overall objective that guides a business's decision making. An organisation's mission statement is normally set out at the front of its annual report. Sainsbury's, for example, set out part of their mission as:

'to discharge the responsibility as leaders in our trade by acting with complete integrity, by carrying out our work to the highest standards, and by contributing to the public good and to the quality of life in the community.'

Sainsbury's Annual Report, 1992

The mission statement is intended by management to provide the focus for all the main and sub-objectives that Sainsbury's set out to be successful. However, mission statements, some people argue, tend to be rather vague, lacking the precision and practicality needed to provide a realistic objective. For example, Steve Jobs, the cofounder of Apple Mackintosh, believed the company's mission was to 'make a contribution to the world by making tools for the mind that advance humankind.' Such a broad objective is difficult to put to managers as a goal because it does not give them anything tangible to work towards.

It is argued that an effective mission statement should have a tangible target, combined with a set time period for achievement. For example, the Pepsi company's mission has long been simply to 'Beat Coke!', a goal it has yet to achieve but one that has given the organisation something tangible to aim at.

DIFFERENT ORGANISATIONAL OBJECTIVES

Business objectives can fall into a number of different categories which are based on the type of organisation that is being considered, and what part of a business is being looked at. The objectives set by a bank will differ considerably from those set by a major charity; as will the objectives set by the sales department of a business, compared to its production side.

Profit maximisation

Many people argue that the aim of most private sector businesses is to make as much profit as possible to reward the owners of the business for the risk they have taken in providing the funds for the organisation's operations. There is no doubt that this is a crucial, if somewhat simplistic objective for private sector firms. Indeed, part of Sainsbury's mission statement states that their aim is:

'to generate sufficient profit to finance continual improvement and growth of the

business whilst providing our shareholders with an excellent return on their investment.'

Sainsbury's Annual Report, 1992

When an organisation is making decisions about the amount it is going to produce, the number of staff it is going to hire, where it will buy its raw materials, and what price it is going to set for its final product, profit maximisation is an important guiding force. However, the time scale for profit maximisation can vary. In a single year a business might decide to use a penetration pricing strategy to establish its product in the market, in the hope that whilst the low price in the short run will reduce profits, it will yield higher profits in the long term once the product becomes established.

Growth

Organisations often pursue growth as their main objective. This can be measured by growth in:

- Sales
- Market share
- Asset value
- Stock market value

Growth is cited as important because it is a way of surviving. A business like the Virgin Group has grown by diversifying into a whole variety of different activities, from financial services to the production of soft drinks. Diversification spreads the risk of the organisation to protect it should one part of their market decline. Growth is also a way of increasing profits in the long term. As the business increases output, economies of scale develop, reducing unit costs and increasing profit margins.

Survival

The need to survive and keep trading is an instinctive objective that exists amongst all organisations. For large multinational corporations the chance of their collapse and extinction is minimal, but for small and medium-sized businesses the objective of survival is as important as all others. It is particularly critical when:

- A business is just starting up and it needs to establish itself in a market
- There is a period of expansion and cash flow becomes tight
- Trading becomes difficult in a particular market, such as the betting industry after the introduction of the National Lottery
- The economy is in recession
- An organisation might be under the threat of a take-over by another firm and needs to take action to prevent this

Cost minimisation

Whilst this might be considered as part of the objective of survival or profit maximisation, organisations, particularly as markets become more globally competitive, have set out to reduce their costs to the lowest possible level to make their businesses as competitive as possible. This has been the driving force behind the process of downsizing, where businesses reduce their level of activity to a lower demand level, stripping out superfluous parts of the organisation to leave a more efficient, competitive core business. The IBM corporation has made huge redundancies as it has tried to get back to its core business of manufacturing and selling computers.

Satisficing

This objective means trying to run the organisation to satisfy the needs of the business's owners and managers. It is often the case that sole traders, partnerships, and small private limited companies, are run to benefit the owners from the point of view of the satisfaction of running the business. A sole trader that runs a photography business might

have the primary aim of only taking work that is creative and interesting, as opposed to being profitable.

Quality

Maximising the quality of the product the business produces has become an increasingly important objective for many organisations who see the quality of what they do as being a key to the long-term success of their business. First introduced by Japanese businesses in the 1970s, quality is a customer-led objective, where the final product or service is of the highest quality possible. This principle should flow through each function of the organisation whether it be distribution, production or buying. Once quality is achieved in all these areas, the product will fulfil consumer expectations. The business is then more likely to win new customers and retain existing ones.

The key to achieving quality lies in the business's workforce, and its ability to deliver quality. A workforce that is going to deliver quality needs to be well motivated and in tune with the aim of satisfying the consumer. Companies such as the TSB, British Airways and Rover have all successfully adopted total quality management (TQM) as a way of delivering quality.

Image and social responsibility

In 1976 Anita Roddick started the Body Shop; a company that personified the objective of image and social responsibility. It specialised in retailing only natural cosmetic products that had not been tested on animals, and that came in refillable containers. The idea of social responsibility as part of an organisation's objectives has become increasingly important as consumers have become more environmentally aware. The reference in Sainsbury's objectives to 'the quality of life in the community' shows how aware companies are of this as an issue.

The growth of business ethics in recent years has heightened the awareness of ethical objectives amongst managers. There are a number of factors behind this:

- The rise of environmentalism has meant that business needs to be more reactive to consumer concerns on environmental issues
- Privatisation, and the decline of public enterprises, has left private businesses with the responsibility of protecting the wider interests of society
- Growing media coverage of business means that firms have to behave ethically or risk the glare of bad publicity

Achieving ethical objectives is seen as important, because organisations that are seen to behave ethically reap the rewards of higher profits as their support from staff, customers, suppliers and the community at large improves.

Public service

Organisations in the public sector have a different set of objectives from those in the private sector. Private sector businesses ultimately have to make a return on the capital provided by their owners, so this shapes the objectives which they set. In the public sector, however, the state owns the capital and is not driven by the need to make a return on it. Public sector organisations such as the Post Office have, traditionally, been more concerned with providing a service to the nation. This often conflicts with the objective of profit because a number of the services provided by public sector organisations are non-profit-making. Postal services operated to outlying country areas are extremely unprofitable, but are provided because of the Post Office's public service objective.

Many former public sector organisations or nationalised industries have been transferred to the private sector during the 1980s through the Conservative Government's privatisation programme. This has led to a conflict between profitability and public service, because the rules of privatisation have meant that privatised organisations like British Telecom and British Gas have had to provide unprofitable services, whilst still trying to make a return for their shareholders. The Government has ensured that unprofitable services are still provided by the privatised industries by using regulatory bodies, such as OFTEL that regulates the telecommunications industry.

■ THE HIERARCHY OF OBJECTIVES

The hierarchy of objectives represents the structure of objectives the organisation needs to achieve to reach its overall mission. Once the organisation is clear about its overall mission it needs to set firstly its long- and short-term goals, and secondly specific objectives for each part of the organisation. The business then needs to set out its policy or strategy on how it is going to achieve its objectives. Once the strategy is in place, managers need to set out the tactics they are going to use to carry it out. This process can be summarised as follows:

- Mission statement
- Long-term objectives
- Short-term objectives
- Departmental objectives
- Set strategy
- Set tactics

For the mission to be achieved successfully, each level of the hierarchy must be achieved. It is also crucial that the people within the organisation are clear on the objectives set, and that they apply the tactics and strategies set out by the organisation in order to achieve them.

Part of the mission statement for a major food retailer could be:

> *'to provide unrivalled value to our customers in the quality of the goods we sell, in the competitiveness of our prices and in the range of choice we offer.'*

In order to achieve this mission, the company has set the long-term objective of opening 80 new superstores in the next five years.

In the short term, it has set an objective of making sure that the waiting time at any checkout is not more than 12 minutes. This objective has been set for each store in the group.

To achieve the waiting time objective it is now company policy that if more than three people are at a queue on a checkout, a new checkout will be opened.

In terms of tactics, this means that all shop floor staff should try to make sure they are available to open new tills as they are required.

Conflict of objectives

One of the problems an organisation comes up against when setting out its hierarchy of objectives is conflicts that arise between objectives. In the case example above, there is an obvious conflict between management's responsibility to its shareholders in terms of profit, and its responsibility to customer service. Making sure that the maximum waiting time at a checkout is 12 minutes increases costs because more staff are needed at any one time to open the new checkouts. The higher costs reduce profit, although the quality of service is improved.

One of the major conflicts that arises when organisations set objectives is the conflict between risk and profit. Typically, the higher the profit a project yields the greater the risk associated with it. For example, if a company moves into a completely new market where there are few competitors, the risks tend to be high because the market is untried, but success will yield high returns because there is little competition.

A classic example of the conflict between risk and profit was the decision taken by Coca Cola in 1985 to launch New Coke to replace the original Coca Cola. During the 1960s and 70s Coca Cola had been cautious in its decision making, being reluctant to take risks by making changes to its core business. As a result of this Pepsi-Cola was able to make deep inroads into its US market share. The decision to launch New Coke was made after intensive market research involving 190,000 consumer opinions, using taste tests. However, the market's reaction did not match the research and within days it became apparent that consumers overwhelmingly preferred the original Coca Cola.

On reflection the company had misinterpreted the research which hypothetically backed the new product. In reality, consumers were too attached to the original taste to allow it to be replaced. Coca Cola reacted to the consumer protest by relaunching original Coca Cola as Coca Cola Classic. The relaunch quickly resulted in Coca Cola Classic regaining its position as market leader, while the new formula brought in extra sales of its own. Coca Cola's US market share expanded from 39 percent to 41 percent after years of decline.

The example clearly shows how the low-risk decision to remain with the original product without major change would have maintained profitability, although this may have declined in the long term as sales fell gradually. However, by taking a risk with a new taste, Coca Cola broke with its traditional strategy, risked profitability, but in the end was successful.

In many organisations the conflict between taking the conservative route and taking risks causes considerable conflict between managers.

CHANGING OBJECTIVES

Over time, both internal conditions within the organisation and the external business environment changes.

Internal changes

An organisation may alter its objectives because the management style, or corporate culture of the organisation changes. This alteration often takes place when a new chief executive is appointed to run the organisation. The new management style used by the leader sets a different agenda as far as objectives are concerned, which leads to a change in objectives.

In the early 1980s the German company Porsche appointed an extrovert German-born American called Peter Schutz as chief executive. His objectives differed from the original ones set by the company of producing quality cars with an exclusive image. He set about trying to compete with new competition for Porsche cars from Japan by producing the 924 which was considerably cheaper than its existing models. Initially, the car sold very well, particularly in the US market. However, the 1987 economic downturn, combined with a rise in the Deutschmark, led to a dramatic fall in sales of the 924. In addition to this, original Porsche drivers became disaffected with the new, cheaper models that made their own expensive models seem cheap. In 1989 Porsche replaced Mr Schutz with Mr Branitzki, their former finance director, who took Porsche back to its original objectives.

External changes

Changes to the external environment often force organisations to change both their long-term and short-term objectives. PEST analysis (political/legal, economic, social, technical) can be used to look at how the external factors can affect objectives.

Political/legal

Changes in the law often force organisations to reassess their objectives. For example, a relaxation in the laws governing finance in 1986 allowed banks and building societies to broaden their product portfolios. Banks could now offer mortgages to home buyers.

Social

Growing environmentalism amongst consumers in the 1980s has led many businesses to include environmental considerations as part of their objectives. Many companies in the chemical and pharmaceutical industries now have some reference to the environment as part of their objectives.

Economic

As the economy moves through the business cycle, organisations have to reappraise their objectives. In a recession, for example, a business's short-term objectives turn more towards survival. This may well mean setting specific objectives for a secure liquidity position. In a period of economic growth, objectives may well move in favour of growth in revenue, and increase in profit margins.

Technological

As technology advances, many organisations will alter their objectives to deal with the opportunities and threats that result from this. In the 1980s IBM had to completely reappraise its objectives as its core business of mainframe computers declined as new, high powered PCs were developed.

OBJECTIVES WITHIN THE ORGANISATION

Functional objectives

In order to achieve its overall mission, objectives set for each part of the organisation need to be achieved. Organisations are usually split into a number of functional areas, each of which has its own objective. Typically, most organisations are divided into the following functions:

Sales

The sales department has the objective of maximising the sale of what is produced by the organisation. The sales director will be responsible for setting strategies that will maximise sales.

Production

The production department will aim to produce units in the most efficient way possible. Production systems will be set up to ensure that resources used in the production of the product are utilised efficiently. The production department will also aim to ensure that the quality of production is as good as possible.

Buying

The buyers within a business need to ensure that inputs are acquired in the right quantity and quality to meet the objectives set by the production department. The buying department will also aim to gain the greatest value for money from the inputs purchased.

Finance

The finance department aims to provide the finance needed for the business to operate. It also aims to control all the financial aspects of the organisation. This involves reporting profits, asset values and cashflow. The finance department also sets up budgets for the organisation.

Marketing

The objective of the marketing department is to ensure that the product produced by the organisation is marketed effectively. This involves managing the marketing mix to ensure that the product is bought by its target group of consumers.

Human resources

The human resources department strives to set up systems that allow the organisation to get the best out of its workforce. These systems involve pay, working conditions, promotion and discipline.

Each functional area within the organisation is dependent on the others. For example, the level of sales achieved by the sales department determines how much the production department needs to produce. In the same way, the quality of inputs obtained by the buying department has a major impact on the quality of what is produced by the production department. It is vital that each function works in the same direction for the organisation to achieve its mission, but it is easy to see how conflicts arise from the pursuit of functional objectives. The sales department will be looking to achieve the highest sales possible, but this may mean extending credit to customers who do not have a particularly good credit record, and this conflicts with the finance department which seeks to manage the organisation's cashflow effectively.

The structure of the different functional areas within the organisation is very much dependent on the nature of the industry within which the business operates. In retailing, for example, there is no production department because the firm buys in finished products and sells them. In service-based organisations, like law firms, there are no production, sales, or buying departments. However, there are departments that specialise in different types of law.

Individual objectives

Within each of the different functional areas of an organisation there are individuals who have their own objectives associated with being part of the organisation. Ideally, the business wants the individual's objectives to be targeted in the same direction as the department within which they work, which in turn fits in with the organisation's overall mission. Thus, it is important that the organisation understands what individuals set as their own objectives, so that they can be harnessed to fit in with the whole organisation. A great deal of work has been carried out by human behaviour theorists to analyse how individuals set objectives.

Scientific management school

Perhaps the most simplistic notion relating to individual objectives within the organisation is that workers aim to achieve the highest financial return from their work. F.W. Taylor (1856–1915) founded the Scientific Management School which put forward the view that workers were really only motivated by money, and so any reward scheme set up by an organisation should reflect this. Many organisations have payment systems that are based on this objective: they offer commission, bonuses and incentive payments.

Human relations school

Elton Mayo (1880–1949) founded the Human Relations Movement which viewed individual working objectives in a different way. The Human Relations Movement found evidence that workers aimed for personal satisfaction from work. This came in the form of good group inter-relationships, staff morale and effective management. Mayo's work was based on research called the Hawthorne studies. This was a research project carried out over five years on a group of women that worked at the Hawthorne Plant of the Western Electric Company. It concluded that improvements in worker productivity were due to greater cohesion and communication between workers as they interacted and worked together.

Abraham Maslow (1908–70) summarised individual objectives in the hierarchy of needs. Individuals set out to achieve a higher and higher level within the hierarchy.

Physical needs
The objective of earning enough income to provide a basic level of subsistence such as eating and sleeping.

Security needs
This need falls into two areas: physical and psychological. Individuals can be threatened physically at work through the nature of their tasks, which could be working with dangerous machinery. They can also be threatened psychologically by, for example, a lack of job security.

Social needs
Within the working environment individuals need to feel accepted and to be part of a social group.

Esteem needs
Individuals need to have both the respect of others, and possess their own self respect. In the work place this could be derived from recognition for doing a good job.

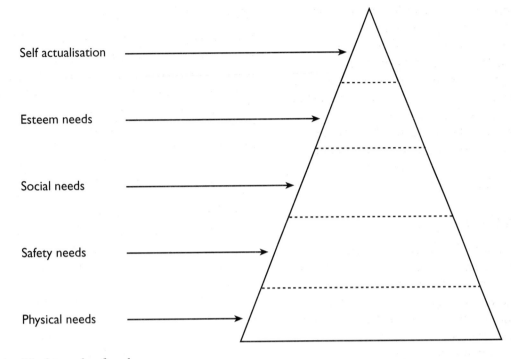

Fig 2.1 *The hierarchy of needs*

Self actualisation

This is the highest order need and is achieved when individuals fulfil their own potential through their actions and achievements. Individuals may achieve this through promotion or when they are given more responsibility.

Maslow argued that the lower order needs within the hierarchy must be achieved first before an individual can move onto higher levels. For example, an employee who is threatened with redundancy will not be concerned with promotion. Maslow believed that it was impossible for individuals to fulfil totally their needs, in that even individuals who had reached the point of self actualisation still strove to develop further and to achieve more.

Theory X and Theory Y

Douglas McGregor developed the work of the Scientific Management and Human Relations School in 1960 in 'The Human Side of Enterprise'. He looked at the work of the Scientific School under the heading of Theory X, where workers were considered to be motivated by money. In Theory Y worker needs were considered to be more complex and in line with the work of the Human Relations School.

The work of the Scientific Management and Human Relations School demonstrates the complexity of objectives set by individuals within the organisation. This complexity raises important issues for organisations in terms of the way that they manage and motivate workers. If organisations view individual objectives in a simplistic way, using money as a motivator, then as evidence shows, they risk not getting the best out of their workforce. If, however, organisations take on board a broader range of objectives set by their workforce, then they will have to develop ways of allowing workers to achieve these objectives.

In 1987 the Ford Motor Company introduced the EDAP: the employee development and assistance programme. This is a joint union and management initiative aimed at developing the Ford workforce. The scheme aims to improve the education of the Ford workforce by offering company-funded education courses. The courses available include computing, foreign languages, art, fitness and health. Employees are encouraged, but not forced, to take up the programme, and by 1994 over one third of Ford employees were involved in the scheme. By allowing their employees to develop their own personal objectives, Ford is developing a more educated workforce whose performance has improved in the workplace. Workers involved in the scheme developed teamwork and communication skills and they have become more responsive to specific job training as a learning culture develops. The EDAP scheme illustrates the company's awareness of individual objectives and how these need to be realised to raise the morale, and subsequent performance, of the workforce.

Conflict of objectives

Once the objectives of individuals within the organisation are considered, an inherent conflict often arises between the objectives of individual employees and the objectives of the organisation itself. An individual who strives for career development may well use a training scheme set up by the company to acquire skills that will allow him or her to leave the company and get a better paid job with another firm. A conflict often arises between groups of workers represented by trade unions who try to maximise their wages. Higher wages increase costs which forces down the profits of the business, or lowers employment.

Managers can often be more concerned in achieving the objectives they set for their part of the organisation at the expense of achieving the organisation's overall objective. For example, if a company produces a range of products, and one manager works so hard to put forward the case of a particular product that resources are drawn away from the other products, then one area of the organisation will do well, while the rest of the organisation suffers.

The challenge to management is to try to harness the drive individuals have to achieve their own objectives so that they fall in line with the overall objectives of the organisation. Many organisations choose to do this through profit-related pay, where the pay of employees is closely related to the financial success achieved by the organisation.

The John Lewis Partnership is one of the largest retailers in the UK with 23 department stores and 112 Waitrose supermarkets. John Lewis differs from other major high street retailers in that it is owned by its employees, who each have a share in the ownership of the business. In 1995 John Lewis had 34,000 partners. This means that the profits made by the business belong to the employees rather than shareholders. The founder of the firm, John Spendan Lewis, believed that the success of the business should be compatible with the objectives of its employees, who in a partnership have some democratic influence over the way the business runs.

The company generates profits from its trading which are first ploughed back into the business for investment in capital; whatever is left is paid to the partners in the form of an annual bonus. In 1995 £51 million was retained in the business and £43 million paid in bonuses.

John Lewis considers the sharing of information between managers and other partners as critical in the successful operation of the business. This is done through local journals called Chronicles, which are distributed in each of the organisation's branches. The in-house journal *The Gazette* is used to communicate the overall progress of the company to all its partners.

John Lewis has been a successful retailer since the 1920s, demonstrating the success over time of this type of organisation. By allowing all employees to have a say in the way the organisation is run, the objectives of the individual are more compatible with the overall aim of the organisation than is the case in traditional shareholder-owned businesses.

A COMFORTABLE FIT

Levi Strauss has prospered by combining an individualistic style of marketing with a gentle approach to management.

Imagine a model of modern American capitalism: a company, stuck in a declining domestic market that has sacked a third of its workforce over the past decade. In the mid-1980s it took itself private in a billion dollar buyout. Since then its after tax profits have soared to $250 million. This is no greedy LBO fund but Levi Strauss; a family firm characterised by philanthropic as well as profit-making goals.

The number of pairs of jeans bought by Americans over recent years has been declining, yet Levi's profits have risen rapidly – explained in part by the expansion of overseas sales, but also by the growth and development of its casual-clothes business: Dockers. The business is led by the great-great-grandnephew of Levi Strauss, Bob Haas. The Haas family owns 95 percent of Levi – as well as the Oakland Athletics basketball team.

The most striking feature of Haas's future plans is his attempt to build what he calls in his mission statement an 'empowered company', founded on a list of six long-term aims set out in 1987. These six qualities entitled ethical management, diversity, new behaviour, recognition, communications and empowerment, might not appear to be consistent with financial success. But Levi appears not only to believe in them, it also spends money on them. The end result is a company with a Japanese-style focus on the long term.

When Mr Haas took over the company in 1984, Levi had diversified unsuccessfully into a range of businesses including skiwear, men's suits and hats. In 1985, supported by $1.65 billion of bank debt, Mr Haas took the firm back into private ownership with the aim of consolidating the manufacture of denim goods. Highlighted for attention was the button-fly trouser: 501 jeans. Through a series of grainy, realist adverts, the sales of 501s more than doubled in America. In order to protect its brand image Levi also restricted distribution, avoiding the large mass-merchandising stores like K-Mart used by its rivals Lee and Wrangler.

At the time of the buyout some advisers reckoned that Levi should sell its then-unprofitable foreign denim business. Once again an effective advertising campaign renewed this declining business. Today over half Levi's profits come from abroad. In countries like France and Japan, Levi jeans are fashion statements sold for fashion prices.

▶ ▶

▶ ▶

The Levi Dockers range has enjoyed similar success. Built on the realisation that all young Americans need at least one pair of smart trousers to supplement the stacks of jeans found in their wardrobes, it has filled a market niche most impressively. But the brand has also succeeded due to the immense amount of money invested in advertising – much more than the public shareholders may have tolerated.

However, Mr Haas feels his greatest challenge is to implement his mission statement – to make Levi an even stronger company. He explains that historically Levi separated 'the hard stuff', which was 'getting pants out of the door' from 'the soft stuff', which was the company's paternalism towards its workers and charitable activities. He now wants to mix the two – to create a company that succeeds by looking to the long term and by handing more power to its employees. It is tempting to dismiss Levi's mission statement as psychobabble, but there are approximately 80 separate task-forces at work, each charged with softening divisions between managers and managed. Responsibility has been channelled downwards. The firm has introduced profit partnerships with production-line workers in which gains are shared. It is also encouraging workers to reorganise their own workplaces, reflecting Japanese practices. Levi has even started to give some production workers small computers to show how rapidly work-in-progress is being completed. Despite this being questioned initially by financial planners, the scheme appears to be paying

dividends by encouraging employees to become more involved in production control. Similarly, even when times were hard, the company justified keeping uneconomic plants because Levi incorporated into its calculations the likely cost of closure to the local community. As there are no obvious family members ready to succeed Mr Haas, he hopes to make every worker a part-owner and to thus ensure the firm keeps its character.

Mr Haas intends to ask his employees in the near future if the current mission statement needs altering. He admits that to include all his business beliefs is impossible, however, the fundamental aim at Levi to reduce the gap between what the company says and what its employees feel, remains paramount. As has been mentioned earlier, the management practices at Levi bear many similarities to that of a Japanese firm. However, critics are quick to point out that the company benefits from its existing reputation for paternalism. Unions elsewhere might be highly sceptical of offers to 'empower' them. Secondly, and of even greater importance, has been Levi's private ownership, thus limiting any predatory activities from corporate raiders intent on making a fast buck at the expense of advertising and philanthropy.

Mr Haas's ideas are not original and are frequently cited in the annual reports of other American companies. That Levi Strauss is such an exception is merely a reflection of Mr Haas's commitment to implementing his mission statement.

QUESTIONS

1 **a** Explain what you understand by the term 'mission statement'. [5]
 b Explain why a mission statement is important to the long-term direction of Levi. [5]
 c What difficulties are likely to arise as Levi attempts to apply its mission statement? [5]

2 Haas wants to fulfil his mission by handing more power to Levi's employees.
 a Using your own examples, outline how a business might do this. [7]
 b Discuss the advantages and disadvantages Levi might face as it hands over more power to its employees. [8]

3 Levi is a privately owned company.
 a What is the difference between a privately owned company and a publicly owned company? [6]
 b Who owns the majority of shares in Levi? [4]
 c Analyse the advantages and disadvantages of Levi being a privately, as opposed to publicly, owned company. [10]

Total [50]

THE FITNESS PLANT SETS STRATEGIC OBJECTIVES

The Fitness Plant is a privately owned fitness and leisure club located in the centre of a large city in the North of England. The business specialises in offering high quality sports facilities to people who work in the city centre. The Fitness Plant has a gym, fitted with state-of-the-art exercise machines, an aerobics studio, a 25 metre swimming pool, sauna and jacuzzi. Since it was opened three years ago the company has built on its membership, achieving a turnover of £1.5 million in 1997.

Andrew Elms, the business's Chief Executive, set up a planning group six months ago to produce a five year plan designed to make the club implement 'total quality management'. The group, made up of Andrew himself, two major shareholders, and another manager, have produced the following plan.

The mission of the Fitness Plant is to 'give its members the best environment possible to achieve their own personal fitness goals.'

From this the following strategic objectives have been set.

1 To keep the club's equipment as up-to-date as any fitness club in the country. This means replacing machines as soon as new, more advanced, machines become available, or replacing machines every two years as they wear out.

2 To train new and existing staff in all the latest fitness techniques. Every employee will have at least two weeks of training each year.

3 To keep the physical appearance of the buildings and its fittings in the best condition possible. This means: cleaning equipment and fittings twice a day,

replacing any damaged fittings and equipment immediately and instituting a rolling programme of refurbishment that refits each part of the building every two years.

4 All staff have to undergo a customer service training weekend, that institutes a complete set of guidelines on all aspects of working with the company and dealing with customers. Employees must follow these guidelines precisely.

The plan was presented to all the shareholders, along with the club's 30 employees. The document's proposals will be implemented with immediate effect. The proposals were met by a good deal of discussion amongst all the employees. Helen Aspen, the company's Finance Director, felt the proposals would add 20 percent to operating costs, reducing margins significantly, and/or leading to a rise in prices. The head of the swimming centre, David Elstob, was horrified that new rules would be imposed on his team of employees which would significantly reduce his freedom to manage. David had worked incredibly hard since the centre was opened to develop his side of the Fitness Plant. He had gained much publicity by inviting celebrities to use the pool, arranging charity events and competitions. Indeed, there was some resentment from other managers in the club that he was running his department in a separate direction to everyone else. The general feeling amongst all the employees was that they felt they had not been consulted on what was a major change to the way the Fitness Plant was going to be run.

QUESTIONS

1 Using the Fitness Plant as an example, explain what you understand by the hierarchy of objectives. [10]

2 Andrew Elms wants to apply 'total quality management' to the Fitness Plant.
   a What do you understand by 'total quality management'? [7]
   b Explain how 'total quality management' might affect profitability in both the short run and long run. [8]

3 The swimming centre, according to other managers at the club, has been working to achieve its own objectives. Discuss the advantages and disadvantages to the Fitness Plant of the swimming centre trying to achieve its own objectives. [8]

4 a What mistakes do you think Andrew Elms has made in trying to implement the development plan? [7]
   b Write a report for the directors of the Fitness Plant on how Andrew Elms' plan could be introduced more successfully. [20]

Total [60]

The Internal Organisation of Business

SUMMARY

1 Businesses may be structured in a number of ways in order for efficient management to take place. The best structure will depend upon the size and type of business concerned.

2 Organisation by function involves the departments being based upon the main functions in which the business is involved, such as production, marketing, financing and personnel.

3 Organisation by product, or product line, involves establishing a parent company and then devolving the responsibility for products, or product lines, to individual divisions that are run as separate units and are responsible to the parent company. Some functions, such as transport, might remain centrally run in order to benefit from economies of scale.

4 Organising by system or process involves the setting up of departments or divisions based upon distinct processes in the production system.

5 Businesses may also be organised on the basis of geography or customer type.

6 Matrix organisation might be employed to combine two or more methods of internal organisation.

7 An organisation chart can be used to show the formal structure of a business. The essential concepts involved are those of levels of hierarchy, span of control, and line and staff employees.

8 The informal structure of a business may be very different from the formal structure.

9 Businesses must consider the degree of centralisation, as opposed to decentralisation, that they will employ. Authority, delegation and responsibility/accountability must be considered.

10 The main activities of management were identified by Fayol as technical, commercial, financial, security, accounting and managerial activities.

11 Managerial activities include forecasting and planning, organising, command, coordination and control.

12 Employee participation can be a great motivator and also highly beneficial for the firm. Methods might include workers' cooperatives, worker-directors, joint consultation, works councils, quality circles and kaizen groups.

DIFFERING BUSINESS STRUCTURES

There are three main ways in which businesses may be structured. These are by function, product or system. The reasons for the eventual choice of structure will become obvious as each form of structure is examined. There are other possibilities, such as by geographical departmentation, customer departmentation or matrix organisation, and these must also be considered.

Internal organisation by function

Many businesses organise themselves along the lines of the functions that they carry out. Since most enterprises are in the business of producing a good or service that customers want and then selling it to them, the main functions tend to be production (of the good or service), marketing (in order to sell the good or service), financing (in order to fund the activities of the business) and staffing (in order to provide the personnel necessary to enable the business to operate).

Organisation by function is still the most common method of structuring a business and it is, in many ways, the most simple to organise since almost everyone has a basic understanding of the functions of a business. As with any method, there are advantages and disadvantages to this method of organisation.

The principal advantage is that organisation by function is, as stated above, a logical method which is understood by the majority and has been proven to be effective over time. However, there are other important advantages. It allows departmental specialisation, which enables members of departments to gain expertise in their respective areas and thus the organisation benefits from the efficiency of the utilisation of its workforce. It also avoids the duplication of effort. As long as the activities of each department are clearly detailed, then each department will deal with its own allocated functions and there should be little overlap and, thus, little repetition of effort. On top of this, training will be simplified and more specific, since it will be carried out by departmental specialists, and the ability to associate themselves with an obvious departmental area should generate strong group feeling and all the Mayo-esque advantages that go with it.

There are, however, disadvantages that may be associated with this method of organisation. Specialisation may lead to an over-developed sense of group feeling and an inability for the members of the department to understand the aims of the organisation as a whole, preferring instead to follow short-term and possibly incestuous internal objectives. This may also lead to conflicts between departments as each department follows its own direction, oblivious to, or uncaring about, the aims of other departments or the business as a whole.

Internal organisation by product

This form of organisation tends to be employed by larger businesses who have a range of products or product lines. In this situation, it is often difficult to organise by function because the business is simply too big and diverse for individual functional managers, such as the production manager, to cope. It is then that businesses tend to reorganise based upon a product line system.

This method enables the senior management executives, such as the managing director and the board of directors, to delegate responsibility for each of the products or product lines to an executive who will take responsibility for all of the functions in respect of that product or product line. Usually, the product group will be set

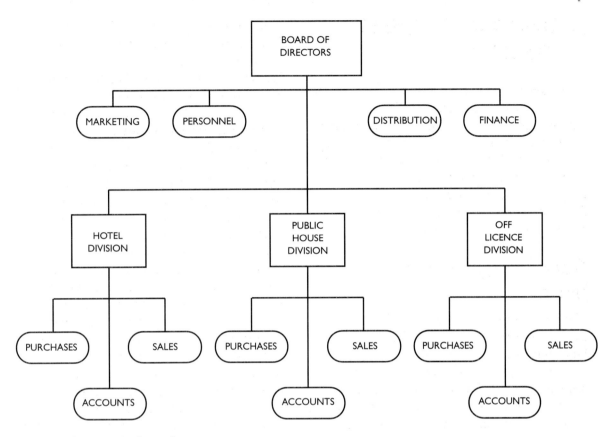

Fig 3.1   *Organisation by product*

financial targets and the executive in charge will be answerable to the main board of the 'parent company'. An example of this might be a leisure group that operates in the hotel and licensed trades industry, running an assortment of retail outlets. One product area may be hotels, another may be public houses and the third may be off-licences. Each of these might become a division of the overall business, with its own chief executive and clearly defined workforce.

The advantages of this are numerous. It enables divisions to employ specialised capital, facilities, market knowledge and skills in order to operate more efficiently. It is especially important that the divisions will have in-depth knowledge of their specific market and will thus be able to formulate an effective marketing strategy, specifically geared to their market segment. It encourages the growth of new products within product lines as each division seeks to expand its operations and it allows greater use of specialisation. It also enables the profitability and performance of each product line to be more easily assessed. It may produce 'healthy' competition between divisions and divisions may be able to share certain services, such as a central research and development section or a group transport section, in order to benefit from economies of scale.

There are possible disadvantages in this method of organisation. It may be difficult for the parent company to maintain sufficient control over the different divisions and those in charge of the divisions may begin to resent what they see as interference in the running of the division. There may be the duplication of activities, within each division, that were previously carried out by a single department before the organisation by product. This may lead to a cost disadvantage. As with functional organisation, there may be the development of a divisional ethos that ignores the ethos of the business as a whole and leads to conflict between divisions and between one division and the management of the parent company.

Internal organisation by system

Manufacturing firms often base their internal organisation upon the processes or systems involved in the production of the commodity. Departments are then set up based upon each process. This is only appropriate where there are obvious stages of production and each stage flows on naturally to the next. It may be applied to service industries, but examples do not occur too frequently.

The advantages are that there is scope for increased specialisation and it is much more simple to pin point problem areas in the production process. Training is simplified and it is thus easier to introduce new methods and technology.

Disadvantages also exist. It is still necessary to organise non-productive departments, such as finance, on some sort of alternative basis and so the coordination of departments becomes difficult. The increased specialisation might lead to monotonous or repetitive jobs and a subsequent loss of motivation. Problems in any one process area, such as a work stoppage, will cause problems in related areas.

Internal organisation by other means

There are a number of other possible ways to organise the structure of a business.

Geographical or territorial departmentation

This is common in businesses whose activities range over a wide geographical area. It is similar to organisation by product or product line and has very similar advantages and disadvantages. It can, however, have large advantages in situations where transport costs are very high because of central production and where the markets are very diverse and so specialist marketing knowledge is of great use. Transport costs may be greatly reduced by regionalised production and delivery times might also be shortened. Specialist knowledge of regional or national markets may enable marketing to be much more specific to each region and therefore increase its effectiveness. There is the disadvantage of the possible duplication of services and also the fact that, because of the wide geographical spread, the parent company may find it difficult to exercise overall control effectively.

Customer departmentation

This tends to relate to businesses that provide services, although this is not always the case. The business is organised in divisions that service, or produce for, different groups of customers. In many cases, organisations may be run on a different system and then have certain divisions that operate on a customer basis. For example, a firm producing building materials might be organised on a functional basis, but may then split its sales department into divisions relating to industrial sales, wholesale sales and commercial sales. The advantage of this is that the needs of each group of customers will be more clearly understood and customers will feel that their needs are being specifically dealt with. There are, however, problems of coordination between these divisions and others that might be organised on a different basis.

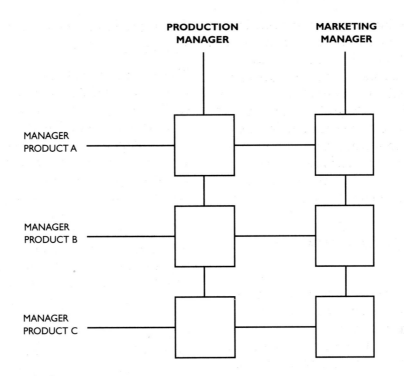

Fig 3.2 *Matrix organisation*

Matrix organisation

As has already been said, many organisations will combine two or more methods of internal organisation. Most often, this will be the combining of function and product line systems, but it might be a combination of any of the previously mentioned systems. Under a matrix system, each individual will be in two or more distinct organisation groups. This has the advantage of making the system more flexible and of enabling individuals to be influenced by more than one group aim. However, there is always the danger of individuals becoming confused as to where their loyalties and priorities lie. An example of matrix organisation is shown above.

Thus an employee involved in the marketing of Product B would be answerable to both the manager of Product B and to the marketing manager.

■ THE FORMAL AND INFORMAL STRUCTURE OF BUSINESSES

Organisation charts – the formal structure

Formal business structures can be shown by means of an organisation chart. This is a chart that shows the structure of the business in terms of how individuals or departments are linked together, using the principal lines of authority. It normally displays the answerability of individuals. There are clear advantages to be gained by expressing the structure of a business through the medium of an organisation chart. First, employees have a clear idea of where they fit into the organisation, who is responsible to them and who they are responsible to. It is especially useful for new employees. Second, simply compiling an organisation chart can often show up inconsistencies or bottle necks that might need attention. Disadvantages may also exist. An organisation chart cannot show how much authority exists at each stage of the business, nor can it show the existence of informal relationships that might cut across the formal structure. A simple organisation chart is shown below.

There are some essential concepts that relate to organisation charts.

Levels of hierarchy

These are the number of different levels of authority that exist within a business. The total levels of hierarchy would be represented by the number of rows in an organisation chart. Thus, in the example below, there would be four levels of hierarchy.

Span of control

This is a measurement of the number of people who are directly responsible to a given individual in a business. For example, a production manager may have three foremen, a stock controller, the person in charge of packing and the person in charge of despatch answerable to him or her. In this situation, the manager would be said to have a span of control of six. There is not a perfect span of control. One cannot say that the ideal situation is where a person has exactly five people answerable. There are four important factors that should determine the span of control of an individual in any given situation. First, the calibre and ability of the person involved should be considered. Some people are capable of managing people more easily than others and may thus be able to deal with responsibility for larger numbers.

Second, the quality of the people being controlled should be considered. Some subordinates will be intelligent, able, trustworthy and motivated, high ranking in Maslow's hierarchy of needs. In this situation, a manager might find that they are very easy to control and so the span of control could be reasonably large to reflect the ease of handling. On the other hand, the subordinates might be more representative of McGregor's Theory X or the ideas of F.W. Taylor. They

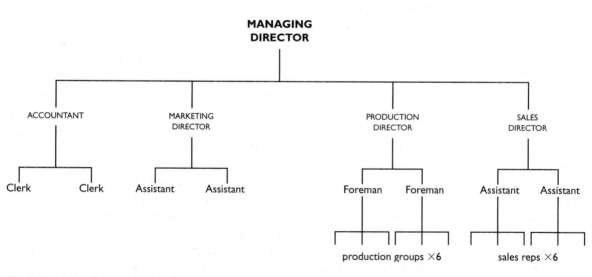

Fig 3.3   *A simple organisation chart*

might be less able, lazy and demotivated. In this situation, it might be fair to assume that they would be difficult to control and so the width of the span of control should be fairly narrow.

Third, the actual task being undertaken should have a bearing upon the width of the span of control. If the task is a simple one, well within the capabilities of the subordinates, then it is fair to assume that a wide span of control could be utilised. Alternatively, if the task is of great importance to the firm and difficult to carry out, then it is likely that close control will be necessary and so the span of control employed would be fairly narrow in order to allow the controller to ensure that the task was being carried out properly.

Fourth, the usual practices of the firm might be an important, and unavoidable, factor. In some situations, a managing director might have decided that no manager should have a span of control of less than six. This might mean that a perfectly good manager, with a difficult set of workers and a hard task to control might struggle. In the same way, it might be decided that a manager should not have a span of control above six. This might mean that a talented manager, with good subordinates, supervising a simple task, is under utilised. The rigidity of decision making in businesses can sometimes be counter productive.

Line and staff concepts

There has been much confusion in business writing and in discussion about exactly what line and staff are. There tend to be two views. The first is that line functions are those that have a direct bearing on the achievement of the principal objectives of the business, whereas staff functions are those that help the line employees to work in the best way to achieve those objectives. This does give cause for discussion since some departments and

employees are difficult to categorise. Some writers would claim that the purchasing department acted in a staff capacity, simply facilitating the functioning of the production department. Others would claim that the objective of production cannot be achieved without the purchasing of materials and so purchasing should be classified as a line department.

The second view is that line and staff concepts are a matter of relationships. Line concepts relate to the authority given to a superior over a subordinate. It is the relationship where a superior directly supervises a subordinate and there is a clear line of authority. Staff authority, however, is advisory. Those people who operate in a staff capacity are there to carry out investigation and research and to give advice to line employees.

Many people now believe that, certainly in large businesses, the different functions are so complex and entangled that it is impossible to classify employees or departments in such simplistic terms.

Organisation charts – appropriateness in different situations

The classic organisation chart tends to take the form of a pyramid. The actual height and width of the pyramid will depend upon the number of levels of hierarchy and the width of the spans of control.

As we have seen previously, when discussing the 'perfect' span of control, different situations demand different approaches. For many years, organisation charts tended to be quite tall. This reflected a fairly authoritarian and bureaucratic approach to management with lots of levels of hierarchy and very distinct reporting patterns. This approach tends to lead to one-way, downward, communication with orders being passed down the structure and little coming up. This in turn can be demotivating for the workforce and thus harmful to the efficient running of the firm. It means that the views and experiences of the workforce are not heard and considered.

In more recent times, mainly as a result of Japanese influence, there has been a trend towards reducing the number of levels of hierarchy in order to increase the two-way communication between those at the top of a business and those at the bottom. It is hoped that, in this way, workers will feel more involved, will contribute more, and will improve the efficiency of the business. The process has been further advanced by the use of such things as worker panels and quality circles.

Organisation charts and the informal structure

As was suggested earlier, organisation charts have a major weakness in that they do not show the informal relationships that might exist within a business. The informal structure of a business is bound to be different from the formal and it is essential that the good manager is aware of the differences. The informal structure exists when members of the business or department know one another well enough to pass on information in directions that are not prescribed by the formal organisation chart. The best known form of this informal organisation is the 'grapevine'. In most businesses or departments, people gain much security, status and social satisfaction from contributing to the grapevine. The information tends to be news that is not freely available to all members of the group, usually because it is confidential or because the formal structure of the firm is not working well in terms of efficient communication. Many management thinkers now feel that the grapevine performs an essential function in terms of communication needs and that it is a vital and

valuable tool. Managers who can manipulate the grapevine may find that their communication improves and that they can give information more quickly than through formal channels.

There are disadvantages to informal structures, however. First, if the informal structure becomes too opposed to the formal one, individuals become confused and are unaware of their positions. This can lead to uncertainty and inefficiency. Second, it is not unusual for individuals to find that they are isolated as the informal communication channels bypass them. This often happens if people are thought to be unpopular or not very good at their jobs. Those who work above and below them then tend to ignore the formal reporting structure and to use the informal channels to bypass the unpopular or incompetent individual.

FEATURES OF BUSINESSES

Centralisation and decentralisation

We have already discussed the reasons why businesses might organise themselves in terms of different structures, depending upon the different situations that the businesses could face. One of the decisions that must be made by larger businesses is whether the managing of the business is going to be centralised or decentralised. In smaller businesses, managing is almost invariably centralised.

There are three main kinds of centralisation. First, there is centralisation as an aspect of management theory. This reflects the tendency to resist the delegation of decision making. If centralisation exists, then a very autocratic style of leadership is taking place and most responsibility is held at the top of the management structure. Second, there is performance centralisation, which tends to be geographical and refers to a business that has all of its operations in one location. Third is departmental centralisation, which refers to the concentration of certain specialised activities within one department. For example, maintenance for all departments of a business might be carried out by one department. In this section, we are especially interested in centralisation as an aspect of management theory. If people have authority within an organisation, it means that they have the discretion to make decisions and to issue commands as they see fit. Decentralisation is the dispersal of authority to lower levels of an organisation. Without a degree of decentralisation it would be impossible to have a sensible organisational structure, since all decisions would have to be taken at the top. In the same way, if there is complete decentralisation, then the status of the person who has delegated all authority will disappear and the position could, in fact, be eliminated. Thus it is clear that one of the important decisions to be made in any business is the degree of decentralisation of authority that is to take place.

Authority, delegation and responsibility/accountability

We have already seen that authority, within an organisation, is having the discretion to make decisions and to issue commands. Along with this authority goes the responsibility for the outcomes of those decisions and commands. The decision maker is normally held to be accountable for the outcomes of the decisions. Managers may delegate their authority by allocating some of their own tasks and decisions to subordinates. However, this raises the question of whether the delegation of authority is also the delegation of accountability or whether the delegator is still responsible for the outcomes.

Delegation of authority is necessary for an organisation to exist. It is impossible for one person to take all of the decisions and to issue all of the commands and so there must be delegation. Delegation is, quite simply, where a superior gives a subordinate the discretion to make certain decisions. Although this may seem to be a simple process, many managers fail because of poor delegation.

Delegation introduces two other concepts, those of control and trust. If a manager is accountable, then it is unlikely that delegation would take place without some degree of control being held. However, if delegation is to be successful, then the delegator must have a degree of trust in the subordinate concerned or the delegation will be pointless. In reality, there needs to be a balance of trust and control. Too much trust may give the subordinate excessive scope in which to make a costly mistake. Too much control and the delegator may as well be doing the job personally. In addition to this, the subordinate is likely to lose motivation and morale and to resent the fact that trust is not forthcoming. If one could express trust and control in a quantitative sense, the sum total of the two would always be the same. Where trust is high, there is only a need for minimal control. Where trust is not strong, there will be a need for a great deal of control. In mathematical terms, it could be said that trust plus control would be a constant value.

Delegation can be specific or general. It may also be handed over in a written or unwritten form. A delegated assignment may have a specific written delegation of responsibility or job description attached to it. This might itemise all the activities and functions for which the subordinate is responsible. This sort of written delegation should be extremely helpful to both the delegator and the subordinate. It is an aid in terms of charting progress, spotting areas of overlap and allocating accountability.

In some cases, it is not so simple to be

specific about areas of delegation. This is especially true where a new job comes into being. For example, if a firm appoints a marketing manager for the first time, the managing director may be unsure as to what amounts of authority are necessary. In this situation it is difficult, in the short run, to be specific about areas of responsibility. However, this is obviously not a situation that should continue for long and one of the first things that the new employee should be asked to do is to establish a job description and clarify that description with the managing director and, if possible, with all those other employees who would be affected and whose cooperation would be necessary. Delegation based upon general terms and agreed verbally, with no written confirmation, is obviously a very dangerous ploy and requires great trust on both sides. If things go wrong in this situation, then it is almost impossible to establish responsibility. In these sorts of cases, it is very often the subordinate who ends up getting the blame and bearing the consequences! In the final analysis, the quantity and quality of delegation will depend upon four factors.

1 **The character of the delegator**   Some people simply find it very difficult to delegate. They are not keen to accept other people's ideas and they do not like the concept of decisions being made by subordinates. They find it difficult to trust subordinates and they are not willing to let subordinates make mistakes, even though making, recognising and coping with mistakes is often an important part of managerial development.
2 **The quality of the subordinates**   If delegation is to take place, it is important that there are sufficiently qualified subordinates available to handle the authority that is being delegated. If this is not the case, then delegation can be a dangerous process. However, the lack of suitable talent is often used as an excuse to avoid delegation by

managers who do not want to reduce their own authority. If suitable talent is lacking, then a long-term objective of the business should be to improve the quality of the workforce.
3 **The task or decision being undertaken**   The importance and cost of the task or decision will have a large impact upon the extent of delegation that takes place. Generally, the more important a task or decision, the more likely it is that control will be held at the top levels and delegation will be minimal.
4 **The nature of the business and external factors**   Various factors such as the history, culture, management philosophy, size and character of the business will have an effect upon the degree of delegation that takes place. The way that the business has been built up over the years and the culture and management philosophy that have emerged will be important factors. For example, firms that have grown from small to large, with no mergers or takeovers, tend to be more centralised than those that have grown by a process of merger and takeover. Large firms tend to have more scope for delegation than small firms and the character of a firm, the way that it is organised, tends to dictate the degree of decentralisation that can take place.

THE ROLE OF MANAGEMENT AND EMPLOYEE PARTICIPATION

The main tasks of management

These concepts were probably best covered by Henri Fayol (1841–1925). He was a French mining engineer who worked with Commentry-Fourchamboult-Decazeville, but he moved into general management and eventually became the managing director. He published the influential work *Administration Industrielle et Generale – Prevoyance, Organisation, Commandement, Coordination, Controle*, which was published in 1916. Fayol spent a long time considering the main tasks of management and he split his ideas into three distinct areas:

1 **The activities of the business**   Fayol felt that the activities of a business could best be divided into six areas. First came technical activities, which were to do with the actual production, manufacture and possible adaptation of the commodities involved. Some might be tempted to describe these as line activities. Second were commercial activities, to do with the buying, selling and exchange functions of the business. Third were financial activities, involving the search for, and optimum use of, capital. Fourth were security activities which related to the protection of property and persons. Fifth were accounting activities, involving stocktaking, balance sheets, costs and statistics and last were managerial activities involving forecasting and planning, organising, command, coordination and control.

   Fayol was of the opinion that all, or certainly most, of these activities were taking place in any business at any given time. However, the balance of the activities would vary with the type of organisation and the moment in time. He felt that the most important activities were those relating to management and it was upon these elements that he concentrated.

2 **The elements of managing the business**   As has already been stated, Fayol determined five areas of management activities. First, he identified forecasting and planning. The importance of sensible and objective planning cannot be over-emphasised and, for planning to be

effective, forecasting needs to be realistic and accurate. (Some methods of forecasting are looked at in more detail in Unit 4.) The second element was organising. By this, Fayol meant the actual setting up of the structure of the organisation, both in terms of material resources and human resources. The third element was commanding. This involved the setting up of a clear organisational structure of command and then maintaining activity among the personnel in the business. Coordinating was the fourth element, which involved putting together the various activities and efforts in the organisation and then overseeing the flow. The last element, and possibly most important, was controlling. This should ensure that the other four elements are occurring as they were intended and planned. The organisation will not run efficiently unless proper control procedures are implemented.

3 **The general principles of managing the business**   Fayol made a number of observations, based upon his own experiences in management, that he felt applied to the majority of organisations at some time or another. He identified unity of direction as an important principle. He felt that people in a business should have the same objectives and aims. Although he did not mind them showing initiative, he did feel that the general objectives of the organisation should be paramount. If individuals or departments are working towards different objectives, then conflict is bound to occur and the efficient management of the organisation is almost impossible. Unity of command was also identified by Fayol. He wanted each individual to be answerable to a single person in order to avoid split loyalties and also confusion in terms of reporting patterns. Fayol also discussed degrees of centralisation and the concepts of order, morale and equity. He felt that material

and social order were essential for the efficient running of an organisation. He also recognised the importance of the development of morale within an organisation and felt that this would be helped if the business was run equitably, i.e. fairly.

Employee (worker) participation in decision making

Employees can find participation in decision making to be extremely motivating. Participation implies recognition and fulfils the need for affiliation and acceptance. However, it is important that participation is real, rather than paying lip service to the workforce. Asking for ideas and then ignoring them is possibly more demotivating than not asking for ideas at all. Research does seem to show that commitment is intensified if the persons concerned participate in the decision making that affects them personally. There has been a movement towards increased participation in the last ten to fifteen years, mostly influenced by Japanese managerial ideas, but some forms of participation have been in existence for a lot longer. The degree of participation varies from organisation to organisation and we need to look at some of the possible ways in which workers might participate in decision making.

Workers' cooperatives

These are businesses that are owned and run by the workers who work in the business. Small cooperatives sprang up during the recession of the 1980s and many have been successful. Larger scale cooperatives have tended to fail, partly because of their lack of management expertise and partly because the businesses were not viable options in the first place.

Worker-directors

These are workers who represent the workforce on the board of directors. They are very common on the mainland of Europe, but they are rare in the UK. In Germany, one third of the board must be appointed by workers or by their representatives and in Holland, there is an aim to balance representatives from management and workers. Surprisingly, in many cases, the concept of worker-directors is unpopular with both management and trade unions. Managers worry about loss of confidentiality and authority, whereas unions feel that it reduces their power to negotiate.

Joint consultation

This is discussion of the problems of an organisation between representatives of the employers and employees. It takes place at all levels and consultative committees can be found in many UK firms, especially larger organisations. Production, employment, pay and working conditions tend to be the most discussed matters.

Works councils

This is another situation where representatives of employers and employees meet for discussion, but wage bargaining, terms of employment and productivity rates are not included in the agenda. These are, instead, dealt with by the respective trade unions.

Quality circles

There is some debate about the origination of quality circles. Some say that they were first instigated at the Toyota Motor Company in the late 1950s. Others suggest that they started in Japan with the publication of *Genba-To-QC (Quality Control for the Foremen)* in 1962. Either way, there is no doubt that they were a Japanese invention and that they have assumed a global importance in recent times as firms have chased improvements in quality and productivity. Quality circles are small groups, usually between five and ten people, who meet on an entirely voluntary basis in order to consider ways of improving quality and productivity in their work areas. Usually a facilitator works with the group and the average time for meeting would be around four hours a month. The theory behind quality circles is simple. First, workers are motivated by their involvement in problem solving and decision making. Second, those who work on the production process must have the best idea of the problems that are arising and of possible solutions to those problems. It should be remembered that quality circles are not a quality control system, but more a method of improving quality, amongst other things.

Kaizen groups

Kaizen programmes and groups are another Japanese concept and they have become important in many large firms throughout the world. A kaizen programme has the main target of eliminating waste of all kinds. The programme attempts to use the mental abilities of the workers as well as improving their manual skills. Workers are encouraged to assess their roles in the production process and to make suggestions – perhaps through quality circles, management meetings or suggestion schemes – in order to attempt to improve their part of the production process. Any idea that can cut half a second or more from the production process is considered and, if possible, adopted. This approach and the use of worker participation leads to a process known as 'continuous improvement'. This is in marked contrast with the traditional Western approach, which has depended upon a series of major inventions or alterations. Continuous improvement has allowed Japanese firms to adjust such things as the size of their workforce in a gradual manner, avoiding much of the unrest and uncertainty attached to the managing of major change.

No matter what the form of worker participation used, it is essential to specify the main objective of the process. Participation must be to do with the sharing of power in

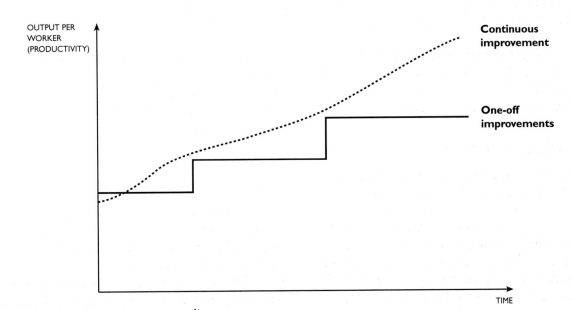

Fig 3.4 *A continuous improvement diagram*

order to allow employees to influence decision making. The decisions may be specific, that is relating to an individual and influenced by the individual concerned, or general, relating to groups of employees who make decisions affecting whole sections of the workforce.

In order for employee participation to be effective, it is important that the right atmosphere and culture exist within the business. Mutual confidence and trust between management and workforce is of paramount importance. If this does not exist, then the employee participation is unlikely to be successful. Management must believe that participation is beneficial to the business and that the workforce have a great deal to offer. The workforce must believe that they can trust the management and that the needs of the organisation are more important than individual or sectional interests. It is important that both sides can understand that a partnership will be productive and that an improvement in the state of health of a business should be good for all. Perhaps what is needed is the complete disappearance of the concept of 'sides'? However, this would not be a simple task to undertake.

THE RESTRUCTURING OF THE HUNTER GROUP

The Hunter Group PLC is an aircraft manufacturer located in the East Midlands. The company was founded in 1952 by two brothers, Mark and Anthony Forbes, both of whom had fought in the Second World War. The company began by building small, light aeroplanes, but gradually developed into the production of passenger jets in the late 1960s. In 1973 the company went public, selling shares on the Stock Exchange. However, it retained many of the traditional management techniques and structures originally put into place by the founders of the company. By the end of the 1970s the company was turning over £400 million. However, the 1980s was a period of decline for the company as it was first hit by recession and then fierce competition from the USA. A period of relatively good performance at the end of the 1980s was followed by a huge decline in the 1990s. The recession of the early 1990s along with new competition from the Far East, has made it difficult for the Hunter Group to survive. Indeed, the company has failed to make an operating profit for three years. A new Managing Director, Oliver Evans, has been appointed by the company to initiate change and turn the company around. To begin this process he has invited a firm of management consultants to report on the problems the company faces, and to produce a business plan on how the company needs to change as it approaches the Millennium.

Here are the major findings of the management consultants.

1 Hunter is structured on a functional basis. However, the business has grown to such a size over the last 30 years that it needs to reorganise itself to be structured by product.

2 Hunter needs to redefine its organisation chart from the one shown in Fig (i) to the one shown in Fig (ii).

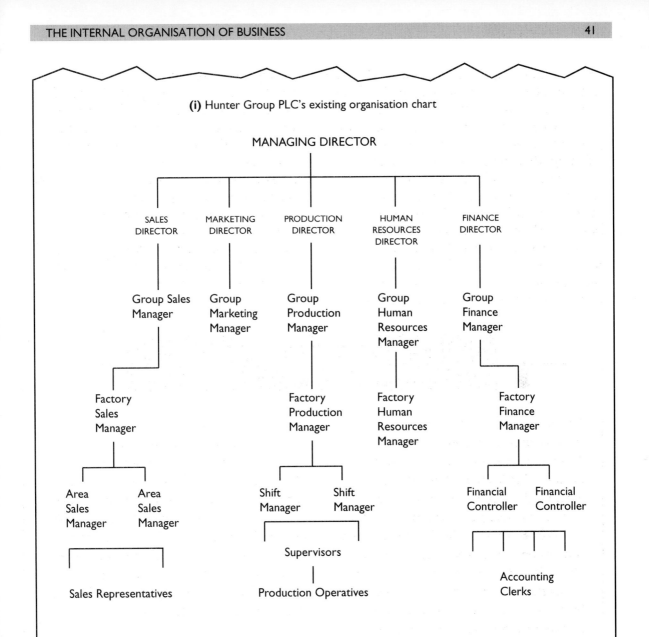

(i) Hunter Group PLC's existing organisation chart

3 The number of layers in the organisational hierarchy needs to be reduced, and the span of control of each manager increased.

4 The decision making within the organisation is to be decentralised with more responsibility being delegated to the managers in charge of the different product groups. These managers will be set specific cost and revenue objectives for their product group.

5 Within each product group, quality circles will be set up. These groups will be encouraged to improve productivity through kaizen programmes.

These recommendations have been treated rather lukewarmly by Hunter's directors, many of whom have been with the company for over 20 years, and have been brought up using the management structure set up by the business's founders. The proposals will

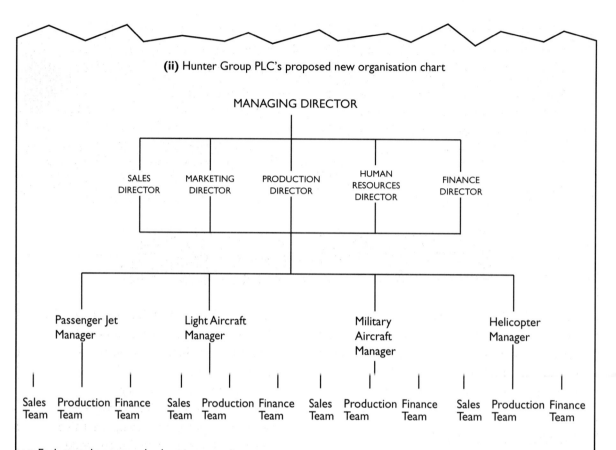

(ii) Hunter Group PLC's proposed new organisation chart

NB Each team has a team leader to manage it

also mean redundancies. The engineering workers union is opposed to the proposal and any decision to implement it will lead to industrial action. Middle management is also opposed to it because many middle management posts are going to be removed.

However, the newly appointed Oliver Evans is determined to force the proposal through. He recently spoke at a board meeting saying 'without these changes the company will not see the Millennium'.

QUESTIONS

1 What do you understand by the following terms?
   a Organisation by function
   b Span of control
   c Decentralised structure
   d Organisation chart
   e Quality circle   [20]

2 Discuss the advantages and disadvantages of the company moving from a functional

organisation structure to a product organisation structure. [15]

3 Discuss the factors that Hunter will need to consider as it appoints managers to head the new product divisions created by the structural reorganisation. [10]

4 How might the introduction of the kaizen programme benefit the organisation? [10]

5 a Analyse the difficulties Hunter will come up against in trying to introduce the structural changes. [10]

  b Evaluate the ways in which management could implement the structural changes. [15]   Total [80]

MANAGING FUTURE SUCCESS AT DIXONS

The Dixons Group is one of the largest publicly quoted companies in the UK. It has a turnover of over £2 billion, and is part of the FT–SE 100, the index of the UK's leading 100 companies on the Stock Exchange.

Corporate Structure

The company's structure is based on the four major retail chains which make up the group: Dixons, Currys, PC World, The Link and Mastercare. The corporate structure of Dixons is shown in the organisation chart below.

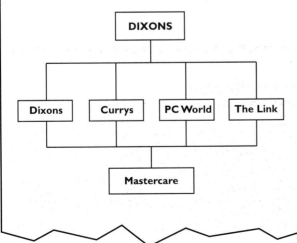

- **Dixons** This is the UK's largest retailer of consumer electronics products. It specialises in video, audio, personal computer, photographic and communications technology.
- **Currys** This is another leading UK retailer that provides a comprehensive selection of domestic appliances, video, audio, computers and communication products.
- **PC World** This is the UK's largest computer superstore retailer. It sells a comprehensive range of personal computers, printers, software and computer accessories.
- **The Link** This chain specialises in communications products, including: phones, faxes, personal organisers, pagers and the Traffic Master navigation equipment.
- **Mastercare** This business specialises in customer service. It employs over 1,300 technicians and engineers who service and repair products purchased through Dixons stores.

Dixons has developed its market power

through external rather than internal growth. This means that Dixons took over the established names of Currys, PC World and Mastercare. The consumer electronics market segment that Dixons specialises in is extremely competitive and subject to considerable change due to advances in technology. It is a non-bureaucratic organisation, that sees its strength in its ability to respond to change.

Decision Making

Major policy decisions that shape the direction of the whole group are taken by Dixons' directors. This could be a decision about overall pricing policy for the group. Policy decisions relating to specific stores in PC World and Currys are taken by the management of the relevant division. This could be decisions on particular product lines to stock in each branch. These decisions are implemented by area managers who are responsible for groups of stores within the division. Day to day decision making is taken by individual store managers, who will, for example, be responsible for ordering stock for their shop.

QUESTIONS

1 a Give an example of another retailer that owns chains of shops under different names. List the names of the stores in the chain. [5]

  b Why do you think Dixons has different names for each of its chains of stores, rather than calling all its stores Dixons? [7]

2 a Dixons describes itself as 'a non-bureaucratic organisation, that sees its strength in its ability to respond to change.' What do you think the characteristics of the organisation's structure need to be to achieve this strength? [7]

  b Analyse the constraints in the organisation that will hinder its ability to respond to change. [8]

3 a What is the span of control? [5]

  b Comment on the span of control a store manager working for Dixons will have. [8]

  c Discuss the factors that determine the manager of a Dixons store's span of control? [10]

Total [50]

UNIT

4 Information and Business Decision Making

SUMMARY

1 Information is data that is relevant to a problem that needs to be solved or a decision that has to be made. It can be classified as qualitative or quantitative. It can also be classified as primary or secondary.

2 Marketing research considers consumer reactions to all of the marketing areas and also analysis of customer needs, attitudes and buying behaviour. Market research is the study of a specific market and tends to concentrate upon the areas of customer needs, attitudes and buying behaviour.

3 Market research can be quantitative and/or qualitative. There are three main ways of collecting market research: observation, experimentation and surveys. Surveys can be split into personal interviews, telephone interviews and postal surveys. All of these methods would usually employ some form of questionnaire. Qualitative research may also be carried out by the use of consumer panels of various types.

4 Market research is normally carried out by means of taking a sample of the market. Sampling may be based on probability, such as random, systematic, stratified or cluster samples, or non-probability, such as quota, convenience or judgement samples.

5 The presentation of data is of great importance and should be given much thought. The four main methods of data presentation are tables, diagrams, graphs and reports.

6 Information technology is becoming an important aid to business decision taking. Applications such as spreadsheets, databases and word processing should be considered.

7 Forecasting can reduce uncertainty, if accurate. There are two main types: qualitative forecasting, which tends to be used for longer term forecasts, such as market research, the Delphi technique and panel consensus, and quantitative forecasting, which tends to be used for short-term forecasts, such as time series analysis.

8 Measures of central tendency, such as the mode, the median and the arithmetic mean, may be helpful tools for use as an aid to business decision taking.

COLLECTION OF DATA FOR DECISION MAKING

Information and data

There is a distinct difference between data and information and it is important that students should understand the two concepts. Data is quite simply the total sum of knowledge available. This is an enormous amount of facts and opinion, most of it of no interest to the individual. It does not become information until it is relevant to a problem that needs to be solved or a decision that needs to be made. For example, it is relatively easy to get hold of the population figures for a town and the socio-economic groupings of the relevant areas in the town. This data is of little use to the person in the street, but if a business decides to conduct a marketing survey of the area, then the data becomes important and necessary information. The business will need to know the population and socio-economic groupings of relevant areas, if it is to conduct an effective stratified sample.

There are two basic ways that information can be classified. First, it can be split into quantitative and qualitative information. Quantitative information contains measured or estimated numerical values. The suggestion that the distance from London to Portsmouth is about 80 miles would be classified as quantitative information. Qualitative information does not contain numerical values and is more a matter of opinion or judgement. A suggestion that it is too far to walk from London to Portsmouth would be qualitative information. There is a tendency to assume that quantitative information is more useful than qualitative information, but this is not actually the case. Both have their uses in certain situations. Bare numerical figures do not necessarily make things clear and an opinion from someone who a person knows well might be much more informative. If a

person was considering walking from London to Portsmouth for charity, the fact that it was about 80 miles might mean nothing. However, a friend that the person knows well saying that it was too far to walk might be good information if the person considering the walk knows that the friend is much fitter than they are. In an ideal world, there should be a mixture of quantitative and qualitative information, balanced as necessary to solve the problem posed or to make the decision required. Care should also be taken not to have so much information that it becomes difficult to analyse and use. The old saying 'unable to see the wood for the trees' should not be forgotten.

The second way to classify information is as primary and secondary information. Primary information is relevant data that is collected by a business for its own, specific, use. Thus, a business selling toys to wholesalers might get information from its customers relating to how well the customers thought that they were being supplied. This would be primary information. Secondary information is relevant data that has been collected elsewhere, but that might be used by a business. All published statistics are a source of secondary data and, when relevant to the decision making or problem solving of a business, they become secondary information. Thus, government statistics on the number of children of certain ages might be useful secondary information for the toy business mentioned above. There are many sources of secondary data. The most common might be:

- Newspapers, such as the *Financial Times*
- Specialist economic and business publications, such as *The Economist*
- Trade publications and professional magazines
- Published company reports
- Market intelligence reports
- Government statistics, such as 'Population Trends', the 'Blue Book on National

Income and Expenditure', or the Bank of England 'Quarterly Review'

The advantages and disadvantages of primary and secondary information tend to be the exact opposites of each other. Primary information should be more accurate and well-fitted to the exact requirements of the business that has collected it. However, it is very expensive to collect and analyse. Secondary information is much cheaper to collect, but the business will not know how it was collected and it may not be exactly the information desired. It tends to be the best approximation.

A business which is looking for information will have to weigh up the situation that it faces, when deciding between primary and secondary research. The key factor will usually be that of cost. Small businesses will not usually be able to afford expensive primary research and, indeed, even larger businesses might find the expense difficult to justify. The importance of the decision or problem will also be a factor. If the problem or decision is not very important, then expenditure on primary research might again be difficult to justify. The expense of primary research usually only makes it worthwhile for big projects. Large businesses might have their own market research departments but, on the whole, businesses tend to use professional research companies to conduct their required market research. In either case, it is a very expensive process.

■ MARKETING RESEARCH AND SURVEYS

Marketing research versus market research

There has, for some years, been confusion between the concepts of marketing research and market research. In reality, the difference is quite simple. Market research is a sub-set of marketing research.

Marketing research involves the research of every aspect of the whole marketing process. It considers consumer reactions to all of the marketing areas, i.e. the product, price, packaging, promotion and distribution, and also analysis of customer needs, attitudes and buying behaviour. Market research is the study of a specific market and tends to concentrate upon the areas of customer needs, attitudes and buying behaviour. However, it has to be said that the difference between marketing research and market research is sometimes quite difficult to classify. It is hard to be specific as to the point at which research becomes wide enough to move from the heading of market research to marketing research.

Market research methods

Market research is essential to a business if the business wishes to reduce risk. It can be the difference between great success and terrible failure. In many cases, financial disaster might well have been avoided if sufficient market research had been carried out. No business studies text would be complete without mention of the Sinclair C5, one of the most spectacular failures of the twentieth century. Whilst there is no guarantee, it is likely that the C5 would not have been launched onto the market if sufficient customer research had been carried out. However, it would have taken a brave man not to put such a new and innovative invention onto the market, especially after the investment that had gone into it. Indeed, market research is not infallible. The original Sony Walkman was predicted to be a complete flop by the market researchers and we all know what has happened since!

Once the decision has been made to conduct market research, one of the first

Fig 4.1 *This product was initially predicted to be a complete flop!*

decisions has to be whether the research is to be quantitative or qualitative. We have already considered the difference between quantitative and qualitative information. It should thus be obvious that quantitative research involves the use of numerical values and statistical techniques and analysis, whereas qualitative research is concerned with discovering the views and opinions of consumers and potential consumers. As we look at different methods of conducting market research, we will see that some fall into the quantitative category and others into the qualitative.

There are three main ways of collecting information for market research.

1 **Observation**   This is where trained observers watch consumers in order to analyse what they do. This is often carried out by the use of 'hidden' cameras. For example, cameras may be positioned in a shop to see how consumers move around the store, which articles interest them, and which promotional activities seem to catch

their eyes. Observation is especially useful because the observer is able to see how people really behave rather than how they say that they behave. However, the main weakness of observation is that it shows what people do but it cannot explain why they do it. In order to discover why people behave in the way that they do, other methods have to be employed.

2 **Experimentation**   This tends to work on the *ceteris paribus* (all other things being equal or constant) assumption. Businesses try to assess the effect of altering one variable, for example price, on a measured factor, for example sales revenue. In order to do this, it is essential that as few other changes are made as possible, otherwise it will be difficult to judge whether any resultant change in sales revenue is caused by the change in price or changes in one of the other variables, such as the quality of the product. The main weakness of experimentation is that, in the real world, it is difficult to behave as if one were in a laboratory. Markets tend to be too volatile and unpredictable and so controlling single factors is almost impossible. Even if all internal factors can be controlled, changes in external factors, such as the state of the economy or tax changes, can easily ruin the validity of the experiment.

3 **Surveys**   These are the most frequently used methods of collecting primary information. A survey takes place when a section of the market, selected to be representative of the whole market, is questioned about their behaviour or views. In an ideal world, the whole market, or population as it is known, would be asked. However, this would normally be too expensive and time consuming and so a sample is selected. (Methods of sampling are considered later in this section.)

Surveys

There are three main types of survey. First, there are personal interviews. This produces the best responses and quality of information. People are asked questions, face to face, by an interviewer. In quantitative research, closed questions are usually used in order to limit the possible responses and to facilitate analysis of the information. In qualitative research, open questions tend to be used so that respondents can explain in depth their behaviour and views. However, the use of the personal interview is an expensive method of gaining information and there is always the danger of interviewer bias. Respondents may simply give the answer that they believe the interviewer wants to hear.

Second, there are telephone interviews. It is a quick and efficient way of conducting a large number of interviews. It is a relatively inexpensive method and the members of the sample can be drawn from a wide geographical area, if appropriate, with ease. Also, in these days of computers and information technology, information can be entered directly onto the database, thus saving a great deal of time. The main weakness of telephone surveys is that respondents often have a built-in distrust of the method, usually based upon a bad experience to do with telephone selling as opposed to market research. Also, the interview needs to be kept short because the respondents do not like to be on the telephone for a long time. In days when the telephone was less common, a drawback existed because only people with telephones could be surveyed. Nowadays, however, this is less of a weakness.

The third method is the postal survey. It involves the sending of a questionnaire through the post with a reply-paid envelope, so that the respondent can return the completed document. This is the cheapest method of surveying large numbers and it also enables the sample to be drawn from a wide geographical area. It tends to provide accurate and full information because the forms are completed in confidence. Also, there is no fear of interviewer bias affecting the responses. However, there are drawbacks. It is an inefficient method, because the average response rate for a normal postal survey is around 20 percent. This may be improved by offering incentives for the return of the completed questionnaire, such as free gifts or vouchers. In addition, there is no guarantee that the person who has been sent the questionnaire is the one who fills it in and the forms have to be simple, because there is no one there to explain them if they are not understood.

The questionnaire

All of these methods usually make use of some sort of questionnaire as the main vehicle for collecting the information. The quality of the questionnaire is therefore of paramount importance to the eventual quality of the information collected. It is perhaps easiest to think of the questionnaire in terms of its usual sections.

1 **Title and preamble**   The preamble is an introduction that makes it clear to the respondent what the aim of the questionnaire is and also explains what the information will be used for. It may also explain the level of confidentiality. The main purpose of this section is to gain the confidence of the would-be respondent.

2 **Questions relating to the respondent**   These are classification questions which might determine things like sex, age, marital status or socio-economic status. These questions are used to stratify the respondents into different groupings and factions. They are a great help when the responses are being analysed.

3 **Information questions**   These are the questions designed to gain the information that will help to solve the problems or

make the decisions that the research is all about. There are three types of questions that might be used. Open or unstructured questions allow the respondents to express themselves as fully as they wish in any way that they think suitable. The replies give true depth, but they tend to be difficult to analyse because no two people respond in exactly the same way. Semi-structured questions allow some leeway to the respondent. They tend to ask for the finishing of half-written sentences or some sort of word association. Closed or structured questions demand exact, short responses. They are the most common form of questions employed in questionnaires. In many cases, the questions only offer two responses, such as true/false or yes/no, and the respondent has to choose one. The information from this sort of question is easy to collate and analyse, but the topics that lend themselves to it are limited by the nature of the questioning. In some closed questions, the strength of agreement or disagreement is measured by offering a scale of possible replies to the respondent. It is then possible to measure the strength of preference being expressed. There are different scales in use, such as the Likert Scale and the Semantic Differential Scale. The Likert Scale usually gives five possibilities, ranging from strongly agree to strongly disagree, whereas the Semantic Differential Scale offers numbers, usually from one to seven, which represent levels of satisfaction. These scales are popular because the preferences can be mathematically totalled and then analysed.

4 **Thanking the respondent**   The final section of a questionnaire should thank the respondent for taking part, explain how the questionnaire should be returned (if necessary), and also explain any reward that might be being offered for the completion and return of the questionnaire.

Panels

There is one further type of qualitative research which should be considered and this is the use of a 'panel'. A panel is a group of consumers, who are used on a regular basis in order to conduct research into a specific market or a wide range of markets. The main point is that the panel allows the researcher to gain the views of the same people over a period of time. Some panels are put together for a limited period of time, but others are run over many years. The advantages of using panels are fairly obvious. Most importantly, it is possible to discover trends, because the information is collected over time and the same respondents are used. These trends may then be analysed and acted upon. The main disadvantages relate to the panel members. Loss of panel members is bound to occur over time and this affects the balance of the panel. Also, being a panel member for a long period of time might affect the individual's attitudes and lead to behaviour that is not typical.

There are a number of different types of panel.

1 **Consumer product testing panels**   Here, consumers are asked to test new products and to give their opinions upon them. This testing may take place in a group at the producer's business, or at the market research establishment, or it might take place in the home of the consumer.
2 **Consumer purchasing panels**   In this case, the consumers report regularly upon their purchasing habits, purchasing intentions and views on products. The information is usually collected by postal questionnaires, the keeping of a diary or interviews.
3 **Audience panels**   This is where TV and radio audiences are monitored using a representative panel of viewers or listeners. The results are used by advertisers and producers, as well as the TV and radio companies.

4 **Focus groups**   These tend to be used in the USA, where small groups of people are brought together for discussion about their purchasing habits, purchasing intentions and views on products.

SAMPLING METHODS

As has already been stated, it is unlikely that a whole market (or population) will be tested and so it is necessary to select a sample of that population. The sample needs to be representative of the whole market, so that the results gained from the research will reflect the views of the whole group, and it needs to be large enough to give a statistically valid result. There are two methods of sampling, probability sampling or non-probability sampling, and these need to be considered in detail.

Probability (random) sampling

In a probability, or random, sample, all members of the population have an equal chance of being selected to be part of the sample group. Because of this, the sample tends to be very representative of the population as a whole and the results are therefore likely to be statistically valid. The larger the sample taken, the more statistically valid will be the results. It should be remembered that sometimes, although samples may appear to be random, it is not always the case. For example, samples based upon telephone users exclude all those who do not have a telephone and samples based upon the electoral register exclude those who are not eligible to vote, perhaps because of age or domestic arrangements. All probability samples are identical in that they provide a list of names that must be surveyed. The researcher or interviewer does not make the choice. There are a number of different types of probability samples.

1 **Basic random samples**   In this situation, names or numbers are drawn at random, usually by computer, from a list of the whole population. This may cause cost problems if the population is geographically widely spread.

2 **Systematic random samples**   Here, a set numerical formula is used to select the members of the sample. This could be the selection of every tenth or twentieth name, for example.

3 **Stratified random samples**   In this case, the population is stratified and then a random sample is taken in each strata. The stratification may be carried out using such discriminating factors as age, sex, socio-economic status or geographical location, for example. This is an important method because not all markets contain exactly identical members and so a simple random sample would not reflect this. If we were to consider the market for aerobics classes, the concept should become clear. In this case, some customer types account for a higher proportion of sales than others. In the aerobics market, this would be more women than men and also more younger women than older women. If the stratified sample is designed to take this into account, then the sample will be much more representative of the population.

4 **Cluster samples**   In order to avoid the problem of a wide geographic survey, the population is sometimes split into clusters and then a cluster is chosen on a random basis. For example, it may be assumed that the market for aerobics courses is identical in all parts of the country. If this is the case, then the country might be split into supposedly identical areas and then one of these areas, or clusters, might be selected at random to be the sample. It may be that once the cluster has been selected, the strata in the market might be considered, e.g. that the market is female dominated and appeals more to the young. If this is the

case, then there would be a random, stratified, cluster sample.

Non-probability sampling

In a non-probability sample, all members of the population do not have an equal chance of being selected to be part of the sample group, because the researcher or interviewer has some say in the choice of the people who will make up the sample. This means that the sample may not be as representative of the population and so it is likely to be less statistically valid. There is always a risk of bias by the researcher or interviewer. Unlike probability samples, the methods do not generate a list of names that have to be sampled and so the cost tends to be less. There are a number of different types of non-probability samples.

1 **Quota samples**   The population is split into a number of different strata, such as age, sex, socio-economic status or geographical location, for example. An interviewer is then given a quota of people to interview in each stratum. It is up to the interviewer to choose the interviewees. The interviewer finishes the survey when the quota in each stratum has been reached. Interviewer bias is still, therefore, a serious factor here. This method is effective in terms of minimising time and money costs, but statistical validity is debatable.

2 **Convenience samples**   This is a very cost conscious method. The researcher selects an area where there are large numbers of people to be discovered, such as a shopping complex or an airport.

3 **Judgement samples**   The people to be included are chosen by the researcher, based upon the researcher's judgement of which consumers will most realistically represent the whole population. Obviously, this is a very subjective form of sampling and much will depend upon the accuracy of the researcher's knowledge of the market.

PRESENTATION OF INFORMATION

Factors for consideration when presenting information

Once research has been carried out and information has been collected, thought needs to be given as to how the information should be presented. There are a number of 'rules' that might apply in any situation when presenting information.

- The information needs to be easy to read. It should not be confusing or over-complicated
- The information needs to be presented in a way that the intended audience can understand. There is no point in making the presentation complicated, if the audience is not able to understand it, e.g. young children. In the same way, there would be no point in expressing information in a very simplistic manner to an audience of top academics
- The information should be well labelled. This will make it easier to understand what the information is trying to explain
- The presentation should create a good visual impact. In this way, the intended recipients will find it attractive and it will take their interest

Methods of presentation

There are four main methods of presenting information and it is necessary to look at each in turn.

Tables

This is where information is organised in terms of vertical columns and horizontal rows. There would usually be more rows than columns, but there are no set rules for the drawing up of tables. As far as possible, the

Year & Quarter	Northern Sales (£000s)	Southern Sales (£000s)	Western Sales (£000s)	Eastern Sales (£000s)	Total Sales (£000s)
1997–1	46	72	38	50	206
1997–2	48	77	39	52	216
1997–3	44	66	35	52	197
1997–4	51	91	42	65	249
Total Quarterly Sales (£000s)	189	306	154	219	868

Fig 4.2 *Sales figures, by quarter and district, for ABC Ltd in 1997*

table should comply with the 'rules' for presenting information that are mentioned opposite. The major drawback of tables is that they are rarely attractive to the eye. The very format tends to mean that they are rather dry and unexciting. An example of a typical table is shown in Fig 4.2.

Diagrams

There are a number of different diagrams that can be used to show business information. In all cases, the diagrams should attempt to fulfil the 'rules' for the presentation of data.

Organisation charts

These show the structure of a business in terms of how individuals or departments are linked together, using the principal lines of authority. They are dealt with in detail in Unit 3, where an example is also shown.

Pictograms

These are a simplistic form of information presentation, where quantitative information is represented by pictures. They usually have good visual impact, but they are not very accurate and can easily be used to distort information by altering the relative sizes of the images without changing the scale. For example, a political party in power might wish to convince the electorate that there was less unemployment under them than under their rivals, when they were in power. However, they might know that this was not really the case. If the government was corrupt, they might use a small figure representing 250,000 unemployed for their total and a large figure representing 100,000 unemployed for the total of their rivals. They can then put up four figures for their rivals and two small figures for their own total. Thus, their total would be 500,000 and the total for their rivals would be 400,000. However, unless the reader looked carefully at the key on the diagram (if one was provided!), he or she would think that the rivals had higher unemployment than the government. This situation is shown in Fig 4.3.

Pie charts

A pie chart uses a circle to present total data and then divides up the circle to represent the different contributions to the total. The area of the circle represents the total amount and the segments are then drawn so that their angles at the centre, out of 360 degrees, are the same as the proportion of the segments to the total. Thus, if we take the total sales for the year from the earlier table, we can draw a pie chart to show the proportion of sales from

AVERAGE UNEMPLOYMENT
UNDER THE GOVERNMENT

AVERAGE UNEMPLOYMENT WHEN
THE OPPOSITION WERE IN POWER

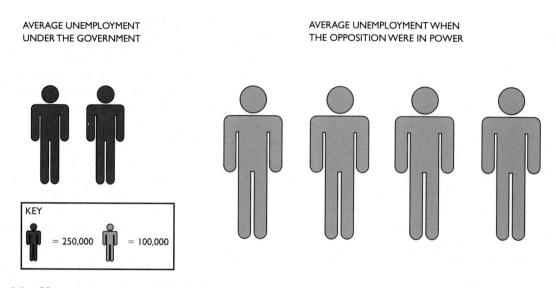

Fig 4.3 *Using a pictogram can distort information*

each district. The degrees of each section will be calculated by the formula:

$$\frac{\text{District total}}{\text{Total sales}} \times \textbf{360 degrees}$$

- The angle for Northern Sales will be 189/868 × 360 = 78.4 degrees
- The angle for Southern Sales will be 306/868 × 360 = 126.9 degrees
- The angle for Western Sales will be 154/868 × 360 = 63.9 degrees
- The angle for Eastern Sales will be 219/868 × 360 = 90.8 degrees

The pie chart to show this can then be drawn and is shown in Fig 4.4.

Pie charts give a good visual impact, but they are difficult to draw and to read accurately. It is also difficult to compare them over time, because the area of the circle will change if the total changes and so segments may remain the same size in terms of degrees, but represent different amounts.

Bar charts

A bar chart displays the information by means of bars of different lengths and it is simply the height of the bar that represents the amount. There are three different types of bar chart that may be used. The first is the simple bar chart that shows total amounts and nothing else.

Thus, it would be possible to show the quarterly totals for sales from the previous data, but not the district figures (see Fig 4.5).

District sales figures for ABC Ltd–1997

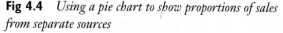

Northern
Southern
Western
Eastern

Fig 4.4 *Using a pie chart to show proportions of sales from separate sources*

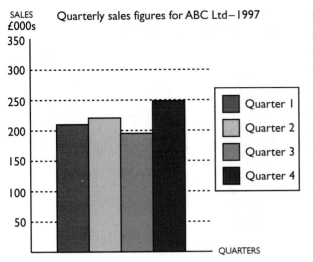

Fig 4.5 *Use of a simple bar chart*

The second is the component bar chart. This is used to show the totals and to break down the figures into components showing the contributing amounts. The main advantage of this type of bar chart is that it shows the totals clearly, but it is difficult to compare any but the bottom components as one moves up the bars, as each component starts at a different level. As a result of this, it is usual to show the most important component first in each bar. Thus, in our example, it would be possible to show the quarterly totals and the relative sales for each of the districts in each quarter and it would be sensible to show the southern sales first as they are the largest. This is shown in Fig 4.6.

The third is the parallel (or compound) bar chart. This is used to show the components clearly in any given area, but the totals are not simple to read and it is necessary to read off and total each component value to attain the total value. Thus, in our example, it is possible to show the district values for each quarter as separate amounts, but the quarterly totals are not clear. This is shown in Fig 4.7.

It should be remembered that bar charts of

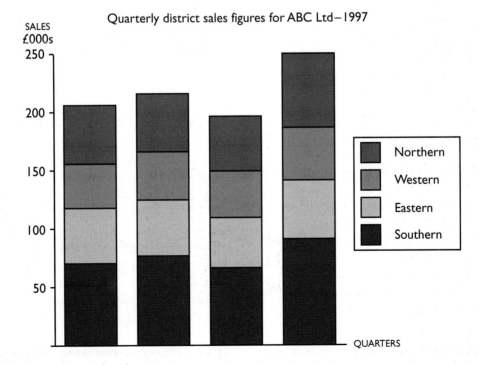

Fig 4.6 *Use of a component bar chart*

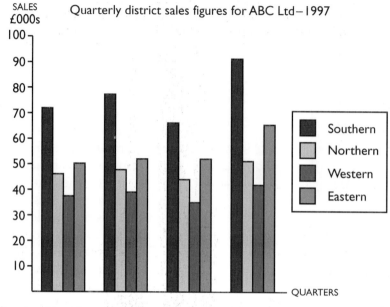

Fig 4.7 *Use of a compound bar chart*

all types may be drawn with the bars horizontal to the x-axis, but this does not change the theory behind them, or their names. For example, the original simple bar chart could have been drawn as in Fig 4.8.

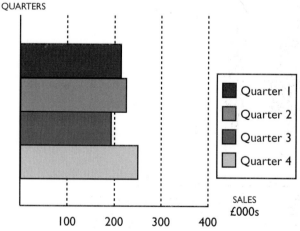

Fig 4.8 *A simple bar chart showing bars drawn horizontally to the x-axis*

Histograms

Histograms are the final method that we shall look at in terms of diagrams. Although at first glance histograms may seem to be the same as bar charts, they are in fact very different. In a histogram, the bars may be of different widths and they also touch. In addition, it is therefore the area of the rectangle that represents the value being portrayed rather than simply the height. They are most frequently used to show grouped frequency distributions and the width of each rectangle will vary if the size of the groups varies. This is best shown by an example. We can see below the breakdown of sales value, per salesperson, for a very large car salesroom which employs 40 salespersons. The figures are for one month.

These figures can now be shown on a histogram (see Fig 4.9). The width of the rectangles on the histogram will vary with the width of the bands used to represent sales. Thus, the last three rectangles will be three times the width of the first three.

In some cases, it might be considered worthwhile to show the information as a

Monthly sales in £000s	Number of salespeople achieving each level
Up to £5,000	I
£5,000 to £10,000	3
£10,000 to £15,000	8
£15,000 to £30,000	16
£30,000 to £45,000	8
£45,000 to £60,000	4

Task element	No of days required	No of workers required
A	2	I
B	6	3
C	4	6
D	7	3
E	9	4
F	3	2

single curve and so the mid-points of each rectangle of the histogram are joined. This is known as a frequency polygon and is also shown in Fig 4.9.

Histograms can be used for a number of different purposes, one of the best being to show worker/days required for different elements of a task. For example, a task may be broken down into the elements shown below and the workers required for each element of

the task may be estimated as shown.

This information can then be shown in the form of a histogram (see Fig 4.10), with the area of each rectangle showing the total number of worker/days required for each element of the task.

Thus, we can see that element C requires 4 days × 6 workers = 24 worker days. This sort of table and/or histogram is very useful for planning purposes.

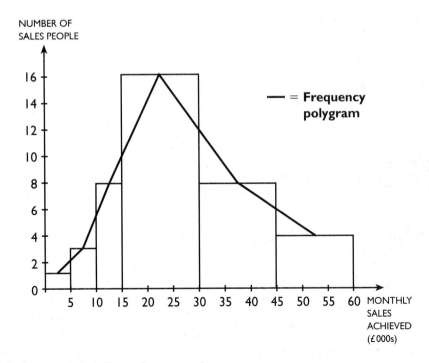

Fig 4.9 *Use of a histogram, including a frequency polygon*

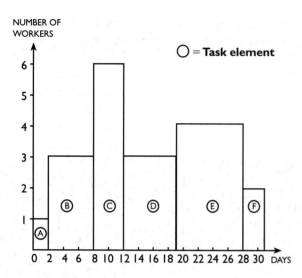

Fig 4.10 *Use of a histogram to show worker/days required for each element of a task*

vertical axis (or y-axis) usually represents the dependent variable, such as sales. The dependent variable will alter with changes in the independent variable. Thus, we could draw a graph of how sales alter over time using the figures from the table below (see Fig 4.11).

Sales figures for **XYZ Ltd** – 1987 to 1996 – £000s	
Year	Sales (£000s)
1987	242
1988	264
1989	238
1990	210
1991	214
1992	236
1993	284
1994	312
1995	324
1996	367

Graphs

Graphs are usually drawn using two axes. The horizontal axis (or x-axis) usually represents the independent variable, such as time. The

Sales figures for XYZ Ltd–1987 to 1996

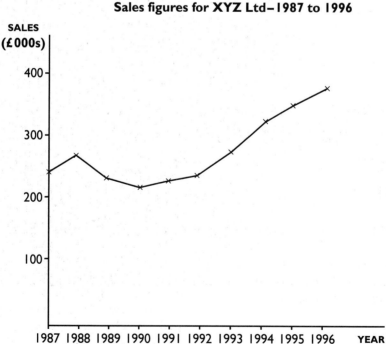

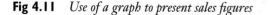

Fig 4.11 *Use of a graph to present sales figures*

Reports

Information does not have to be delivered in a pictorial manner. Indeed, the most common means of presenting information in business is the use of a written report. Although there are no hard and fast rules relating to report writing, there are some conventions that are normally adhered to. The report should have a clear heading and state the names of the people who have been involved in its preparation. The terms of reference, or objectives, should be explained, as should the methods used to collect and analyse any data. The findings of the investigation should be clearly stated, as should the conclusions drawn from the findings. There should be recommendations made that relate to the terms of reference and the conclusions. Sections should be clearly headed and numbered in a consistent fashion, with the use of footnotes where necessary. Any detailed statistical or mathematical information, and all support documents, should be placed in appendices at the end of the report. The report should be signed and dated. It should be remembered that reports tend to be very subjective and so often have a biased approach, reflecting the views of the compiler/s.

MANAGEMENT OF INFORMATION THROUGH INFORMATION TECHNOLOGY

In this day and age, the role of information technology as an aid to business decision taking should not be ignored. There are a number of applications of information technology that might be considered.

Spreadsheets

A spreadsheet is a visual display on a computer that represents an inputted set of numerical data. The data is organised in such a way, through the use of programmed formulae, that a change in any one piece of data will update all connected figures. Thus, it would be possible to set up a spreadsheet for the projected accounts for a firm for the coming year. Once this had been done, the management could alter various figures in order to see what effect this would have on the other variables. They could run through different borrowing scenarios or different fixed asset investment scenarios and then formulate the predicted financial and accounting outcomes. This is obviously a great help in decision making.

Databases

A database is simply a collection of information that is stored on a computer. The best sort is a single, cross-referenced database. A single version of each information item is stored and these items are related to other information items as required. Once the data storage has taken place, application programs can be used to access the database. For example, a firm may input the names, addresses, credit ratings and bank details of all of its customers. Each customer would be inputted. The database can then be accessed by application programs as required. So, if the firm wanted a list of all customers, this could be accessed. In the same way, a list of all of those with suspect credit ratings could also be accessed. Indeed, this could be a multi-search process and the firm might be looking for all customers, with a suspect credit rating, situated in Scotland. With the right application program, this would be simple to generate. As we can see, the correct storage and retrieval of information on a database would obviously be a great help to decision making. The applications range throughout a business, from ordering to selling to marketing.

Word processing

This separates the input of information from written input. It also enables the mixing of numerical information and written text in the compilation of final documents. The evolution of the computer-based word processor has had an enormous impact upon clerical and secretarial functions in business. The clear presentation of information should make it easier to make decisions.

The cost of information technology, both financial and human, should not be ignored. Many businesses cannot afford the required level of investment. Also, there is a belief that the implementation of information technology leads to unemployment. This may not be true, but it does lead to the employment of computer-literate workers and the redundancy of more traditionally skilled workers. This in turn, whilst not affecting total unemployment, may have a severe impact upon human resource management in businesses.

There are also limitations and problems in the use of information technology. Much has been written about the security of information stored on computers and there have been a number of firms where confidential data has been accessed by outsiders. Also, technical breakdowns or the arrival of a computer virus may have disastrous effects upon the storage, analysis and use of information within a business.

METHODS OF SALES FORECASTING

We have already discussed the concept of forecasting, when we were looking at uses of spreadsheets. It is appropriate, at this stage, to consider it in more detail. Forecasting is the estimation of future events or outcomes. If a business can estimate what is to happen in the future, then it is possible to plan for the expected outcome and uncertainty will be reduced. Thus a business might try to estimate its future sales or it might try to estimate the effect of future economic events, such as a government Budget, upon its financial future. In this way, the firm will be able to look at the forecasts and plan accordingly. It should be remembered that forecasting is only useful if it is relatively accurate. If forecasting is inaccurate, then firms will be planning ahead to deal with situations that are not going to arise. This may be more damaging than not forecasting at all. It should also be remembered that forecasting may be accurate, and so reduce uncertainty, but then be negated by unexpected and non-forecastable random occurrences. Forecasting may reduce uncertainty, but it cannot eliminate it.

Quantitative and qualitative forecasting

We have already dealt with quantitative and qualitative concepts, when we looked at information types and research methods. Now we need to consider these in terms of forecasting.

Quantitative forecasting analyses numerical figures and then projects them into the future in an attempt to forecast an outcome. These methods only tend to be useful in the short run, i.e. predicting two or three time periods ahead. We shall look at one method of quantitative forecasting, time series analysis, later in the unit.

Qualitative forecasting uses opinions to forecast future events. There are three main methods employed by businesses.

1 **Market research**   Businesses will often use market research to attempt to forecast future trends in their markets. This is done by collecting the views of consumers in relation to what they think their future

needs might be and what products they would like to see.

2 **The Delphi technique**   This is a process named after the most famous of the Greek oracles. Experts are employed by the business and they are sent a number of postal questionnaires, which they fill in with their views and then send back to the business. These returns are then analysed and used to forecast future trends. Obviously, the method will only be as effective as the quality of the experts employed.

3 **Panel concensus**   In this method, experts are brought together and they are asked to discuss the future trends as they see them. It is a form of brainstorming. It is often used as a second phase of forecasting, after the Delphi technique has been employed. The two together are an effective form of qualitative forecasting. Again, the quality and accuracy of the experts is of paramount importance.

Time series analysis

Time series analysis is a form of short-term quantitative forecasting that uses moving averages to establish a trend. This trend is then extrapolated into the future to enable a forecast to be made.

In any series of data, there are three elements. These are the trend, the cyclical (or seasonal) variation and unpredictable occurrences. The trend is the general direction that the data is taking; this tends to be simply upwards, downwards or stable. Cyclical variations are regular highs and lows that occur over a period of time. Thus, a firm selling holidays might expect to see high sales in the summer and around the Christmas period, and lower sales in the other two quarters of the year. Unpredictable occurrences are happenings that cannot be forecast, such as a war or unusual weather changes.

Time series analysis follows three simple steps. The first is to identify the trend and the cyclical variations. The second is to extrapolate the trend into the future, i.e. take the trend line and extend it into future periods. The third is to make a forecast by taking the extrapolated trend and adding to it the expected average cyclical variation for the period being predicted. This process is best understood by looking at an example and we shall consider two sets of data in order to do this. Firstly, let us look at the sales figures for a business over a period of 20 years.

Sales figures for ABC Ltd – 1977 to 1996 – £000s			
Year	Sales (£000s)	Year	Sales (£000s)
1977	34	1987	53
1978	35	1988	54
1979	36	1989	59
1980	40	1990	60
1981	39	1991	57
1982	43	1992	61
1983	45	1993	64
1984	48	1994	66
1985	50	1995	70
1986	47	1996	68

The first task, when attempting a time series analysis is to spot the trend in the data. If data is in quarters, as will be the case in our later example, then this is quite simple. However, this is not always the case. Here, on careful observation, we can see that the data is peaking every five years, in 1980, 1985, 1990 and 1995. The trend of the data determines the **moving average** that should be used. Here, we will use a 5-point moving average. This means that we will take the average figure for each of the five years surrounding any given year and call this the trend. The whole process is shown in Fig 4.12 and will then be explained.

Year	Sales (£000s)	5-year total	Trend [5-year total divided by 5]	Cyclical variation
1977	34			
1978	35			
1979	36	184	36.8	−0.8
1980	40	193	38.6	1.4
1981	39	203	40.6	−1.6
1982	43	215	43	0
1983	45	225	45	0
1984	48	233	46.6	1.4
1985	50	243	48.6	1.4
1986	47	252	50.4	−3.4
1987	53	263	52.6	0.4
1988	54	273	54.6	−0.6
1989	59	283	56.6	2.4
1990	60	291	58.2	1.8
1991	57	301	60.2	−3.2
1992	61	308	61.6	−0.6
1993	64	318	63.6	0.4
1994	66	329	65.8	0.2
1995	70			
1996	68			

Fig 4.12 *Determining trend and moving average*

The first task was to calculate the five year totals, since a 5-point moving average is being used. Thus, for 1979, the total is the sales figures for the years from 1977 to 1981 inclusive, i.e. 34 + 35 + 36 + 40 + 39 = 184. This figure relates to 1979, since 1979 is the middle figure of the five years. We say that the data *centres* on 1979. When we use a moving average, we then simply drop the first piece of data and add in the next. Thus, we will now drop the figure for 1977 and add on the figure for 1982. This will give a five year total of 193, which centres upon the year 1980. This process is continued until we have five year totals for all of the years from 1979 to 1994. As we can see, there are not totals for the first two years and the last two years.

The trend figure for each of the years can then be calculated by taking the five year totals and dividing each of them by five. Thus, the trend figure for 1979 is 184/5, i.e. 36.8, and the trend figure for 1980 is 193/5 or 38.6.

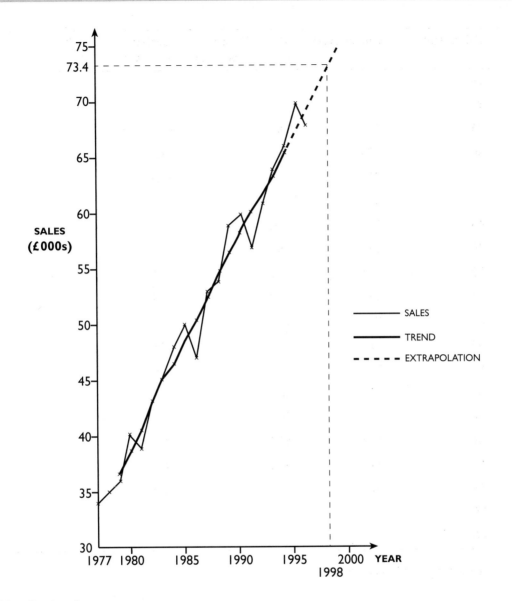

Fig 4.12 *Continued*

The cyclical variation is the difference between the actual figure for a period and the trend figure. Thus, the cyclical variation for 1979 is 36 − 36.8, which is −0.8, and the cyclical figure for 1980 is 40 − 38.6 or 1.4.

Let us now assume that the business wishes to predict the sales figures for 1998. The next step is to draw a graph of the trend and then to extend the line (extrapolate) into the future using the line of best fit. In this way, it is

possible to predict a trend for the year 1998. The graph is shown in Fig 4.12.

When we look at the graph, we can see that the extrapolation of the trend line gives a predicted trend figure for 1998 of £73,400. However, if we were to take this as the forecast, we would be ignoring the concept of cyclical variation. In order to make an accurate forecast, we need to take into account what has happened in similar years to

1998. If we take each peaking year, i.e. 1980, 1985, 1990 and 1995 as the first year in each five year sequence, then 1998 would be a fourth year, along with 1978, 1983, 1988 and 1993. We have cyclical variation figures for three of these years, 1983, 1988 and 1993, and they are 0, −0.6 and 0.4 respectively. If we add these and divide by three, then we can gain an average cyclical variation. In this case, it would be −0.2 divided by three, i.e. −0.067. This then needs to be added to the predicted trend figure for 1998 in order to get the true forecast. Remember that the formula for a forecast is:

Forecasted value = Forecasted trend + average seasonal variation

Thus, in this case, it would be 73.4 + (−0.067) = 73.333 or £73,333. The business has an idea of what their sales ought to be in two years' time, i.e. in 1998. If another year was being considered, e.g. 1997, then the reading would be taken from the extrapolation on the graph and then the average cyclical variation for a third year in the sequence would be added to the forecasted trend. This would be the average of the cyclical variations for the years 1982, 1987 and 1992. The figure would be 0 + 0.4 + (−0.6) divided by three which, by coincidence, gives the same figure as for a fourth year in the sequence, i.e. −0.067.

It should be remembered that it is difficult to predict much further ahead using this method and, if the business wished to do so, then it would be better to use some form of qualitative method.

A problem arises when the data is in a cyclical pattern that is even numbered, for example, quarterly data. This is because the averages do not centre upon an exact point in time. Again, this problem is best explained through the use of a worked example. Let us consider the sales data for another business that is shown below.

This data is expressed in quarters and so it is necessary to use a 4-point moving average. This means that we will add the first four sales figures, in order to get the first total, and then drop the first figure and add in the fifth and so on. However, a problem occurs when we do this. All of the calculations have been carried out in the table shown in Fig 4.13. We can see that the first four figures total to 71, but when

| Quarterly sales figures for XYZ Ltd – 1993 to 1996 – £000s | | | |
Year/Quarter	Sales (£000s)	Year/Quarter	Sales (£000s)
1993 – 1	14	1995 – 1	20
1993 – 2	19	1995 – 2	25
1993 – 3	16	1995 – 3	22
1993 – 4	22	1995 – 4	28
1994 – 1	18	1996 – 1	24
1994 – 2	22	1996 – 2	28
1994 – 3	20	1996 – 3	26
1994 – 4	24	1996 – 4	30

Year/Quarter	Sales (£000s)	4-quarter total	8-quarter total	Trend [8-quarter total divided by 8]	Cyclical variation
1993 – 1	14				
1993 – 2	19				
		71			
1993 – 3	16		146	18.25	−2.25
		75			
1993 – 4	22		153	19.13	2.87
		78			
1994 – 1	18		160	20	−2
		82			
1994 – 2	22		166	20.75	1.25
		84			
1994 – 3	20		170	21.25	−1.25
		86			
1994 – 4	24		175	21.88	2.12
		89			
1995 – 1	20		180	22.5	−2.5
		91			
1995 – 2	25		186	23.25	1.75
		95			
1995 – 3	22		194	24.25	−2.25
		99			
1995 – 4	28		201	25.13	2.87
		102			
1996 – 1	24		208	26	−2
		106			
1996 – 2	28		214	26.75	1.25
		108			
1996 – 3	26				
1996 – 4	30				

Fig 4.13   *4-quarter moving average for the quarterly sales figures of XYZ Ltd – 1993 to 1996*

we look at the table, we see that this figure is between the second and third quarters of 1993. It does not centre on an exact time period. The same applies for all of the other 4-quarter totals. In order to centre the data, it is necessary to find another average. The first two 4-quarter totals centre either side of the third quarter of 1993. By adding these together and dividing by eight, instead of four, we are able to get an average figure which centres upon the third quarter of 1993, i.e. 18.25. We can do this for all the time periods which can be calculated by using the 8-quarter total column.

Thus, we can see that when a moving average has an even number of points, it is necessary to find two averages, in effect, in order to find the trend. Once this has been done, then the forecasting is carried out in exactly the same way, i.e. by drawing a graph, extrapolating the trend line, reading off a predicted trend figure, and then adding in the appropriate average cyclical variation. You might like to try to calculate a forecasted sales figure for the first quarter of 1997 from the data above.

Remember that time series analysis is only of use in the short term. It is based upon the assumption that history repeats itself and so can be extrapolated into the future. It can also be completely negated by the occurrence of unpredictable events. When all of these facts are taken into account, we can see that whilst it is better to attempt to predict and plan than not to, predictions must not be considered to be guaranteed outcomes. They are simply a means of reducing uncertainty and they cannot eliminate it.

Monthly sales figures for the sales staff of ABC Ltd to the nearest £1,000	
Salesperson number	Monthly sales (to nearest £1,000)
1	2
2	3
3	4
4	4
5	4
6	4
7	6
8	7
9	9
10	19
Total sales	62

THE IMPORTANCE OF THE AVERAGE

In any section on information and decision taking, the importance of an understanding of measures of central tendency, or averages, should not be underestimated. It is especially useful, when making comparisons of figures, to have a single figure that is representative of the group of figures. This figure is usually a measure of central tendency.

We do not need to go into great detail here, but we should look briefly at the three main measures of central tendency. These are the mode, the median and the arithmetic mean. Let us look at each in turn and, in order to do so, we shall use the following sales figures for ten different salespeople in the same business over a period of one month.

We can now consider each of the measures of central tendency:

1 **The mode**   This is the most frequently occurring figure in a group of figures.

Thus, in this case, the mode will be £4,000, since these were the sales figures achieved by four of the salespeople.

2 **The median**   This is the middle figure in a group that has been sorted into ascending or descending order. In this case, we have the sales figures for ten salespeople, arranged in ascending order. Thus, the median value will be that which is between the fifth and sixth salesperson. Here, each has sold £4,000 for the month, so the median value is the same as the modal value, i.e. £4,000.

3 **The arithmetic mean**   This is calculated by taking the total of all the values given and then dividing that total by the number of figures. In this case, total sales are £62,000 and there are ten salespeople, so the average sales are £6,200 per person.

The best, i.e. most appropriate, measure of central tendency will depend upon the situation being considered. The mode is used when we are trying to discover the most common figure. This would be very useful when considering clothes sizes or shoe sizes. In our example, most salespeople, 40 percent of them, achieve monthly sales of £4,000. This might be a useful figure for comparison relating to relative performance. The median is useful when there are extreme values that will distort the arithmetic mean. In our example, the salesperson who achieves sales of £19,000 for the month distorts the average,

pulling it up well above the other two measures. This is a major weakness of the arithmetic mean and so, in this case, the mode and the median figures are likely to be more useful. The arithmetic mean does have strong advantages over other measures of central tendency, however, because it takes into account all of the values that have been measured and it can be used as the basis for further analysis, such as the standard deviation.

RELAUNCHING THE POLO

Nestlé, the food and confectionery manufacturer, produce the famous household brand name Polo. This product has dominated the mint market for many years with its distinct product design and packaging. However, Nestlé had seen the market share and the sales of Polo decline in the four years up to 1993. This decline is shown in the table below.

Market shares %	1990	1991	1992	1993
Polo	17.4	17.5	16.2	15.8
Trebor extra strong mints	15.9	16.1	17.4	17.3
Trebor mints	3.6	3.3	2.6	3.0
Trebor spearmints	1.5	1.5	1.3	1.5
Softmints	5.7	7.1	7.7	8.5
Others	55.9	54.6	54.8	53.9

Nestlé were seeing a decline in the demand for Polo from consumers as taste changed and there was an increase in competition from other brands such as Trebor's Extra Strong Mints. In order to analyse Polo's decline more closely, Nestlé embarked on

some extensive market research. The key findings of this research relating specifically to Polo were:

- Polo was seen as a predictable brand that had not been developed
- Consumers were no longer associating mints solely with Polos but with other products as well
- Polo does not offer a taste to suit more diverse consumer tastes

The research also identified some key findings relating to the market. These were:

- There was a growing demand for spearmint flavour in the youth market
- There was an increasing demand for strong mints in the adult market
- Sugar-free mints were a small but growing segment

In response to this market research, Nestlé remarketed the Polo brand. The company launched three new brands to support the traditional Polo mint. The new brands, along with the traditional Polo mint, were targeted at the following market segments.

Product	Target Segment
Polo Original	All adults
Polo Strong	All adults with a male bias
Polo Sugar Free	16–24 with a female bias
Polo Spearmint	16–24

The strategy has widened and deepened the mint market, allowing Nestlé to target its marketing more specifically at certain groups of consumers. The results of this change was successful in that Polo's market share increased from 15.8 percent of the mint market in 1993 to 19.8 percent of the market in 1994.

QUESTIONS

1 a Outline the different types of market research survey Nestle could have used. [5]
  b Explain which type of survey you think would have been the most appropriate for Nestlé to use. [7]

2 a Explain what you understand by the term 'sampling'. [5]
  b Explain the advantages and disadvantages associated with each method of sampling. [8]
  c Which method of sampling do you think would have been most appropriate for Nestlé to use when researching the Polo market? [10]

3 a What do you think are the qualities of a good questionnaire? [5]
  b Taking into account the findings of Nestlé's market research, design a questionnaire that could have produced these findings. For each question you have asked, write a note explaining the purpose of your question. [10]

4 a Draw a series of pie charts to show the market share of each brand in the mint market for 1990 to 1994. [7]
  b Why are pie charts used in market research? [8]

5 Many companies have followed the results drawn from market research when launching new products only to see the products fail when they actually reach the market. Evaluate the usefulness of market research as a basis for launching new products. [15]

Total [80]

PROMOTING ASPEN'S COMMUNICATIONS EQUIPMENT

Aspen communications is a wholesaler of communications equipment. The company was started in 1982 by two brothers, Edward and Mark Lampeter. They tried to exploit the newly emerging market of telecommunications which had been opened up to competition by the Government. Aspen sell a range of telephones, telephone systems (PABX), mobile phones, answering machines, modems and telecom accessories. Their target market is telephone shops, electrical retailers, department stores, and businesses who need communications equipment for their own use. The market, and Aspen's business, expanded rapidly during the 1980s with the growth in communications, and the company's turnover had reached £40 million by 1990. However, the early 1990s saw recession and increased competition both domestically and from abroad. Aspen saw its sales and profits decline as a result of this. In 1996 Edward and Mark Lampeter appointed a new marketing director, Sarah Miles, who they had head-hunted from a rival company. Sarah put forward a plan in December 1996 that completely changed the image of the company. It involved promotion through trade magazines, exhibitions, direct mail and personal selling. However, the plan met with a great deal of scepticism from some members of Aspen's board of directors when Sarah demanded a 20 percent increase in her marketing budget to fund her plan. Edward and Mark supported Sarah and the plan was put into place, with promotional activity beginning in April 1997. The sales figures for the 18 months following the plan's implementation are contained in the table below.

Month	Sales £ million
April 1997	3.25
May	3.11
June	3.46
July	3.55
August	3.34
September	3.54
October	3.89
November	3.23
December	3.88
January 1998	3.76
February	3.77
March	3.20

After 12 months of the promotions campaign a stormy board meeting took place, during which a number of Aspen's directors called for Sarah Miles' resignation on the basis that sales at the end of the year were no higher than at the start of the year, despite her expensive promotion campaign. Sarah countered these criticisms by saying that average sales for the year were 15 percent higher than the previous 12 months.

QUESTIONS

1 a Draw a graph of monthly sales revenue against time in months. [5]

  b Calculate a 4-point moving average for the 12 months shown in the table. [8]

  c Plot the 4-point moving average sales figure on the graph you plotted in part a. [5]

  d On the basis of the information you have calculated as a moving average and plotted on your graph, comment on whether the promotional campaign was a success or failure. [5]

  e What other factors would you need to take into account before you could judge the success of the marketing campaign? [5]

2 a Calculate the average monthly sales for the period in the table using both the arithmetic mean and the median. [7]

  b Using the mean average you have calculated above, calculate the average monthly sales figure for the previous 12 months. [5]

3 Explain how you would go about producing a comprehensive assessment of how successful the promotions campaign was. [10]

Total [50]

Financial Accounting – Section A: Accounting and finance

SUMMARY

1   An introduction to accounting. What accounting is, why it is used, and who accounts are prepared for.
2   What accounting information is available to stakeholders? The main document produced by accountants is the annual report.
3   The balance sheet is a major accounting document available to stakeholders. It is a summary of what the company owns and owes at a particular point in time.
4   The balance sheet balances because of the accounting equation that is followed each

time a business makes a transaction. The accounting equation states that fixed assets + current assets = owner's capital + long-term liabilities + current liabilities.
5   The profit and loss account measures the organisation's trading performance over the accounting year.
6   The profit and loss account is produced following the principle of accrual accounting.
7   Non-profit-making organisations produce income and expenditure accounts.

WHAT IS ACCOUNTING AND FINANCE?

Accounting and Finance can be defined as the measurement of the performance of an organisation and the resources used by them, in money terms, in a set past, current or future time period, for the users of accounts. This definition can be broken down and examined in the following way.

Users of accounts

These are people who use accounts to provide information to form the basis of decision making. They are also known as stakeholders. They are all people that have a stake in the success or failure of the business. This could be the sales director of an organisation measuring the money value of sales in order to judge the success or failure of the organisation's sales force, or it could be suppliers to the business who are concerned about getting paid for the goods they supply.

Users can be split into two groups as follows.

1   **External users**   This is the group of users who lie outside the organisation's management. It includes:

- Shareholders and potential shareholders, who will be interested in the return they might earn on funds they have tied up in shares
- Workers, who will be concerned with

the potential wage rise the company could or could not afford

- The local community, who might be interested in the success or failure of the organisation and the consequences this might have for the local community
- The Government, who will be compiling the national statistics on economic output
- The tax authorities, who will need to calculate the organisation's tax liability
- Other organisations, who will want to measure their own performance against others
- The bank and other creditors, who will wish to assess the organisation's ability to repay funds they have loaned to them

2 **Internal users**   This group of users are part of the organisation's management and need financial information to help them make decisions about the way the organisation is run. This could be the production manager who needs to know the money value of raw materials required for the coming period, or the marketing director who wants to see how the sales have been affected by a new advertising campaign.

Money terms

Expressing all items in money terms is a key accounting convention, which means using the currency of a country to value items. Buildings, stock, wages and expenses are all expressed in money terms because it provides a standard for users of accounts to make an objective assessment of an organisation's financial situation. If a shareholder was comparing the sales of Marks & Spencer and British Home Stores, effective comparisons can really only be made if money value of sales is compared.

Past, current and future time periods

Accountants work in the three time periods. Past figures for sales or profits provide a user

such as a potential shareholder with information which can be used to assess the past performance of an organisation. In the current time period the organisation's cash position is vital information for a manager deciding on whether to buy a new piece of machinery. The finance department of an organisation spends a great deal of time producing budgets which are the future plans for the organisation in financial terms. For example, the future cost and revenue figures associated with the launching of a new product provide managers with an objective basis on which to decide whether to go ahead with the project or not.

Measurement of resources used

Organisations use the resources of land, machines, raw materials and components, workers, managers and cash. Use of these resources is often measured in money terms because of the need for a standard value. For example, an organisation such as Ford will measure the value of its land and machinery because it gives the users of accounts a basis on which to value the worth of the organisation. An organisation's management will need to be able to assess the money value of machinery it will need for the coming year to see whether it has the funds available to acquire it.

The performance of the organisation

Financial performance of organisations is frequently measured in terms of profitability. This information is provided by the profit and loss account statement in the organisation's accounts. However, performance can also be assessed in terms of cost and revenue figures. The marketing director of Cadbury's Schweppes PLC would, initially, have been more concerned with the revenue gained from the launch of a new product when trying to penetrate a market and establish market share, than with profitability as a measure of performance. Similarly, the bank that has loaned funds to a small computer software company would perhaps be more concerned with the amount of cash the organisation has, as opposed to its profitability, in order to give an idea of its ability to repay a loan.

Financial information

All organisations from sole traders to partnerships to PLCs have to produce documentation which provides a record of their activities in financial terms. This information, in its simplest form, will be given on a tax return produced by a sole trader, so that the tax authorities can assess how much tax the organisation has to pay. Larger organisations, such as partnerships and private and public limited companies, have to produce more formal sets of accounts.

Auditing

In the case of public limited companies like Shell, ICI and BP, the organisation must by law publish a set of accounts which is available to the general public. The accounts are contained in a document called the annual report. This report is produced by an independent accountancy firm which specialises in a process called auditing. Auditing means that all the financial records of an organisation are checked by a firm of accountants to make sure they are correct and provide a 'true and fair view' of the organisation's financial position at that point in time. This is important because the stakeholders in the organisation must be confident that any decisions they make relating to the organisation are based on accurate information. Just consider the disastrous consequences for a company which supplies another company with goods

on credit, relying on information contained in the annual report which suggests the company is financially secure, only to find that this information was wrong and the company is in fact bankrupt. It is in the auditors' interests to make sure the accounts are accurate because they are liable if the accounts are found to be wrong. Figure 5.1 overleaf illustrates the layout and format of an annual report on the retailer Sainsbury's PLC.

■ THE BALANCE SHEET

What does the balance sheet show?

The balance sheet is a statement of an organisation's value at a given point in time. It does this by putting a money value on what an organisation owns, in the form of assets, and owes, in the form of liabilities. The amount of funds owned in the form of assets always equals the funds generated through borrowing and the owner's funds (liabilities) because of a concept known as the accounting equation. This states that:

Liabilities + Owner's Capital = Assets

This equation is followed for each transaction which an organisation makes. For example, if a company purchases a machine for £200,000 and finances it by borrowing the £200,000, then you can see that:

+£200,000 liabilities = +£200,000 assets

The same process applies each time you make a transaction. If you buy a CD using a credit card then you have a loan that is a liability of £12 and your CD asset of £12.

+£12 liabilities = +£12 assets

The process continues to work if you were to use £50 cash asset to buy a pair of jeans. The

Sainsbury's
Annual Report
& Accounts 1996

Company Objective; To provide unrivalled value to our customers in the quality of the goods we sell.

Page 1

Many companies use the annual report to state their missions as an organisation

Chairman's Statement

I am delighted to report another year's good performance. Group profits increased by 25% to £632m. This brings compound growth over the last 20 years to 23%. This year's results reflect better than expected sales over the second half of the year, improving productivity and close control over costs. For many years our investment in large modern stores has brought about improving profit margins. Dividends per share have increased by 20% and are now two and a half times greater than 5 years ago.

Page 3

This statement is a general summary of the organisation's performance over the year and provides the management's public view of how it feels about its overall performance. It will communicate information about any possible changes in policy or future plans the organisations might have.

Ten Year Record

£m	86	87	88.......
Group sales	3,572	4,043	5,009......
Group profit	186	237	298......
Dividend per share	2.72p	3.46p	4.15p......

Page 2

All organisations carry a summary of their financial performance over previous years. This is useful to users of accounts who can pick out trends and changes in performance.

Report of the Directors

Profit and Dividend; Profit on the group's activities amounted to £623m. After deducting £184m for taxation and £153m for dividends, £253m has been transferred to reserves. The directors have proposed to pay a dividend of 6.35p per share.

Principal Activities; The principal activity of the group is the retail distribution of food and home improvements and garden products.

Share capital; The principal changes in share capital was that £158m was issued by the way of a rights issue to shareholders at 312p per share.

Page 4

The directors of the organisation are legally required to report on major aspects of the organisation's activities. Unlike the Chairman's statement, the directors' report is more objective and does not express a view.

Fig 5.1   *Summary of an annual report produced by Sainsbury's PLC*

Sainsbury's PLC Annual Report 1996

value of your assets in the form of clothing rises by £50, but your cash asset falls by £50.

Liabilities = +£50 assets (jeans)
= −£50 assets (cash)

In the same way, a company which buys stock valued at £60,000 using cash assets sees its cash assets fall by £60,000 and its stock assets rise by £60,000.

Liabilities = +£60,000 assets (stock)
= −£60,000 assets (cash)

Every transaction made by an organisation is recorded by the accounting function of the business in a series of ledgers that summarise changes in each item in the balance sheet. The process, called double entry book-keeping, takes place on computers, but it still follows the principle of the accounting equation shown above.

OWNER'S CAPITAL OR SHAREHOLDERS' FUNDS

Small businesses

In a small organisation, such as a sole trader or partnership, the owner's capital will simply be money put into the business by the owner(s). When a graphic designer decides to open a studio on his or her own using £60,000 to buy the latest computers and software, then this would be entered into the firm's accounts under the heading of owner's capital. If these funds were held as cash in the firm's bank account, then, following the accounting equation, this would be entered in the following way.

Owner's capital and liabilities	Assets
+£60,000 Owner's capital	+£60,000 Cash

Larger businesses

In a larger organisation, like a private limited company or a public limited company, the owner's capital would be in the form of shareholders' funds. Unlike the ownership of a sole trader or a partnership, the ownership of larger organisations is split into units, each unit representing part ownership of the company and called a share. Share capital is sometimes referred to as equity. The number of shares issued depends on the size of the company; some of the privatised utilities such as British Telecom and British Gas have issued so many shares, and have so many shareholders, that their annual general meeting, which all shareholders may attend, has filled Birmingham's NEC arena!

Share capital

Ordinary shares

Fig 5.2 *The value of stocks and shares reported in a newspaper*

Ordinary shares are the most common form of share capital issued by organisations. Each share gives the owner the right to a proportion of the organisation's profits, in the form of dividends. The amount of dividend is recommended by the directors of the company who base their decision on the profit earned over the accounting period. Sainsbury's paid 8p per share in 1996. Each ordinary share carries a voting right that can be cast when there are major decisions which need to be made. This could be the acceptance of a merger with another company, the election of a new director, sacking of an existing director and the acceptance of dividends. Ordinary shares are permanent capital because they cannot be cashed in, although they can be sold on through the Stock Exchange if they are in a public limited company.

Preference shares

Preference shares, represent a much smaller part of share capital than ordinary shares. They are lower risk than ordinary shares because they carry a fixed rate of dividend that has to be paid each year. Preference shares do not carry a voting right.

The impact of share issues on the balance sheet

If a company issues £509 million of new ordinary shares, assuming these funds are put into a bank account, then the transaction would be recorded in the following way in the balance sheet.

Shareholders' funds and liabilities	Assets
Ordinary shares +£509 million	Cash +£509 million

Reserves

Reserves represent part of the owner's capital which is not in the form of shares. The majority of reserves tend to be in the form of profit that has not been distributed in the form of dividends. Profit added to the reserves is known as revenue reserves. When the local BMW dealership sells a new series 5 for £25,000, a car they had originally bought for £18,000, then the £7,000 profit made on the sale would be recorded in the accounts in the following way.

Shareholders' funds and liabilities	Assets
Revenue reserves +£7,000	Cash +£25,000 Stock −£18,000

Capital reserves, on the other hand, are funds generated outside normal activities, such as the revaluation of assets. Most individuals see their wealth rise when the price of their house goes up. The same thing applies to businesses who see the value of their assets rise. So if the value of the London Hilton, as a property, goes up by £100,000, then this would be added to the capital reserves of the Hilton organisation. In the balance sheet this would be shown as follows.

Shareholders' funds and liabilities	Assets
Capital Reserves +£100,000	Buildings +£100,000

Business entity

When considering owner's capital or shareholders' funds, it is important to understand the accounting concept of business or separate entity. This means that the business is considered to be a separate legal person in its own right, with an identity which is different from the owner's. In the case of a sole trader, any funds put into the business are now part of the business, and are owed by the business to the owner. The same principle applies to public and private limited companies whose funds are put in by shareholders. On a practical level, it is important that users of accounts, such as the tax authorities, can distinguish between the personal funds of the owner and the funds of the business.

LIABILITIES

Long-term liabilities

Liabilities differ from owner's capital because they are funds borrowed from an outside third party. Long term means they are not due for repayment by the organisation for more than 12 months.

Interest payments represent the cost of financing loans and its level depends on the size and length of repayment, and whether it is secured or not. The key difference between interest and dividends is that interest has to be paid each year no matter what the performance of the organisation is like, whereas dividends do not.

Loans

Loans are generally obtained through banks, although there are other organisations, such as Investors in Industry, who provide funds. Loans such as a mortgage, are sometimes secured, which means that if the firm does not meet the repayments of the loan then an asset can be taken from the organisation, and sold to cover the repayment.

Debentures

An organisation can also issue units of debt called debentures. These are rather like shares in that they are a certificate which is part of a loan, but the buyer is lending the organisation money rather than taking part ownership in it. Many major soccer clubs like Arsenal and Leeds United have used this type of scheme to raise funds to improve their stadiums. When Twickenham Rugby Ground sold debentures to the value of £15 million to cover the cost of

Fig 5.3 *Loans are most often obtained through banks*

new stands, the balance sheet would have changed accordingly.

Shareholders' funds and liabilities	Assets
Long-term liabilities +£15 million	Buildings +£15 million

Current liabilities

These are borrowed funds that have a repayment date of less than 12 months. They are important to businesses because they provide short-term funds that can be used to allow a business's payment system to function efficiently. A good example of this is trade creditors, where stock can be obtained on credit without cash being used immediately.

Cash is the life blood of all businesses because they cannot trade without it. Anything that makes cash management by firms easier is very important. There are five sources of current liabilities.

1 **Trade creditors or accounts payable** This is funds owed by an organisation to its suppliers which have not been paid at the balance sheet date. When a retailer takes delivery of £80,000 worth of stock from a supplier, it is entered as an £80,000 creditor in the balance sheet. The double entry for this would be:

Shareholders' funds and liabilities	Assets
Current liabilities +£80,000	Stock +£80,000

2 **Overdraft** When an organisation draws more funds from its bank account than there are funds available to it, then it will go overdrawn. Most companies will agree a certain figure with the bank for an allowable overdraft.

3 **Accrued charge** This is rather like creditors, except it refers to services the business receives rather than stock. The electricity bill at the local Chinese takeaway, which is unpaid at the balance sheet date, is an example.

4 **Tax payable** Corporation tax, paid on company profits, is normally due 12 months after it has been earned. From the time it was earned to the time it is actually paid it is considered a current liability.

5 **Dividends payable** The directors of the organisation decide on a dividend to recommend to shareholders based on the profitability of the company that year and what it can afford. This is put to the organisation's shareholders at their AGM, who vote to accept or reject it. So, at the balance sheet date, the dividend is outstanding and thus carried as a current liability.

FIXED ASSETS

An asset is any object which has a value to its owner. In a business context, this means an item that belongs to a business, which can be expressed in money terms. Most individuals consider their assets as the car, house, CD system, computer and clothing that they own. The same applies to the machinery, buildings and stock that the business owns. In the balance sheet, assets represent a use of the funds acquired from owner's capital and liabilities, and are split into fixed and current assets.

Historic cost

Accountants need to be objective about the value of fixed assets if they are to give a true and fair view of the organisation's worth, so a concept known as historic cost is used. This means the basis for valuing all fixed assets is at the price they were paid for, since this price represents the only really objective measure of the asset's value. When a bank spends £100 million on a new computer system, this is the basis for valuing that asset in the balance sheet.

Fixed assets

A fixed asset is an asset that will be used by the business for some considerable time and will not be used up in the normal course of trading. Such assets can be split into two types.

Tangible fixed assets

These can be physically touched, existing as machinery, plant, buildings, and fixtures. A school's fixed assets would be its classrooms, playing fields, video equipment, sports hall and music equipment.

If your school spends £500,000 on a new astro turf using a loan from central

Fig 5.4 *Two examples of intangible fixed assets*

government, then the balance sheet entry would look like this:

Liabilities	Assets
Long-term liabilities	Fixed assets
+£500,000	+£500,000

Intangible fixed assets

Trademarks, patents and copyrights are all examples of intangible fixed assets. In 1988 accountants became aware of the value of brand names as assets and started to record them in their company balance sheets. Rank, Hovis McDougall value brands such as Mothers Pride and Hovis at £560 million. Part of the reason for doing this arises from a need to value the company when it is being merged or taken over.

This leads us to another intangible asset, goodwill. When a business, such as your local pizza restaurant, is being sold, the owner is likely to price the firm at more than the money value of the building, kitchen equipment and tables. Obviously, a successful business will also have the customer base that has been built up over time included in the price. The difference between the value of all other assets, and the purchase price of the business, is called goodwill. It represents an estimated value put on the firm's customer base. Because goodwill is impossible to measure accurately, organisations only enter it into their balance sheet when the organisation is being sold.

Many organisations also own shares in other organisations and the value of these shares is included as an intangible fixed asset.

CURRENT ASSETS

Unlike fixed assets, current assets are not permanent and are constantly being turned over as the company trades. Current assets are considered to be more liquid than their fixed counterparts because of the comparative ease with which they can be turned into cash. The more easily an asset can be turned into cash the more liquid it is considered to be. There are three types of current assets that are laid out in the balance sheet on the basis of how easily they can be turned into cash, the least liquid coming first.

Stock

Stock can either be in the form of raw materials and components, work in progress or finished goods. For a company like Ford UK, engine parts for the Fiesta would be their stock of components, Mondeos on the production line their work-in-progress, and Scorpios waiting to be shipped out their finished goods.

Debtors or accounts receivable

When a firm sells goods on credit, allowing them to leave the factory before they are paid for and then waiting for payment at a future date, typically 30 to 90 days, the outstanding debt is considered to be debtors in the balance sheet. For example, when Chanel sells

£30,000 worth of women's suits to Harvey Nicholls store in London for £50,000 on credit payable in 30 days, then the accounting entry for Chanel would look like this.

Shareholders' funds and liabilities	Assets
+£20,000 Revenue reserves	−£30,000 Stock +£50,000 Debtors

Prepayments

These are payments made for services that have not been fully received at the balance sheet date. Most companies pay for insurance before its benefit has been fully received. That is to say, if a payment of £500 made for insurance to run from 3 May, 1996 to 3 May, 1997 and the balance sheet date is on 31 December, 1996 then not all of the insurance benefit which has been paid for has been received. The money value of this is carried as a prepayment in the balance sheet.

Cash

This is the most liquid of the current assets. Most firms carry a small amount of petty cash for everyday expenses, along with cash in current bank and deposit accounts. Businesses cannot survive without sufficient amounts of cash, so its effective management is absolutely vital.

■ LAYOUT OF THE BALANCE SHEET

All companies have an accounting year that starts and finishes on set dates. The balance sheet is drawn up so that the organisation's worth is reported at the end of the accounting year. For many organisations it begins on the 1 April and ends on the 31 March to coincide with the tax year, although other dates can be used. So on 31 March the balance sheet is drawn up by summarising the changes in assets, liabilities and owner's capital over the year, following the double entry accounting principle.

Horizontal format layout

Up to now, we have worked on the two column principle of owner's capital and liabilities on one side of the balance sheet and assets on the other. The balance sheet of Hardy Amps Ltd, a company which manufactures sound equipment for the music industry, is illustrated in Fig 5.5.

Vertical layout 1

Over time accountants have moved away from the horizontal format to a vertical format which involves laying out assets and liabilities down the page instead of across it (see Fig. 5.6). However, they have also reordered assets and liabilities, so that long-term liabilities and shareholders' funds are grouped together as the long-term source of funds, with current assets and liabilities, along with fixed assets, grouped as the use of these long-term funds. The accounting equation has been reorganised in the following way:

shareholders' funds + long-term liabilities + current liabilities = fixed assets + current assets

with current assets moved to the other side of the equation as follows:

shareholders' funds + long-term liabilities = fixed assets + current assets − current liabilities

Hardy Amps Ltd

Shareholders' Funds	£	£	Fixed Assets	£	£
Ordinary Shares	80,000		Tangible		
Reserves	25,000		Buildings	110,000	
		105,000	Machinery	40,000	
Long-term Liabilities			Intangible		
Mortgage	75,000		Patents	15,000	
Debentures	20,000		Shares	20,000	
		95,000			185,000
Current Liabilities			Current Assets		
Trade Creditors	10,000		Stock	30,000	
Overdraft	12,000		Debtors	25,000	
Tax payable	18,000		Prepayments	6,000	
Dividends payable	15,000		Cash	16,000	
Accrued charge	7,000				77,000
		62,000			
Total liabilities		262,000	Total assets		262,000

Fig 5.5 *Horizontal format balance sheet for Hardy Amps Ltd: 31 March, 1996*

The vertical format balance sheet gives us three new figures to consider.

1 **Net current assets** The figure for current assets less current liabilities gives us net current assets or working capital. This figure tells us how much capital (funds attributable to the shareholders) is available to the organisation in the short term. In the case of Hardy Amps Ltd, there is a surplus of £15,000. In other words, £62,000 of short-term sources of funds have been made available for £77,000 of short-term assets. The more working capital an organisation has the more funds it has to acquire stock and pay bills and wages.

2 **Net assets** This is simply the addition of fixed assets to net current assets or working capital. This net figure shows the net value of what the company owns.

3 **Capital employed** This is the sum of the two long-term sources of finance, long-term liabilities and shareholders' funds that are used to finance the net assets.

Vertical layout 2

The Companies Act 1981 slightly altered the vertical presentation to isolate the shareholders' funds. Thus, restating the accounting equation we can now see that:

shareholders funds + long-term liabilities = fixed assets + current assets − current liabilities

becomes:

shareholders funds = fixed assets + current assets − current liabilities − long-term liabilities

This means that the balance sheet of Hardy Amps Ltd is now laid out as in Fig 5.7.

The differing formats are confusing, so it is vital to understand the importance of each item included. The layout may have changed over time, but the accounting equation has not.

Hardy Amps Ltd

Fixed Assets	£	£	£
Tangible			
Buildings	110,000		
Machinery	40,000		
Intangible			
Patents	15,000		
Shares	20,000		
		185,000	
Current Assets			
Stock	30,000		
Debtors	25,000		
Prepayments	6,000		
Cash	16,000		
		77,000	
Less			
Current Liabilities			
Trade Creditors	10,000		
Overdraft	12,000		
Tax payable	18,000		
Dividends payable	15,000		
Accrued charge	7,000		
		62,000	
Net Current Assets: CA − CL		15,000	
Net Assets: FA + (CA − CL)			**200,000**
Shareholders' Funds			
Ordinary Shares	80,000		
Reserves	25,000		
		105,000	
Long-term Liabilities			
Mortgage	75,000		
Debentures	20,000		
		95,000	
Capital Employed: SF + LL			**200,000**

Fig 5.6   *Vertical layout 1 balance sheet for Hardy Amps Ltd: 31 March, 1996*

Why is the balance sheet important?

Information in the balance sheet that measures the organisation's value is important to the users of accounts for a number of reasons depending on the user.

1   From the point of view of managers and shareholders it shows how much the organisation they are responsible for is worth. The growth in this worth will be seen as a positive sign of progress over time; an individual would look at the money value of their own personal worth in the same way.

Hardy Amps Ltd

	£	£	£
Fixed Assets			
Tangible			
Buildings	110,000		
Machinery	40,000		
Intangible			
Patents	15,000		
Shares	20,000		
		185,000	
Current Assets			
Stock	30,000		
Debtors	25,000		
Prepayments	6,000		
Cash	16,000		
		77,000	
Less			
Current Liabilities			
Trade Creditors	10,000		
Overdraft	12,000		
Tax payable	18,000		
Dividends payable	15,000		
Accrued charge	7,000		
		62,000	
Net Current Assets: CA − CL		15,000	
Net Assets: FA + (CA − CL)			**200,000**
Less			
Long-term Liabilities			
Mortgage	75,000		
Debentures	20,000		
		95,000	
NA − LL			**105,000**
Shareholders' Funds			
Ordinary Shares	80,000		
Reserves	25,000		
			105,000

Fig 5.7 *Vertical layout 2 balance sheet for Hardy Amps Ltd: 31 March, 1996*

2 It gives shareholders and managers a measure of the firm's size in money terms, and how it should be performing in terms of profitability. Obviously, larger organisations should make larger profits.

3 If an organisation is being sold it provides the shareholders or owners with a money value on which to base the purchase price of the company.

4 A bank which is considering a loan for an organisation would be interested in its balance sheet, because the balance sheet provides the bank with information on how much the firm has borrowed already; this could give it some idea of the firm's ability to repay the loan.

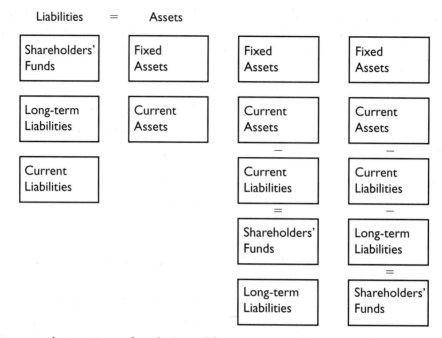

Fig 5.8   *Diagram to show movement from horizontal format to vertical layouts 1 and 2*

THE PROFIT AND LOSS ACCOUNT

What is the profit and loss account?

The profit and loss account is a statement which shows the surplus of sales revenue earned, above expenses incurred, over the financial period. It is a legal requirement of all companies to produce this statement. Ultimately, many stakeholders within an organisation will judge its trading activities' success or failure on the basis of the amount of profit made over a period of time. As such, the profit and loss account is very much a statement that reflects performance of the organisation over the financial year.

Measuring sales

Realisation

A good is sold as soon as there is a transfer of ownership of goods from the seller to the buyer. This normally takes place when goods are delivered. Once this transfer of ownership takes place, the sale is recorded, and any profit made on the good. At the same time as the ownership has been transferred, all the expenses associated with getting the good or service to a point where it can be sold are subtracted, and this figure is entered into the profit and loss account. Accountants say that profits have been realised at the point of sale, a concept called realisation. The key point to notice here is that cash does not have to change hands for the profit to be realised. When a company, such as Nike, delivers £500,000 worth of training shoes to Olympus, the sporting goods retailer, this will be recorded in Nike's profit and loss account as a sale whether or not cash has been paid. If it has been, it is a cash sale. If, on the other hand, Olympus took the goods on credit, then the sale would be a £500,000 debtor in Nike's balance sheet, but it would still be recorded as a sale and the profits realised in Nike's profit and loss account.

Measuring expenses or costs

Matching

An expense is a money value put on goods and services used by an organisation as it operates. An expense is incurred in the profit and loss account when it is matched with the sale of the product produced by the company. When, for example, Nike delivers training shoes to Olympus, all the costs associated with the trainers are matched and then subtracted from their sales revenue to give the profit. These costs would include labour, raw materials, rent, heat and light and administration. This process of matching sales and their related costs is called the matching principle.

Accrual accounting

Matching and realisation are carried out on a time basis, so that revenues and expenses are matched with the accounting period when the goods were sold. This concept is called accrual accounting. By using accrual accounting, the profit figure for the period should reflect the success or failure of the company, in terms of profitability, over the period. Here is an example of the concept of accrual accounting.

A small wholesaler of china plant pots buys in 50,000 units at £12 each during the accounting period 1 January, 1996 to 31 December, 1996 and sells 30,000 units at £18 during the same period. It also incurs labour costs of £65,000, and overheads of £49,000 in the same period, although £19,000 of the overhead had not been

paid for by 31 December, 1996. The profit and loss account drawn up on 31 December, 1996 would look like this.

	£000s
Sales revenue (30,000 × £18)	540
Cost of stock (30,000 × £12)	360
Labour	65
Overheads	49
Total cost	474
Profit	**66**

You should note the following important points.

1 Only the 30,000 units of stock sold are counted as expenses. This is because the remaining 20,000 units will be carried in stock and sold in the following year when they will be considered a cost.
2 Despite the fact that £19,000 of the overheads remained unpaid by the date of the account, they were still included because the services included in the overhead, such as heat and light, had already benefited the company in terms of generating the sale of goods in that period. This is a clear indication of how the profit figure can differ from the cash figure the organisation has.
3 The figures are in £000s so the sales revenue is £540,000. This type of number expression is frequently used by accountants.

Direct costs

Direct costs, or prime costs, are defined as those costs that take place as a direct result of the production of a good or service. Labour and material costs are normally considered to be direct costs, and are identified as direct labour and direct materials in the profit and loss account. The leading international hairdressing company, Vidal Sasoon, will have

Fig 5.9 *A hairstylist at work is incurring direct costs*

direct labour in the form of its stylists and direct materials in the form of shampoo, hair mousse and spray.

Direct materials
This is sometimes known as the cost of stock or cost of sales in the profit and loss account. Accountants have to establish how much stock has passed through the business during the accounting period to establish how much to match with the sales revenue generated from its sales. It is calculated in the following way:

opening stock + purchases − closing stock = cost of sales

By adding opening stock at the start of the accounting period to the amount of stock bought in the form of purchases, the

accountant can tell how much stock the company had available to sell during the period. By subtracting the closing stock left at the end of the period the accountant can tell how much stock has been sold during the period. If the television shop, Epsom Visual, which sells televisions at a price of £450, starts the year with an opening stock of 110 televisions valued at £200 each, purchases 400 televisions during the year at £200, and has 80 televisions in closing stock, then the cost of sales will be calculated as shown below.

opening stock + purchases − closing stock = units sold

		£
Opening stock	110 @ £200	22,000
Purchases	400 @ £200	80,000
Total stock available	510 @ £200	102,000
Less closing stock	80 @ £200	16,000
Cost of sales	**430 @ £200**	**86,000**

The figure of £86,000 would be matched with sales revenue for the period:
430 @ £450 = £193,500.

Direct labour
This is the cost of labour directly associated with producing the product or providing the service of the organisation. In the example used in direct materials, this would be the sales force who sell the televisions in the shop. There are three full time sales people employed by the shop who are paid £12,000 each per year, giving a total direct labour cost of £36,000.

Indirect costs

Indirect costs or overheads are costs that are incurred by an organisation which cannot be directly related to the production of the good or service it produces. They are grouped into two areas.

1 **Fixed overheads** This is indirect costs that do not change as output changes, such as rent, depreciation of building and machinery (this is discussed in greater detail on p. 95), advertising and management salaries. Epsom Visual incurred the following fixed overhead costs in 1996: rent of £22,000, advertising costs of £10,000 and an allowance for depreciation of £15,000.

2 **Variable or production overheads** Indirect costs like maintenance, heat and light and transport, do tend to rise as the firm increases output. Epsom Visual has indirect expenses in 1996 of £3,000 for heat and light, £2,000 for transport, £1,000 for maintenance and £4,000 for administration.

Measuring profit

Gross profit

Gross profit is sometimes called gross operating profit or gross trading profit. It is calculated as:

sales revenue − cost of goods sold (direct costs + production overheads) = gross profit

Direct costs and production overheads in the profit and loss account are often called the costs of goods sold because they represent the expenses of actually getting the product to a position from which it can be sold, excluding the fixed overheads associated with running the business.

		£	£
Sales	(430 @ £450)		193,500
Cost of sales	(430 @ £200)	86,000	
Direct labour		36,000	
Production overheads		10,000	
Cost of goods sold			132,000
Gross profit			**61,500**

Net profit

Net profit can also be known as net operating or net trading profit. It is calculated as:

gross profit − indirect costs = net profit

The net profit figure represents the profit which the organisation has generated from its normal course of trading.

	£	£
Gross profit		61,500
Rent	22,000	
Advertising	10,000	
Depreciation	15,000	
Indirect costs		47,000
Net profit		**14,500**

Profit before tax

Once the net profit has been established, other expenses and income that are not directly associated with the company's normal course of trading are included.

Non-operating income

Most organisations will generate income from activities other than their normal business of producing whatever their product or service is. Here is a list of possible sources:

- Income from dividends on shares owned in another company
- Interest received from loans made to other companies
- Income received from the sale of fixed assets such as land, buildings or machinery

Non-operating expenses

As with non-operating income, organisations will also incur expenses outside their normal course of business. Interest, which is not included as an operating expense because it is a cost of financing, normally represents the bulk of this cost.

Epsom Visual have earned £8,000 from a portfolio of shares they own. They also received £6,000 from the sale of a company van. Their interest costs were £12,000.

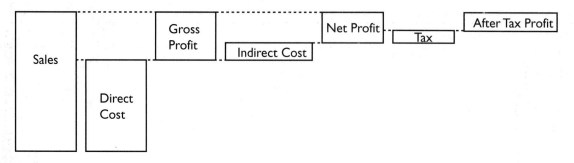

Fig 5.10   *The different types of profit*

Profit after tax

Corporation tax is the tax companies pay on the profits they earn. The rate paid depends on the level of profits earned; the more profit earned, the higher the tax payment. The after tax profit figure is then available for appropriation to shareholders as dividends with the remainder being kept as retained profit in the business. The retained profit is added to the revenue reserves figure in the balance sheet.

Epsom Visual paid tax at a rate of 40 percent and paid 30 percent of the remainder as dividends.

LAYOUT OF THE PROFIT AND LOSS ACCOUNT

The basic structure of the profit and loss account is pretty much the same for most organisations, although you will come across slight differences in presentation. The profit and loss account in published accounts only includes main items and misses out the detailed breakdown of costs and revenues. However, when it is produced for managers all of the detailed information required is included.

The layout breaks down the profit and loss account into three sections.

1 **Trading account**   This is the section which relates to income and expenses generated through the normal course of trading and is section 1 in Fig 5.11.
2 **Profit and loss**   In this part, income and expenses from non-trading activities, along with the tax deduction are included. This is shown in section 2 in Fig 5.11.
3 **Appropriation account**   This summarises the distribution of after tax profits as dividends or retained profit and is shown in section 3 in Fig 5.11.

Published accounts

Figure 5.12 shows what the published accounts of Epsom Visual would look like. The trading account carries far less detail than the account available to managers. The reason for this is that organisations only really want to provide as much information as legally required, for fear that it might be used against them in the wrong hands.

How is the profit and loss account used?

As stated earlier in this section, the profit and loss account provides the user of accounts with measure of the organisation's success or failure in terms of profitability. Although the idea that greater profits as a measure of success is somewhat simplistic, and many other factors should be taken into account, it

Section 1 Trading Account			
Sales revenue	430 @ 450		193,500
Cost of sales	430 @ 200	86,000	
Direct labour		36,000	
Production overhead		10,000	
Cost of goods sold			132,000
Gross Profit			61,500
Rent		22,000	
Advertising		10,000	
Depreciation		15,000	
Total overhead			47,000
Net Profit			**14,500**
Section 2 Profit and Loss Account			
Non-trading income		14,000	
Interest		(12,000)	
Net income			2,000
Profit before Tax			**16,500**
Tax 40%			6,600
Profit after Tax			**9,900**
Section 3 Appropriation Account			
Dividends 30%			2,970
Retained Profit			**6,930**

Fig 5.11 *Profit and loss account for Epsom Visual: 31 December, 1996*

is impossible to hide the fact that most people would consider a more profitable company to be comparatively more successful. Here are different ways stakeholders would use the profit and loss account.

1 The sales director of the organisation would consider the sales figures to see how these have changed over time and how they compare with other, similar organisations.
2 The production director would be interested to see how cost of sales have behaved in comparison with previous years.
3 Existing and potential shareholders would look closely at the after tax profits and how much dividend has been made available to them.

4 Employees negotiating wage increases would show considerable interest in the rise in net profit, as a basis for any wage demands they might have.

INCOME AND EXPENDITURE ACCOUNTS

As we know, only a proportion of organisations have profit as a major aim of their operations. Charities, sports clubs, social clubs, pressure groups and political parties, all earn income and incur expenses as a result of their activities. The income and expenditure

Section 1 Trading Account		
Sales revenue	193,500	
Cost of goods sold	132,000	
Gross Profit	61,500	
Total overhead	47,000	
Net Profit	**14,500**	
Section 2 Profit and Loss Account		
Non-trading income	14,000	
Interest	(12,000)	
Net income		2,000
Profit before Tax		**16,500**
Tax 40%		6,600
Profit after Tax		**9,900**
Section 3 Appropriation Account		
Dividends 30%		2,970
Retained Profit		**6,930**

Fig 5.12   *Published account for Epsom Visual: 31 December, 1996*

account is used by the non-profit-making organisation in very much the same way a company will use the profit and loss account. The account itself works on essentially the same principles, following the concept of accrual accounting. These organisations are often legally required to publish their accounts for members' use.

Layout of the income and expenditure account

The account is laid out in a vertical format like the profit and loss account with income received at the top having expenditure deducted from it. The only difference is that, because non-profit-making organisations generate income from such a wide range of sources, the return of each activity is grouped together. The example of the Vine Hockey Club is given in Fig 5.13.

The net surplus figure earned by the Hockey Club would be added to the reserves in their balance sheet in the same way that the retained profit of a company would be.

Vine Hockey Club					
	£	£		£	£
Bar takings		25,000	Less		
Opening stock 1/1/97	2,800		Pitch hire	4,000	
Bar purchases	20,000		Transport	10,000	
	22,800		Other expenses	5,200	
Closing stock 31/12/97	5,500		**Total Expenses**		**19,200**
Bar expense		17,300	**Net Surplus**		**11,000**
Bar surplus		7,700			
Subscription income	150 @ 50	7,500			
Sponsorship		15,000			
Total Income		**30,200**			

Fig 5.13 *Income and expenditure account for the Vine Hockey Club: 31 December, 1997*

THE AUDIT OF FOCUS 2000

Focus 2000 camera equipment is a company that specialises in the production of all different types of camera equipment. It is currently being audited, and this has produced the following accounting data.

Accounting data
Stock 300, debentures 500, mortgage 200, plant and machinery 400, buildings 350, fixtures 180, cash 240, creditors 400, taxation payable 120, accounts receivable 280, overdraft 190, ordinary shares 400, retained profit 210, patents 150, vehicles 170. Investments in other companies 400, revaluations 250, general reserves 200. All items are in £000s and were recorded on 31 December, 1998.

During the year 1.1.98 to 31.12.98 the following transactions were recorded.

Transactions
Wages of £200,000 were paid, overheads of £210,000 were paid, stock of £600,000 was purchased, marketing costs of £100,000 were incurred, administration costs were £120,000 and depreciation of £300,000 was charged. The company earned £80,000 from interest and dividends associated with its investments. Sales revenue from credit sales was £1.7 million and cash sales were £0.4 million. The current rate of corporation tax is 30 percent and the company retains 40 percent of after tax profits. Interest of £90,000 was paid. Opening stock on the 1 January, 1998 was £200,000.

QUESTIONS

1 Organise the items shown under 'accounting data' into a vertical format balance sheet. [10]

2 Produce a profit and loss account for the year ending 31 December, 1998. [10]

3 List the users who would be interested in looking at the accounts produced above. [4]

4 What might be the particular interests of the accounts produced for three of the users you have listed? [6] Total [30]

FORTUNA EDUCATION RECONSIDER PRODUCTION IN CHINA

Fortuna Education market educational cassettes and books for the home learning of foreign languages. They are an established **private limited company** based in London, where they produce all their material. The tapes and books are manufactured in China by two companies that specialise in this area of production. Fortuna chose to out-source this area of production in 1989.

The company has had three extremely successful years since 1994, when it launched CD versions of its tapes. Fortuna chose to expand into CDs using funds raised partly through the issue of **debentures**, and partly by selling new shares to existing shareholders. The company's performance over the three years are shown in summarised **balance sheet** and **profit and loss accounts** for each of those years.

Profit and Loss Account £000s	1994	1995	1996
Sales	3,500	5,000	8,000
Cost of goods sold	1,200	1,500	1,900
Gross Profit	**2,300**	**3,500**	**6,100**
Indirect costs	1,400	1,600	2,000
Net Profit	**900**	**1,900**	**4,100**
Interest	100	200	200
Profit before Tax	**800**	**1,700**	**3,900**
Tax	200	500	1,100
Profit after Tax	**600**	**1,200**	**2,800**

Balance Sheet £000s	1994	1995	1996
Fixed Assets			
Machinery	500	550	600
Buildings	1,000	1,100	1,300
Copyright	700	900	1,000
	2,200	**2,550**	**2,900**
Current Assets			
Stock	400	500	700
Debtors	300	600	700
Cash	300	400	600
	1,000	**1,500**	**2,000**
Current Liabilities			
Overdraft	350	400	400
Creditors	250	300	400
	600	**700**	**800**
Working Capital	**400**	**800**	**1,200**
Net Assets	**2,600**	**3,350**	**4,100**
Shareholders' Funds			
Ordinary shares	1,200	1,400	1,400
Reserves	400	700	1,450
	1,600	**2,100**	**2,850**
Long-term Liabilities			
Bank loans	500	500	500
Debentures	500	750	750
	1,000	**1,250**	**1,250**
Capital Employed	**2,600**	**3,350**	**4,100**

John Ellis, Fortuna's Chief Executive, is concerned about the production of tapes and books in China. After visiting the production site in China last summer, John Ellis was worried about the ethics of buying in from China, when their workers were forced to

▶ ▶

produce under such poor conditions. At the company's annual general meeting he claimed that 'higher **direct labour costs** in the UK are a price worth paying for better public relations.' As a result of this meeting the company plan to stop buying in from their Chinese supplier, and are going to produce the tapes themselves in the UK.

QUESTIONS

1 What do you understand by the following terms highlighted in the text: **a** private limited company; **b** debentures; **c** direct labour; **d** balance sheet; **e** profit and loss account? [20]

2 **a** Explain what you understand by the term 'reserves' in the balance sheet. [4]
  b Account for the rise in Fortuna's reserves over the last three years. [6]

3 Using the figures from the balance sheet and profit and loss account, explain why the managers of Fortuna are pleased with the company's performance. [10]

4 Analyse the impact of Fortuna's decision to move production back to the UK on its balance sheet and profit and loss account. [20]

Total [60]

THE REDBRICK WINE DISTRIBUTORS' BALANCE SHEET

The Redbrick Wine Distributors import wine from all over the world into the UK. They specialise in selling to independent off-licences, restaurants, pubs and bars in the UK. They have recently investigated the opportunity of opening an office in Ireland which would open up a new market for them.

The Redbrick Wine Distributors balance sheet: 31 December, 1996

Fixed Assets	£000s
Buildings and machinery	200
Vehicles	150
	350

Current Assets	
Stock	80
Debtors	60
Cash	20
	160

Current Liabilities	
Creditors	50
Overdraft	40
	90

Working Capital	**70**
Net Assets	**420**
Owner's Capital	
Ordinary shares	200
Reserves	120
	320
Long-term Loan	**100**
Capital Employed	**420**

QUESTIONS

1 Explain what you understand by the following terms in the balance sheet:
   a Creditors
   b Ordinary shares
   c Fixed assets   [12]

2 The company earned a £120,000 profit last year. Explain where this would have been entered into the balance sheet. [8]

3 a Explain what you understand by the principle of historic cost. [4]

   b Why is it important to use historic cost in the production of a balance sheet? [6]

4 When the balance sheet was being drawn up a mistake was made. It was discovered that a cheque for £5,000 from a major customer had not been received as first thought. What effect would this mistake have had on the balance sheet shown above? [10]

Total [40]

THE SALE OF LAND CRUISER MOTORS LTD

Land Cruiser Motors Ltd is a car dealership that specialises in new and used four wheel drive cars. The business carries all makes of four wheel drive vehicles, but it specialises in Land Rovers and Range Rovers. The owner, George Anton, is looking to sell the business as he comes up to retirement. He has called in a firm of chartered accountants to value the business for him. They have calculated that the business has a net asset value of £1.4 million. However, they have recommended to George that he sets a price of £2 million for the business.

QUESTIONS

1 a What do you understand by the term 'net assets'? [5]

   b Using examples that specifically relate to the case study, explain how the accountants would have gone about calculating the net assets figure of £1.4 million. [10]

2 a Explain fully the concept of goodwill. [5]

   b What is the value of goodwill in this case? [3]

   c Where would this goodwill be entered in Land Cruiser Motors Ltd's balance sheet? [2]

   d What are the problems of measuring goodwill in accounts? [5]

Total [30]

Financial Accounting – Section B: Techniques used in the preparation of accounts

SUMMARY

1. Depreciation is used to value fixed assets in the balance sheet.
2. The depreciation expense is applied in the profit and loss account to account for the cost of using fixed assets.
3. Depreciation has to be used to account for the fall in the value of fixed assets to follow the prudence concept and the matching principle.
4. There are two main methods of calculating depreciation: the straight line method and declining balance method.
5. Stock is valued at the lower of historic cost or net realisable value (NRV).
6. The two techniques used to identify stock to value it in accounts are LIFO and FIFO.
7. Cashflow is vital for the survival of all businesses.
8. There are three sources of cash: sales, share issues and borrowing.
9. The cashflow statement in the annual report summarises the movement of cash through the business in the accounting year.

In the preparation of final accounts there are a number of accounting techniques that need to be followed to give the accounts consistency over time, and between organisations. Three crucial areas are the valuation of fixed assets, stock valuation and cashflow. Only by carefully following set accounting principles set out in the Statements of Standard Accounting Practices for these techniques can organisations provide a 'true and fair view' of their financial position, which can be applied by users of accounts or stakeholders, to make a genuine assessment of a business's finances.

DEPRECIATION OF FIXED ASSETS

What is depreciation?

Most fixed assets fall in value over time due to general ageing, wear and tear and obsolescence. For example, ICI will own plant and machinery which, with age, will go down in value, as will their computer systems which gradually become outdated as new developments in technology take place. This fall in value will need to be accounted for in the balance sheet to give a 'true and fair view' of the value of the company's assets.

Why is depreciation used?

Prudence

Depreciation is used to follow the prudence concept. This states that:

'accounts should be prepared in a conservative way so that the value of profits and assets are not overstated.'

By doing this, the picture given to stakeholders is one that leaves them in no doubt of any financial problems the organisation might face, so they are aware of difficulties and can take decisions accordingly. If depreciation of fixed assets is not taken into account then the value of assets will overstate the worth of the organisation to its owners, who would realise less than they might hope if the business was, for example, being sold. The value put on assets in company accounts, after depreciation has been subtracted from the assets' historic cost, is called the assets' net book value.

Matching

When an organisation buys an asset, it is used to produce goods and services for the business over the asset's life. The sound systems bought by a nightclub will provide music for their customers over three years. The cost of the asset will be maintenance, which is on-going, but also the fall in the value of the asset from the time it was bought to the time it was eventually scrapped or sold on. If a nightclub spends £60,000 on sound equipment that lasts for three years, and can be sold on for £6,000, then the £54,000 fall in value will be another expense associated with owning the asset. Because the sound system brings in customers over its three year life then this depreciation expense should be matched with revenue gained from these customers over the three years. Hence, the matching principle.

If this was not done then the expense would either be written off as a cost when the asset was purchased, which means £60,000 would be taken off profit in the year when it was bought, or the £60,000 could be written off as an expense when the asset was disposed of, less the £6,000 resale income. In each case, the profit figure would be understated when the expense was written off. If £60,000 was taken off the nightclub's profit in the first year it would end up making a loss, which would not reflect its performance in that year and would not give a 'true and fair view' of the firm's financial position. Thus the cost of the asset should be spread over its life.

Methods of depreciation

There are a variety of different techniques used to calculate depreciation, and we shall consider the two main methods: straight line and declining balance.

Straight line depreciation

This method involves depreciating the value of an asset by equal amounts in each year of the asset's life. In the case of the nightclub's sound equipment, the annual allowance for depreciation would be calculated using the following equation:

$$\frac{\textbf{historic cost} - \textbf{residual value}}{\textbf{useful life}}$$

$$= \textbf{annual depreciation expense}$$

In the case of the nightclub's sound equipment the calculation would be:

$$\frac{£60,000 - £6,000}{3} = £18,000$$

where:

- **Historic cost** is the purchase price of the asset when it was originally bought by the organisation
- **Residual value** is the scrap or resale value of the asset
- **Useful life** is the time period when the asset will be used by the organisation to produce goods and services

The nightclub in our example will subtract £18,000 from the value of the sound equipment in each of the three years of the equipment's life.

The strength of this method is its simplicity, it is easy to use, and it can be applied consistently with each asset the organisation owns. However, it fails to reflect accurately the true way in which assets depreciate. Most assets tend to depreciate more in value in the early years of their life. New cars, for example, lose something in the region of a third of their value in the first year of their lives. Straight line depreciation fails to account for this.

Declining balance

By taking off a constant percentage of an assets' value as an allowance for depreciation, declining balance depreciation takes into account the way assets tend, in reality, to depreciate by more in the early years of their life. The percentage rate is calculated using the following equation:

% rate of depreciation

$$= \left(1 - \sqrt[n]{\frac{\text{residual value}}{\text{historic cost}}}\right) \times 100$$

n = useful life

In the first year of the life of the nightclub's sound equipment, the equipment would lose 53.6 percent of its value, which is £32,160, and this would be the depreciation allowance in the first year. In the second year, the depreciation allowance would be calculated by taking 53.6 percent of the asset's net book value of £32,160, which is £17,237. This method gives a truer reflection of the way depreciation actually occurs, but its increased complexity is a clear disadvantage, especially when one considers how inaccurate the calculation of depreciation is likely to be anyway.

Figure 5.14 compares the two methods of calculating depreciation for the nightclub example.

Straight line depreciation	£	£	£
Year	1	2	3
Net book value at the start of the year	60,000	42,000	24,000
Depreciation	18,000	18,000	18,000
Net book value at the end of the year	42,000	24,000	6,000
Declining balance depreciation			
Net book value at the start of the year	60,000	27,840	12,918
Depreciation	32,160	14,922	6,924
Net book value at the end of the year	27,840	12,918	5,994

Fig 5.14 *A comparison of straight line and declining balance depreciation*

Depreciation in the accounts

Balance sheet

Once the depreciation allowance has been calculated for each year it is subtracted from the asset's historic cost to give the asset's net book value, which is entered into the balance sheet. In the nightclub example, the end of year two is 31 December, 1998, thus the net book value of £12,918 would be entered under fixed assets in the balance sheet. The accounting entry can be summarised as:

historic cost − accumulated depreciation = net book value

Profit and loss account

The annual depreciation allowance made on an asset represents the expense of using the asset to generate revenue. Therefore the total depreciation allowance for all the assets a business owns is subtracted as an expense under indirect costs in the trading section of the profit and loss account.

Depreciation and cash

Depreciation is sometimes called a paper cost because no cash actually leaves the business when the expense is incurred. Cash that leaves the business to purchase an asset does so when the asset is actually purchased. This means that depreciation in the accounts does not relate to any movement of cash. Moreover, some accountants see depreciation as a source of cash. When a company reports its profit at the end of the year, depreciation has been taken off the profit figure as an indirect cost, but no cash has left the business, which means the depreciation figure can be added back to the profit figure to give the total amount of cash the business should have.

■ ACCOUNTING FOR STOCK

Net realisable value (NRV)

Like other assets, the basis for stock valuation is historic cost. The car components carried by Ford would be valued at the price they were purchased, in the same way as oil bought by the retailer Halfords, or as coffee bought by the makers of Nestlé's Nescafé would be. Where work has been carried out on the stock, the labour and overhead cost must be included in its valuation. For example, where a carpet maker buys £220,000 worth of materials and incurs £340,000 of overheads and labour costs, the stock valuation would be:

£220,000 + £340,000 = £560,000

However, under certain circumstances the value of stock may fall below its historic cost. This could be because the stock has become damaged in some way, it may have become obsolete, or it could have gone out of fashion. An example of this would be a computer retailer holding 386 PCs bought for £350 each, but, because they have been superseded by new Pentium and 486 computers, can only

be sold for £300 each. The £300 is used to value the stock and is known as the net realisable value or NRV. The rule that **stock is valued at the lower of historic cost or net realisable value** is used to follow the prudence concept where assets are valued in a conservative way. Normally one would expect the NRV to be greater than historic cost because stock is sold at a profit, but when occasionally it falls below the historic cost, NRV is used.

LIFO and FIFO

Last in first out (LIFO) and first in first out (FIFO) are both methods used by organisations to calculate the value of stock to be entered into the balance sheet and profit and loss account. The techniques are used because the price at which firms buy stock changes over time. Consider this example. Zenra Ltd import and then sell cocoa to food manufacturers. During the first four months of 1997 they receive the following quantities of cocoa at the following prices.

- 15 January   40,000 kg @ £1.40
- 4 February   80,000 kg @ £1.60
- 27 February   70,000 kg @ £1.70
- 15 March   50,000 kg @ £1.75

At the start of the year Zenra has 50,000 kg @ £1.30, and during the period 220,000 kg was sold. This means that 70,000 kg are left at the end of the period, but at what price will it be valued? Logically, you would assume that it would be valued at the latest prices of 27 February and 5 March assuming the stock acquired earliest is sold first, leaving the later purchases still in stock. However, it would be practically very difficult to prove this unless cocoa bought at a different time is stored separately. Accountants overcome this problem by using LIFO and FIFO. These are purely accounting techniques, in that they do not necessarily represent the true movement of stock, but assume a certain movement.

How FIFO works

First in first out is the logical way stock moves with earliest stock purchased assumed to be the first to be sold. In this case, Zenra would be assumed to sell the opening stock first, then the stock purchased on the 15 February and so on. This means that the closing stock will be valued at the latest prices, which, in this case, is stock valued at £1.75.

How LIFO works

Last in first out is an alternative to FIFO, and is used by American companies. It is slightly illogical, but it is based on the assumption that the latest stock purchased is sold first; that means that the closing stock is valued at the earliest price, which, in this case is, the opening stock valuation of £1.30 and the stock bought in first at £1.40.

The implication for accounts

Profit and loss account

The last two rows in Fig 5.15 show that the differing values of closing stock realised by LIFO and FIFO, change the cost of sales and gross profit figures for the company. When the price of stock is rising, FIFO gives a greater value of closing stock compared to LIFO, because stock is valued at the latest price. The greater value of closing stock, reduces the cost of sales and increases the reported profits. This does not mean that the company will make more profit because over time the reported profit will be the same whichever method is used. However, the greater profit shown by FIFO when prices are rising would not be considered as prudent as LIFO. The situation is reversed when the price of stock purchased is falling.

Balance sheet

As Fig 5.15 shows, the value of closing stock using FIFO is greater when prices are rising compared to LIFO. This situation would be reversed with falling prices. Again, LIFO would be more prudent using the example above.

Thus, some accountants prefer LIFO because it is more prudent when prices are rising, but FIFO more accurately reflects the real movement of stock.

■ CASHFLOW

Why is cashflow important?

Cashflow represents the amount of cash a business has at its disposal to finance its activities.

The importance of cashflow was touched on in the sections on profit and loss and the balance sheet, but will now be considered in greater depth. An organisation can only continue to operate if it can meet the demands of its creditors by paying them the money they are owed. If an organisation fails to meet this obligation to any one of its creditors, then they can take the organisation to court, file for bankruptcy or liquidation and, if the court agrees, the company will become insolvent and will have to cease trading. Its affairs will then be run by a trustee, normally from a firm of accountants, who will sell the assets of the business to cover outstanding debts owed to creditors; if there is still outstanding debt after this is done then the business goes bankrupt and is wound up.

As you can see, without cash businesses cannot survive. Thus it is absolutely vital that the cashflow of all organisations is managed effectively.

Cashflow and profit

Credit trading

One of the most important concepts in accounting is the difference between cashflow and profit. Because firms almost always conduct at least some of their trade on credit there will

Date	FIFO	LIFO
(a) Opening stock	50,000 kg @ £1.30 £65,000	50,000 kg @ £1.30 £65,000
(b) 15.1.97	40,000 kg @ £1.40 £56,000	40,000 kg @ £1.40 £56,000
(c) 4.2.97	80,000 kg @ £1.60 £128,000	80,000 kg @ £1.60 £128,000
(d) 27.2.97	70,000 kg @ £1.70 £119,000	70,000 kg @ £1.70 £119,000
(e) 15.3.97	50,000 kg @ £1.75 £87,500	50,000 kg @ £1.75 £87,500
(f) Stock available a + b + c + d + e	290,000 kg £455,500	290,000 kg £455,500
(g) Closing stock	70,000 kg **50,000 kg @ £1.75 £87,500** **20,000 kg @ £1.70 £34,000** **£121,500**	70,000 kg **50,000 kg @ £1.30 £65,000** **20,000 kg @ £1.40 £28,000** **£93,000**
(h) Cost of sales f − g	£334,000	£362,500
(i) Sales revenue	220,000 kg @ 2.50 £550,000	220,000 kg @ 2.50 £550,000
Gross profit i − h	**£216,000**	**£187,500**

Fig 5.15 *The effect of LIFO and FIFO on cost of sales and gross profit figures*

always be a time lag between sales and the cash receipts of those sales. In the same way, firms receive goods on credit, so again there will be a time lag between expenses and payments.

Depreciation

Because organisations spread the cost of their fixed assets over a forecasted useful life rather than deducting the cost of an asset when the cash was paid for it, there will again be a huge discrepancy between the cash an organisation has and its profit.

Kevin Hurd is a sole trader who runs a meat dealing business. During the month of April 1997 the firm made the following transactions. The firm started the period with £5,000.

1 **5 April** Stock of £25,000 worth of turkeys was purchased on credit.
2 **9 April** A van valued at £20,000 was purchased for cash. An allowance of £400 was made for a month's depreciation.
3 **15 April** All the stock of turkeys was sold for £40,000 – half on credit, half for cash.
4 **22 April** Wages of £2,000 were paid in cash.
5 **28 April** Overheads of £1,500 were paid in cash.
6 **29 April** £25,000 was paid to suppliers.

The effects of these transactions on the company's profit and cash positions are illustrated in Fig 5.16.

A stakeholder would get a totally different impression from the profit and loss account than they would do from the cashflow statement. Kevin Hurd, whilst looking profitable on the one hand, is in a very vulnerable cashflow position. He has to find £23,500 from somewhere, probably a bank overdraft or loan. His position would look even more precarious if the buyer of his goods could not pay.

Cashflow Statement: 30 April 1997		Profit and Loss for April 1997	
	£		£
Opening balance	5,000	**Sales Revenue**	**40,000**
Cash inflow	20,000	Cost of sales	25,000
Total available cash	25,000	Direct labour	2,000
Cash outflows		**Cost of Goods Sold**	**27,000**
Stock purchases	25,000	Gross profit	13,000
Van purchased	20,000	Overheads	1,500
Wages paid	2,000	Depreciation	400
Overheads paid	1,500	**Total Indirect Costs**	**1,900**
Total	48,500	**Net Profit**	**11,100**
Closing Balance	**−23,500**		

Fig 5.16 *Illustration of the flow of cash during trading*

Working capital

This was defined in the balance sheet as current assets less current liabilities. It tells the accountant how much short-term cash and liquid assets, such as stock and debtors, there are to cover short-term demand on those assets in the form of creditors and overdraft. The more working capital there is, the more secure the company is against becoming insolvent.

Sources of cash

There are three main sources of cash or funds accessible to organisations.

Sales

This is internal finance generated by the organisation itself through producing and selling its product and is the major source of short-term finance for the organisation. However, the realisation concept of recognising sales even if the cash for them has not been paid, means that actual cash only flows into the firm when the goods are paid

for. This could be cash sales and payments made by debtors. Once all the costs associated with its activities have been paid, the net cash left represents funds available to the firm. Accountants often consider retained profit as a source of funds for a company, but this is only the case if cash received from sales has actually been received.

It is also important to realise that the profit made by organisations may well understate the amount of cash available because of the depreciation expense. Depreciation is the cost allowance made to cover the fall in value of fixed assets, but the cash for these assets flows out of the business normally when the assets were purchased. This means that the depreciation taken from profits each year does not reduce the cash available. For example, if Virgin PLC buys a Boeing 747 for £14 million and writes off £2 million a year for the seven year useful life, then its profit in each year will fall by £2 million a year. However, the cash used to buy the plane would have been spent when it was bought at the start of its life. Thus the £2 million deduction from profit does not actually reduce the amount of cash available. So £2 million could be added back to the retained profits as available cash. This is why depreciation is sometimes seen as an internal source of funds.

Share issue

The sale of shares by companies represents a major source of long-term finance. All limited companies issue at least two shares, but most large companies issue millions of shares. Sainsbury's, for example, has around 200 million shares in circulation. Private companies can raise substantial amounts of capital by 'going public' and having their shares issued on the stock market; a move made by the furniture retailer Allied Carpets PLC in 1996.

Shares represent permanent capital, so once they are issued they do not need to be repaid (see shareholders' funds, p. 75). The directors of the company also decide on the amount of dividend to be paid each year, which can be altered depending on the organisation's performance and this means dividend can be reduced in lean years. Thus share issues have major advantages over borrowing where interest payments, along with a repayment schedule, have to be made. However, shares carry voting rights at the company's AGM that can be used to influence the direction of the business. This means that a share issue dilutes the control of existing shareholders, and new owners may want to force the business in a direction that the existing shareholders may not wish to go. In the mid 1980s, the Virgin Leisure Group was floated on the stock exchange by Richard Branson in an attempt to raise new funds to expand the company. However, after a turbulent year, Branson bought back the shares issued turning the business back into a private company because he felt the new shareholders were trying to take the company in a direction he did not want it to go.

Borrowing

Borrowing, or debt, is cash borrowed from third parties such as banks. In the short term, borrowing from banks on overdraft or taking trade credit is a major source of cash (see current liabilities, p. 77). In the long term firms can obtain secured loans in the form of a mortgage, or issued debentures (see long-term liabilities, p. 77).

The advantage of debt is that in the short term it is flexible, allowing an organisation to operate without having huge stocks of cash, which has the cost of being tied up unprofitably, when it can be used to buy stock to sell. In the long term borrowing is far easier for most companies to organise than a share issue. Most small- and medium-sized companies simply do not have the reputation to attract shareholders in the way Virgin or Sainsbury's might. Even for large companies borrowing for certain projects is much cheaper than incurring all the costs of the administration of a share issue. Borrowing also means that the organisation retains more control than would exist when shares are issued, although banks may have a say in how any funds borrowed are spent. Interest as an expense is also allowable against tax, whereas dividends are not.

The problem with borrowing is that the money has to be paid back in the end and firms, no matter how poor their profitability is, have to pay the interest.

Other sources

Factoring

This is often used by small businesses who are looking for short-term funds. Small firms often struggle because they are not paid on time by their debtors, normally larger, more liquid organisations. One way around this is to sell the debtors to a business who specialise in collecting debts. This is called factoring. Obviously, there is a cost and the factoring company will normally take a commission which is a percentage of the value of the debts to be collected.

Leasing

This is a way of obtaining assets like buildings, cars and photocopiers without having to use large amounts of cash to cover the cost of buying the asset. Essentially, the asset is being rented in the same way as an individual may rent a television from Radio Rentals. The other advantage is that, depending on the lease agreement, the leasing company will maintain the asset. The leasee can, again depending on the lease agreement, send the asset back if it is no longer needed, or have it replaced if a new, more up to date, version of the asset becomes available. However, the cost of leasing exceeds the cost of purchasing an asset in the long run.

Venture capital

These are funds made available by companies who are interested in new or expanding businesses that need finance. They normally involve funds being provided on a share rather than debt basis, and this means that the venture capitalist may wish to have a significant say in the running of the organisation.

Government funding

Organisations in the public sector gain automatic access to UK Government funds. Grant maintained schools, hospital trusts and local authorities all run on UK Government money. The main problem with this is that the funds are set on the basis of what the Government can afford and/or wishes to pay, which is often at odds with the cost of the service the organisation wants to provide. Universities are a prime example of this; they are facing a huge increase in student numbers which is not matched by increased funding. As a result they are forced to seek other sources. The National Lottery has generated a whole new pool of funds which are being made available to sport and the arts.

Private sector companies often benefit from Government funds if their activities are in the national or local public interest. A Korean manufacturer received a large grant from the Welsh Office for a £2 billion investment in South Wales.

The cashflow statement

What is the cashflow statement?

The cashflow statement now produced by companies replaced the old funds flow statement produced by companies in 1991. As part of the published accounts, companies are now required to produce a statement which summarises the changes in the inflow and outflow of cash during the accounting period.

As stated earlier, there are a variety of sources and these are considered under the following headings in the cashflow statement.

1 **Operating activities**   Cash generated from sales less operating expenses incurred.
2 **Returns from investment and servicing of finance**   This would be inflows from interest on loans made and outflows of dividends paid.
3 **Taxation**   Corporation Tax paid.
4 **Investment activities**   This involves cash outflows spent on tangible and intangible fixed assets, purchase of shares in other companies and loans made to other companies.
5 **Financing**   This is the loan and share capital changes made to finance activities. This could be an issue of shares or a loan taken out.

The layout of the cashflow statement

Scott's is a major home and wear retailer. It received cash inflows from the following sources: operating activities £790 million, interest received £110 million, dividends received £40 million, receipts from the sale of tangible fixed assets £70 million. Cash outflows were spent on: interest paid £144 million, dividends paid £115 million, Corporation Tax paid £124 million, £700 million on tangible fixed assets and £190 million on debentures and shares. This has been financed by the issue of ordinary shares of £610 million and £123 million of long-term borrowing, although £123 million has been used to repay a long-term loan.

Scott's	£ million	
Net inflow from operating activities		**790**
Returns from investment and servicing of finance:		
Interest received	110	
Interest paid	(144)	
Dividends received	40	
Dividends paid	(115)	
Net cash outflow on investment and servicing of finance		**(109)**
Corporation Tax paid		(124)
Investment activities		
Tangible fixed assets purchased	(700)	
Receipt from sale of tangible fixed assets	70	
Purchase of debentures and shares	(190)	
Net cash outflow on investment activities		**(820)**
Not cash outflow before financing		**(263)**
Financing		
Issue of ordinary shares	610	
Proceeds from long-term borrowing	123	
Repayment of long-term borrowing	(150)	
Net cash inflow from financing		**583**
Increase in cash		**320**

Fig 5.17 *The layout of Scott's cashflow statement: 14 March, 1997*

A vertical format is used to lay out the cashflow statement with cash inflows and outflows resulting from the organisation's activities grouped at the top half of the account. Under each section inflows from particular sources are netted against their related outflows, for example interest received and interest paid. The financing of these activities is in the bottom half, with a figure for the change in the company's cash position. Scott's have experienced an increase in the amount of cash they held from the previous year of £320 million.

MANAGING CASHFLOW

From the manager's point of view, the effective management of cash or working capital is of vital importance. Carry too little cash and the business is vulnerable to insolvency; carry too much cash and the business is tying assets up unprofitably. In this section there are three case examples of organisations with different liquidity problems and how they might go about solving them.

Case 1 – Raising finance

The Chammon is an Indian restaurant run by Omar Unis and Asif Sharma in partnership. The company is currently in a sound cash position, carrying £70,000 cash at 1 April, 1996. The partners wish to expand by purchasing a second restaurant. They have premises in mind which would cost them £120,000 plus £40,000 in refurbishment.

How would they raise the finance to go ahead?

1 Share capital is not an option here because the business is too small to sell shares.
2 They could put in their own money in the form of owner's capital and this would be a popular option.
3 A loan could be taken from a bank, but this would have to be secured because they are such a small business. The bank may well ask the partners to use their first restaurant to secure the loan which could be a risk they do not want to take. Loans could also be obtained from friends or other sources. However, because the firm does not have limited liability, if it goes into liquidation the creditors could force the partners to sell their personal assets to pay their outstanding debts.
4 They could use some of the cash they have available, sell stock and factorise their debtors. However, this would leave them in a vulnerable position as the value of their working capital has fallen.
5 Inviting a new partner to join the business who would put in extra funds is an option. However, the new partner would dilute the control of the existing partners and reduce the profit for existing partners because it would now have to be split three ways.

The low risk option is for them to put in their own funds because it maintains their working capital and avoids them having to take out a loan with the interest and repayment costs. They have also maintained control by not inviting a new partner in. However, there is the opportunity cost of the return this money could have earned in the bank, or the alternative private uses it could have been put to. Asif and Omar chose this option.

Case 2 – Overtrading

Susan Tully Ltd is a small landscape gardening business. Much of the firm's work is for the gardens surrounding company offices. The company has just signed a major contract with a large brewery to work on a number of their pub gardens in the London area. The contract is worth £30,000 which will be paid after the work has been completed in April. Susan Tully will have initial expenses of £5,000 to buy in shrubs, grass seed, fertiliser, etc. and this has to be paid for immediately. The business also has to pay a monthly wage bill of £3,000 for staff taken on to do the work and who have to be paid weekly. With this major job on, resources for other work will be squeezed and will drop to a few hundred pounds per month. The cashflow for the business for the four months to April is set out in the table below.

£	Jan	Feb	Mar	Apr
Opening balance	10,000	2,500	200	(2,200)
Cash inflow from sales	500	700	600	30,000
Cash outflow for expenses	8,000	3,000	3,000	3,000
Net cashflow	(7,500)	(2,300)	(2,400)	27,000
Cash balance	2,500	200	(2,200)	24,800

Susan Tully has just received a telephone call from the brewery to ask her whether she can do the Southeast region.

Should Susan accept the contract to do the Southeast region?

1 The profit on the London region contract is:

Sales	£30,000
less:	
Materials	5,000
Labour	12,000
Total Cost	**17,000**
Gross Profit	**13,000**

If the Southeast is taken on as well, then the profit will rise to £26,000. If the company turned the contract down it may well jeopardise future work or even the London contract. On the basis of this information you may well suggest acceptance of the contract.

2 The cashflow, on the other hand, means that the company will require an overdraft of £2,200 in March and its cashflow over the months to April will leave it in a vulnerable position. This problem will be doubled if the new contract is taken on. If the cash is forthcoming in April, then the firm's cash position will be strengthened by both contracts. However, if the brewery delays payment, then the firm will require a further £3,000 overdraft in April, which will be doubled if the new contract is taken on and also not paid. This situation is called overtrading, a situation where an organisation trades at a level it does not have the cash funds to support. In other words, too high a volume of business reduces liquidity and threatens solvency. In Susan Tully's case, the bank may refuse the overdraft and file for insolvency if her business goes ahead with the contract without first agreeing the overdraft with the bank.

In the end, Susan Tully agreed to take on both contracts by organising her finance in the following way. A £3,000 overdraft facility was agreed with the bank to cover the £2,200 cash shortfall in March. The firm also organised an agreement with a company which specialises in factoring, to factor the debt if it was not paid on time.

Case 3 – A medium-sized expanding company

Meditec Ltd is a medium-sized limited company employing 100 staff. It is a private business with 15 shareholders, who all work for the company. It specialises in developing laser technology involved in surgery. It has recently made a breakthrough in a new type of laser used for keyhole surgery. However, the development cost required to bring the new product to a marketable position requires an investment of £7 million. How should the company raise the capital?

The retained profit for the company last year was £1.2 million, which, even with a £500,000 allowance for depreciation, is nowhere near enough to cover the investment. However, a certain amount can and should be used and with the understanding of all the shareholders that little dividend will be paid this year, the company earmarked £1 million.

The company does have the option of going public by applying to float their shares on the Stock Exchange. This is an exciting young company which may well attract Stock Exchange interest. However, the existing shareholders, whilst standing to make considerable personal financial gains, would lose control over the direction of the company. There is also the cost of administering the issue, along with the risk that potential investors may not be interested in the shares.

An alternative to this is selling more shares to existing shareholders and inviting new shareholders to buy shares. New shareholders would dilute control, and asking existing shareholders to buy several million pounds of new shares may be optimistic. However, it is felt £2 million could be raised this way.

A venture capitalist organisation has

expressed a great deal of interest in the project and is willing to put up £2 million. However, they will want a major say in how the product is marketed and they will want 30 percent of any profit earned by the venture over 7 years. These conditions proved too much for Meditec who decided against this option.

A ten year bank loan of £4 million could be organised and this would need to be secured against the property owned by the company.

A favourable rate of interest was negotiated with the bank. However, the interest cost would have to be paid each year, adding considerably to expenses.

The company decided to raise £1 million internally from profits, £2 million through a share issue to existing shareholders and new shareholders, who all worked for the company. The remainder was organised through a secured bank loan.

BODY CARE CONSIDERS AN ATTRACTIVE OFFER

Amanda Jenkins has just started a new business manufacturing moisturising creams that she sells on to department stores and chemists. She set up Body Care herself 12 months ago and has seen the sales of her products grow quite steadily. She employs three full time staff who work in production, a part time marketing assistant and a part time secretary. Body Care's balance sheet at 31 December, 1997 is shown below.

During 1997 the company sold 95,000 1 litre bottles at a price of £2.50. Four deliveries of stock were taken by the company during the year.

•	1 January	25,000 ltrs @ £1.10
•	3 May	30,000 ltrs @ £1.20
•	3 September	38,000 ltrs @ £1.25
•	5 November	15,000 ltrs @ £1.28

The opening stock of 12,000 litres was originally purchased at £1.10.

During the year the following expenses were incurred:

	1997
Fixed Assets	**£000s**
Vehicles	25,000
Machinery	60,000
	85,000
Current Assets	
Stock	15,000
Debtors	9,000
Cash	10,000
	34,000
Current Liabilities	
Trade Creditors	8,000
Overdraft	6,000
Tax payable	3,000
	17,000
Net Current Assets	17,000
Net Assets	102,000
Owner's capital	
Share capital	40,000
Reserves	12,000
	52,000
Long-term Liabilities	
Mortgage	38,000
Unsecured loan	12,000
	50,000
Capital Employed	102,000

- Production workers were paid £1,200 per month each
- The marketing assistant was paid £5,000
- The secretary was paid £8,000
- Heat and light was £1,500, although £500 was left unpaid at 31 December, 1997
- An advertising campaign costing £8,000 was launched
- Leasing and rental expenses for the machinery and buildings was £20,000
- Interest expenses on the mortgage and other borrowing was £8,000
- The company vehicle was originally bought for £30,000 – it has a three year life and an estimated second hand value of £9,000

Amanda Jenkins has been approached by a major retail chain who want to supply Body Care moisturiser under the retailer's own label. The contract would be for 60,000 litres at the £2.50 selling price. This is an attractive offer by the retailer, however, they do have a notorious reputation for late payment. Accepting the order may mean the company could face the problem of overtrading.

QUESTIONS

1 a Explain the difference between LIFO and FIFO in stock valuation. [5]
  b Calculate the cost of sales using FIFO. [10]
  c Explain why accountants might prefer to use LIFO when producing accounts compared to FIFO. [5]

2 a Explain why accountants use depreciation to calculate the expense of using fixed assets. [10]
  b Calculate the depreciation expense of the company vehicle. [5]
  c Discuss how Body Care would have decided on the useful life and residual value used to calculate the depreciation expense. [5]

3 a Draw up a profit and loss account for 31 December, 1997 (use FIFO to calculate the cost of sales). [15]
  b On 31 December, 1997 £40,000 of the sales made remained unpaid. What impact would this have on the firm's accounts? [5]

4 a What do you understand by the term 'overtrading'? [10]
  b Explain how Body Care might deal with the problem of late payment from the retail chain. [5]
  c Discuss, using financial and non-financial arguments, whether Body Care should accept the order or not. [15]

Total [90]

SUNSHINE CREEK MOVES INTO A NEW MARKET

Sunshine Creek is a vineyard located in France. It was bought by two English entrepreneurs in 1990. The business has performed reasonably well over the last five years, but there is certainly room for development. Sunshine Creek's accounts for the year ended 31 December, 1997 are set out below.

Fixed Assets	1997
	£000s
Land	700
Machinery	85
Buildings	200
	985
Current Assets	
Stock	95
Debtors	12
Cash	15
	122
Current Liabilities	
Trade Creditors	7
Overdraft	6
Tax payable	16
	29
Net Current Assets	93
Net Assets	1,078
Owner's capital	
Shares	500
Reserves	160
	660
Long-term Liabilities	
Mortgage	300
Other borrowing	118
	418
Capital employed	1,078

Profit and Loss Account

Sales revenue	500
Materials	230
Direct labour	100
Cost of goods sold	330
Gross Profit	**170**
Depreciation	30
Advertising	40
Administration	20
Total overhead	90
Net Profit	**80**
Interest expense	24
Profit before Tax	**56**
Tax	16
Profit after Tax	**40**
Dividend paid	10
Retained Profit	**30**

The owners, David Weller and Tony Aston, are looking to expand into the holiday market by opening a bed and breakfast lodge on the vineyard. This will all be financed internally through money generated by the business and David and Tony putting in their own funds. The lodge will cost £120,000 to build and £70,000 to furnish. The lodge will have 20 rooms which the brothers have decided to charge on average £40 a night for, although this rate will vary depending on the time of the year. The average occupancy rate in the first year for the lodge is forecasted at 60 percent throughout a 50 week year. All rooms let are assumed to be paid in cash. The overhead expense is £15,000, which again is paid in cash. There are minimal direct costs that are forecasted to be 9 percent of sales revenue.

QUESTIONS

1 a Explain what you understand by the term 'reserves' in the balance sheet. [5]
  b Under what circumstances will the value of reserves rise? [5]

2 When the provisional balance sheet and profit and loss account was produced a few items were left out:
  • Cash sales of £10,000
  • A telephone bill of £2,000
  • A bill for £4,000 was paid to a creditor for stock that had been received
  • A cheque was received from a debtor for £3,000
  By including the alterations outlined above, draw up the final balance sheet and profit and loss accounts for Sunshine Creek. [10]

3 Using the information forecasted for the building of the new lodge, produce a cashflow statement for the lodge's first year of trading. (Assume all the cash inflows and outflows occurred in the same year. Do not include the cost of building or furnishing the lodge in your forecast.) [20]

4 Using financial and non-financial points, discuss whether you think Sunshine Creek should open the new lodge or not. [20]

Total [60]

CHEMCLEAN TAKES IN NEW STOCK

Chemclean makes carpet cleaning liquids by converting raw material called Chemdry crystals into the finished product. At 1 April, 1997 there was no opening stock. Quantities of Chemdry taken into stock and issued to production from the period 1 April, 1997 to 31 March, 1998 were as follows.

Month	Raw material Chemdry (litres)	Purchased price per litre $	Issued to production (litres)
April	200	2.00	
May			100
July	500	3.00	
August			300
September	800	4.00	
October			400
January	900	5.00	
March			1,400

QUESTIONS

1 Use both LIFO and FIFO conventions to calculate the value of issues to production, and closing stock values at each stage. [15]

2 Some accountants prefer the use of LIFO when prices are rising. Why is this the case? [10]

Total [25]

BODDOR UNDERTAKES A PROGRAMME OF COST CUTTING

As part of a programme of cost cutting, a large mining corporation, Boddor, decided to close 50 of its mines worldwide. A group of middle managers at a small mine targeted by Boddor for closure, believed that there were markets that had not been fully exploited by Boddor. The management of this mine proposed a buyout. After lengthy negotiation with a number of electricity generators, it was established that new markets did exist, although demand was not large enough to retain existing employment levels. The number of employees would have to be reduced by one third and several levels of management removed to cut costs and bureaucracy. Each manager was prepared to put up their redundancy (retrenchment/lay-off) payments, but this was not sufficient to fund the new venture. Additional finance would have to be found.

QUESTIONS

1 Outline four potential sources of finance for the proposed buyout. [7]

2 Discuss the advantages and disadvantages of each source of finance you have identified for the managers who are proposing to buy Boddor. [8]

3 As the manager of a bank approached for a loan by the managers at Boddor, analyse the factors your bank would need to consider before it makes the loan. [15]

Total [30]

Financial Accounting – Section C: Analysing accounts

SUMMARY

1 Analysing accounts by stakeholders gives them the information on which to base their decisions relating to the organisation.
2 Financial ratios enable the stakeholder to manipulate the final accounts to provide meaningful figures on which to make judgements about the organisation's performance.

3 There are three types of ratio analysis: performance analysis, capital analysis and shareholder analysis.
4 Ratios only provide a financial assessment of the business's performance, which means other factors need to be allowed for in making a true assessment.

One of the key reasons for producing financial information in the format of the balance sheet, profit and loss account, and cashflow statement, is to provide information that can be used as a basis for decision making by the different stakeholders in the organisation. In order to do this effectively, accurate interpretation of accounts needs to be carried out. This can be done through the use of financial ratios, providing a more meaningful picture of financial data than that offered by the raw figures contained in the final accounts.

WHAT ARE FINANCIAL RATIOS?

A financial ratio expresses one figure in accounts in terms of another. For example, accountants express net profit as a percentage of net assets. Net profit, in this case, is a measure of performance, and net assets a measure of size. Thus net profit as a percentage of net assets, is business performance as it relates to size. Larger organisations will normally make more profits than smaller ones because they have the capacity to sell more, so just saying that Marks & Spencer's net profit at £420 million is better than a £20 million profit for a regional chain of clothing shops would be misleading. However, if profit is expressed as a percentage of net assets a different picture emerges.

Marks & Spencer: $\dfrac{420 \text{ m}}{1,700 \text{ m}} \times 100 = 24.7\%$

Regional shop: $\dfrac{20 \text{ m}}{65 \text{ m}} \times 100 = 30\%$

The regional shop has on the surface used its assets more effectively to generate profits. The financial ratio has been used in the same way that you might use to compare the distance travelled by two cars. A Landrover Discovery can travel 600 km on a tank of petrol, whereas a Nissan Micra can only travel 300 km. However, the Discovery holds 95 litres which is rate of 6.3 kilometres to the litre, whereas the Micra holds 25 litres, a rate of 12 kilometres to the litre. You would therefore conclude that the Micra uses its fuel more effectively than the Discovery.

The importance of ratios to stakeholders

The way stakeholders interpret accounts depends very much on who they are and what they are trying to find out. A potential shareholder will consider closely the after tax profits of the company and how they relate to the number of shares issued. A bank manager would look at the liquid assets an organisation has, and how their value compares to the short-term debts the organisation has to cover. The sales director of the organisation will consider how the sales of the organisation relate to the profits it has made.

Accountants often split ratios into three distinct groups.

1 **Performance ratios**   These ratios are concerned with how successful the organisation has been at generating sales and profits from its trading activity.
2 **Capital ratios**   This group concentrates on the way the firm manages its capital in the short term in the form of cashflow, and in the long term in the way it raises finance.
3 **Shareholder ratios**   Shareholder ratios look specifically at the profit attributable to the owners and the way it relates to their investment.

■ APPLYING RATIO ANALYSIS

Performance ratios

All the ratios calculated are based on the accounts of Varsity Sports PLC, a company that specialises in sports clothing. The company supplies clothing for all sports, aiming at serious participants in areas such as athletics, rugby, soccer, basketball, hockey and gymnastics. Many professional individuals and teams use the kit provided by the company. For Varsity Sports' balance sheet and profit and loss accounts, see Fig 5.19. All figures contained in the accounts, and used in the following ratio calculations are in £000s.

Return on net assets or capital employed

$$\frac{\text{net profit}}{\text{net assets}} \times 100 \text{ or}$$

$$\frac{\text{net profits}}{\text{capital employed}} \times 100$$

$$\frac{750}{2,400} \times 100 = 31.25\%$$

We touched on this ratio in our introduction, and as stated there, this ratio shows how much net profit the organisation has generated from the assets it has employed. Net profit is used as opposed to after tax profits because the ratio concentrates on trading performance. Net assets is working capital + fixed assets and illustrates the value of assets employed by the firm. This is equal to capital employed, which is long-term liabilities + shareholders' funds, and this shows the long-term finance the firm has employed. Varsity Sports has a return on net assets (RONA) of 31.25 percent which means that for every £1 of assets employed net profit is 31p. The higher this value, the more successful the organisation has been at generating net profits from its net assets.

The RONA is generated in two ways. It is

partly contributed by the level of sales generated by the assets and partly by the profit made on each unit sold.

Asset turnover

This ratio shows the level of sales generated by the assets employed.

$$\frac{\text{sales}}{\text{net assets}}$$

$$\frac{6,900}{2,400} = 2.875$$

This figure tells us that Varsity Sports creates £2.87 of sales revenue from each £1 of assets employed. The higher the ratio, the more sales are generated from each £1 of assets employed, and the more successful the business has been. If the asset turnover rises, other things remaining equal, the RONA will rise. As with all ratios, asset turnover will vary from industry to industry. Some firms, particularly those which are labour rather than capital intensive, have a relatively high asset turnover ratio because their asset value is relatively small compared to the value of sales they make. This often applies in service industries, such as travel agents, law firms and accountancy firms.

Profit margin

Profit margin represents the amount of profit made on each item sold by a company. It is expressed as follows.

$$\frac{\text{net profit}}{\text{sales}} \times 100$$

$$\frac{750}{6,900} \times 100 = 10.87\%$$

This figure means that for each £1 of sales 10.87p of profit is made. The greater this value the more successful the firm is at generating profit from each unit it sells.

There is a relationship between asset turnover and profit margin, in that organisations which work on lower profit margins may well sell more and obtain a higher asset turnover because their prices are lower. A company that works on a low asset turnover, such as retailers who sell specialist designer clothing, will demand a much higher profit margin.

Stock turnover

$$\frac{\text{cost of sales}}{\text{stock}}$$

$$\frac{2,700}{300} = 9$$

$$\frac{365}{9} = 40.55 \text{ days}$$

The cost of sales tells you the value of stock sold over the accounting period, which, when divided by the closing stock figure gives you the average number of times stock is sold in a year. By dividing this figure into 365 the average number of days' stock held in the business is derived. Most firms would want to see stock moving through the business as quickly as possible. However, if the figure is too high and the day sales in stock is too low, then the business may suffer because it does not carry enough stock and may regularly run out. Certain industries will have quicker turnover than others, for example retailers like greengrocers have a particularly rapid turnover.

Debtors' turnover

$$\frac{\text{sales}}{\text{debtors}}$$

$$\frac{6,900}{350} = 19.71$$

$$\frac{365}{19.71} = 19 \text{ days}$$

Like the stock turnover ratio, debtors' turnover gives an indication of how long, on average, debtors are carried by the business. By calculating the day sales in debtors, the average length of time it takes to collect from debtors is given, which in the case of Varsity Sports is 19 days. The more quickly cash can be collected from debtors, the better from a liquidity point of view, although a debtor period which is too short may cost the company sales because its credit policy is over restrictive.

Efficiency ratios

These ratios are of particular interest to management because they give them a quantitative measure of the organisation's overall efficiency, and the efficiency of different parts of the organisation. The basic calculation is as follows.

$$\frac{\text{cost of goods sold}}{\text{sales}} \times 100$$

$$\frac{4,100}{6,900} \times 100 = 59.42\%$$

This means that for every £1 of sales, cost of goods sold is 59.42p. The lower this ratio is, the more efficient the business is at managing its costs during the period. This ratio can be developed by breaking down costs to see how efficiently direct labour or materials are managed and it can be extended to indirect costs as well.

$$\frac{\text{direct labour}}{\text{sales}} \times 100$$

$$\frac{1,400}{6,900} \times 100 = 20.28$$

Varsity Sports has a direct labour cost of 20.28p per £1 of sales.

Varsity Traders PLC: Profit and Loss Account 31/12/97	
£000s	
Sales	6,900
Cost of sales	2,700
Direct labour	1,400
Cost of goods sold	4,100
Gross Profit	**2,800**
Indirect costs	2,050
Net Profit	**750**
Interest expense	50
Profit before Tax	**700**
Tax	150
Profit after Tax	**550**
Dividend	100
Retained Profit	**450**

Varsity Traders PLC: Balance Sheet 31/12/97		
£000s		
Fixed Assets		
Machinery		800
Property		1,200
		2,000
Current Assets		
Stock		300
Debtors		350
Cash		50
		700
Current Liabilities		
Creditors		50
Tax payable		150
Dividend payable		100
		300
Net Current Assets		400
Net Assets		2,400
Shareholders' Funds		
Ordinary shares 5,000 @ 5p		250
Reserves		550
		800
Long-term Liabilities		
Mortgage		600
Debentures		1,000
		1,600
Capital Employed		2,400

Fig 5.18 *Profit and loss account and balance sheet for Varsity Sports*

Capital ratios

These ratios are used to examine the way the organisation finances itself, and are broken down into two areas, short-term and long-term finance.

Short-term finance

Current ratio

This is a short-term financial ratio that focuses on working capital by identifying the value of current assets available to cover current liabilities.

$$\frac{700}{300} = 2.33$$

→ Current assets
→ Current liabilities

This figure tells us that the firm has £2.33 of current assets to cover every £1 of current liabilities it has. In other words, they have cash, and access to assets that can quickly realise cash, to cover the demands of their creditors. The higher the value the safer the company is in terms of liquidity compared to a low ratio which indicates a vulnerable liquidity position. However, if the ratio is too high, the business is tying up liquid assets in a non-earning capacity. The company could use surplus liquid assets to invest in new machinery. Again, as with other ratios, values will vary from industry to industry. However, accountants tend to view a current ratio between 1.5 and 2 as a rough guide for firms to aim at.

Acid test or quick ratio

$$\frac{\text{cash} + \text{debtors}}{\text{current liabilities}}$$

$$\frac{400}{300} = 1.33$$

As a measure of liquidity, the current ratio has one major weakness for organisations, in that including stock as a liquid asset can be misleading. Stock, for many organisations, may prove very difficult to turn into cash in the short term because the stock has to be sold and cash has to be collected from debtors. For a food retailer, this may be relatively easy, but consider the difficulties facing a house builder, such as Barratt Homes, whose stock of raw materials, houses under construction and even finished houses, might take months or even years to turn into cash. The current ratio, under these circumstances, is inappropriate as an accurate guide to liquidity. For this reason, accountants often exclude stock from the ratio and use cash and debtors as sources of short-term funds to cover creditors. The 1.33 figure means that for every £1 of current liabilities, Varsity Sports has £1.33 in cash and debtors to cover them. On the face of it, Varsity Sports is in a relatively healthy position in terms of liquidity, but the figure achieved by other firms in the industry needs to be considered before any conclusions can be drawn. An even more accurate picture of liquidity could be established by just looking at cash divided by current liabilities. This may be worth doing if there are concerns about debtors paying on time.

Long-term finance

Capital gearing

As we discussed in the section on cashflow, we know that firms can either raise long-term funds through owner's capital or by borrowing. Owner's capital involves the owners of sole traders or partnerships putting in their own money, whereas limited companies and PLCs would issue shares. Long-term liabilities are normally in the form of bank loans and debentures. The proportion of funds raised either through owner's capital or long-term liabilities is called gearing and it is measured by the ratio:

$$\frac{\text{long-term liabilities}}{\text{shareholders' funds} + \text{long-term liabilities}} \times 100$$

$$\frac{1,600}{800 + 1,600} \times 100 = 67\%$$

The figure of 67 percent tells us that for every £1 of long-term capital raised 67p is borrowed. The larger the proportion of long-term finance raised, the more highly geared the company is said to be. There are certain risks associated with high gearing, linked with the costs of financing the organisation through borrowing. Firstly, borrowed funds have to be repaid, whereas share capital does not. Secondly, interest must be paid each year on borrowed funds, whereas dividends are paid at the directors' discretion. If profits are low in any year the directors can reduce the dividend payment they make, but the interest payment will be exactly the same. However, this needs to be traded off against the advantages of high gearing. Where there is less share capital, there may be more dividend to pay out amongst shareholders because there are fewer of them when the company is highly geared, and with fewer shareholders, the existing ones retain more control over the organisation. Typically, small, young, expanding companies tend to be highly geared because they rely on borrowed funds for their long-term finance.

Interest cover

$$\frac{\text{net profit}}{\text{interest payable}}$$

$$\frac{750}{50} = 15$$

This ratio illustrates the ease with which Varsity Sports can cover its interest payments with net profit. A figure of 15 means that for every £1 of interest payments, Varsity has £15 of net profit to pay them. The higher the figure, the more secure the firm is in terms of covering its interest payments with net profit. More highly geared firms will tend to have a lower interest cover because their interest expense on a larger amount of borrowing will reduce the value of the ratio.

Shareholder ratios

Return on shareholders' funds or return on equity

$$\frac{\text{profit after tax}}{\text{shareholders' funds}} \times 100$$

$$\frac{550}{800} \times 100 = 69\%$$

Return on equity or shareholders' funds is a measure of the organisation's after tax performance in terms of the funds put in by the owners. It tells the shareholder how much return they have earned on their investment in the company. Varsity Sports has earned 69p for every £1 invested by their shareholders. Profit after tax is used because this is attributable to the shareholders, but remember not all this will be distributed to them in the form of dividends because some of the profit will be retained for reinvestment in the business.

Earnings per share (EPS)

The return to shareholders can also be viewed in terms of the amount of profit earned on each share issued.

$$\frac{\text{profit after tax}}{\text{number of shares issued}}$$

$$\frac{550}{5,000} = 11\text{p per share}$$

The return here is expressed as an amount of money earned on each share issued, which in the case of Varsity Sports is 11p per share. The higher this amount is, the better from the shareholders' point of view, although this will not all be distributed in the form of dividends.

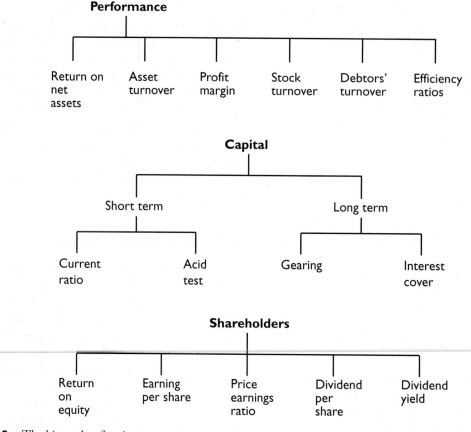

Performance

- Return on net assets
- Asset turnover
- Profit margin
- Stock turnover
- Debtors' turnover
- Efficiency ratios

Capital

- Short term
  - Current ratio
  - Acid test
- Long term
  - Gearing
  - Interest cover

Shareholders

- Return on equity
- Earning per share
- Price earnings ratio
- Dividend per share
- Dividend yield

Fig 5.19 *The hierarchy of ratios*

Price earnings ratio (P/E ratio)

$$\frac{\text{market price}}{\text{earnings per share}}$$

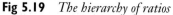

$$\frac{70p}{11p} = 6.36$$

The price earning ratio or P/E ratio relates the stock market's valuation of the company to the amount of profit earned on each share. The market price of the share is determined continuously by changes in the demand for the shares on the stock market, whereas the earnings per share is reported once at the end of each financial year. If demand for the shares rises, the market price of the shares will rise, and, with a constant earnings per share, the price earnings ratio will rise. Thus if the stock market's view of the company improves,

its P/E ratio will rise. In this case, Varsity Sports' current share price is 70 pence.

Dividend per share

$$\frac{\text{dividend}}{\text{number of shares}}$$

$$\frac{250}{5,000} = 5p \text{ per share}$$

Dividend per share tells the shareholder how much they will earn on each share they own. Varsity Sports has paid 5p per share in this instance. The amount paid on each share depends on the amount of profit the company earns and the proportion of this profit the directors choose to pay as dividends. The higher the amount the happier the shareholders are likely to be in the short term, although the more the company retains, and subsequently reinvests in the business, the higher profits are likely to be in the future.

Dividend yield

$$\frac{\text{dividend per share}}{\text{market price}} \times 100$$

$$\frac{5p}{70p} \times 100 = 7\%$$

This final shareholder ratio tells the shareholder the dividend they are earning related to the market price of the share. The higher the value, the greater the return the shareholder is earning on the stock market valuation of the shares. A potential shareholder would see that for each £1 they spend on shares they would earn 7p in dividends. If the demand for the shares rises, its price rises, and the yield will fall. The dividend yield and P/E ratio are often used by existing and potential shareholders to measure the stock market performance of companies' shares. Its performance on the stock market is important because this is the place where a company will look to raise new funds in the future. Shareholders also have the power to sack directors if the performance of the company and the shares is unsatisfactory.

Evaluating performance

As with any statistic, in any field, the only real way to draw conclusions from the information provided is to make comparisons. If a student scores 70 percent in a maths exam, the general consensus might be that this is a good result, but further investigation shows that the student came 25th out of 30, and, out of the maths exams she has sat this year, this was her lowest mark. The new conclusion drawn would be much more critical of her performance, except that this was a particularly weak section for her, and she was aiming to get only 60 percent. The same type of situation faces the managing director of Varsity Sports. A 31 percent return on net assets in 1997 is a respectable result, given that other comparable firms in the same industry had an average return on net assets of 27 percent. This was also their highest RONA figure over the last five years. However, the company's directors, who had invested heavily in new products over the last two years, were expecting a return of 35 percent. From this we can see there are three standards on which a firm can judge its performance.

Inter-company comparisons

The nature of any inter-company comparison depends on the stakeholder's objective when looking at the business. From the point of view of managers wishing to assess general company performance, it is important that any comparisons made between firms are done comparing firms of similar size in the same industry. Marks & Spencer's, for example, would compare itself with C&A and British Home Stores because of the similar nature of their businesses. A comparison with Tesco or Sainsbury's would not be as meaningful because these organisations concentrate more on food than clothing and home furnishings. A potential shareholder, on the other hand, would perhaps make comparisons across industries for return on equity because they would be looking for companies in industries with high return on equity values as a basis for buying shares.

Time comparisons

Trends in performance are again considered closely by stakeholders who are looking to see whether things are improving or deteriorating. Figures considered over four or five years provide a useful basis on which to establish trends, although periods longer than this may be misleading because the nature of the business could have changed. For example, a business may well have diversified into another area, or sold off a major part of its operations.

Budget comparisons

Organisations will set themselves targets for overall performance, and performance of individual parts of the business. These targets will be based on the manager's assessment of prevailing market conditions and the capability of the organisation based on available resources. Asda, for example, may well set itself a high target for return on net assets based on a boom in consumer spending that they expect to continue.

Ideally, any evaluation of performance would be based on a combination of all three comparisons. However, external users of accounts will not have access to budgets; some firms may be too young to consider trends, and figures for inter-company comparison may not be available for smaller organisations.

DIFFICULTIES ASSOCIATED WITH APPLYING RATIO ANALYSIS

Non-monetary information

The strength of financial analysis is its use of figures which provide a relatively objective view of an organisation's trading performance and financial position. However, this is a one dimensional way of looking at these parameters, that totally ignores important factors underlying the strength of the organisation. The quality of the firm's products, skill and motivation of its workforce, up to date nature of its capital and the amount of customer loyalty the firm has, will not be included in any financial analysis,

although they will contribute to the organisation's success.

Accounting periods

The accounting year varies between firms and this can have an important impact on the results derived from different ratios. If an off-licence chain, such as Threshers, produced its end of year accounts in September, its net assets figure is likely to be inflated by stock levels that have been built up to cover high demand for Christmas. However, in January the net asset figure will fall when stock levels are run down. Since profits are reported for the whole year, this would lead to a relatively lower RONA in September when compared to accounts produced in January.

Here is an example for a regional chain of off-licences where a lower stock value in January inflates the RONA.

September $\dfrac{500}{2,500} \times 100 = 20\%$

January $\dfrac{500}{2,100} \times 100 = 24\%$

Accounting methods

Different organisations may well produce their accounts using different methods, such as declining balance and straight line depreciation. This will alter profit and asset values that will give different accounting ratios depending on the method chosen. This problem will be even more marked when users are looking at multinationals, where international differences exist in the production of accounts. The USA, for example, use LIFO for stock valuation, whereas the UK uses FIFO.

Business environment

Before users of accounts make any drastic decisions because an organisation has shown a dramatic fall in RONA, asset turnover and profit margin, it is important to consider the trading conditions within which the business is operating that will not be directly indicated by the ratios. Trading performance is inevitably affected by booms and recessions, and these conditions need to be considered in any analysis. External industry shocks, such as the beef crisis, which affected cattle farmers in 1996, will obviously have a major impact on their trading performance.

Essentially these weaknesses mean that stakeholders should draw their conclusions on accounts with the difficulties discussed above borne in mind. If the RONA has suddenly increased for a company, then close analysis should be carried out to see why this might have happened.

NELSON FORGES AHEAD

Three companies operate in the road haulage market in the South West of England: Nelson Road Carriers, Redman and Son and Apex International. The market is extremely competitive and each firm is trying to increase its own market share. The adjacent table highlights the financial performance of each company in 1996.

The total sales in the market are estimated to be £64 million, with Nelson increasing its market share to 48 percent in 1996. With operating profits up 25 percent to £7 million, Nelson's directors believe that their policy of using a new computerised system for organising their fleet of vehicles, along with a

1966			
%	RONA	Profit margin	Asset turnover
Company			
Nelson	22	20	1.1
Redman	17.2	17.8	0.97
Apex	18	17	1.06

more flexible pricing policy, has accounted for their improved performance. The company is now looking to upgrade much of its fleet to reduce maintenance costs and improve reliability.

QUESTIONS

1 a Explain what you understand by the following ratios:
  • Return on net assets
  • Profit margin
  • Asset turnover [15]
 b On the basis of the above ratios, discuss which company has the best performance. [15]

2 a Using the information in the text, calculate the net asset figure for Nelson. [7]
 b Explain the impact rising sales might have on the return on net assets. [8]

3 a Calculate Nelson's profitability in 1995. [5]
 b Explain the advantages to Nelson of a growing market share. [10]

c Assuming the profit margin was the same for Nelson in 1995 as in 1996, calculate the company's sales in 1995. [5]

4 a Explain what ratios you would have used to measure the efficiency of Nelson, Apex and Redman. [10]
  b Discuss the problems associated with using ratio analysis to compare the performance of Nelson, Apex and Redman. [15]

  c What further information would you require to make a more meaningful analysis of the performance of Nelson, Apex and Redman? [10]

Total [100]

HARRISON COMPONENTS CONSIDERS MAJOR INVESTMENT

Harrison Components Ltd manufacture water filters for swimming pools. The company has been in existence for 30 years and has grown rapidly over the last five years. Its major customers are construction firms which specialise in building swimming pools for leisure centres, but it also supplies filters for the home swimming pool market.

The company is currently considering whether to invest in a major new piece of equipment used in the production of filters. It is state of the art technology, and would improve both the efficiency of production and the quality of the filters. However, it is an investment of £1.4 million, which is a major capital expenditure for the company. The accounts of the company are laid out below.

Profit and Loss Account: Harrison Components Ltd: 31 December, 1996 and 1997

	1997	1996
Sales revenue	5,500,000	5,000,000
Cost of sales	1,500,000	1,400,000
Direct labour	1,200,000	1,000,000
Production overhead	900,000	850,000
Cost of goods sold	3,600,000	3,250,000
Gross Profit	1,900,000	1,750,000
Management salaries	800,000	750,000
Advertising	400,000	400,000
Depreciation	260,000	240,000
Total overhead	1,460,000	1,390,000
Net Profit	440,000	360,000
Net interest expense	60,000	70,000
Profit before Tax	380,000	290,000
Tax	160,000	150,000
Profit after Tax	220,000	140,000
Dividends	140,000	120,000
Retained Profit	80,000	20,000

Balance Sheet: Harrison Components Ltd: 31 December, 1996 and 1997

	1997	1996
Fixed Assets		
Tangible		
Buildings	1,000,000	1,100,000
Machinery	800,000	700,000
Fittings	200,000	250,000
	2,000,000	2,050,000
Current Assets		
Stock	420,000	300,000
Debtors	120,000	110,000
Cash	150,000	120,000
	690,000	530,000
Current Liabilities		
Trade creditors	100,000	110,000
Overdraft	90,000	90,000
Tax payable	160,000	150,000
Dividends payable	140,000	120,000
	490,000	470,000
Net current assets	200,000	60,000
Net assets	2,200,000	2,110,000
Shareholders' funds		
Ordinary shares	900,000	900,000
Reserves	400,000	310,000
	1,300,000	1,210,000
Long-Term Liabilities		
Mortgage	700,000	700,000
Debentures	200,000	200,000
	900,000	900,000
Capital Employed	**2,200,000**	**2,110,000**

QUESTIONS

1 a Account for the increase in the reserves of Harrisons at the year ended 31 December, 1997. [5]

b Suggest a reason for the rise in the depreciation expense in Harrisons' profit and loss account. [5]

c Why is the £160,000 tax expense carried in the 1997 profit and loss account also carried as a current liability in the balance sheet? [5]

2 a Calculate the following ratios for each year: Return on net assets; Profit margin; Asset turnover. [9]

b On the basis of your calculations explain whether performance has improved or not. [6]

3 a Explain what you understand by the term 'liquidity'. [5]

b Which ratios would you use to measure liquidity and why? [10]

c On the basis of the ratios you have selected, make an assessment of the company's liquidity over the two years shown. [10]

4 a Suggest different ways in which Harrison Components could raise the funds to buy the new piece of machinery. [5]

b What are the advantages and disadvantages associated with each method you have suggested? [5]

c What impact will the machinery bought have on the company's return on net assets in the short and the long run? [15]

Total [80]

NOIR LTD GROW WITH THE SKIING INDUSTRY

Noir Ltd manufacture skis. They are an English company that has been very successful since they began manufacturing in 1990. They have benefited from the growth in the skiing industry, and the high prices of their main competitors. Their accounts for 1996, 1997, and 1998 are set out below.

Profit and loss account: Noir Ltd, 1996–1998

£000s	1996	1997	1998
Sales revenue	3,500	5,000	8,000
Cost of goods sold	1,200	1,500	1,900
Gross Profit	**2,300**	**3,500**	**6,100**
Indirect costs	1,400	1,600	2,000
Net Profit	**900**	**1,900**	**4,100**
Interest	100	200	200
Profit before Tax	**800**	**1,700**	**3,900**

Balance sheet: Noir Ltd, 1996–1998

£000s

Fixed Assets			
Machinery	500	550	600
Buildings	1,000	1,100	1,300
Copyright	700	900	1,000
	2,200	2,550	2,900
Current Assets			
Stock	400	500	700
Debtors	300	600	700
Cash	300	400	600
	1,000	1,500	2,000
Current Liabilities			
Overdraft	350	400	400
Creditors	250	300	400
	600	700	800
Working Capital	400	800	1,200
Net Assets	2,600	3,350	4,100
Shareholders' Funds			
Ordinary shares	1,200	1,400	1,400
Reserves	400	700	1,450
	1,600	2,100	2,850
Long-term Liabilities			
Bank loans	500	500	500
Debentures	500	750	750
	1,000	1,250	1,250
Capital Employed	**2,600**	**3,350**	**4,100**

QUESTIONS

1 Using financial ratios, write a report to Noir's directors commenting on the company's financial performance over the period shown. Use the following headings to structure your report: profitability, liquidity and efficiency. [30]

2 What further information would you have required to make a truer assessment of the business's performance? [10]

3 Discuss the strengths and weaknesses of using ratio analysis to judge business performance. [20]

Total [60]

Management Accounting –
Section A: Budgeting

SUMMARY

1 A budget is a financial plan that sets out the way a business is going to use its resources in different enterprise activities, in a given future time period.

2 Budgets have three purposes: to aid resource planning, to help set organisational objectives and to allow managers to exercise control.

3 There are operating budgets, summary budgets, master budgets, flexible budgets and capital budgets.

4 The budgetary process is made up of: preparation, implementation and review.

5 Flexible budgets are used to measure the performance of the whole organisation and individual parts of the organisation.

6 Capital budgeting investment appraisal is used to assess the financial costs and benefits of a particular business project.

7 The costs and benefits in capital budgets come in the form of cash inflows and outflows.

8 There are four techniques used to apply investment appraisal: payback, average annual rate of return, net present value (NPV) and internal rate of return (IRR).

One of the most important aspects of business decision making is trying to work out what the consequences of a decision taken now might have in the future. The quality of the way in which a business plans for the future has a major bearing on the success or failure of a decision. The financial consequences of future decisions are set out in an organisation's budgets.

WHAT IS A BUDGET?

A budget is a financial plan, that sets out the way a business is going to use its resources in different enterprise activities, in a given future time period.

In simple terms, a budget sets out how an organisation will use its resources, such as

labour, raw materials and capital, to achieve the objectives set by the company in the coming financial period. Budgets are set up for each aspect of a firm's operations, including revenue, expenses, profit, cashflow and capital expenditure.

The use of budgets

Budgets exist for a number of reasons. These include the following.

Resource planning

Budgets provide managers with a plan on how resources, such as labour and capital, are going to be used in the coming financial period. These plans help managers to organise resources efficiently during the period. This might be using the forecasted sales to work out how many units of a product need to be produced, and how many labour hours are needed to produce those units.

Objective setting

Budgets provide the organisation with targets that can be used to motivate people in the organisation. Revenue targets can be used to motivate the salesforce, and production goals can be used to motivate the production department.

Control

Because budgets provide targets, they can be used to judge individual areas of the organisation against those targets. When a sales budget is set, the performance of the sales department can be assessed according to how successful they were against their budget. The same principle can be applied when production cost targets are compared against the actual production costs achieved by the production department.

Decision making

By setting out the financial consequences of a particular decision, the budget provides some insight into the financial success or failure of a decision. For example, when a decision about whether a new product should be launched is made, the costs and revenues generated by the product can be forecast, giving a financial measurement of whether the product will be a success or failure, and whether the product launch should go ahead or not.

■ TYPES OF BUDGET

There are a variety of different types of budget that can be used for different aspects of the firm's operations, depending on its objectives.

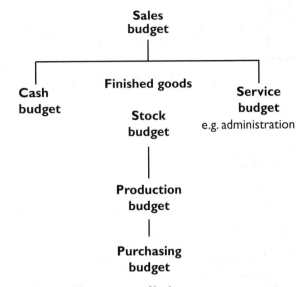

Fig 6.1   *The structure of budgets*

Operating budgets

This is a budget designed specifically for the company's trading activities in the coming year. It deals with each aspect of operations including: sales, production, labour, raw materials, cash and stock. The main objective of an operating budget is to plan the efficient use of the organisation's resources over the financial year, so that it meets its overall trading objective. An operating budget is produced by budgeting for each interdependent aspect of the organisation's operations in a structure set out in Fig 6.1.

Sales budget

This is sometimes called the principal budgetary factor, because the sales budget provides the starting point upon which all other budgets have to be set. Sales determine the level of business activity upon which the amount that needs to be manufactured is made, along with the amount of labour required, the capital requirement, and so on.

Finished goods stock

Once the level of sales has been set the business needs to set out how much stock it will need to meet sales. Any stock the company already has does not need to be produced, but the shortfall on sales will need to be made up by production.

Production budget

This means setting up budgets for the raw materials and components, labour and capital used to produce the output required by sales.

Cash budget

The funds required by the organisation over the budgetary period is a vital aspect of the budgetary process, because any shortfall in liquidity makes it very difficult for the organisation to trade.

Service budgets

Finally, the business needs to budget for administration, personnel, accounts and any other parts of the firm that service the main functional part of the business.

Summary budgets

Once budgets have been produced for each part of the organisation, they can be brought together as summary budgets.

- The budgeted profit and loss account
- The budgeted balance sheet
- The budgeted cashflow statement

These summary budgets are set out in the same way as the normal financial statement provided by the organisation at the end of the financial period, except they are based on budgeted figures. Once the summary budgets have been accepted by the management they are set out as master budgets.

■ PRODUCING A BUDGET

The budgetary process can be broken down into three stages; preparing, implementing and reviewing. The process can be illustrated by the following case example. Glass Vase Ltd manufacture high quality glass vases that they sell to a variety of different retailers including home furnishing shops and department stores.

They set up their budget in the following way.

Preparing

Setting objectives

The objectives set by organisations can vary from achieving as much profit as possible to maximising market share, obtaining high market growth and increasing sales revenue. Objective setting is normally carried out using the following criteria:

- The long-term strategic objectives of the business
- The results achieved by the business in previous years
- The results achieved by similar companies in the same industry
- The prevailing economic and market conditions
- The given internal conditions of the business – what managers feel they can achieve

It is important that the objectives set are tough enough to stretch the organisation, but not so difficult that managers feel they are unattainable.

Glass Vase Ltd want to achieve a 12 percent return on capital employed. This was an objective that management felt they could achieve given the buoyant state of the economy and the home furnishing market. The managing director, Tim Flowers, has a close association with similar companies in the industry who are achieving around the same level of return. He also feels that this level of return will allow them to achieve the growth in size that was set up in their five year business plan.

Allocating responsibility

To ensure that the company achieves the budgeted objectives that are set, different areas of the organisation have the responsibility of achieving their own objectives to make sure the overall objective is achieved. Within the organisation there are three different types of centre.

1 **Revenue centres** This is normally the sales department, which is responsible for generating revenue from its activities.
2 **Cost centres** This would be an area like the production department which is responsible for generating costs.
3 **Profit centres** A profit centre is an area of the organisation responsible for generating both costs and revenues. This

would be, for example, an individual store in a chain of retailers.

Setting policies and strategies to achieve objectives

In order to achieve a target rate of return in the budget, the business will need to operate in a certain way, following the policies and strategies set by the firm. For Glass Vase Ltd, this would involve following the production, marketing and sales strategies that have been employed so successfully over the last five years. One new strategy would be to include garden centres as an extra area of distribution.

Preparing forecasts

This stage of the process involves filling in the detail of the budget, working from the targets set in the objectives. The table below shows how Glass Vase Ltd has set each of its budgets to achieve the target rate of return.

Sales budget

Product	Budget units sold	Budget price	Budget revenue
1	230,000	£25	5,750,000
2	100,000	£20	2,000,000
3	150,000	£32	4,800,000
Total revenue			12,550,000

The sales budget then allows the company to set its production budget based on the number of units sold. Direct costs are

relatively easy to budget because they are directly related to the output the company produces.

Production budget

Product	Budget units produced	Budgeted direct labour cost per unit	Budget direct labour cost
1	230,000	£6	1,380,000
2	100,000	£7	700,000
3	150,000	£9	1,350,000
Total direct labour cost			3,430,000

Direct materials budget

Product	Budget units produced	Budgeted direct materials	Budget direct cost
I	230,000	£4	920,000
2	100,000	£6	600,000
3	150,000	£5	750,000
Total direct labour cost			2,270,000

Indirect costs, which are fixed costs, are in this case forecast on the basis of previous years' figures, as well as the firm's desire to meet its objectives.

Indirect costs	£
Depreciation	650,000
Production overhead	700,000
Marketing expenses	600,000
Rent	200,000
Transport expenses	500,000
Selling expenses	350,000
Total indirect cost	3,000,000

From the sales, production, and overhead budgets, Glass Vase Ltd have produced the budgeted profit and loss account in Fig 6.2. Glass Vase Ltd have budgeted for changes in both assets and liabilities to produce the budgeted balance sheet shown in Fig 6.3.

Glass Vase Ltd Budgeted Profit and Loss Account: 31 December, 1997		
£000s		
Total sales revenue		12,550
Direct costs		
Total direct labour cost	3,430	
Total direct material cost	2,270	
Cost of goods sold		5,700
Gross profit		6,850
Indirect costs		3,000
Net Profit		**3,850**

Fig 6.2 *A budgeted profit and loss account for Glass Vase Ltd*

Glass Vase Ltd Budgeted Balance Sheet: 31 December, 1997		
£000s		
Fixed Assets		
Machinery	8,000	
Property	12,000	
		20,000
Current Assets		
Stock	3,000	
Debtors	3,500	
Cash	500	
	7,000	
Current Liabilities		
Creditors	500	
Tax payable	1,500	
Dividend payable	1,000	
	3,000	
Net Current Assets		**4,000**
Net Assets		**24,000**
Shareholders' Funds		
Ordinary shares 5 million @ 50p		2,500
Reserves		5,500
		8,000
Long-term Liabilities		
Mortgage		6,000
Debentures		10,000
		16,000
Capital employed		**24,000**

Fig 6.3 *A budgeted balance sheet for Glass Vase Ltd*

From the budgeted balance sheet and profit and loss account the budgeted return on capital employed will be:

$$\frac{3,850}{24,000} \times 100 = 16\%$$

The 16 percent return on capital employed exceeds the target rate of return set in the company's budget objectives of 12 percent, so the budget is accepted.

Implementing the budget

Once the budget has been accepted by the company's senior management, it becomes a management order and is communicated to managers who are responsible for carrying it out. As the financial year progresses each cost, revenue and profit centre will have the responsibility of meeting their budgets, so that the overall target rate of return can be achieved.

Reviewing – final assessment

Once the budgeted period is over, the business can review its performance against the budget. This has two purposes: firstly, the organisation can make some kind of judgement on how well it has performed during the year against its budgeted figures, and secondly, the quality of the budget set can be assessed. Any mistake made can then be rectified for subsequent years.

BUDGETARY CONTROL – FLEXIBLE BUDGETS

Prepared budgets are also known as fixed budgets because they are set, and do not allow for changes in the level of activity achieved by the business. Because they are fixed, operating budgets are of limited use when it comes to measuring the performance of the organisation. For example, if the production department of a firm budgets for a total cost of £200,000 and its actual cost over the period is £220,000, then the department's

performance could be seen as poor because costs are higher than they should be. However, this budget takes no account of sales which could have been 50 percent above those budgeted for, which would have led to much higher production costs.

Flexible budgets change to take account of different levels of business activity, making them much more appropriate for measuring the performance of an organisation against its budget.

Preparing a flexible budget

This is how a flexible budget is produced.

1 Costs are divided up into their fixed and variable elements. This is crucial because variable costs will change with different sales or activity levels.
2 Budgets are set for different activity levels. In the example overleaf, 100 percent activity relates to the budgeted normal level of activity. Fifty percent activity is for half the normal level of activity.

Fig 6.4 shows what happens to fixed and variable costs, along with sales revenue at different activity levels. It is clear that variable costs will change with the activity level and fixed costs remain the same. Because the flexible budget allows for the activity changes, it can be used to measure performance.

After the budgetary period is over, the actual performance of the organisation can then be compared with the flexible budget to make an assessment of the organisation's performance. In this case, Glass Vase Ltd has had a good year and achieved a 150 percent activity level. Its actual cost figures are now compared with the budgeted figures at this level (see Fig 6.5).

Variance

The final column in Fig 6.5 shows the difference between the budgeted figure and the actual figure achieved, and is called the

	Glass Vase Ltd		
	£000s	£000s	£000s
	50%	100%	150%
Total sales revenue	6,275	12,550	18,825
Direct costs			
Variable direct labour cost	1,715	3,430	5,145
Variable direct material cost	1,135	2,270	3,405
Cost of goods sold	2,850	5,700	8,550
Gross profit	3,425	6,850	10,275
Fixed Indirect costs	3,000	3,000	3,000
Net Profit	**425**	**3,850**	**7,275**

Fig 6.4   *The effect of different activity levels on sales revenue, fixed and variable costs*

variance. A favourable variance (F), is one which means that the actual profit figure is higher than the budgeted figure, whereas a negative figure is actual performance below the budgeted figure. In this case, Glass Vase Ltd has a favourable profit because of a favourable variance on direct labour costs, which outweighs the adverse variance on direct materials. Management can now take action to appraise the performance of the relevant departments.

CAPITAL BUDGETING – INVESTMENT APPRAISAL

What is investment appraisal?

Investment appraisal is the monetary assessment of all the costs and benefits of an investment project over a given time period. An investment project is the use of resources by an organisation to yield a monetary return in the future. From a business organisation's point of view this would mean increasing future profits, but for charities the returns

	Glass Vase Ltd		
	£000s	£000s	
	Actual	Budget	Variance
		150% activity	
Total sales revenue	18,825	18,825	0
Direct costs			
Variable direct labour cost	4,900	5,145	245(F)
Variable direct material cost	3,600	3,405	195(A)
Cost of goods sold	8,500	8,550	50(F)
Gross profit	10,325	10,275	50(F)
Fixed Indirect costs	3,000	3,000	0
Net Profit	**7,325**	**7,275**	**50(F)**

Fig 6.5   *A comparison of actual cost figures with budgeted figures*

could be looked upon as, say, better public service. Investment appraisal considers the monetary cost and benefits as cash outflows and inflows from the business.

Here are some examples of possible investment projects.

1 An organisation launching a new product that will generate future revenues, profits and cashflow.
2 A new production technique that increases efficiency which reduces costs and increases profits.
3 There could be the choice of two alternative pieces of machinery, and the company wants to know the one which reduces costs the most, or generates the greatest amount of cash.
4 An organisation may be considering the takeover of another company, yielding greater profits in the future.

Investment appraisal means assessing the future quality or success of an investment decision. As capital budgeting it relates to the quantitative planning used in the future allocation of resources. An organisation needs to budget for the future cash generated by a project over the estimated life of the project. For example, a new product being launched may have an estimated sales life of four years. All the cash inflows and outflows would need to be budgeted for over the four year period.

The application of investment appraisal

Investment appraisal has two main applications for organisations:

1 **Decision making** Ultimately, investment appraisal should improve the quality of decision making associated with an investment project. By objectively examining the costs and benefits associated with a project it is possible to make a decision based on some meaningful analysis.

2 **Planning for the use of resources** An organisation needs to know clearly what the demands on its resources will be in the future, so that it can make adequate provision for them. The most important consideration here is cash. Investment appraisal is based on the inflow and outflow of cash from the organisation. This is because any project will involve tying up cash for long periods of time, which has its own costs in terms of interest. The organisation will obviously need to consider how much cash it will need to put a project into place and then how much cash it will need to support the project.

Analysing project cost

The costs associated with an investment decision can be broken down into two types: initial set up costs and project running costs. In the application of investment appraisal we look at these costs in terms of cash outflows since investment appraisal is concerned with the movement of cash.

Set-up costs

These are the costs associated with putting the investment decision into operation. This may take the form of buying and commissioning a new piece of machinery involving the initial cost of purchasing the machine, along with any costs associated with putting it into operation, such as training staff to use the machine, or converting part of the factory to put the machine in. If the organisation is launching a new product, then we would look at the cost of any new machinery bought, the cost of research and development into the product, market research costs and initial marketing costs, such as an advertising launch.

An example would be a decision by a local sports centre to open up a fitness suite. The initial costs associated with this proposal are listed below.

Purchase price of the equipment	£95,000
Training costs	£10,000
Fitting the equipment	£5,000
Total	**£110,000**

Running costs

Once the project has been set up, it will incur running costs during its useful life with the organisation. These costs would be the labour, material and overhead expenses associated with operating the project. For a new product, this would be all the costs associated with producing and selling it. A new piece of machinery would have labour and maintenance costs. The table below illustrates the running costs associated with the building of the sports centre's fitness suite.

You will notice that this project has a forecasted life of four years. The years shown are considered to be at the end of the year, which means that if we look at year 1, we are looking at the running costs which will have been incurred over the 12 months to the end of the first year of the project. The same applies to years 2, 3 and 4. Year 0 is the present moment in time.

Depreciation

A common mistake is to confuse depreciation with the cashflows associated with a product. Depreciation does not represent the movement of cash; it is an accounting technique used to allow for the fall in value of fixed assets over time, and the way this affects the published profit and loss account and balance sheet. Depreciation should be ignored in working out a project's cash flow.

Project benefits
Cash inflows

Project benefits are considered in terms of cash inflows generated by the project. The organisation will need to forecast these inflows in very much the same way it forecasted its running costs. In the case of our sports centre example, the management are likely to have carried out market research about the potential demand for their fitness suite. They would then have looked at this in the light of the potential capacity of the suite and prices for the facility. From this, expected revenue over the life of the project can be forecasted.

The table opposite (top) represents the forecasted revenues of the management team of the sports centre. Again, it is worth noting that revenues are calculated and attributed to the end of each year in the same way as running costs.

Years	0	1	2	3	4
Initial outlay	£110,000				
Labour		£25,000	£25,000	£25,000	£25,000
Maintenance		£6,000	£7,000	£8,000	£8,000
Marketing		£2,000	£2,000	£2,000	£2,000
Total	£110,000	£33,000	£34,000	£35,000	£35,000

End of year	0	1	2	3	4
Forecasted revenues or cash inflows	£20,000	£40,000	£70,000	£90,000	£90,000

Cost savings

Projects can also generate a cash inflow in the form of cost savings. When a business invests in a new machine, or introduces a new production technique, it will gain a cash inflow because of the increase in efficiency it gets from the new machine or method.

Extra revenues

Projects sometimes also earn revenues from outside the normal course of their operations. A typical example is cash derived from the sale of an old machine which makes way for a new one, or a forecasted disposal value for an asset at the end of its life. For example, many organisations will derive income from selling company cars at the end of their useful lives. In our sports centre example, the centre would receive a £20,000 grant from the Sports Council if the project was to go ahead. This is included as a cash inflow at the start of the project in year 0.

■ APPLYING INVESTMENT APPRAISAL TECHNIQUES

Calculating the net cashflow

Once the costs and benefits of an investment decision have been established, it is now possible to apply different techniques to analyse the consequences of the decision. Before these techniques can be applied it is important to draw up a table which summarises the cashflows associated with a particular project. Figure 6.6, using our sports centre example, illustrates how this is done.

Net cashflow

This is calculated by subtracting project cash outflows from cash inflows. In the example, we see that after an initial net cash outflow (which is expressed as a negative value), the project yields a positive net cash inflow over its operating life.

End of Year	0	1	2	3	4
Cash inflows	£20,000	£40,000	£70,000	£90,000	£90,000
Costs or cash Outflows					
Initial outlay	£110,000				
Total cash outflow	£110,000	£33,000	£34,000	£35,000	£36,000
Net cashflow	−£90,000	£7,000	£36,000	£55,000	£55,000
Cumulative cashflow	−£90,000	−£83,000	−£47,000	£8,000	£63,000

Fig 6.6 *A table to summarise the cashflow associated with a particular project*

Cumulative cashflow

This row is useful because it illustrates what happens to the cash position of the company as the project is in operation. We can see that the project makes an overall positive return on the initial investment in the third year of its operation.

Payback

What is payback?

This is a simple way of analysing the returns of an investment project. It involves working out the amount of time it takes a project to pay off its initial investment. In the case of our sports centre example, we would be looking at the amount of time it would take to pay off the initial investment of £110,000.

Calculating payback

The initial outlay is paid off by the net inflows earned by the project. If we consider Fig 6.6, we can see that the cumulative cashflow actually becomes positive in the third year of the project's life, which means that the project pays back in the third year. This method can be further developed to give a more precise payback date. It can be calculated by using the following equation.

$$\frac{\text{outstanding cash flow at the beginning of the payback year}}{\text{net cash inflow in the year of payback}}$$

$$\times\ 365 = \textbf{pay back in days}$$

The fitness suite pays back in the third year:
47,000/55,000 × 365 = 312 days
Two years and 312 days payback.

An evaluation of payback

The advantage of payback is that it is a simple technique to apply. The sooner a project pays back the better for the company. The payback time is crucial to some organisations who have borrowed funds to finance their investment and are concerned with the repayment of any loans. For this reason, payback is extremely useful to small companies.

Payback is limited in that it only considers cash inflows during the payback period, and not over the entire life of the project. Many projects may take a long time to payback, but have substantial returns after the payback date. This is particularly important with large projects which involve considerable initial research and development costs.

Average annual rate of return

What is the average annual rate of return?

This technique of investment appraisal involves calculating the average net cash inflow of a project over its life, and then expressing this as a percentage of the initial cash outlay.

Calculating the average annual rate of return

The average net cashflow is calculated by dividing the total net cashflow generated by the project, by the forecasted life of the project.

$$\frac{\text{total net cash flow/forecasted life of the project}}{\text{initial cash outlay}}$$

$$\times\ 100 = \textbf{average annual rate of return}$$

In our case study example, the average annual rate of return is calculated as follows.

$$\frac{7{,}000 + 36{,}000 + 55{,}000 + 55{,}000 - 90{,}000/4}{90{,}000}$$

$$\times 100 = 17.5\%$$

This means that for every £1 invested the project yields 17.5p. The higher this figure the greater the return of the project.

Evaluation of average annual rate of return

The advantage of this technique is that it takes into account cash inflows over the entire forecasted life of the project. Thus this method would account for cashflows after the payback period. The fact that it gives a percentage return means that it can be used to compare projects of different sizes.

The problem with both average annual rate of return and the payback method is that they fail to take into account the time value of money.

Net present value (NPV)

Discounting

This method of investment appraisal takes into account the time value of money. An investment project means using funds for an initial outlay which will be tied up for a given time period. These funds can be raised through borrowing, from retained profits and from issuing new shares. The funds have a value over time. If the money is borrowed, its value over time will be in the form of an interest payment made to the lender. If the funds were raised from retained profit, then the organisation would be foregoing the interest it could have earned had the money been, for example, put into a bank account.

What is NPV?

The net present value method takes the time value of money into account by discounting cashflows. Future cashflows generated by a project are not worth as much in the future as they are in the present. For example, you would rather have a £1,000 now than in a year's time, because you could have invested £1,000 for a year and earned a rate of interest on it. For each rate of interest there is a set of discount values which can be applied over the useful life of a project. The cashflows are multiplied by the discount factor which applies to the year of the relevant cashflow to give the present value of the cashflow.

For example, at a rate of interest of 10 percent, the discount factor after one year is 0.909. If a project yielded a cash inflow of £10,000 after one year then the present value would be:

£10,000 × 0.909 = £9,090

Choosing the discount factor

Organisations will choose their discount factor based on a number of different factors, for example:

- **Current market interest rates** – the higher market interest rates are, the higher rate chosen for the discount factor: this is because borrowing costs are higher and the firm could earn more from funds put into a bank account
- **Risk** – the higher the risk associated with a project, the higher the return the organisation would want to earn from investment; the project would thus be discounted at a higher rate

Calculating the NPV

The present values in Fig 6.7 are calculated by multiplying the net cashflows by the relevant discount factor.

End of Year	0	1	2	3	4
Cash inflows	£20,000	£40,000	£70,000	£90,000	£90,000
Costs or cash outflows					
Initial outlay	**£110,000**				
Total cash outflow		£33,000	£34,000	£35,000	£35,000
Net cashflow	−£90,000	£7,000	£36,000	£55,000	£55,000
Discount rate 10%	1	0.91	0.83	0.75	0.68
Present values	**−£90,000**	**£6,370**	**£29,880**	**£41,250**	**£37,400**

NPV is calculated by subtracting the initial outlay from the sum of the present values of the net cash inflows.

Fig 6.7 *Calculating present values to produce NPV*

From Fig 6.7 above

Initial outlay = −£90,000
Total present values = £6,370 + £29,880
+ £41,250 + £37,400 = £114,900
NPV: £114,900 − £90,000 = £24,900

If the NPV is positive, then the discounted cashflow generated by the project exceeds the initial outlay and the project is viable when measured against the discount rate set. In this case, the sports centre project yields a greater return than could be earned from a high interest bank account. If the result had been negative, the project would not be viable when measured against a discount rate of 10 percent. The sports centre could have earned more from a high interest bank account.

Assessment of NPV

1 NPV's strength lies in the fact that it considers cashflows for the entire life of the project, and allows for the time value of money.
2 Using a positive or negative figure to judge a project is a fairly simple way of interpreting its result.
3 However, setting a discount rate can be a complicated, inexact science.
4 The NPV gives an absolute value. This

makes it difficult to compare projects of different sizes. A £10 million investment may well yield more than our sports centre example in cash inflows, but because of the size of the project it may not be as profitable per £1 invested.

Internal rate of return

What is the internal rate of return?

The internal rate of return is the discount rate which gives a project a net present value of zero. In other words, the same procedure is carried out for IRR as for the NPV, but the final NPV will be zero.

Calculating the internal rate of return

The internal rate of return can be calculated by finding the NPV of a project at two different discount rates. The NPVs can then be graphed against the discount rate and Fig 6.8 illustrates this. Because the relationship between the NPV and the discount rate is a linear one, we can just extrapolate our linear relationship until it crosses the x-axis where the discount rate which yields a zero NPV will be. In our sports centre example we know that the NPV of the project at a 10 percent discount rate is

End of Year	0	1	2	3	4	NPV
Net Cashflow	−£90,000	£7,000	£36,000	£55,000	£55,000	
Discount rate	1	0.87	0.76	0.66	0.57	
Present values	−£90,000	£6,090	£27,360	£36,300	£31,350	£11,100

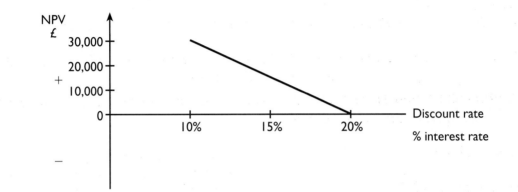

Fig 6.8   *Calculating the internal rate of return*

£30,340, so this is the first point we can plot on our graph. The table in Fig 6.8 gives the NPV of the project at a discount rate of 15 percent, £11,100 (101,100 − 90,000 = 11,100). Plotting the two NPVs and extrapolating the graph gives us an IRR of 20 percent.

EVALUATION OF INVESTMENT APPRAISAL

Accuracy

Investment appraisal involves forecasting cashflows over a number of years. This has inherent difficulties. Actual cashflows can work out to be very different from budgeted cashflows when one considers how the trading conditions of organisations can change. It is important that any investment decision is taken with these difficulties in mind.

This problem is compounded with very long-term projects, where trading conditions can vary markedly from the start of a project into its later stages. Long-term projects often involve very large cashflows which increase their risk even further.

Non-monetary factors

Discounted cashflow and other investment appraisal techniques look at investment decisions in monetary terms. However, other factors, which cannot be considered in monetary terms, have to be accounted for. Examples of the type of factors are outlined below.

Organisation strategy

A decision may or may not fit into a company's overall strategy or policy, so a project may be very profitable in cash terms, but may not take the company in a direction which it wants to take. For example, our sports centre may find that a health suite does not really fit into the 'sports policy of the centre'.

Human influence

The people in an organisation will have a major impact on the investment decisions that take place. A new machine, for example, may require major changes to the working practices of an organisation's workforce. A machine which simplifies a particular task could make a job boring and repetitive for the labour force, which would reduce their motivation. The preferences of managers may also influence an investment decision. For example, an organisation's director may have a close relationship with the potential supplier of a new machine, which would lead them to choose it rather than an alternative.

Economic factors

Any investment project takes place within an economic climate. This climate will have a major influence over the project's success or failure. If overall macroeconomic indicators look promising (stable growth, low inflation) then the project is more likely to go ahead than if the future looks uncertain. Economic factors are particularly important when a company is considering a project which spans national boundaries. For example, an organisation may be looking at buying machinery from overseas or launching a new product abroad. In both cases exchange rate changes, trade barriers and cultural factors will influence the decision.

Government influence

Governments, both at a national and local level, can influence investment decisions in a number of ways. At a national level their economic policies have an obvious impact. If the Government is trying to expand the economy by reducing interest rates, then the discount rates of investment projects will fall. Governments can also try and increase the volume of investment by offering tax incentives. This means that organisations will receive a tax rebate on any profits used to buy new machinery. Government may also offer grants to firms who invest in particular markets or regions. Organisations who invest in certain deprived regions could well receive a grant from the Government for doing so.

THE SHOREHAM NURSERY BUDGET

The Shoreham Nursery is a garden centre based in the Northwest of England. It is a large centre that sells to both domestic gardeners and professional gardeners. It sells a huge variety of different products from plants, shrubs and flowers (its core business), to garden furniture, gardening tools and greenhouses. It has been in business since the early 1970s but has recently begun to grow under the new, dynamic management of Audrey Nuttall who has sought to improve all aspects of the business's approach.

£	March	April	May	June	July	August
Sales	75,000	80,000	90,000	100,000	120,000	125,000
Cost of sales	45,000	48,000	54,000	60,000	72,000	72,000
Labour cost	15,000	15,000	17,000	17,000	20,000	20,000
Overheads	5,000	5,000	7,000	7,000	8,000	8,000

The table above sets out all the costs and revenues the company has budgeted for the next six months.

QUESTIONS

1 a Why is it important for Shoreham Nursery to use budgets? [10]
  b Discuss the factors Shoreham Nursery should take into account when setting up its budgets. [15]

2 a Why are sales so important in setting up a budget? [5]
  b Account for the forecast set by the Shoreham Nursery that both sales and costs will rise over the six months considered. [5]

  c Calculate the monthly net profit budgeted by the Shoreham Nursery. [5]
  d Produce a budgeted profit and loss account for the six months budgeted for. [5]

3 Discuss the problems Shoreham Nursery will incur when setting up its budgets. [15]

Total [60]

THE JB PROCTOR BUDGET

JB Proctor is a partnership that specialises in constructing conservatories. It operates in the Southwest of England, and has exploited the rapid growth in this market over the last ten years. David Edwards, who is one of the partners, has set up a flexible budget for 1997.

	£000s 50%	£000s 100%	£000s 150%
Total sales revenue		200,000	
Direct costs			
Variable direct labour cost		40,000	
Variable direct material cost		90,000	
Total direct costs			
Gross profit			
Fixed Indirect costs		40,000	
Net profit			

QUESTIONS

1 a Explain what you understand by the term 'flexible budget'. [5]
  b Why are fixed budgets unsuitable for assessing business performance? [8]
  c Produce a flexible budget for JB Proctor by completing the table above. [10]

2 The company actually achieved 150 percent of capacity and had the following cost and revenue figures:

  • Sales £320,000
  • Direct material costs £140,000
  • Direct labour costs £80,000
  • Fixed indirect costs £42,000

  a Product a profit and loss account for the actual level of activity. [5]
  b What do you understand by the term 'variance'? [5]
  c Calculate the cost and revenue variances, and state whether they are favourable or unfavourable. [7]
  d Suggest why you think the labour costs exceeded their budgeted figure by so much. [5]
  e Suggest why you think the fixed cost changed at the higher level of activity, when it was forecast not to change. [5]

  Total [50]

A NEW STAND FOR WALTHAM TOWN FC

Waltham Town FC, who play in the Football League Third Division, are considering whether to build a new stand. The stand would have a capacity of 10,000 people and it is forecast that it will yield the following revenue figures over the next five years:

Year 1 – £2.1 million
Year 2 – £2.3 million
Year 3 – £2.4 million
Year 4 – £2.4 million
Year 5 – £2.4 million

The initial cost of the project is £4.9 million and its annual running costs are forecast to be constant at £200,000.

QUESTIONS

1 a What costs would be included as part of the initial costs? [3]

b What costs would be included as part of the running costs? [4]

c Analyse how the Club would have gone about forecasting the revenue set out above. [8]

d Discuss the particular problems of forecasting revenue in this case? [10]

2 Produce a cashflow table that summarises the cashflow position of the project over its useful life. [7]

3 a Use the following investment appraisal techniques to assess the feasibility of the project: [20]

- Payback

- Average annual rate of return

- Net present value (use a ten percent discount rate).

Year	1	2	3	4	5
Discount rate 10%	1	0.91	0.83	0.75	0.68

b On the basis of the techniques used, explain whether the project should go ahead or not. [8]

4 What other factors would the Club need to consider when deciding whether or not to go ahead with the project? [10]

Total [70]

WARWICK LTD REPLACE THREE VANS

Warwick Ltd wish to replace three vans in their distribution fleet. The vans cost £11,000 new, have a useful life of five years and have a residual value of £1,000. There are three alternative ways of replacing the vans which are:

1 Outright purchase, payment terms being cash one year after delivery.
2 Leasing, rental £30,000 per annum, 30 percent tax relief one year in arrears.

3 Hire purchase, total price to be paid calculated as 130 percent of the outright purchase cost; 20 percent of this total price to be paid at once and the balance in five equal instalments.

Year	1	2	3	4	5	6
Discount rate 10%	1	0.91	0.83	0.75	0.68	0.62

QUESTIONS

1 Construct a table showing cashflows, for each alternative, for each year. [20]

2 Using appropriate investment appraisal techniques, calculate the cheapest way of replacing the vans. [20]

Total [40]

BEDWYN LTD CHOOSE A PROJECT

The managing director of Bedwyn Ltd is keen to expand into new markets. A group of management consultants were employed by Bedwyn to look into two markets. One is to start exporting fire detection equipment into Europe and the other is to diversify into the mass UK market, having currently specialised solely in the industrial sector. There is considerable potential in the European market with the removal of trade barriers through the EU. The figures for these two investment opportunities are summarised below. Project A covers the movement into the European market and Project B represents expansion in the UK. One director supports Project A since the revenue potential is much greater than B. However, another director is more cautious since the company has little knowledge of selling overseas. He is also worried about changes in the exchange rate, which would affect the projected figures given. On top of this, the director believes that the production techniques associated with A would upset the workforce.

Year	Project A £000s	Project B £000s
0	−400	−500
1	−300	300
2	100	200
3	200	100
4	200	100
5	200	50
6	300	
7	300	
8	250	
Net Cashflow		

Average annual rate of return	15.2%	10%
Payback end year	5	2
Internal rate of return	18%	22%
NPV @ 10%	£261,000	£112,000

QUESTION

1 Write a report to the directors of Bedwyn Ltd outlining which project they should choose. [40]

Total [40]

Management Accounting – Section B: Costing

SUMMARY

1 Costs are the money value of resources used by the organisation in producing a good or service.
2 Costs can be used as a basis for: setting prices, measuring efficiency, recording profits and making decisions.
3 Costs can be classified in terms of resources, departments, products, output, jobs and units.
4 Absorption costing is a way of ascertaining costs for individual cost centres.
5 Marginal or contribution costing is applying direct costs to cost centres. It can

be used to make decisions on: special orders, whether to make or buy components and the measurement of cost centre performance.
6 Break-even is a costing technique used to assess whether a project will make a profit or loss. The break-even point tells managers how many units have to be sold for a project to start making a profit.
7 The break-even diagram gives a pictorial view of the costs and revenue generated by a project.

An understanding of costs is absolutely critical for a whole variety of different functions within business. Being able to measure the costs associated with the whole organisation's operation, as well as individual areas within the organisation, allows business people to set prices, measure performance and produce budgets, all of which improves the quality of decision making.

WHAT ARE COSTS?

Accounting cost

Costs are the money value of resources used up in the activities of an organisation, when it produces goods and services. This could be the wages paid to labour, expenditure on raw

materials, the acquisition of capital or the payment of overheads.

Opportunity cost

Business people often use the term 'opportunity cost', which looks at costs in terms of the highest value alternative given up to achieve the option the business chooses. This is a much broader concept than accounting costs in that it can be used to assess the real cost associated with taking a decision. For example, when a firm invests £220,000 in new plant machinery, its cost as a decision can be assessed in terms of what these funds could also have been used for, such as an extension to a factory, or research and development.

Application of costs in organisations

Setting prices

Costs are critical in setting prices, because the price set by the business needs to exceed the cost of producing the product in order to make a profit. The cost of producing one unit (cost per unit) of output achieved by the company provides the basis for setting prices. If Ford can produce an individual car for £7,000, then this will be the basis of setting the price for that individual car.

Measuring efficiency

The efficiency with which a business uses resources can be measured by using costs, since costs are the money value of resources used. The cost per unit figure is critical here because the lower the cost of producing each unit achieved by business, the more effectively it has used its resources.

Recording profits

Because sales revenue less costs gives profit, the value of costs incurred during a period is vital in calculating profits during the period.

Decision making

When a firm is considering all types of decisions, like launching a new product, buying a new piece of machinery or trying to sell overseas, it needs to assess the costs associated with each alternative to make a decision about which one to choose.

Cost classification

Within businesses costs are considered in a variety of different ways. The term used to describe a particular type of cost depends on the way costs are being used.

Resource

A labour cost, material cost, or capital cost identifies the cost in terms of the resource being used.

Department

Costs for particular sections of the organisation, such as a production, personnel or marketing cost.

Relation to the product

Direct or prime costs are those costs that can be directly attributed to the production of a product by the organisation. For example, workers who assemble computers on a production line are considered to be direct labour costs.

Indirect costs or overheads are costs that cannot be attributed to the production of a product by the organisation. An indirect labour cost is attributed to wages paid to those in personnel or administration.

Relation to output

A fixed cost is one that does not change whatever the level of output by the business. If the business produced nothing it would still incur its fixed costs. For example, no matter what a firm's level of output is, it has to pay the same rent and capital costs.

A variable cost is one that changes with output. For example, as a business increases output it uses more raw materials and their costs increase.

The distinction between fixed and variable costs can vary between organisations, for example workers who are salaried in one organisation are considered to be fixed costs, whereas in another organisation where they work flexible hours they are a variable cost.

Job costs

When specific jobs are carried out for

customers, like the servicing of a car or building work, then the job itself is costed out. This is normally done to set a price for the job done for the customer.

Unit costs

Accountants and managers frequently express costs per unit of output by calculating:

total cost/output

This is done for pricing and measuring efficiency. Any type of net cost can be calculated by dividing any specific cost by output, such as unit direct labour cost, or unit direct material cost.

ASCERTAINING COSTS

When business organisations set prices, measure efficiency or calculate profits, they have a relatively simple task if they are based in one place and sell one product. However, once organisations grow and are based in a variety of different locations, producing a number of products, establishing which costs should be attributable to which area becomes more difficult. Consider an organisation like BP who are trying to set a price for their engine oil. How do they set a cost for the organisation's administration or advertising against that single product?

Ascertaining costs means establishing all the costs associated with an area of the organisation or a cost centre.

Cost centres

A cost centre is an area within the organisation that generates identifiable expenditure. This could be a function within the organisation, like the marketing department, or a product produced by the

business, such as two stroke engine oil produced by BP.

Absorption costing

The main problem companies come up against when establishing the costs associated with an individual cost centre involves overheads or indirect costs. If a manufacturer produces four different pens it can calculate the direct costs associated with each type of pen relatively easily, because it will know what materials have been used for the pen's production, and how many direct labour hours have been used to produce it. However, it will have greater difficulty in working out how much of the total overhead generated by the entire organisation should be attributed to a single pen produced. For example, administration costs are incurred by the whole organisation, and so it is impossible to work out how much administration a single product should account for. Absorption costing is an accounting technique used to allocate overheads between cost centres. In the following example, we can consider how RCT Pens allocate or absorb overhead costs to the three products they produce which are all cost centres.

In this example, the base chosen to allocate overheads is total direct cost, although direct labour or direct material could also have been chosen. The allocation of overhead is calculated by working out the proportion of the total direct cost that is accounted for by a particular cost centre, then allocating that proportion of overhead to the centre. In the case of the Author model of pen, a third of the overhead is allocated which is £250,000. From this point it is then possible to calculate the cost per unit of each product and then, by adding the mark-up, the final selling price is arrived at. The choice of total direct cost as a basis for allocation of the overhead is pretty arbitrary, although it could be said that the cost centre that accounts for the greatest

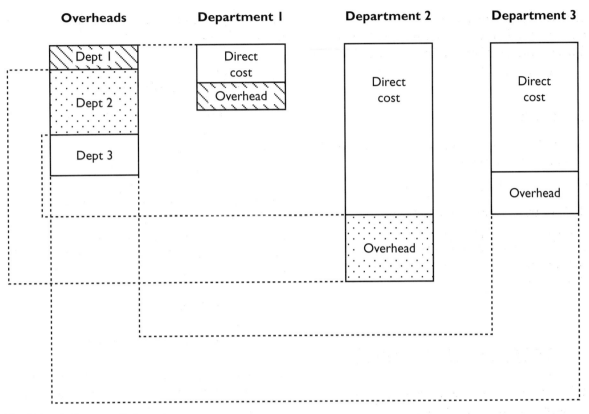

Fig 6.9   *A diagram of absorption costs*

£	Total	Executive	Professional	Author
Direct labour	670,000	120,000	300,000	250,000
Direct material	530,000	180,000	200,000	150,000
Total direct cost	1,200,000	300,000	500,000	400,000
Overhead	750,000	300/1,200 × 750	500/1,200 × 750	400/1,200 × 750
		187,500	312,500	250,000
Total cost	1,950,000	487,500	812,500	650,000
Units produced		120,000	130,000	100,000
Cost per unit		4.06	6.25	6.5
Add mark-up		50%	40%	40%
Selling price		6.09	8.75	9.1

Fig 6.10   *An example of allocating or absorbing overhead costs*

proportion of direct costs is likely to account for more overheads than the other centres, on the basis that greater use of labour probably means more management and administration time is spent on that cost centre.

More advanced absorption costing

The single basis for cost allocation can be made more precise by breaking down the overhead into its principal components. In the

Cost centre	Capital value	Number of employees	Floor space
Executive	150,000	20	100
Professional	200,000	30	120
Author	150,000	30	60
	500,000	80	280

case of RCT Pens, this is marketing, administration, and heat and light. Once this is done a more precise basis on which to allocate the overhead is chosen.

1 Maintenance costs are allocated on the value of assets in each cost centre. This is based on the assumption that the greater the value of capital equipment, the greater its maintenance expense will be.
2 Administration costs are allocated on the basis of the number of workers employed, because it is felt that the more workers employed by a cost centre, the greater the administration cost generated by the centre.
3 Energy costs are allocated on the basis of floor space occupied by a cost centre. The greater the floor area occupied by a cost centre, the greater its energy usage will be.

The table above shows the capital value, number of employees and floor space for each cost centre.

Once the overheads have been listed and the method of apportionment has been chosen, the allocation of overheads to each cost centre can be calculated. Figure 6.11 illustrates how overhead costs are allocated on the basis used above. For each overhead, the proportion allocated depends on the proportion of the basis chosen accounted for by the cost centre. In the case of maintenance, the allocation to the Executive pen cost centre

£	Total	Executive	Professional	Author
Direct labour	670,000	120,000	300,000	250,000
Direct material	530,000	180,000	200,000	150,000
Total direct cost	1,200,000	300,000	500,000	400,000
Overheads				
Maintenance	200,000	150/500 × 200 60,000	200/500 × 200 80,000	150/500 × 200 60,000
Administration	200,000	20/80 × 200 50,000	30/80 × 200 75,000	30/80 × 200 75,000
Energy	350,000	100/280 × 350 125,000	120/280 × 350 150,000	60/280 × 350 75,000
Total overhead	750,000	235,000	305,000	210,000
Total cost	1,950,000	535,000	805,000	610,000
Units produced		120,000	130,000	100,000
Cost per unit		4.45	6.19	6.1
Mark-up		50%	40%	40%
Selling price		6.68	8.67	8.54

Fig 6.11 *A more advanced method of absorption costing*

is calculated by working out the proportion of capital value present in the costs centre.

This more advanced method of absorption costing means that overheads are allocated on a more scientific basis, and this makes a difference to the total cost of each cost centre, which in turn alters the final selling price for each product. However, it is argued that trying to allocate this scientifically is perhaps something of a futile exercise, given the arbitrary nature of allocating overheads.

Marginal costing

Marginal costing or contribution costing is the process of ascertaining costs for a cost centre using only direct costs. The allocation of indirect costs to cost centres is ignored, and only those costs that can be directly attributed to the cost centre are considered. To ascertain the marginal cost associated with a cost centre involves ascertaining the following.

1 All the direct costs associated with the cost centre: labour, materials and components.
2 Variable overheads directly attributable to the cost centre. This is quite difficult to identify, but it would include any management salaries and maintenance costs that can be tracked down to the cost centre.

Marginal costs are particularly useful to managers because they show managers:

- Exactly what happens to total costs when one more unit of output is produced

- What costs a cost centre is actually responsible for

Figure 6.12 shows the marginal cost statement for RCT Pens. It shows the marginal cost of producing each pen, and the selling price which is based on a mark-up on the marginal cost. The difference between the selling price and the marginal cost is called contribution.

Application of marginal costing

Marginal costing is useful to managers in the following decision making situations.

Special orders

Businesses are frequently faced with a situation where a customer wants a special order, normally a bulk purchase, and they also want a discount. RCT Pens was faced with just such a decision when a buyer wanted to take 10,000 Executive pens at a price of £3 per unit. Based on a marginal cost of £2.50, the decision to accept a price of £3 and earn 50p contribution per unit would make an additional contribution of £5,000, which is used to cover fixed costs.

Sales price	£3
less:	
Marginal cost	£2.50
Unit contribution	£0.50
Contribution × units sold	10,000 × £0.50 = £5,000

	Total	Executive	Professional	Author
Direct labour	670,000	120,000	300,000	250,000
Direct material	530,000	180,000	200,000	150,000
Total direct cost	1,200,000	300,000	500,000	400,000
Units produced		120,000	130,000	100,000
Marginal cost		2.5	3.85	4
Selling price		6.5	8.85	8.4
Contribution		4	5	4.4

Fig 6.12 *An illustration of a marginal cost statement*

However, there are other factors the firm should consider before it decides to accept the order.

1 Is there enough capacity to produce the special order? If there is not, will taking on extra staff, or using overtime, mean paying a higher rate of pay? In RCT's case there was spare capacity, but if they had to use overtime the rate of pay for direct labour would increase by 50 percent.
2 Could the special order be sold at the normal price to another customer? If this is the case, then there is no point in accepting the order. Indeed, the special deal offered may mean that other customers will also want the price reduction.

Make or buy decisions

Companies are frequently faced with the decision to make their own components, or buy them in from an outside supplier. Marginal costing is a useful way of assessing the decision. If the marginal cost of producing the unit is greater than the price charged by an outside supplier then it may well be worth buying in the component. RCT, for example, had the option of buying nibs for their Executive pens at a cost of 30p per unit, which is less than the marginal cost of 35p that it cost to make them. However, there were other factors they needed to consider.

1 Is the quality of the component produced by the outside supplier of sufficient quality? It may be the case that the quality of the outside supplier is higher if they specialise in the component. In RCT's case the quality was not high enough.
2 Is the supplier reliable enough? If the company produces the good itself, it has greater control over the supply of the component. This may be particularly important if the good is being imported. In RCT's case, the supplier was considered to be very reliable.
3 Does using an outside supplier mean making workers redundant? The company would need to consider both the consequences for morale, and the financial costs of redundancy. This was seen by RCT's management as a major disadvantage in terms of staff morale.
4 Would the use of an outside supplier free up resources for the production of a product with a higher contribution. In RCT's case, they could produce more of their Author pen which earned them a contribution of £4.40.

In the end RCT chose to turn down the chance to buy in the component, despite the fact that it would have reduced costs, because it would have adversely affected staff morale.

Measuring performance

Because direct or variable costs can be specifically identified with a cost centre, and are to a certain extent under the control of the cost centre, the performance of the cost centre can be measured by their marginal cost. A cost centre with a relatively high marginal cost and low contribution may need to be looked at carefully by management to see whether it is viable. If marginal costs have been rising over time then this may indicate a deterioration in the cost centre's efficiency, and a situation where managers have to step in to improve it.

Key factors

Under certain situations, the sales of a product may not be constrained by sales, but by the scarcity of labour or raw materials. One of RCT's major problems is a shortage of skilled labour. By looking at the contribution per labour hour of each of its pens, RCT can decide which product to specialise in when output is constrained by the shortage of man hours. The table opposite shows that the Author pen gives the highest contribution per man hour, and if a decision has to be made to concentrate on a product, then this is where the labour resource should be channelled first.

In RCT's case the Professional product yields the highest contribution per labour hour, so

	Executive	Professional	Author
Contribution	£4	£5	£4.40
Labour hours per unit	0.04	0.03	0.06
Contribution per labour hour	£100	£166	£73

when there is a shortage of labour this is where the labour resource should be channelled.

Absorption costing versus marginal costing

The strength of marginal costing is that it does not involve the arbitrary allocation of fixed overheads to cost centres. Using even the most relevant of bases to allocate overheads, still means there are inaccuracies in the final calculation. Marginal costs are under the control of the managers in charge of the cost centre whereas they have no control over fixed costs, thus marginal costing is useful for control purposes. Marginal costs allow the organisation greater flexibility when setting prices, because they give the manager a minimum price to work from when they want to discount prices.

However, it is absolutely vital that organisations cover their fixed costs in the end, because the business will fail if they do not. If managers become obsessed by contribution rather than profit, the return the business earns in the end will leave them in a loss-making situation.

■ COSTS AND DECISION MAKING – THE BREAK-EVEN MODEL

A key area of business planning is being able to forecast at what point a profit or loss is made on a decision. The decision could be launching a new product or expanding into a new market. The point that separates profit and loss, the break-even point, is critical both in terms of whether a project is viable or not, but also in terms of managing the project to a successful outcome.

Break-even occurs when neither a profit nor loss is made on a project.

The break-even model involves looking at how costs and revenues behave at different levels of output and then forecasting what happens to profit at these different levels of output.

Costs

In the break-even model it is critical to divide costs into their fixed and variable elements. Variable costs are those that change with output, and fixed costs remain constant.

Campus Promotions' Summer Ball: Fixed and Variable Costs

Variable costs

Food – this has been quoted by a catering company at £4 per ticket sold.

Drink – this has been calculated to be £7 per ticket sold.

Fixed costs

Hire of a marquee	£3,000
Labour cost	£1,000
Live Music	£500
Printing costs	£100
Administration	£200
Power	£50
Total	**£4,850**

Campus Promotion is a small organisation that organises social events, such as balls, dinners and parties. It markets itself at the corporate hospitality market, where companies are happy to sub-contract social events. Campus have identified the fixed and variable costs associated with a summer ball they are organising for a corporate client.

Revenues

In the simple break-even model, revenue is relatively simple to calculate because price is assumed to remain the same at each level of output. Thus, by calculating the product of output and price at each level of output, a linear relationship between revenue and output is produced. Campus plan to charge £30 per ticket for the event.

Campus plans to sell a maximum of 600 tickets which would give the following cost and revenue figures.

Sales revenue	600 @ £30	£18,000
Variable costs	600 @ £11	£6,600
Contribution		£11,400
Fixed costs		£4,850
Net profit		£6,550

These figures can be developed further in the break-even model, which show what happens when fewer than 600 tickets are sold.

The break-even diagram

This is a graphical representation of the relationship between cost and revenues, and output. It is an effective pictorial representation of the financial results projected in the model. As such, it can effectively be used in reports and presentations relating to a project. The diagram is built up by graphing each monetary variable against output.

Revenue

The break-even diagram illustrates the relationship between costs and revenues and different levels of output. The sales figure is plotted first by taking sales at 600 units and drawing a line through the origin, because no ticket sales means no revenue.

Fixed costs

Fixed costs for Campus Promotions stay constant at £4,850, because they do not vary with output and even if no tickets are sold they still have to be paid.

Variable costs

Variable costs for Campus Promotions are plotted at £6,600 at 600 units sold and then through the origin, because no ticket sales mean no variable costs.

Total costs

Total costs are found by adding fixed and variable costs. For Campus Promotions, this line begins at £4,850, where zero sales just gives the fixed cost. At 600 ticket sales the total cost is £4,850 + £6,600 = £11,450.

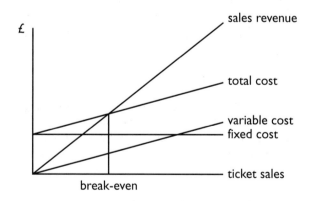

Fig 6.13   *The break-even diagram*

Calculating the break-even point

The level of ticket sales where total revenue covers total cost is the break-even point. This is shown in the break-even diagram, and with an accurate diagram the break-even point can be taken from the diagram. However, the break-even point can be calculated more accurately by using the following equation.

$$\frac{\text{fixed cost}}{\text{selling price} - \text{unit variable cost}} = \text{break-even}$$

Campus has calculated the break-even for its event as:

$$\frac{4,850}{30 - 11} = 255 \text{ tickets}$$

The break-even point is calculated by working out the unit contribution of the project (selling price − unit variable cost), which can be used to pay its fixed cost. Once the fixed costs have been covered by the unit contribution the project will break-even.

Margin of safety

The margin of safety is the difference between the target level of output and the break-even level of output. In the case example this would be:

$$600 - 255 = 345$$

The margin of safety gives the business an idea of how much room they have for sales to fall below the target level of activity before there is a danger of the project making a loss.

Changes in costs and revenues

When either costs or revenues change, the break-even level of output changes. A rise in fixed costs, for example, will, assuming price and variable costs remain the same, increase

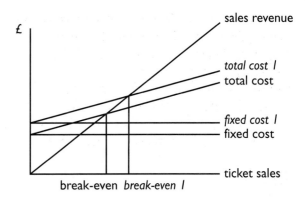

Fig 6.14   *The break-even diagram after a change in fixed costs*

the break-even point. In the case example, an increase in the cost of the marquee by £500 would raise fixed costs to £5,350.

$$\frac{5,350}{30 - 11} = 281 \text{ tickets}$$

Figure 6.14 illustrates the impact of a rise in fixed costs.

If selling price rises then contribution per unit is increased, which, assuming fixed costs remain the same, reduces the break-even point. Campus, in response to the rise in marquee costs, increased the ball price by £3 to £33.

$$\frac{5,350}{33 - 11} = 243 \text{ tickets}$$

If the variable costs change, then the slope of the total cost curve will alter because the rate at which total cost rises or falls will change as the variable costs alter. For example, if Campus revised the cost of drink upwards from £7 to £8, then the break-even point will become:

$$\frac{5,350}{33 - 12} = 255 \text{ tickets}$$

The target rate of profit

The break-even model can be further developed to allow the organisation to work out how to achieve a target rate of profit. Campus are looking to earn a profit of £2,500 on the project. This can be calculated by adding £3,500 to the fixed cost, and then working out how many tickets they would have to sell in order to cover this.

$$\frac{\text{fixed costs} + \text{target profit}}{\text{unit selling price} - \text{variable cost}} = \text{target ticket sales}$$

$$\frac{5,350 + 3,500}{33 - 12} = 412 \text{ tickets}$$

■ EVALUATION OF THE BREAK-EVEN MODEL

Strengths of the model

1 The break-even model is a simple planning tool that provides managers with a guide to the costs and returns of a project or decision.
2 It gives a graphical interpretation of a project's costs and revenues that can improve the quality of a presentation or report on the project.
3 It can be used quickly and easily to forecast the impact of a change in costs and revenues on the project.

Weaknesses of the model

The main problem with the break-even model lies in its simplicity. Most decisions do not provide the business with such simple relationships between revenue and output, and costs and output, that the model predicts.

1 In the case of price, it is possible that the business will charge different prices for the product depending on, for example, how many units are sold in a single order. Businesses often offer bulk purchase discounts in such circumstances. Campus normally offer one free ticket with every ten purchased together.
2 Variable costs do not always change at the constant rate assumed in the model. Businesses that buy in bulk can often achieve discounts. The rate of pay of labour can also change if, for example, workers are required to work weekends which means they are paid at a higher rate for that extra time.
3 Fixed costs are also not necessarily as fixed as it is assumed in the model. Maintenance of capital, which is considered a fixed cost, will often increase if the firm operates at a higher level of output. In the case example, Campus has assumed that the labour cost is fixed because it assumes that it will use all its staff whatever the level of ticket sales. However, in reality it would use the staff on other events if the ball fell short of capacity.

Whilst the changes in costs and revenues can be built into the model, the fact that the model loses its simplicity does reduce its effectiveness. Remember, break-even is often used as a planning tool which often means forecasting costs and revenues which introduces inherent inaccuracies.

NINKA LTD'S TWO COST CENTRES

Ninka Ltd manufacture computer printers. They are a young expanding company that has taken advantage of the big expansion in the IT market in the last ten years. They produce two types of printer in their Swindon factory: ink jet and laser. The two products have been set up as individual cost centres and there is quite a bit of competition between the managers of the two departments to achieve the greatest level of efficiency. The following table sets out the monthly direct costs associated with each cost centre.

The total annual overhead expense is £4.8 million. Forty percent of the overhead

	Ink jet £	Laser £
Direct labour	45,000	60,000
Direct materials	250,000	960,000
Total	295,000	1,020,000
Units produced	10,000	12,000

expense is made up of depreciation of capital used to produce the printers.

The market for computer printers is a very competitive one, and in both the home market and the business market, consumers are extremely price sensitive.

QUESTIONS

1 Explain what you understand by the following terms contained in the case study: **a** direct cost; **b** cost centre; **c** depreciation. [15]

2 **a** What other expenses are included under the heading of overheads other than depreciation? [3]
   b Calculate Ninka's monthly overhead expense. [5]
   c Calculate the monthly depreciation expense. [4]
   d Why do you think the depreciation expense accounts for such a high proportion of the overhead costs? [8]

3 Ninka Ltd uses direct material as a basis for allocating overheads.
   a Explain the principle of absorption costing. [7]
   b Calculate the overhead to be allocated to each cost centre. [6]

c Calculate the unit cost for each type of printer. [7]

4 The manager of the ink jet section claims that his department is the most efficient based on the unit costs of production. Explain why this claim may well be misleading. [10]

5 Ninka's accountant believes the depreciation expense should be allocated separately from the other overhead costs.
   a Why do you think this is the case? [6]
   b Explain on what basis you would choose to allocate the depreciation expense. [4]

6 Ninka normally works on a mark-up of 20 percent for both products.
   a Calculate the selling price of each type of printer. [5]
   b What other factors should they take into account before setting price, other than cost? [10]   Total [90]

OLYMPIC SPORTS SHOE LTD WISHES TO RAISE SALES

Olympic Sports Shoe Ltd produce three types of sports shoe with the following costs for 1998.

	Squash pro	Tennis elite	Badminton squad
Direct labour	35,000	22,000	15,000
Direct materials	52,000	46,000	25,000
Units produced	6,000	5,000	3,000

Overheads are £45,000. Olympic believe in absorption cost pricing and allocate overheads on the basis of direct labour costs. The company works on a mark-up of 32 percent on unit cost. The marketing director of the company is interested in raising the sales of the Tennis elite shoe to increase the firm's profile in this area. To do this the market research department has come up with the following figures on the demand for the tennis shoe.

Mark up	Demand
20%	6,000
25%	5,800
30%	5,600

The company are about to launch a new running shoe targeted at the serious club athlete.

QUESTIONS

1 a Explain what you understand by absorption cost pricing. [7]
  b Calculate the overhead allocation for each product. [8]
  c Calculate the price for each shoe. [10]

2 A new manager in the accounting department feels that the method of allocating overhead needs to be carried out more precisely.
  a Explain how this could be done. [7]

  b What are the problems of using this new method? [8]

3 a For the tennis shoe, work out the revenue for the four different levels of mark-up price. [9]
  b On the basis of the revenue figures, which mark-up would you choose? [6]
  c Analyse the different pricing strategies you would consider before you changed the price of the shoes. [15]

Total [70]

FINANCIAL DATA FROM THE MINI OHMS COMPANY

The Mini Ohms Company supplies electric motors to washing machine manufacturers. For production levels of between 10,000 and 30,000 units per year, variable costs are in direct proportion to revenues. Key financial data is as follows:

- Unit selling price £25
- Variable costs are 65 percent of revenue per year
- Fixed costs £150,000

QUESTIONS

1 a Explain the difference between fixed and variable costs. [4]

  b Calculate operating profit for Mini Ohms at 10,000 units. [5]

  c Calculate operating profit as a percentage of revenue at 30,000 units. [6]

2 a Draw a break-even chart for the Mini Ohms Company. [9]

  b Calculate the break-even point in units. [6]

3 A new buyer has approached Mini Ohms with an order for 6,000 units, but they have asked for a discount on the order.

  a What is the lowest price you would advise Mini Ohms to accept? [5]

  b Argue the case for and against Mini Ohms accepting the new buyer's offer. [15]

Total [50]

A NEW SPEAKER FROM MOBILE PHONE ACCESSORIES

Mobile Phone Accessories manufacture add-on gadgets to mobile telephones. For example, they produce clip stands used to hold the phones when a user is driving. The directors have decided to manufacture a speaker to be used with a mobile phone that can be used for hands-free speech when someone is driving. The product will be produced in their Birmingham factory where an extra unit has been rented on an industrial park where they already have a factory. The costs associated with the speaker are given below.

Fixed costs

Capital	£30,000
Rent	£4,000
Heat and light	£900
Marketing	£15,000
Administration	£6,000
Management salaries	£5,000

Variable costs

Direct labour per unit	£1.30
Direct materials per unit	£1.20

The company has a maximum output of 200,000 units, but their target sales is 150,000.

QUESTIONS

1 a Explain how the company would have forecasted the fixed costs of producing the product. [5]

 b How would the company have forecast the demand for the product? [5]

2 Mobile Phone Accessories work on a mark-up of 30 percent on total unit cost.

 a Calculate the unit cost of production if the firm achieves capacity. [4]

 b Draw a break-even diagram to represent the costs and revenues associated with the project. [8]

 c Calculate the break-even output. [5]

 d Calculate the margin of safety. [3]

3 The company have been approached by a Korean manufacturer claiming it can make the product at a cost of 90p per unit. However, the transport costs of 200,000 units would be £100,000. As a result of this, Mobile Phone Accessories would only have the costs of marketing, management salaries and administration to cover at home. Using numerical and non-numerical arguments, analyse the costs and benefits of using the Korean manufacturer. [20]

Total [50]

Human Resource Management

SUMMARY

1 Human resource management is involved with all of the factors that affect the personnel of a business, attempting to organise and develop the personnel in such a way that the individuals, and the groups within which they work, are at their most efficient and effective.

2 Human resources should be looked upon as an investment, not as a cost. The human resource objectives of a business should reflect the overall objectives.

3 The forecasting and planning of human resources is essential and should be based upon the present resources, the projected growth of the business and external factors which might influence human resources.

4 Personnel management deals with the management of the human resources within a business. The main functions of personnel management are recruitment, induction, appraisal and training, promotion, departure, protecting the physical and social welfare of the workforce and conducting industrial relations.

5 A motivator is something that induces a person to perform. It is a reward or incentive that drives someone towards achieving results. People are motivated towards achieving results by motivators. Motivation can be achieved through external motivators, i.e. incentives, or internal motivators, i.e. intrinsic human nature.

6 There are various motivational techniques that might be employed. They may be split into monetary and non-monetary techniques. There are many different methods of money payment. Non-monetary techniques are usually based upon some method of participation or an attempt to improve the quality of the work being undertaken.

7 Leadership is the ability of a leader to get subordinates to maximise their own potential and to work towards group objectives with zeal and confidence. Leadership can be formal or informal.

8 The most appropriate leadership approach in any situation will depend upon the leader's personal traits, the type of subordinates, the task to be completed and the business environment.

THE WORKFORCE AND WORKFORCE PLANNING

Human resource management

Human resource management is involved with all of the factors that affect the personnel of a business. It is an attempt to organise and develop the personnel in such a way that the individuals, and the groups within which they work, are at their most efficient and effective. This organisation and development may be carried out by a specific department, usually called the personnel department, or by individual departments. The modern trend is very much Japanese influenced; modern Japanese businesses seldom have personnel departments. The effective management of human resources is considered to be the responsibility of all individual managers within a business. It is felt that managers should be responsible for the individuals in their departments and should understand the importance of human resource management to the running of the department and the achievement of personal, departmental and company based objectives.

The current trend reflects the significant change in attitudes that has taken place in recent years. In the past, human resources were seen to be a cost to the business. They were looked at solely in terms of wages and any other relevant costs, such as recruitment and/or training. This approach reflected the rather combative 'them and us' attitude that was prevalent in management and workforce relationships 20 or more years ago. These days, human resources are often looked upon as an investment. Some theorists, such as Likert, have even suggested that businesses should include the value of employees as a tangible resource in the accounts. Whilst this would be difficult to evaluate, we should not lose sight of the fact that a business is often only as good as the quality of the individuals who make up the human resource base. We shall look at the management of the human resources of a business in more detail when we consider the activity of personnel management.

It is worth stating the idea that, in an ideal world, the human resource objectives of a business should reflect the overall business objectives. Let us assume that the overall objectives of a certain business are to produce a quality product at an acceptable profit. If this is the case, then the human resource objectives would be to have a workforce that is capable of producing and selling a product of the required quality, at a cost that will provide a profit. The staff members of the workforce should be capable of supporting the line members in this aim. If the human resource objectives are not met, then it is unlikely that the business will be able to achieve the overall objectives.

Workforce planning

As well as the management of human resources, it is also important that there is effective planning for the future needs of the business in terms of its personnel. There are a number of factors that need to be considered.

1 **The present situation**   In order to plan for the future, it is essential that there are detailed records of the present personnel. These records should try to do more than simply record the basic personal details of existing employees. They should attempt to include some assessment of factors such as education, experience, wider interests and, most importantly, potential. In this way, it is possible to plan how much of future human resource needs can be met internally and how much needs to be gained from outside.

2 **The projected growth of the business**   This is a means of attempting to assess the future human resource demand. In most firms, changes in forecast sales will

indicate the likely necessary changes in human resource demand. If sales trends can be accurately forecast, then the business can begin to adjust the workforce accordingly, rather than attempting to change the workforce after the sales changes have taken place. (This is where forecasting techniques such as those considered in Unit 4 can be especially useful.) This is essential in situations where the human resource supply is not abundant. For example, a business involved in the supply of Voice Mailbox computer software will not find it quick or easy to discover suitably qualified workers. Thus, effective forecasting would enable the process of recruitment to begin early and would give more time to fill the difficult posts.

3 **External factors**   When workforce planning, factors which are external to the business, but nevertheless influential, must be considered. This can be done by the use of basic PEST analysis, i.e. the consideration of **p**olitical, **e**conomic, **s**ocial and **t**echnological factors. Political factors, especially those relating to the law and employment legislation, may affect future needs. For example, complying with EU legislation by limiting maximum working hours might lead to a requirement for a larger workforce. Changing economic factors, such as an expected boom period, might lead to changes in consumer expenditure patterns, sales, and thus human resource requirements. Social changes, in such areas as population trends, education or social mores, can have the same sorts of effects as changing economic factors. Technological changes can be very influential. Changes in materials, production techniques, mechanisation levels, computerisation and information technology can radically affect the human resource requirements of a business.

Personnel management

Personnel management quite simply means the management of the human resources within a business. The personnel function may be carried out by an individual within a small organisation or by individual managers, or a specialised department within larger organisations. Whichever the case, the functions involved will not be very much different; it is simply the scale which alters.

It is easier to perceive the functions of personnel if one considers the usual route taken by an individual as the person goes through a career in a business.

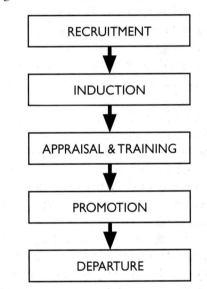

Fig 7.1   *The usual career route in business*

Personnel management involves all of the above functions relating to a normal career. In addition, there are two other, over-arching, functions which usually apply. These are protecting the physical and social welfare of the workforce and conducting industrial relations. Each of these personnel functions is of great importance if human resources are to be managed efficiently.

Recruitment

Recruitment usually takes place for one of two

reasons; either to replace a worker who has left the business, or to employ a worker as an addition to the existing workforce. No matter what the reason for the appointment or the size the business is, recruitment should follow a number of logical, simple, steps if it is to be carried out efficiently.

Discussion and assessment

Discussion with appropriate individuals and an assessment of the job involved is very important. In a small business, the owner, or manager, will be aware of the human resource requirements and will thus make the decision as to whether or not it is necessary to employ an extra worker.

However, in larger organisations, it is not quite so simple. If there is a personnel department, then there is a need for much liaison between the manager of the department requiring extra workers and the personnel department. Even if there is no personnel department, the manager of the relevant department will still have to liaise with senior staff before initiating the employment of a worker.

In many businesses, job analysis is used so that the requirements of the job are discovered and a job specification can be drawn up. Job analysis is a study of the tasks that make up a job. The tasks are normally grouped under the headings of physical requirements, mental requirements, skill requirements, areas of responsibility, physical working environment and job hazards. Once this has been done, then a job specification can be drawn up. This is a list of all the qualifications that a person will need if they are going to do the job. It will include things such as age, sex, educational level and relevant experience. The job specification might also include things that would prevent a person from being employed to do a job, such as colour blindness or height restrictions. It must be said that great care has to be taken to ensure that job specifications do not

contravene the law on equal opportunities. If a job analysis has been carried out, it can also be used to determine pay levels to be offered for the job. This is done by comparing the job in question with other, similar, ones. The process is known as job evaluation and the starting point is often a comparison of job analyses. After this, jobs are usually ranked in some way and this ranking is used to formulate a sensible pay structure and to determine appropriate wage and salary differentials. There are weaknesses to this method, since it is the job that is being evaluated and not the person doing it and, also, the whole process is very subjective. In addition, it is an expensive process and so it is only viable in large businesses.

Advertising the job

When a job becomes available, or is created, then one of the first decisions to be made is whether the job should be filled internally, by an existing worker, or whether a person from outside the business should be appointed. In some cases, the firm might consider both. In either case, it will be necessary to bring the existence of the job to the attention of those who might be interested. For an internal appointment, this is usually fairly simple and can be achieved by a number of methods, ranging from word-of-mouth in small firms to the use of notice boards and in-house magazines in larger firms. For external appointments, a suitable recruiting channel must be chosen. Most often, this tends to be advertising in the press, local or national, and in suitable professional or trade magazines. However, there are many other channels that might be employed, such as job centres, employment agencies, public notice boards, direct contact with education and training establishments or personal contacts of existing employees.

Selecting appropriate candidates

Once an effective recruiting channel has been employed and the business has received a realistic number of applications, then the candidates need to be assessed and a shortlist of candidates suitable for interview needs to be drawn up. If a job analysis and specification process has been carried out, then this can be done by comparing the applications with the job specification. If not, then it is up to the individuals involved in the selection to use their judgement to choose suitable interviewees. The depth, length and number of interviews will, to a large extent, depend upon the importance of the job concerned. For menial, basic jobs, the interview may be little more than a brief chat. For high-flying posts, there might be a series of interviews spread over quite a long period of time. These might include various psychometric and sociological tests, as well as more traditional interviews. Interviews allow two-way communication to take place and the candidates can use them to discover whether the business is one in which they would like to work. This is just as important as the interviewer getting the right candidate. If this does not take place, then the successful candidate might find that they are working in a business that does not suit them. In these cases, labour turnover tends to be fairly rapid. Once the interviewing and selection has been carried out, it is then necessary to ensure that the successful applicant is offered the post and, on acceptance, that the correct legal procedures are followed. References should be checked and then contracts of employment should be drawn up and signed. The lack of a suitable contract of employment, including a written statement of the conditions of service and terms of employment, can cause great problems if there is a subsequent disagreement with the employee.

Induction

Induction is the process of introducing a new employee to a business and ensuring that the employee understands the objectives,

workings and rules of the organisation. The induction process should also ensure that the employee is aware of their own responsibilities and position in the business. The employee should be made aware of the physical environment in which he or she will be working and should be introduced to the goods and services which the business provides.

The length of the induction process can be very variable. In some cases, a worker can be introduced to all of the above in a matter of minutes. In other cases, induction can be a long training process taking months. The length of the process tends to be determined by the experience of the employee, the difficulty and importance of the post and the size of the organisation.

If a job is very simple and the worker has previous experience, then induction may be very quick. It might be little more than a brief chat with a superior or a fellow worker. An example of this might be a shop assistant, with previous experience, starting work in a small newsagents. At the other end of the scale, induction might include a tour of the business, videos and presentations, and specialist training courses. For example, large photocopier manufacturers often employ engineers to carry out repairs to machines that they rent out to clients. When employed, these engineers are usually given training courses that last as much as three months in order to become acquainted with the company machines. Without these induction courses, the engineers would not be able to function within the firm.

Appraisal and training

An increasingly important part of the personnel function is the administration of an appraisal system. In times gone by, appraisal tended to be a fairly informal process, which only took place when an employee was being considered for promotion or for the sack. In recent times, however, the importance of staff development in terms of improving skills, efficiency and motivation, has been realised and it is now much more common to come across formal appraisal systems. Appraisal is seen as an important facilitator. It can identify employees who are promising and those who need help or special attention. It enables superiors and subordinates to communicate and to understand each other's views and problems. It shows areas of strength and weakness and points out any training that might be necessary. There are many types of appraisal system, but most would include the same basic elements. The appraisal needs to be on an agreed, regular basis. This might be as often as four times a year or as little as once. The process normally begins with the person being appraised writing some form of self-appraisal or filling in a standard pro-forma. This, together with any previous appraisal letter, is then usually used as the basis for an interview with the superior designated to conduct the appraisal. The interview normally attempts to analyse how well the worker has achieved the targets set in the last appraisal and what aims and ambitions the worker has for the future. It is at this stage that any training necessary to achieve objectives can be identified and discussed. As a follow up to the interview, an appraisal letter is usually produced by the interviewer and, if agreed, signed by both parties. If there is disagreement, then another interview might be held or the person being appraised might be able to ask for appraisal by an alternative person. Some sort of built-in appeal system is to be recommended, since it is not unusual for a person not to get on with the superior chosen to be the appraiser.

This form of appraisal is, in many ways, a type of 'management by objectives'. Management by objectives is a management control system where every employee has objectives set for the coming time period and is expected to attempt to achieve those targets

if at all possible. This system works reasonably well in businesses and occupations where targets can be easily set and outcomes simply measured. Thus, it tends to work for production workers and salespeople but is much harder to apply to those who are involved in staff occupations and the provision of services.

As we have already said, appraisal can often identify areas where training is necessary. Training is the process of helping workers to develop the skills and knowledge necessary to perform their required tasks as efficiently as possible. In all cases, the business management will need to weigh the cost of training against the perceived and expected benefits to be gained, in order to decide if training is worthwhile.

There are four basic reasons for training to take place. The first is the introduction of workers to the business, and we have already dealt with this under induction. The second reason is to enable employees to carry out their present tasks more efficiently. This is obviously of great benefit to a business, since it will improve the efficiency of the workers. The third reason for training is to cope with changes in jobs. Change is always taking place, and whenever there are changes in the structure of a business, in working procedures, in production methods or technology, training may well be necessary so that employees are capable of dealing with the new situation. The fourth, and possibly most important reason for training is to prepare people for future promotion. It is very much in the interest of a business to improve the skills and abilities of its employees, so that they will be able to move up within the organisation, accepting more complex and difficult posts and dealing with them efficiently. However, it must be remembered that training is expensive and there is always the danger that a business will pay for the training of an employee who will then leave and that another organisation may benefit from the training without having to pay for it. There are two main methods of training:

1 **On-the-job training**   This is the most simple form of training and takes place within the business itself. The employee is given training by someone who already has the necessary, required skills. This is attractive because it is a relatively cheap form of training. However, it is only as effective as the quality of the people who do the training, and it may be the case that the trainers are not highly skilled or motivated and that the training is therefore inadequate.

2 **Off-the-job training**   This usually takes place in specialist educational units outside the business but, in some cases, businesses may have their own internal training units where employees are sent to learn required skills away from the actual workplace. The advantages of this method are that the training is carried out by specialist, qualified trainers and that the trainees are allowed to work at their own speed, usually speeding up as they become more skilled. This is important because, with on-the-job training, trainees are often expected to work at the same speed as everyone else from the beginning, which can cause problems of confidence, morale, motivation and quality. The obvious disadvantage is that this sort of training is very expensive, especially if the business has its own training centre. It also means that once the trainees have been trained, they still have to go through the process of becoming acclimatised to their actual workplace.

A compromise form of training is pyramid, or trickle-down, training, which is now quite often employed in larger organisations. This is where an employee is trained outside the firm and then comes back into the business and trains someone else. These two then train two others and so on, until all those people needing the specific skills have been trained.

In this way, the costs are not as high as sending all employees out to be trained and yet the original employee will have been trained by an expert. The weakness still exists, however, that the internal training will only be as good as those who pass on the knowledge and also that the communication may become distorted as the knowledge is passed down through a number of levels.

The departure of employees

Employees may leave a business for a number of different reasons but, whatever the cause may be, it is essential that the departure takes place with the minimum of disturbance to the running of the organisation. Whoever is responsible for the personnel function must ensure that the post that is being relinquished is filled or, if this is not necessary, that the workforce is reorganised to cover the departure.

There are four usual reasons for the departure of an employee.

Resignation

This is where an employee leaves a business voluntarily, usually to go on to another job elsewhere. In this case, it is simply necessary to ensure that all legal requirements are carried out in relation to the resignation and that all relevant payments are made.

Retirement

This is similar to resignation, but it occurs where an employee leaves the business in order to end work altogether, because the employee has reached a certain age. The most common retirement age in the UK is 60, although many people still carry on until 65, or even longer in some occupations.

Redundancy

This takes place where an employee, or a group of employees, are dismissed as a result of a readjustment of the workforce requirements of the business. This may come about as a result of the closure of a business or a part of the business. It may also be caused by the reorganisation of responsibilities, so that a certain post or posts become unnecessary. If a large number of redundancies is necessary, the management will normally ask for people to volunteer for redundancy, offering financial incentives. If this is not successful, then decisions will have to be made about which employees should go. Often, this is done on a last-in first-out basis, but this does mean that a number of good employees might be lost and so management prefer to have the choice if possible. Because the employees are losing their jobs through no fault of their own, there are legal payments to which they are entitled, based upon the age of the employee and the number of years of service with the business. These are minimum amounts and it may well be that the management and trade unions involved will work out a scheme that pays more than the minimum. If a firm makes an employee redundant, it is illegal then to readvertise the job. Redundancy necessarily implies that the post no longer exists.

Dismissal

This is where an employee is dismissed from a business because the employee is not competent to carry out the required duties or has breached the rules of the organisation, either an unacceptable number of times or in a very serious way. The law relating to dismissal is very complex and may also be very costly for a business if dismissal is found to be unfair. Because of this, it is essential that a business should have a laid down dismissal procedure which is clear, consistent and, above all, legal. The procedure should detail the situations in which the employer would terminate employment for incompetence or misconduct. It should make clear what will lead to dismissal, who has the authority to make the decision, and what right of appeal the person being dismissed will have.

The physical and social welfare of the workforce

An important and original function of personnel management is to look after the physical and social welfare of the workforce. The physical welfare of the workforce is protected by law. Employees have the legal right to be protected from harm when they are at their place of employment. The main piece of legislation relating to this is the Health and Safety at Work Act (1974), which was mostly based upon the findings and recommendations of the Robens Report. The Act sets up a legal system which attempts to protect workers' health, safety and welfare. It imposes certain duties upon employers, but it also imposes certain duties upon employees as well. In this way, it is hoped that employers and employees, acting together, will minimise the risk of danger in the workplace. The Act attempts to ensure that workers are protected in three main areas. First, that they are protected from accidents that may occur. Second, that they are not asked to take part in production processes that might be injurious to their health and third, that they should be protected from fire.

The social welfare of the workforce is not really covered by the law, but it does make sense for management to attempt to ensure that the workforce is socially happy, since a happy workforce displays high morale and all of the benefits that go with it, such as reduced absenteeism and conflict. There are two main areas where management are involved in the social welfare of workers. First, workers often have personal problems and they look to management for advice and help. This counselling function may be formalised or on an *ad hoc* basis. Formal counselling services tend to be found in larger firms, with big workforces. Whatever the method, workers feel happier if they know that there is someone who is prepared to offer advice and help when they have problems. The problems encountered may be monetary, legal or social, but if they affect the performance of a worker, it is in the interest of the business to solve them. The second area relating to social welfare is the provision of social amenities and opportunities for the workforce. This will vary enormously from business to business. A small organisation might have a few social events during the year and little else. Larger organisations might offer social clubs and sports facilities for the workforce and their families. Whatever the scope, the aim is to make the workforce happier with their employment and also to generate a sense of belonging and involvement with the business. Many Japanese firms have realised the importance of the provision of social welfare and have attempted to use it to generate loyalty to the company. In some cases, they have used the firm to replace the traditional family. Thus, as the role of the family as a support and satisfier has been reduced in modern times, the company has taken over. Workers now identify with the company as their 'family' group.

Industrial relations

In some large firms, a department exists specifically to deal with industrial relations. However, in most organisations, it is part of the personnel function. Industrial relations covers all aspects of the relationships between employers and employees, although it is often thought of in a much narrower sense as dealing with the relationships between employers and trade unions.

Industrial relations is the study of job regulation in all areas where paid employment takes place. This could be large industrial concerns, but it could also be much smaller businesses, such as supermarkets or schools. Industrial relations covers a number of possible areas of conflict and problem relating to relationships between employees and their employers, relationships between different employees, relationships between different groups of employees, relationships between trade unions and employees, and relationships between groups of trade unions and groups of employees, e.g. the Trades Union Congress and employers' associations or the Confederation of British Industry.

MOTIVATION OF THE WORKFORCE

There are many different opinions about what motivation actually is. Some theorists feel that it is anything that leads to people achieving more than they would otherwise do. Others feel that motivation is the process of satisfying the needs of a person, so that the person is motivated to carry out his or her duties as well as can be done. If the second opinion is taken, then it follows that if one can identify an individual's needs, then it should be possible to motivate that person. However, individual needs are both complex and changeable and so motivation is not as simple as it would first appear. For many years, management theorists have considered the concept of motivation and there has been much disagreement on the matter.

A motivator is a thing or action that induces an individual to perform. Motivators are the rewards or incentives that drive people towards achieving results. Thus, people are motivated towards achieving results by motivators. When results have been achieved, then satisfaction is experienced. Much of the discussion regarding motivation is based around the question of what things actually work as motivators.

A motivated workforce is more likely to achieve the objectives of a business, as people strive to attain whatever motivators they are being offered. Thus, effective motivation is of great importance in any organisation and should not be overlooked.

Theories of motivation

Satisfaction

Early theories of motivation were based upon the concept of satisfaction. The theory worked on the idea that a satisfied worker was a productive worker. However, over time it was realised that satisfaction is not really a motivator. The fact that workers are satisfied does not seem to mean that workers will then work harder; it tends instead to lead to the workers continuing at the same level of intensity. However, there are advantages to be gained from having a satisfied workforce, such as loyalty to the business, low staff turnover, high morale and low absenteeism, so the importance of satisfaction should not be overlooked.

Incentives as motivators

Later theories were based upon the idea of incentives as motivators. This was known as the 'carrot' approach.

The belief is that workers will try harder in order to obtain an offered reward. There is no doubt that rewards can work as effective motivators, but they tend to do so only in the short run. Also, to be effective motivators, certain conditions must apply. First, the individual must think that the reward being offered is worthwhile and desirable. If the reward is considered to be of too little value or not worth having, then it will not be an effective motivator. Second, performance must be capable of being clearly measured, so that the performance of the individuals can be judged and rewarded. If it is difficult to discern individual performance, then individuals will not be motivated to perform well because they will know that it will not be obvious that they are doing so. Lastly, the desired new level of performance must not be used as a new minimum standard, if it is reached. If the standards are continually

raised, it will soon act as a disincentive to the workforce.

The main theorist in this area was probably F.W. Taylor (1856–1915), who put forward the idea of scientific management. It is important to realise that Taylor, although he was an American, was a Victorian and that he seemed to hold the usual Victorian attitudes towards the working classes. Taylor felt that workers were basically rather lazy and unmotivated and that they would be motivated primarily by money. He encouraged managers to develop techniques for the study of work and the determination of the most efficient way of performing tasks and then to use the standards discovered as the basis for incentive systems, where workers would be rewarded for exceeding the standards and penalised for falling below them. In reality, Taylor's ideas were far from 'scientific', but they did hold sway for a long time and concepts such as work study and production engineering are still in use today.

Human needs – intrinsic motivators

The leading theories of motivation, however, are now mostly based upon the idea of intrinsic motivators. The theories work on the basis that people can gain satisfaction simply by performing well. Thus, good performance and achievement act as motivators, since they give satisfaction. One of the first writers in this area was Abraham Maslow (1908–1970). Maslow believed that human needs could be presented in the form of a hierarchy, beginning with basic needs and going up to more complicated ones. He felt that as each set of needs was satisfied, they would cease to act as motivators and so it would be necessary to offer the chance to satisfy higher needs in order to continue to motivate workers. The needs are shown in Fig 7.2.

Physiological needs
Physiological needs are the basic

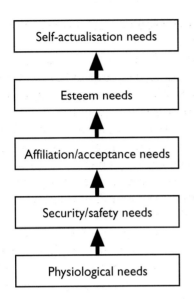

Fig 7.2 *Maslow's hierarchy of needs*

requirements for sustaining life, such as food, water, shelter and clothing. Maslow was of the opinion that the fulfilment of these needs was absolutely essential and that nothing would act as a motivator until these basic needs were satisfied. It is normally recognised that physiological needs are satisfied by means of money and so, in this case, it can be argued that money acts as a motivator.

Security needs

Security, or safety, needs are the needs to be safe from physical danger and secure in one's employment and ownership of property. Firms can attempt to fulfil these needs by convincing workers that their jobs are secure. This might be the basis for the 'jobs for life' approach of many Japanese firms in the 1980s. However, whatever the motivation for the approach, it should be remembered that many of the firms who adopted this approach are now finding it hard to keep to their promise in the different economic climate of the 1990s.

Affiliation needs

Affiliation or acceptance needs are the needs of individuals to belong to groups and to be socially accepted by others. Businesses might attempt to create an atmosphere where these needs can be satisfied by setting up social events and ensuring that there is a caring atmosphere in the work environment.

Esteem needs

Esteem needs are a natural progression from acceptance needs. Maslow felt that once people felt accepted, the next obvious need was to be valued, i.e. held in esteem. If this can be achieved, then the individual will grow in confidence and be a more effective worker.

Self-actualisation needs

Self-actualisation needs are the highest level of needs in Maslow's hierarchy. They are the internally generated needs to maximise one's own potential. They are the ultimate intrinsic need. Intrinsic theorists, such as Likert and McGregor, believe that higher order needs have grown in importance in the modern worker and are now much stronger than they were. If this is true and satisfaction from the job itself is an important factor in motivation, then it is essential that businesses do all that they can in order to make jobs more interesting. It is also important that workers have genuine participation in decision making. (We shall deal with the concept of participation later in the unit.) Although intrinsic theories are quite persuasive, they will only really be successful where the job is truly capable of being interesting and challenging. They work best where intelligent and independent-minded people are employed in challenging occupations. They will not apply well where technology stops the individual from having true control over the job, such as in mass, flow production. They will also not apply well with individuals who do not want involvement in decision making and who like to be led by an authoritarian manager. Many workers fall into this category.

Other management theories

Before leaving the topic of motivation, we should consider the ideas of a few more management theorists. Elton Mayo (1880–1949) was the founder of the human relations movement and of industrial sociology. He carried out research on work groups in Chicago between 1927 and 1932 at the Hawthorne Works of the Western Electric Company. In the main project, he concentrated upon one group of women workers and altered their working conditions in order to assess the effect of this upon output. He implemented changes such as new payment systems, different rest breaks, different lengths to the working day and offering food and refreshments. In each case, when the changes were made, the output of the group of six rose. At first, Mayo thought that this was a direct response to the motivators being offered. However, when the initial experiment was over, the six women were returned to their original conditions of work, which were far from ideal To the surprise of all, production in the group continued to rise. It soon became apparent that the major cause of the production rises had been based upon group dynamics rather than the motivators being offered. The women had felt important because they had been singled out and they had developed good group relations, where each of them wanted to work hard for the others. They had also been given a say in developing their own working patterns and dividing up the tasks in the way that seemed to be best for them. So, Mayo highlighted the importance of the group in which a person works and showed that informal social relations are of great significance. One could argue that he showed the importance of the fulfilment of acceptance and esteem needs.

There are two other writers on management theory and motivation that should be considered: Douglas McGregor and Frederick Herzberg. Douglas McGregor (1906–1964) was another advocate of the human resources approach and another American. He did, however, realise that people were different and that, whilst some were capable of intrinsic motivation, others were not. He put forward a view of a worker type that he called 'Theory X'. The view owed much to the ideas and opinions of F.W. Taylor. The Theory X type has an inherent dislike of work and will avoid it if possible. Because of this dislike, Theory X types need to be coerced, controlled, directed, and threatened with punishment if they are to make an adequate effort to achieve the objectives of the business. Indeed, the Theory X type actually prefers to be directed, wishes to avoid responsibility, has little ambition, and desires security above all else. As an alternative to the Theory X type, McGregor proposed an alternative type known as 'Theory Y'. For the Theory Y type, the expenditure of effort in work, both mental and physical, is as natural as play or rest. Theory Y types will exercise self-direction and self-control if they are committed to achieving objectives, and the level of commitment will be in direct proportion to the size of the rewards associated with the achievement of the objectives. Thus external control and punishment are not an effective means of producing effort. Theory Y types learn, under proper conditions, not only to accept but also to seek authority. In modern industrial life, the intellectual potentialities of most people are only partially utilised and many more people are capable of contributing creatively to organisational problems and objectives than currently do so. Theories X and Y are a set of assumptions, stressing the fact that, in order to be effective motivators, managers must recognise the differences between people in the workforce and their varying capabilities. Effective motivational techniques must take into account the working situation and the types of people concerned.

Frederick Herzberg (b. 1923) was yet another follower of the human resources approach. He took Maslow's hierarchy of needs and very much modified the concepts. He proposed a two-factor theory of motivation. He called the first group of factors that he considered maintenance, or hygiene, factors. He said that these factors were not motivators but, if they were removed or absent, they acted as dissatisfiers. These hygiene factors are things such as working conditions, salary, job security and a stable personal life. The existence of these does not make the workforce strive harder, but their absence can lead to demotivation. It is almost a return to the early satisfaction theories of motivation. In many ways, these maintenance factors fulfil Maslow's three lower order needs and this is shown in Fig 7.3.

Maslow's hierarchy	Herzberg's two-factor approach
	Motivators
Self-actualisation needs	Interesting work
	Achievement
Esteem needs	Recognition
	Promotion
	Growth in the job
	Maintenance factors
Affiliation/acceptance needs	Working conditions
	Salary
Security/safety needs	Job security
	Company policy
Physiological needs	Status
	Personal life

Fig 7.3 *Maslow's hierarchy compared to Herzberg's two-factor approach*

The second group of factors identified by Herzberg were known as motivators or satisfiers. These were the factors which would act as motivators, lead to satisfaction, and fulfil higher order needs. They are related to job content and include such factors as achievement, recognition, promotion and growth in the job. Herzberg felt that it stressed the importance of job content to intrinsic motivation and that the ideal work situation would be where the job had challenging content in order to motivate and that there existed 'hygiene' factors, in both quantity and quality, to ensure that dissatisfaction was avoided.

Motivational techniques

Having looked at where the basis for motivation derives, it is now fitting to consider some of the main techniques and rewards used to act as motivators.

Money as a motivator

Money has a double effect as a motivator. It can be used to satisfy basic needs and it is also an indicator of success, status and power. The scientific management followers would say that money was the most important motivator available. However, those who follow the human resources approach, and believe in the importance of intrinsic motivation, would see money as being no more important than any other motivator. Indeed, some would see it as being relatively unimportant. There is no doubt that money can be used to satisfy Maslow's lower order needs but, in reality, much will depend upon the individual concerned. Some people do not see money as being important, above a certain level of income, and so it will not greatly motivate them. Money tends to motivate those who are on their way up and who are ambitious and the amount offered must be substantial by comparison with the normal payment, otherwise it will not be seen as a positive motivator. If the amount is relatively small, then it will simply act as one of Herzberg's hygiene factors, i.e. it will be a reinforcement, rather than a motivator. Indeed, this is often the case with money payments. Research has shown that rewards, given on a regular basis, become expected and simply act as reinforcements; they are seen as a condition of work rather than an impetus to work harder.

There are a number of different methods of monetary payment that might be considered. A salary is an annual, agreed amount that is normally paid to an employee in equal amounts each month. Salary levels may be reviewed each year or sometimes more often. As we have already stated, salary levels tend to be a hygiene factor and not a motivator. A salary increase would have to be very large, and also be capable of being withdrawn, if it were to act as a motivator. Wages can usually be split into two types: time-based wages and performance (or output)-based wages. Wages are generally paid weekly and, in the past, were almost always paid in cash. These days, there is a growing trend towards payment directly into a bank but, even so, the majority of workers are still paid in cash. Time-based wages are where a worker is paid by the hour at a certain rate. Thus, the more hours that the worker puts in, the greater will be the wage. This tends to encourage workers to attempt to spend more time at work. In times gone by, the average working week was 40 hours and anything worked above this figure would be paid at a higher than usual, overtime rate. It is in the interests of the worker, if motivated by money, to attempt to get as much overtime work as possible. Thus it might be argued that time-based wages are a disincentive to hard work. The European Union is attempting to set maximum numbers of working hours and minimum wage rates for all workers and this has caused much debate in member countries. Output-based wages are sometimes known as payment by results. This is where workers are paid for the amount that they produce and so the more they produce, the more wages they will receive. It is also known as piece-work, because workers are paid for each completed piece of work. This method of payment should encourage more effort, but there are a number of serious

drawbacks. In their haste to produce, workers may foresake quality requirements and also forget safety rules. Thus there might be high levels of rejects and also accidents. In addition, this method of payment will only work when workers are producing articles that can be easily measured and attributed to specific workers. The trend in recent years has been away from payment by results towards time-based wages. This trend has been strongly influenced by the views of the larger trade unions. A combination of the two methods is the payment of a basic wage or salary with some sort of performance bonus or commission. Some workers are paid a normal time-based wage and are then paid a bonus based upon output. This is seen as a form of compromise payment. Other employees might work on a basic wage and commission system. This especially applies to salespeople. In these cases, the salespeople receive a salary, usually fairly small, and will then receive a percentage payment based upon their total value of sales for the period concerned. This again is seen to be a motivating method, although much will depend upon the type of individual concerned. Many employees do not like this method because it means that their earnings can vary a great deal from time period to time period and so it is difficult to plan financially.

Non-monetary motivation

There are a large number of different methods of non-monetary motivation, most of them involving either some form of participation in decision making or some means of improving the quality of work in order to lead to intrinsic motivation. Many management theorists now believe that participation in decision making and planning can be a strong motivator. As an additional advantage, it can also lead to an increased likelihood of problem areas being spotted and solutions being devised to deal with them.

The acceptance and recognition that the participators gain helps to fulfil higher level needs, although weaker managers sometimes feel that too much participation might weaken their own positions. Obviously, this does not have to be the case. Confident managers will encourage participation and, having heard all views, will then make decisions from a better informed position. We have already looked at forms of employee (worker) participation, such as worker-directors, joint consultation, works councils, quality circles and kaizen groups, in Unit 3. As we have said, improving the quality of work is another method of non-monetary motivation and there are a number of ways of attempting to do this. Job enrichment is where an attempt is made to enrich a job in terms of giving it a higher degree of challenge and responsibility. It is also called job restructuring. It has been used with success to improve productivity and morale, and to reduce absenteeism and staff turnover, in large firms such as Texas Instruments and Procter and Gamble. Jobs can be enriched in a number of ways. The variety and complexity of tasks might be increased and the role of workers in deciding work methods, work rates and the state of the work environment might also be amplified. In addition, workers may be given more responsibility, such as the right to stop the production line, and increased levels of feedback on performance, in order to make them aware of their progress. As with all things, there are drawbacks to the process of job enrichment. Some jobs, requiring low skills and high levels of repetition, do not really lend themselves to enrichment. This especially applies to tasks on automated flow production lines. There have been attempts to get around this by moving workers between jobs on the line. However, moving from one boring job to another is not really very enriching. Also, many workers do not want job enrichment and extra responsibility and would rather have job security and higher pay.

Another method of non-monetary motivation is job enlargement. This is where the scope of a job is enlarged by adding similar tasks, but not increasing the degree of responsibility. Although there have been some successes with job enlargement, the argument put forward above applies here as well. Adding one boring job to another is little different from moving workers between boring jobs. It is unlikely that the process will act as a motivator. A final approach that might be considered is that of the quality of working life concept (QWL approach). This is a more modern approach that began in the 1970s in a number of large American firms, such as General Motors and the Aluminium Company of America. The QWL approach follows a number of steps. First, a committee is set up containing representatives of management and the workforce, and including a QWL specialist. The committee try to discover methods of improving the dignity, attractiveness and productivity of jobs, concentrating on the job enrichment concept. The recommendations of the committee are then considered and, where possible, implemented. The participation of workers is of paramount importance because they not only feel involved in decision making, but they are also able to make suggestions to enrich jobs, knowing that they are in the best position to understand what will achieve this. In other schemes involved in job enrichment, it tends to be a case of the management deciding what is best for the workers. QWL recommendations can be very widespread, concerning not just the redesigning of jobs. They may well apply to the working environment, changes in organisational structure, leadership styles, quality control and many other areas.

■ LEADERSHIP

There are many different definitions of leadership. They mostly relate to the perceived functions of a leader. A leader has responsibilities to the individuals and group which he or she is in charge of and also to the task or objectives that must be achieved. Thus, leadership might be defined as the ability of a leader to get subordinates to maximise their own potential and to work towards group objectives with zeal and confidence.

Formal and informal leadership

Leadership can be formal or informal. Formal leadership exists where the leader has been delegated authority and is capable of exerting great influence. For example, a person might be appointed to run the production section of a business as the production manager. The person might be given complete control over the section and a place on the management board of the business. Thus, the person would have both authority and influence.

Informal leadership exists where a person can initiate action, but does not possess the same authority. An example of this might be the case of a trade union shop steward in the same production section as above. The shop steward may have influence and the ability to initiate action, such as a withdrawal of labour, without having been given delegated authority in the business. In some situations, informal leaders may have more actual power than formal leaders and this can cause serious difficulties and disruptions.

It is essential for formal leaders to be aware of the existence and strength of informal leaders within their designated areas, and to be able to handle them so that they are a positive influence upon the group and are attempting to achieve the same objectives. Often, it is necessary to negotiate group objectives in order to accommodate the desires of the formal and informal leaders.

Trait theories of leadership

Early theories of leadership suggested that natural leaders were born, not made. The idea is that natural and effective leaders are born with certain characteristics and that without these characteristics, it is not possible to be a good leader. People with these characteristics, or traits as they were known, should be sought out and then put into positions of authority and power.

It is worth considering the main, desired, traits. It was felt that leaders needed above average intellect. However, it was also felt that they should not be too bright, since geniuses tend to be rather eccentric and, in many cases, poor communicators. Leaders should display initiative and inventiveness and also have the ability to be independent. Confidence and decisiveness were thought to be necessary traits, as was the ability to be calm in a crisis. Physical traits were also considered to be important. Leaders should be healthy, physically striking and full of energy. Lastly, it was felt that most leaders would be from the higher socio-economic strata of society.

Whilst there is no doubt that possession of these traits might make good leadership material, trait theories have not really explained what leads to an individual being a good and effective leader. In too many cases, successful leaders have possessed very few of the recommended traits and, in others, people with most of the desired traits have failed as leaders. The general feeling is that this is too simplistic a theory and that the traits are too vaguely defined.

Styles of formal leadership

Later theories of leadership have based their studies upon the behaviour and style adopted by leaders. In the majority of cases, four styles are highlighted and these are explained below.

Autocratic or authoritarian leadership

This style of leader adopts a dominant approach, attempting to make the majority of decisions. The leader will wish to hold onto authority and power and will delegate very little, if at all. There will be little discussion or consultation with subordinates and most communication will be in a downward direction. Although it might be thought that this is a situation that should be avoided, it is not always the case. Some leaders will find it hard to work in any other way and so they will function best by adopting an autocratic style, even if it does tend to alienate some of the subordinates. In the same way, many workers do not wish to be participative and simply want to be led and protected from decision making. If this is the case, then there is no point in attempting to be democratic. Finally, if a task is urgent and is essential to the business, it is likely that there will not be time for consultation and a democratic approach, and that the autocratic style will be the most appropriate and effective.

Paternalistic leadership

This is very like the autocratic style of leadership, although the leader adopts a father-like approach to subordinates and decisions are supposedly made in the best interests of the subordinates. There is likely to be more consultation and discussion than with the autocratic approach, but delegation is still unlikely. The leader makes the assumption that he or she knows what is best for the subordinates. Again, this may be an appropriate leadership style; it will depend upon the leader, the workforce and the task involved.

Democratic or participative leadership

The democratic leader discusses actions and decisions with subordinates and encourages participation. Delegation takes place and so power and decision making are more spread out. This kind of leadership covers a wide range of possibilities, from the leader who will not make a decision without the full agreement of all involved, to the leader who will consult, but still makes decisions centrally. It is generally agreed that this style tends to increase motivation and satisfaction amongst the subordinates and also reduces tension within the group. However, decision making becomes a slower process and so this is not suited to situations where decisions have to be made quickly. Also, as we have said, some workers do not wish to participate and would prefer to be led. Productivity is not always particularly high under this style of leadership, but the quality of output tends to be good. If work is boring and repetitive, output tends to be higher, in the short run at least, under a more autocratic style. However, in the long run, morale tends to fall leading to higher absenteeism, higher staff turnover and greater conflict within the group.

Laissez-faire or free-rein leadership

Here, the leader largely abdicates responsibility, allowing the subordinates to set their own goals and working patterns. The role of the leader becomes largely facilitative and advisory and the leader is mostly a contact point between the outside environment and the group. This form of leadership is rarely successful in the long term.

Leadership and the achievement of business objectives

In general terms, the main aim of leadership should be to achieve the objectives of the business. In order to do this, it is likely that the leader will have to take a number of factors into account, most of which have been mentioned previously. This approach to leadership is known as the jigsaw, or best-fit, approach and involves consideration of four factors.

1 **The leader's personal traits**   In many cases, individual leaders have very strong characteristics and find it almost impossible to adapt to different styles of leadership. Some people cannot be anything but autocratic and some would find it impossible to be so. In these cases, leaders are best advised to adopt their natural style, aware of the pitfalls that may appear.

2 **The type of subordinates**   The leader must be aware of the character of the subordinates in the group and adopt the leadership style that will suit them. Remember that not all workers wish to be participative. Many enjoy the autocratic or paternalistic approach.

3 **The task to be completed**   The urgency, importance and relative simplicity of the task may dictate the leadership approach. The more urgent, important and complicated a task, the more likely we are to see an autocratic approach to leadership.

4 **The business environment**   Any leader will be constrained by the greater environment of the business in which the leader operates. It may well be that the normal working methods, structure and traditions of a business will end up dictating the leadership approach that is universally adopted.

BLUE CIRCLE CEMENT CHANGES ITS WORKING PRACTICES

Blue Circle Cement is the UK's largest cement producer. It accounts for around 50 percent of all the cement supplied in the UK, producing its output from ten cement works. Up until the early 1980s, the industry was characterised by low wages, over-manning and long hours of work. The industry was also heavily unionised with restrictive working practices, and strict demarcation between skilled and unskilled workers. Overtime payments were made when workers were forced to work unsocial hours and this often occurred when systems broke down. Not surprisingly there was no great incentive for workers preventing mechanical breakdowns. The results of these working practices were low levels of staff morale, poor worker/manager relationships, and inefficiency throughout the organisation. These problems increased Blue Circle's costs and reduced its profits but, more significantly, it was losing market share to cheaper foreign competition from European producers. The company's whole existence was in the balance unless something was changed.

Changing working practices

Blue Circle introduced a plan to produce a 'highly skilled, flexible workforce, where all employees work as a team.' The key elements of the plan were:

- Enhanced skills for individuals with a reduction in the number of job grades, leading to greater flexibility
- Introduction of a simple pay structure with the elimination of paid overtime and bonuses and increased basic wage levels
- Significantly reduced manning levels and a reduction in total labour cost

These proposals were drawn up with close consultation with the trade unions present in Blue Circle. Jobs would be defined much more broadly, breaking down the old demarcation lines. Unskilled workers would be encouraged to learn new skills so they could take on the work of skilled workers. Team working was introduced, with all employees being encouraged to work together under a working culture that involved mutual respect amongst workers. The new system would be continuously reviewed by both management and unions to maintain standards and develop it further.

Pay

A new system of pay was introduced. This involved replacing a payment system where workers were heavily dependent on overtime, to one which gave employees a fixed basic salary for a contracted number of hours worked each year. There were also a number of flexi-hours that could be worked if there was an operational need. This new structure made labour costs more predictable for management. It also broke the cycle where workers sought to work longer hours so they could build up

overtime. Teams of workers were required to work full shifts, thus taking responsibility for the work done during the shift. The results of these measures were to increase the efficiency of the workforce.

Team working

Blue Circle realised the importance of team working. To facilitate this the workforce was broken up and into teams. Managers were trained in the skills of team building and team leadership. The workforce was involved in team building workshops, where workers were encouraged to use a cooperative, participatory approach to work and to develop a whole new team working ethos within the organisation.

Skills

In addition to team training all employees were expected to learn new skills. Blue Circle made an initial time period available to workers and put in the necessary resources to allow all workers to do this.

The whole project took Blue Circle two and a half years to implement. However, once it was in place the new working practices, combined with the installation of new equipment and technology increased productivity by nearly 300 percent. The new working practices were also popular with the workforce, who felt more involved in the company's progress and felt a greater sense of pride in their jobs. This increased staff morale and commitment.

QUESTIONS

1 a Explain the views on motivation put forward by F.W. Taylor as part scientific management. [7]

b Illustrate how Taylor's views are reflected by the workers' attitudes within Blue Circle. [8]

c Evaluate the payment system put forward in Blue Circle's plan as a way of motivating the firm's workforce. [10]

2 a Briefly explain the main ideas on motivation of the following management theorists: Maslow; McGregor; Mayo; Herzberg. [10]

b Referring to each of the theorists you have written about from **2a**, analyse how the project used by Blue Circle would have increased staff motivation. [15]

c Comment on the difficulties you think Blue Circle might have faced when implementing their plan. [10]

3 Discuss why staff motivation is important to Blue Circle's performance. [20]

Total [80]

GREAT MILLS – APPOINTING AND TRAINING NEW MANAGERS

Great Mills is one of the UK's leading chains of DIY stores, with over 92 stores open nationally, and employing over 3,000 people. It is one of the companies that has exploited the growth in out of town shopping, operating large superstores and garden centres. Great Mills is part of RMC PLC.

Great Mills believes that its most valuable resource is its employees, so it takes great care in the recruitment and training of new staff. This is particularly true when it is employing and training new managers. Great Mills has set the following specifications for the type of managers they want:

Motivation:

- Is interested in the product
- Likes seeing how much they can get people to buy

- Wants to sort out problems themselves
- Wants to be their own boss
- Wants to see things improve

Communication:

- Is good at talking and listening to people
- Believes in themselves
- Believes in people and is quick to use the best in others

Perception:

- Uses their common sense
- Notices small details
- Notices how people are feeling

Processing:

- Can see the wood for the trees
- Thinks on their feet and can make quick decisions
- Tries out ideas

- Looks at a set of figures and quickly picks out the main points

To develop these characteristics in their managers Great Mills has had a comprehensive management training scheme for the last ten years.

Recruitment and Selection

This is the process that Great Mills goes through in recruiting new managers.

1 **Job advertisement**   The job advertisement is critical in initiating the recruitment process. From the point of view of attracting the right candidates, it is important where the advertisement is placed and also that its content is right.

2 **Shortlisting**   It is not possible to interview everyone that applies, so a shortlist of the most suitable candidates is drawn up.

3 **Preliminary interview**   At this stage Great Mills tries to assess the level of motivation the candidate has. The interviewers try to match the candidate's personal characteristics with their own criteria of what makes an effective manager. The interview lasts about an hour during which candidates are asked questions such as:
   - What attracts you to DIY retailing?
   - How well do you cope when you are faced with many things to do?
   - How do you enjoy making decisions that affect others?

4 **Candidate assessment**   Potential

Great Mills managers are assessed using a number of exercises including:
- Being asked to look at a series of financial information, relating to key retailing issues and make a series of recommendations based on the information
- Being made to undertake a perception interview, where candidates are asked to walk around a store for half an hour on their own and then go round the store with an assessor and tell the assessor what observations they have made
- Having to interview an existing member of staff about their job

Once the selection process is finished the successful candidate is offered a place on the Great Mills management training scheme. Great Mills then finalises the job offer and a contract of employment is drawn up, creating a legal basis for the appointment.

Training

Once new managers are appointed they undergo an induction process that involves them carrying out a variety of different tasks throughout the store to make them familiar with the way the store works. Trainees also have to attend development courses, and undertake weekly assessments. They work with a 'mentor', who is an experienced member of the organisation, whose task is to guide and advise the new trainee. After 10 months on the programme, the trainee is finally assessed before they are appointed as a store manager.

QUESTIONS

1 Outline the main functions of the personnel department within an organisation, such as Great Mills. [7]

2 a Explain where you think Great Mills ought to advertise for its new managers. [5]

b Outline what you would put in an advertisement for a trainee manager for Great Mills. [5]

c Explain why the contents and location of an advertisement are so important in the recruitment process. [8]

3 a In the case study there are three questions that are asked of potential trainee managers at the preliminary interview. Bearing in mind the management criteria Great Mills set for their managers, write out three additional questions you would ask at the interview. Write a note explaining why you have asked each question. [10]

b Evaluate how effective personal interviews are when assessing candidates for a job. [10]

4 a What do you think is the purpose of Great Mills asking candidates to interview existing members of staff? [5]

b Design an exercise Great Mills might use to assess candidates' problem solving and decision making skills. Explain carefully the purpose of your exercise. [10]

5 Analyse the benefits to Great Mills of operating a successful recruitment and training programme. [10]

Total [70]

Operations Management

SUMMARY

1 The location decisions of productive units will be affected by a number of factors. The relative importance of the factors will vary with the individual needs of the businesses concerned.

2 The size of a business may be measured in a number of ways, but usually by either output or sales value.

3 As a business grows in size, there are a number of unit cost advantages that might be experienced. These are known as economies of scale and might be internal and/or external. Unit cost disadvantages may also occur and these are known as diseconomies of scale.

4 Production is the complete process of combining factors in order to satisfy the needs and desires of consumers. Production may be primary, secondary or tertiary.

5 There are a number of possible production methods, such as job, batch, flow, lean and cell production. The choice of method will depend upon the resources available to the firm, the market, the type of product or the kind of service being produced and the quality of the workforce available.

6 Productivity is a measure of how efficiently a business converts its factor inputs into output.

7 Quality is an integral part of making a sale and so efficient quality control must be an essential objective of any firm.

8 Traditional quality control puts the onus on a quality control department. Total quality management (TQM) puts the onus on all workers and management.

9 Stocks may be of raw materials and purchased items, work-in-progress and finished goods. They may also be production process and administration stocks. Firms must always balance the costs and benefits of holding stocks.

10 Stock holding charts can be used to determine stock levels.

11 The just-in-time production system (JIT) has a great influence on stock control, but it is much more than a simple stock control system.

12 Efficient project management is essential if projects are to be finished on time and within budget. Critical path (network) analysis is one way of attempting project management and Gantt charts may be used to give an alternative visual representation of the network.

Operations management is a more modern term for production management. Production management tended to have the image of simply being concerned with the production of tangible goods. However, it was felt that there are sufficient similarities between producing goods and providing services for the two to be treated under the same heading. Since systems for the supply of both goods and services are commonly referred to as operating systems, the title of operations management has been adopted. It encompasses the production of goods, through manufacturing systems, and the provision of services, through service systems.

LOCATION AND SIZE OF THE PRODUCTIVE UNIT

In order to produce a good or provide a service, it is necessary to have a productive unit or base from which to work. The siting and size of the unit will be of great importance. It is especially important since the unit will probably be the greatest single investment that the business will have to make.

The location of industry

There are many factors that an entrepreneur will take into account when considering the location for a productive unit. For small businesses just in the process of starting up, the choice is often very limited. They will normally be sited in the locality of the owner's home, in any suitable location. Providers of services tend to position themselves close to their markets, and consider little else. However, large firms, when planning for the long-term future, may well consider the location of their productive units by weighing up the importance of the following factors.

Production processes and transport costs

Processing costs do not vary a great deal from area to area, although wage rates may reflect regional costs of living. Because of this, one of the most important factors in the location decision is relative transport costs. Firms have to transport raw materials to the productive unit and finished products from it. Much will depend upon whether the production process involved is bulk-decreasing or bulk-increasing. If a production process is bulk-decreasing, it means that the business brings

in high bulk raw materials, which are then processed to produce lower bulk finished products. If this is the case, then it will be more expensive to transport raw materials than it will be to move finished products and it makes more sense to site the productive unit closer to the source of the raw materials. This is why the old staple industries, such as iron and steel manufacture and ship-building, were sited close to their raw materials. Bulk-increasing production processes will lead to the opposite situation. If a firm brings in many low bulk raw materials in order to produce a higher bulk product, then it will make sense to site the productive unit closer to the final market.

A sufficiently skilled workforce

Businesses need human capital and it is vital that they are located in areas where they can find the right quantity and quality of workers. Labour-intensive businesses will consider this to be a more important factor than capital-intensive ones. Thus, large car plants, which even with modern technology still employ large numbers of workers, would have to locate in areas where there was abundant, sufficiently skilled labour.

Suitable infrastructure and amenities

The existence of adequate road and rail links may be of vital importance to a business. This could also apply to port and air transport facilities. Good transport links can be a key factor in the location decision. Businesses are often keen to site their production units close to motorways, an example being the number who have located close to the M4 in the corridor between London and Wales. Other businesses, who export to the continent, have set up close to the south coast of England. There are five basic amenities that most businesses may expect: electricity, gas, water, drainage and waste disposal. In the UK today, the first two are available in the majority of places. However, businesses that require large amounts of water, perhaps for cooling purposes, or that have specialised waste disposal requirements, such as chemical firms, may consider this factor to be of great importance.

Availability of land

The need for suitable land, at a reasonable cost, will always be important. The larger the unit, the more cost will be a factor. In certain cases, the geology of the land will also matter. Some industries, such as power generation, need land that is capable of supporting heavy weights. In other cases, climate may be a factor. Even if the land is suitable, it will be no use without planning permission to build the site and so this must also be an important factor.

The influence of social factors

The importance of available social facilities, such as good housing, acceptable schools, adequate health care and suitable leisure facilities, is often overlooked. It is, in fact, thought to be an important factor because, in the end, it is owners or members of the senior management who will make the siting decision and there is bound to be an element of personal interest involved. It has been known for a productive unit to be sited where it was for the simple reason that the owner was able to gain membership of a local golf club!

The existence of government activity

As well as restricting building in designated zones, a government may attempt to encourage businesses to site in certain areas, most commonly to improve employment in the area and to reduce regional imbalances. This is usually carried out by offering grants or tax concessions.

The need for safety

Some productive processes, such as nuclear power or certain munitions, may be considered to have inherent dangers that need to be considered when making the location decision.

Availability of subsidiary industries

Businesses may consider not just the proximity of suppliers of components and materials, but also the existence of local research facilities and support industries, such as market research and advertising agencies.

The scale of operations and economies and diseconomies of scale

Both of these concepts have already been introduced and explained in Unit 1, but it is important to consider them here as well. There are a number of factors that affect the scale of operations, but the main one is obviously the level of demand for the goods or services produced by the business. Others might be the availability of factors of production, the wishes of the owners or senior management, or the availability of suitable technology. The size of a business is usually measured either by the number of units produced or by the sales value of the output of the firm. If a business is able to increase the scale of its production, then there are usually cost benefits that will accrue. If output can be increased at a faster rate than the cost of inputs, then unit costs (average costs) will fall. Unit cost reductions that are caused by an increase in the scale of production are known as economies of scale. There are five main economies of scale that can be generated internally and these are commercial economies, technical economies, financial economies, managerial and labour economies and risk bearing economies. The above economies are all generated by the act of the business becoming larger. They are caused by the internal action of the business and so are known as internal economies of scale. There are other economies to be gained from increased scale of operations which stem from outside the business and are known as external economies of scale.

External economies of scale are the unit cost reductions that come about because of the increase in the output capacity of the industry as a whole. There are two main types: concentration economies and information economies.

There may be disadvantages attached to an increase in the scale of operations and these are called diseconomies of scale. These tend to fall into two main categories: information diseconomies and human diseconomies.

Diseconomies of scale may have cost disadvantages that need to be set against the advantages gained through economies of scale; however, it should be remembered that research has shown that firms never grow so large that the negative cost effects of the diseconomies actually outweigh the cost benefits derived from the economies.

▰ PRODUCTION

Production is the complete process of combining factors in order to satisfy the needs and desires of consumers. For a business involved in the manufacturing of tangible goods, this will be the whole process including the ordering of necessary raw materials, the setting up of capital equipment, the establishment of a suitable workforce, the choice of a production method, the establishment of quality control procedures and the instigation of an efficient delivery service. Thus, a car firm will select and build a suitable production site, install the capital necessary to carry out the chosen production method, employ a suitably qualified workforce, set up a materials ordering system and quality control system, and then implement a distribution system for finished goods.

For the production of services, it is still necessary to combine factors of production in order to satisfy the service requirements of potential customers. Thus a travel agent will need to locate a business, employ suitable staff, purchase necessary capital equipment, such as computers, and oversee the quality of the service that is being provided.

Production should not be confused with the term 'productivity'. Productivity is a measurement of how efficiently a business converts its factor inputs into output and is dealt with in more detail later in this unit.

Types of production

In Unit 1, the productive part of the economy was split into three sectors: primary, secondary and tertiary. Obviously, production can take place in any of these three sectors and would be given the same classification.

Primary production involves the natural resources and tends to be concentrated in the areas of agriculture, fishing and the extractive industries. Secondary production relates to the production of tangible goods or buildings, which have been manufactured or constructed using a combination of raw materials from the primary sector of the economy. Tertiary production is the provision of services. These services may be direct, aimed at end consumers, or commercial, aimed at the business community. Direct services might be such things as hairdressers or plumbers. Commercial services could be banking or insurance. Obviously, some services might cover both businesses and end users, such as banking.

Production methods

A business will need to choose a production method that is suitable for the good which is being produced. The choice of method will take into account the total output required, the nature of the good, the factors of production available and the level of quality which needs to be attained. There are a number of methods which can be employed and these include the following.

Job production

This takes place when it is necessary to produce a single, one-off product. For larger items, this might be the production of a ship, a bridge or a motorway. However, it can also be applied to smaller, individual items, such as wedding dresses or individual computer systems for businesses. Job production requires the production and completion of the finished product before another product is started.

Fig 8.1 *An example of job production*

The advantages of job production include the fact that the product is exactly suited to the needs of a specific customer and that the product is given the sole attention of the production team until it is completed. The main disadvantage is that the unique nature of the product tends to require high levels of design activities and this leads to high production costs. There is also a lack of opportunity to gain economies of scale and this in turn has cost implications. Because of this, goods made by job production tend to be expensive. However, as long as the product fulfils the needs of the customer, the cost will be met. This is obvious in terms of such items as bridges or buildings, but it also explains why designer clothes can be sold for such high prices.

Batch production

This takes place when items are produced in batches, which go through the different processes of the production system together. At each stage of the system, the whole batch is processed before it passes on to the next stage. A good example is the production of tubular steel supports for bus seats. An order for 20 might pass through the process in the following way. First, 20 base supports may be cut and finished. After this, the side parts may be added to all 20 bases. The angles of the joints may then be tested on the whole batch and then the top bars may be added. Finally, the whole batch may be checked for faults and then despatched. Once this batch has been produced, the next batch might be started.

There tends to be confusion between this process and that of flow production. Products might be produced in 'batches' by flow production. The important distinction is that in batch production, the whole batch is treated as a unit, whereas in flow production the individual products are processed at each stage of the production system and then move straight on. There are numerous advantages to batch production. It usually takes place in industries where demand is for batches of products and so output can be exactly matched to demand and batch design can be altered between batches to ensure that the products match customer requirements. There is scope for the division of labour into specific production tasks and there is the opportunity to gain from economies of scale.

Disadvantages also exist. There are high levels of work-in-progress stocks, because there are batches of semi-finished goods at all points of the production process. The division of labour can lead to boredom, and thus a lack of motivation, for the workforce. Also, batch production requires high levels of organisational planning in order to manage the movements of batches from process to process and to sequence the different batches that are passing through the production system.

Decisions on batch size are of great importance from a cost viewpoint. As batches get larger, the cost per unit tends to diminish. Also, the set-up costs are reduced as the production process needs to be changed less frequently. However, there is a downside to large batches. As goods are produced in greater number, the amount of work-in-progress stocks increases and the cost of this to the business will be great. It is normally necessary to take all of these factors into account when deciding on batch sizes. A useful diagram to show this is given in Fig 8.2. It would suggest that the optimum batch size exists at the point where the benefits to be gained by lower set-up and order costs are negated by the higher stock-holding costs.

Flow production

In flow production, individual products move to the next stage of the production process as soon as they finish the preceding one. The production process must be planned in such a way that there are no bottle necks in the system and that the occurrence of hold-ups is

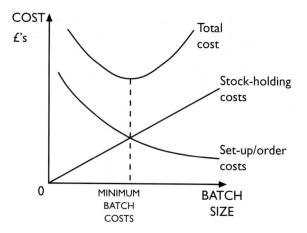

Fig 8.2   *Deciding on optimum batch size*

minimised. Ideally, all stages should be of equal duration, so that the products can flow freely.

Flow production lends itself to industries where demand for the products is high and constant. It also suits the production of a standardised item that only requires minor alterations. Large breweries use flow production to bottle beer. The product is standardised in that the final item is a bottle of beer of a standard size. However, it is possible to make changes to the constituents of the contents and to the labelling of the bottles without significantly altering the manufacturing process.

There are many advantages of flow production. Quality tends to be high and consistent, as products are standardised. It is also easy to check quality at different stages of the process. Labour costs tend to be low and the physical handling of products is minimised.

Work-in-progress stocks are reduced and it is possible to minimise input stocks if suppliers are reliable and production is constant (see just-in-time stock control, p. 197).

The disadvantages tend to be the high level of initial capital investment that is usually required and the de-motivational effects upon the remaining workforce. In addition, there is a need for a comprehensive preventative maintenance programme in order to avoid a shut-down of the system.

The traditional idea of flow production taking place on a conveyor belt that runs through the whole plant area is being questioned at the moment. Toyota, for example, have implemented the idea of flexible workshops based upon a particular type of machine layout and a multi-skilled labour force. The machine layout is based upon U-shaped assembly lines, as shown in Fig 8.3 below.

This layout means that a worker in the enclosed area can theoretically tend two, or more, machines, and is in a good position to help others if they have problems or are falling behind. The success of this system depends upon the flexibility of the workers and multi-skilling is imperative.

Lean production

This is a term that refers to a wide range of measures that have been instigated, mostly by the Japanese, to reduce waste and to improve efficiency in the production process. Lean production ideas can be applied to batch, flow or cell production. The ideas cover all areas of the production process and are aimed at eliminating wastage in terms of materials and time. The first area is product development and the aim is to minimise the time taken between devising the idea for a new product and actually getting the product onto the market. The best example of this is Toyota, who are capable of getting a new car idea into the show rooms approximately 45 percent more quickly than their western rivals, such as

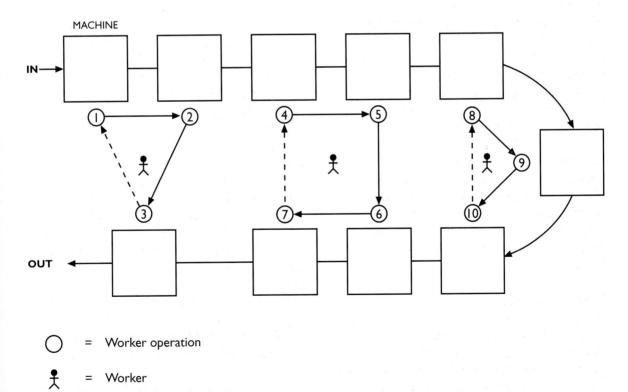

○ = Worker operation

☂ = Worker

Fig 8.3 *Toyota's U-shaped production line*

Ford. The next area is the delivery of stock for the production process. The use of just-in-time (JIT) stock control has revolutionised a number of industries. It is used to minimise the stock-holding costs at all points of production, inputs, work-in-progress and finished goods. It requires very accurate ordering systems and very reliable suppliers. Another area of lean production is in the process itself. A kaizen system is often implemented. Kaizen means continuous improvement and is usually based upon the use of groups of workers (kaizen groups) to improve their own efficiency at the workplace. Kaizen especially lends itself to development in a system that is based upon cell production. (Kaizen groups have already been covered in Unit 3, p. 39.)

Cell production

This is also known as cellular production and involves the separation of a flow production system into a number of self-contained mini factories. The basic idea is thought to derive from the Soviet Union in the 1950s. The performance of each cell is measured in terms of a range of goals – output, quality, lead-time and cash targets. Each cell consists of a cell leader, 'the father of the team', and below the leader a single level arrangement comprising manufacturers, manufacturing craftsmen and product assessors. Reorganisation into a cell system tends to make the cell workers more committed and motivated, leading to significant improvements in production performance. Success depends upon the flexibility of the workforce and this generates a substantial training and development requirement. Lucas Industries introduced cell production in their automotive electrical plants and, after two years, they discovered that there was an 80 percent reduction in work-in-progress stocks; the stock turnover ratio had risen from 7 to 13, productivity was up 25 percent and the reject level was 20 percent of the previous figure. Interestingly, it might be argued that one of the earliest, and most successful, uses of cellular production was in the building of the Great Wall of China. Workers were split into cells and given responsibility for building a distinct section of the wall. In this way, morale was kept up and the enormity of the task did not overawe them.

The choice of production method will depend upon four main factors.

1 The resources available to the firm.
2 The market.
3 The type of product or the kind of service being produced.
4 The quality of the workforce available.

Many firms will combine a number of production systems in the same plant. They might use job and batch production to make components and then use a form of continuous production to assemble the final product. There is no 'best' method.

PRODUCTIVITY

As has already been said, production and productivity should not be thought to be the same thing. Productivity is a measurement of how efficiently a business converts its factor inputs into output. A great deal of operations management is concerned with attempts to improve the productivity of the factors employed.

Productivity is attained in one of two ways. Either, more is produced from the same number of inputs, or the same amount as before is produced using a smaller number of inputs. Either way, the unit cost of production will fall.

Inputs may be raw materials, labour or machinery. Increases in the levels of mechanisation have had great effects upon the levels of productivity, since the time of the Industrial Revolution in the eighteenth century. The same can be said for the impact of specialisation on labour productivity.

Productivity is normally measured in terms of either capital efficiency or labour efficiency. This is best shown by an example. Suppose we take a firm, ABC Ltd, who produce work desks using a combination of machinery and labour. Possible results are shown below:

	1995	1998
Average weekly wage	£300	£350
Average weekly output per worker (labour productivity)	50	60
Unit labour cost	£6	£5.83
Weekly cost of a machine	£2,000	£2,200
Average weekly output per machine (capital productivity)	400	480
Unit machine cost	£5	£4.58

We can see that in the case of both labour and capital, productivity has improved over the period shown and that this has led to a reduction in unit labour and machine costs. In the case of labour, wages have risen by almost 17 percent, but output per worker has risen by 20 percent. Machinery is even better, with costs rising by 10 percent and output per machine by 20 percent.

Capacity utilisation and capital intensity

Capacity utilisation measures the extent to which the maximum capacity of a productive unit is being utilised. Obviously, if a plant is capable of producing 50,000 units per year and is only used to produce 25,000, then the potential of the plant is being under-used and we would say that the capacity utilisation was only 50 percent. The equation used is:

$$\frac{\textbf{Actual output}}{\textbf{Potential output}} \times \textbf{100}$$

The higher the level of capacity utilisation that can be achieved, the more widely the fixed costs of production can be spread. In this case, if fixed costs are £500,000, then the actual fixed cost per unit, at current output and 50 percent capacity utilisation, is £20. If potential output of 50,000 units can be achieved, i.e. a capacity utilisation of 100 percent, then the fixed cost per unit falls to £10. Obviously, this would give the firm a significant cost advantage, but it will only be possible if the firm can produce at full capacity and if the demand is there for the quantity produced.

Capital intensity measures how heavily a firm relies upon capital, in ratio to the other factors of production, to achieve its production. If a firm is heavily capitalised, then it is said to be capital intensive. If it is dependent on large numbers of workers, and little capital, then it is said to be labour intensive.

Capital intensive production is very expensive in terms of initial set-up costs and so it is only applicable in situations where demand for the final product will be high and regular. An example of this sort of production would be the Coca Cola plants that are to be found around the world. Set-up costs are high and the plants are highly capital intensive, but the levels of demand mean that the outlay is soon recovered. Another factor, following on from this, is the availability of funds to pay for the high set-up costs. Obviously, it is only possible to be capital intensive if the machinery can be paid for and this is one of the reasons, although it is not always the case, why it is larger firms that tend to be capital intensive. A third factor affecting the capital intensity of production is the type of product. Highly capital intensive production tends to be used for products that are standardised, requiring little change. Thus, the Coca Cola plant will turn out standard cans of Coke and only small changes, such as different labels and slight changes to the mixture, are required to turn out other products in the range, such as Coke Light.

QUALITY AND QUALITY CONTROL

Quality

In most cases, it is quality that sells goods and services. Quality, in this context, does not have to mean that the product is the 'best', like a Rolex watch, but rather means that the product is best for the particular needs of a customer, determined by the use to which the product will be put and the price for which it is sold.

There are two different approaches to quality.

1 **The production view**   This is where products are produced to exact specifications and, if they match those specifications, then the products are said to be of the necessary quality.

2 **The consumer's view**   This view covers a number of areas, such as value for money, reliability, appearance, utility and back-up services. These are much more difficult to monitor, but no less important if the firm wishes to be successful and to make sales.

These approaches can be combined, and added to, to develop a process which can be used to aid the quest for quality. Figure 8.4 illustrates the system.

The first step in the process is quality of design. Firms must consider how well the design features of the product satisfy customer requirements. The second step is production quality. How well does the production process manage to manufacture products that match the design specifications? The third step is product quality. How well does the finished product, good or service, satisfy the requirements of the customer? The final step is the most important of all, in many respects, and that is customer feedback. This can be used to alter the quality of design and thus gain continuous improvement of the product.

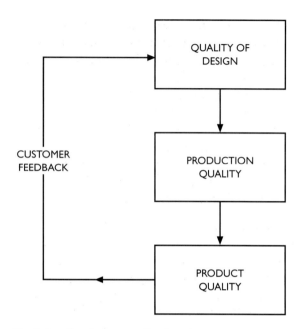

Fig 8.4   *Continuous quality improvement*

Quality is an integral part of making a sale and so its importance cannot be over-estimated. Perceived 'good' quality will lead to high sales, high market share and, presumably, profits. However, in the same way, a perceived lack, or loss, of quality can be a disaster. The collapse of the UK car industry had much to do with perception of low quality and comparisons between UK cars and foreign cars, especially Japanese and German cars. In the same way, health scares at the Perrier bottling plant in France led to perceptions of a loss of quality and a large fall in market share.

When one considers the importance of quality, it is obvious that efficient quality control must be an essential objective of any firm.

Traditional quality control

Traditionally, quality control has been the checking of the quality of work in the production process. There have tended to be three stages.

1 **The checking of raw materials and bought-in components**   The quality of inputs is checked on delivery to ensure that they are fit for purpose.

2 **The checking of semi-finished products**   The work-in-progress is checked at nominated spots through the production process.

3 **The checking of finished products**   The quality of the final products is checked to ensure that they meet specifications.

In all these cases, the checking was normally carried out by taking a sample at each stage, not by checking every unit. The quality control was carried out by inspectors, usually working for a quality control department, and whose job it was to discover faulty items. There are a number of problems with this traditional approach.

1 It is a negative approach, in that the success of the inspector depends upon the failure of the operator. Indeed, there is a danger that the inspector might become too zealous in the quest for faults and begin to fail perfectly good items. Also, operators often see inspectors as being a threat and there may well be problems relating to conflict and tension.

2 If checking is only carried out at certain points on a production line, faulty items may pass through three or four stages before they are picked up. This is a waste of productive capacity.

3 The existence of the inspectors takes the responsibility for quality away from the operator and there is thus less motivation for the operator to work efficiently.

4 The actual checking by inspectors is boring work and can often lead to faulty units getting through the system. This poor product quality may then be transferred into a lack of consumer confidence when the finished units are bought.

Total quality management (control)

The philosophy of total quality management (TQM) is that it despecialises the inspection function and places the responsibility for quality control in the hands of all workers and management in the firm.

TQM aims to produce a system that will lead to marketing, engineering, production and service at the most economical level, but giving full customer satisfaction. An ideal TQM system would, in fact, lead to the disappearance of the traditional quality control department because their role would be completely taken over by the other employees of the firm.

TQM also questions the traditional view of the costs of quality. In the West, quality control has often been seen as an addition to production costs. In TQM companies, the achievement of high quality standards is seen as a means of reducing total costs. The cost of inspection time by employees is more than cancelled out by the cost savings that result from lower reject rates.

TQM, along with other methods such as just-in-time production, quality circles and in-process controls, enables the philosophy of continuous improvement (kaizen) to be achieved. Quality circles have already been considered in an earlier unit and just-in-time will be looked at later in this unit. In-process controls use statistical methods to study variations in products in a different way from the old-style use of statistical error. In the past, upper and lower limits were set for the production of components and, so long as production took place within these tolerances, then the unit was said to be fit for purpose. Once the tolerances were exceeded, the machines were then inspected and re-set. Now, a number of Japanese firms employ statistical process control in a different manner. In effect, the traditional tolerance levels are split into two sets of tolerances, which are calculated and checked. The first is the normal tolerance levels that might be expected from a healthy machine and/or production method. The second is the unnatural variation that might be caused by a specific factor, such as a poorly aligned machine. Japanese workers are asked to check tolerances and to report when the natural variations are being exceeded, even though the components are still within their overall quality limits. In this way, causes can be identified early and action can be taken before products are produced that are outside acceptable limits. Thus costs of wastage, or re-working costs, are avoided.

Training and employee development

In all of the modern methods of quality control, great importance is placed upon the role of the workforce and the acceptance of responsibility. If this is the case, then quality and, indeed, productivity, will only be as good as the quality of the workforce being employed. This means that firms will wish to employ workers who are able, and of sufficient intelligence, to cope with the tasks involved. They will also want to employ workers who share the company's values and philosophy. If they are able to employ such a workforce, the quality of their induction processes and their employee training and development programmes will also need to be first-rate if the employees are to be capable of fulfilling their roles in the quality control process.

■ STOCKS AND STOCK CONTROL

Types of stocks

There are a number of different types of stocks that a firm needs to control. They fall into two main sorts as follows.

Product stocks

1 **Stocks of raw materials and purchased items**   These are held in order to ensure that there is a continuous flow of necessary factors of production into the firm, so that the production process is not stopped. The modern trend is to keep these stocks as small as possible, if not to eliminate them all together. We shall look at this tendency later in this unit. Even though there are obvious advantages to reducing stock levels, these may be outweighed by the economies of bulk buying and so, in some cases, firms will keep large stocks of raw materials and purchased items because the savings from bulk buying outweigh the costs, financial and opportunity, of holding the stocks.

2 **Work-in-progress stocks**   These are the stocks of semi-finished goods that occur, or are kept, at different points in the production process. If stockpiles are simply occurring at different points in the system, then the process should be adjusted in order to eliminate them. However, it may be that work-in-progress stocks are held on purpose to guard against hold-ups at various points in the system. If this is the case, the same logic should apply. As sensible as it might be to try to keep production going, the system should still be examined in order to discover what is causing the hold-ups.

3 **Stocks of finished goods**   These are held to ensure that customers can be supplied, even when there are fluctuations in demand or stoppages in production. An inability to supply customers on demand can be extremely damaging for a business, because the disappointed customer will often find an alternative supplier and will never return to the business that was unable to supply.

Production process and administration stocks

The second type of stocks that firms hold are

production process and administration stocks. Production process stocks would be items such as spare parts for machines, replacement tools and maintenance equipment. Administration stocks would be items such as stationery or computer spares. Whilst these stocks do tie up some money, they tend to be relatively much less important than product stocks in the normal production business.

Costs and benefits of holding stocks

We have already mentioned some of the benefits to be gained by holding stocks. First, stocks of raw materials and bought in goods, as well as work-in-progress stocks, enable the production process to run smoothly when there are unexpected events. Second, stocks of finished goods enable customers to be satisfied and thus goodwill to be retained. A third point is that high stocks of inputs might attract cost savings through bulk buying and also avoid the costs incurred through the frequent ordering and handling that must take place when small stocks are kept.

However, it is felt by most that the costs of stock holding usually far outweigh the benefits. First, and most obviously, stocks tie up working capital. They represent money which could almost certainly be of better use elsewhere. Second, the actual costs of storing stocks are high as they need to be physically handled and stored. Third, there is always the danger that stock will become obsolete or deteriorate in some way.

It is because of the high potential costs of stock holding that much thought has been given to the role of stocks in operations management. In some cases, effort is made to balance costs and benefits, usually through some form of stock-holding chart. In others, efforts are made to minimise stock levels by means of a just-in-time approach. We shall now consider these two approaches.

Stock-holding charts

There are many different charts that might be used to help a business with its stock control system, although they tend to be of two types. The first attempts to show how much of a given stock should be ordered and how often the ordering should take place. The second simply tries to set an optimum stock level. This may be done by balancing stock-holding costs with the costs of running out of stocks and this might apply to a productive or retail situation. Another way of doing this is by attempting to assess the different levels of demand for different items and then working out priority stocks, which should not be allowed to run out. This usually applies to retail outlets. We can look at each of these three possibilities.

Traditional stock-holding charts

Traditional stock-holding charts attempt to set maximum and minimum stock levels and then to plan reorder times so that stocks never fall below the minimum level nor rise above the maximum one. The 'perfect situation' is shown in Fig 8.5.

In theory, stock is ordered and then used at a uniform rate. This continues until the

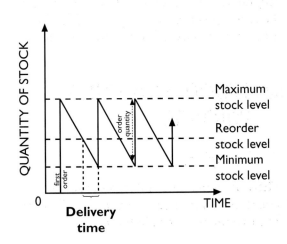

Fig 8.5   *A traditional stock control chart*

reorder level of stock is reached, at which point, the suppliers are contacted and a new order is placed. The size of the order would be the difference between the maximum and minimum stock levels. The new order arrives at exactly the point when the stock level reaches minimum and so the stock is replenished to the maximum level and the process starts anew. Although this is a pleasing, and simple, chart, it is based upon far too many assumptions to be trusted implicitly. It assumes that usage of stock is constant and that there is no faulty stock. It also assumes that the delivery times are always the same and that reorder will be made at exactly the right moment. These assumptions are unlikely to be discovered in reality. Stock usage, or demand, will almost certainly vary and waste almost always occurs, even in the most efficient of firms. Also, delivery is not a guaranteed thing, there are too many variables that might affect it, such as traffic or weather conditions. Finally, reordering is not always carried out at exactly the right moment, although the use of computer technology in stock control has much eased this problem, especially in the retail trade. Cash registers will now often be a part of the stock control process and every sale is registered and a stock count maintained. At a certain reorder level, the new order is put in by the computer, to another computer, with no human intervention.

The assumptions made mean that the traditional stock control chart is unlikely to be perfect at all times, indeed, it is unlikely to be perfect most of the time. It is, however, a useful tool if it is used as an aid to stock control, but with a knowledge of its inherent weaknesses borne in mind.

Setting optimum stock levels

Optimum stock levels may be set in a number of ways. One method is shown in Fig 8.6, where an attempt is made to estimate the costs

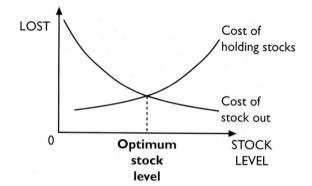

Fig 8.6   *Holding costs versus stockout costs*

of running out of stock, known as a stockout, and the costs of holding stock.

An optimum, safe, level of stock is then discovered by taking the point at which the two lines cross. Again, there are a number of assumptions here, but the concept is another useful aid to stock control.

Prioritising of stocks

The third chart that might be used is shown in Fig 8.7 and tends to relate to stocks of finished goods, although there are applications to inputs.

In a retail situation, the stock is divided into three categories. Category A items are those that sell regularly and account for a high

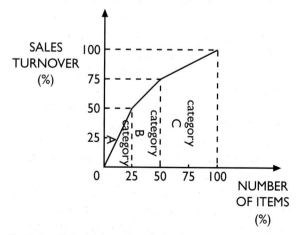

Fig 8.7   *Prioritising of stocks by demand levels*

percentage of sales revenue. Category B items do not sell as often, nor contribute as much, and category C items are the most slow moving. In Fig 8.7, category A items make up 25 percent of the goods on offer, but contribute 50 percent of sales turnover. Category B items are also 25 percent of the goods on offer, but only contribute 25 percent of sales turnover and category C items account for 50 percent of goods on offer, but only contribute 25 percent of turnover. By considering this, it is possible for management to prioritise the items on offer and to concentrate their stock management more on category A goods than on category C. Thus, they will attempt to ensure that they do not have stockouts of category A items, because of their essential nature. It does not mean that it will be impossible to get category C items, but it does mean that they will be missing from the shelves more often than category A goods.

Just-in-time (JIT)

We have already looked at the traditional, just-in-case stock-holding concepts, and so now we should consider the concept of just-in-time. JIT is more than a stock control system, it is a complete production system that is, in effect, used as an umbrella phrase to cover a whole range of concepts and techniques. The aims of JIT are to achieve continuous improvement along with a reduction in stock levels.

There are a number of different theories regarding the origins of JIT. Some say that it was first used in the 1950s by Japanese ship builders. At that time, the Japanese steel industry had huge amounts of unused capacity and ship builders discovered that they could get steel delivered virtually on demand. Because of this, they were able to reduce steel stocks from one month's supply to less than one week. Other writers have suggested that JIT evolved because of the lack of natural resources and land space in Japan. However, the first recorded use of a JIT system is probably to be found in Toyota, possibly as early as the late 1940s. Certainly, by 1954, JIT at Toyota was being extended back to the suppliers and forwards to the sales department, who were given the task of running the planning of production.

In JIT, it is demand that instigates production. If there is no demand, then nothing is produced. The JIT concept is very straightforward. Finished goods are produced just in time to be sold to the customer; sub-assemblies are produced just in time to be assembled into finished goods, component parts are produced just in time to go into the sub-assemblies and materials are purchased just in time to be used to make component parts. Thus, it is the consumer and, therefore, the sales department, who trigger the production process. It is for this reason that JIT is often found to include a 'kanban' system. Under a kanban system, materials, component parts and sub-assemblies are pulled through the production process by cards, known as kanban, which are placed in purpose-built containers designed to hold a specific (usually small) number of items. The cards initiate production and so if there is no kanban attached to a container, then nothing will be produced. The amount of stock and production in the system is thus altered by the number of cards and this in turn will depend upon demand for the final product.

If goods are to be produced so that output perfectly matches demand and production takes place at the last minute, one of two important conditions must hold. Either, the demand must be stable, or at least easy to predict, or the production process must be extremely responsive and produce consistently high quality output. In order to achieve this, Japanese firms will often 'smooth' production schedules over a given time period. For example, Toyota forecast the demand, and thus production, for the coming month and then calculate the total number of components required. The component figures are then divided by the number of working days in the month and the figure arrived at becomes the base-line target for each production cell. The requirements are then modified as the month goes on and it can be seen whether or not the forecasts are accurate. It is rare for Toyota to have significant periods of slack demand and, more often than not, overtime is used to meet increases in demand. Mazda keep their production work forces to the absolute minimum and then use workers from their support member pool. These are workers who have been trained by Mazda and are available for short-term work assignments. They are not on the permanent staff of the firm. An effective JIT system requires a number of conditions.

1 **A reduction in machine set-up times**   This is necessary, because JIT requires relatively small batch sizes for production, ideally batches of one. Small batches will require a large number of machine set-up changes, and so it is important that they are efficiently carried out. At Toyota, for example, they managed to reduce the times for the changeover of dies in the stamping shops from as much as ten hours to a little under three minutes. At Hino Motors, they use a JIT system to produce 1,900 different types of trucks, with 700 engine types, on the same production line. Trucks are assembled one at a time and so one can imagine that the number of set-up changes must be very high indeed.

2 **A basically simple workflow**   JIT systems are most successful when production is organised on a product, as opposed to a process, basis. If a factory is organised on a product basis, then people are grouped around the products that they produce, rather than by the functions that they perform. In systems organised on a process basis, materials often have to revisit work areas, such as the welding department, a number of times and this means that JIT does not work well.

3 **Total quality management (control)**   A JIT system has hardly any room for error. It is essential that each work area passes on goods which are of the required quality to the next. In order to achieve this, a total quality management (TQM) system is often employed. TQM has been covered earlier in this unit. It is worth stating, however, that JIT not only needs TQM, but it is also a method by which it might be achieved.

There are a number of benefits that are derived from the use of JIT system. The main ones are the efficient use of working capital, reductions in waste and improvements in quality. Other gains are reductions in lead-times and machine set-up times. This in turn leads to smaller batch sizes and an ability to be more responsive to changes in demand and the market. It must be remembered that the great possible weakness of JIT is that it is easily ruined if the workforce gives anything less than 100 percent commitment. There are no back-up stocks and so any worker who does not produce on time, to the right quality, will cause a log jam in the system and will affect the whole production process.

PROJECT MANAGEMENT

Any time that a project is being considered, serious thought should be given to its management. No matter how large or small the project may be, it is more likely to be completed quickly, and efficiently, if it is managed in a sensible and planned way. The majority of projects will be planned with two main objectives in mind:

1 To finish the project within the agreed time available.

2 To finish the project within the agreed budget.

There are many different systems of project management that can be adopted, but we shall look at two models that might be of use: critical path analysis and Gantt charts.

Critical path analysis

Critical path analysis (CPA) is also known as network analysis and is a form of operational research. Operational research is the use of model building to represent real-life problems. The models are then manipulated in order to attempt to discover an optimum solution to the problem being represented. The operational research approach to problem solving is shown in Fig 8.8.

CPA shows the best way to go about a project; it identifies the time that the project should take, and it shows the activities where there is slack time available and the activities that are critical, in that they have no leeway at all. The technique was first used in the 1950s, in the USA, for the building of the Polaris missile. The Polaris project was extremely complicated and required the coordination of an enormous number of activities, taking place over many years. No one doubts that the implementation of CPA to the problem was a great aid to the successful completion of the project.

It is probably easiest to describe the workings of CPA by taking a project and using it as an example. Let us consider the building of an extension to a small house and the steps that would be taken in a critical path analysis.

The first steps are to identify the activities that make up the project and to determine, for each activity, what other activities need to be completed before it can be started and what activities depend upon the completion of the activity before they can start. Using our example, if we assume that planning

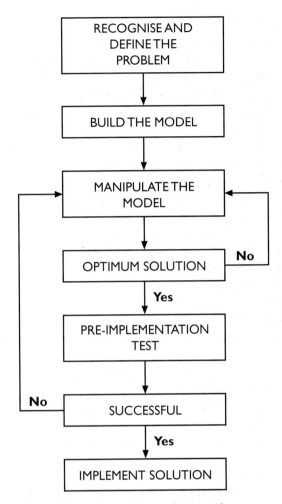

Fig 8.8 *The operational research approach*

permission has already been granted, then we might show the activities and the dependencies as in the table overleaf.

We can see that there are 13 main activities that need to be completed in order to build the extension, each designated by a letter, and that the start of certain activities is dependent upon other activities being finished. For example, it is not possible to build the roof frame (F) until the outer shell has been built (D). In the same way, it is not possible to install electricity and gas (J) until the roof has been tiled and guttered (G) and

Activity letter	Activity	Must be preceded by	Duration (days)
A	Clear the ground	–	2
B	Dig the foundations	A	1
C	Put in the base	B	3
D	Build the outer shell	C	7
E	Put in doors and windows	D	3
F	Build roof frame	D	4
G	Tile roof and install guttering	F	3
H	Build interior walls and floors	D	6
J	Install electricity and gas	G, H	4
K	Install plumbing	G, H	5
L	Plaster walls	J, K	4
M	Decorate exterior	E	3
N	Decorate interior	L	7

the interior walls and floors have been built (H).

The next step is to estimate the duration of each activity and this has already been carried out for our example in the table above. So, we can see that building the roof frame (F) is expected to take four days and decorating the exterior (M) is expected to take three days. Once the activities have been identified, the dependencies recognised, and the durations assessed, it is possible to draw the network diagram. This is shown in Fig 8.9.

In order to understand the concept, it is necessary to be aware of the three basic elements that make up any network diagram. These are nodes, activities and dummies. The first element is the node. A node shows the beginning and end of an activity and is depicted by a circle. The circle is usually split into three parts. The first part, on the left hand side of the node, contains a number that identifies the node. These numbers may be allocated in any sensible manner, but usually from left to right, as in Fig 8.9. The right hand half of the node is split into two segments. The top segment shows the earliest start time (EST) of the activity that is to follow. The bottom segment shows the latest

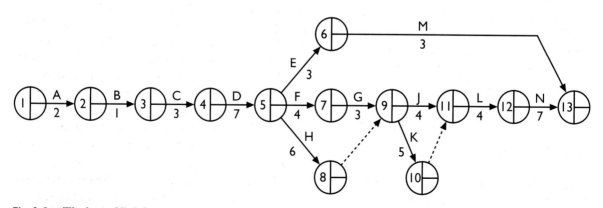

Fig 8.9   *The basic CPA diagram*

finish time (LFT) of the activity that has finished at the node. An example of a node is shown in Fig 8.10 and the concepts of EST and LFT will be dealt with later.

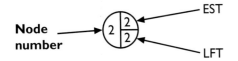

Fig 8.10 *A basic node*

The second element is the activity. An activity is any part of a project that uses up time and/or resources. It is shown by an arrow and runs from left to right. The length of the arrow has no bearing on the duration of the activity. The activity is normally depicted by a letter, which is placed on top of the arrow. The duration of the activity is normally shown by a figure placed under the arrow, below the activity letter. An example is shown in Fig 8.11.

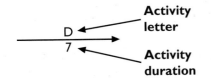

Fig 8.11 *An activity arrow*

The final element is the dummy. This is used where an activity depends upon two or more activities to finish before it can begin. It is also not usual to show two activities leaving and arriving at the same nodes and so a dummy is used. A dotted arrow is used to depict a dummy and the arrow has no letter and a timespan of zero. As we shall see later, a dummy may become part of the critical path. A dummy is shown in Fig 8.12.

Fig 8.12 *A dummy*

If we now consider the basic diagram in Fig 8.9, we can see examples of nodes, activities and dummies. The nodes and the activities are straightforward, but the dummies should be explained. Activity H can start at the same time as F. Activity G needs F to finish before it can begin and J needs both H and G to finish before it begins. By using the dummy between H and G, it is possible to start H at the right time and yet still show the dependence of J on H and G. Activity L requires J and K to be finished before it can begin. If a dummy was not used, J and K would start from node 9 and end at node 11. This would be confusing because they have different durations and so node 10 and the dummy between nodes 10 and 11 are used. This is especially important, as we shall see later, because it enables the critical path to be shown properly.

Once we have the basic diagram, the next step is to calculate the minimum length of the project, by working out the earliest possible start times (ESTs) for each of the activities. A figure of 0 is placed in the upper right hand segment of node 1. After that, the ESTs for the other nodes are calculated by working from right to left, adding the activity time for the next activity to its EST in order to get the EST for the following activity. If there is more than one activity entering a node, the highest EST figure is the one that should be taken as the EST for that node. The ESTs for our example are shown in Fig 8.13.

The diagram shows how simple the method is. We start at node 1 with a value of 0 and then add the duration for activity A. This gives us an EST of 2 for node 2. This means that the earliest that activity B can possibly start is on day 2. In the same way, the earliest that activity C can start is day 3, and so on. Node 9 gives an example of what happens when two activities end at the same node. Activity G gives an EST of 20 for node 9 (17 + 3) and the dummy from node 8 gives an EST of 19 at node 9 (19 + 0). Thus, the higher value of 20 is taken. The same process applies to nodes 11 and 13. The minimum length for the project is shown by the EST in

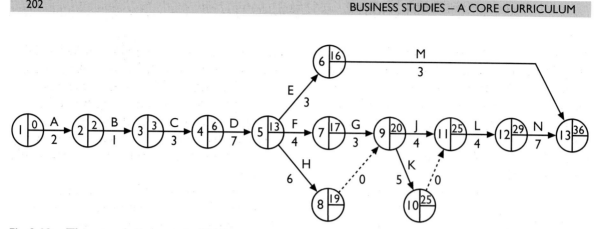

Fig 8.13   *The network diagram plus ESTs*

the final node, which means that the building of the extension should take 36 days.

The final step is to calculate the latest finish times (LFTs) for the activities and then to identify the critical path. The LFT shows the latest time that an activity can finish if it is not going to extend the minimum length of the project. The first step is to give the last node of the project an LFT equal to its EST. It is then necessary to work backwards, from right to left, subtracting the length of the activity from the LFT of the node at the point of the arrow, in order to get the LFT at the node at the start of the arrow. Where a node has more than one arrow starting from it, the lowest figure should be chosen. The process is continued until node 1 is reached, where the LFT must be 0.

Once this has been done, it is possible to identify the critical path. The critical path is the route through the network diagram where there is absolutely no leeway, where activities cannot be delayed without extending the length of the whole project, where the ESTs are equal to the LFTs. The critical path is shown on the network diagram by two parallel lines drawn through the critical activity arrows. It can also be described by node numbers and/or activity letters. The LFTs and critical path for our example are shown in Fig 8.14.

Node 13 is the final node and has an EST of 36 and so the first step is to make the LFT 36 as well. The LFT for node 12 is then calculated by taking the duration of N, 7 days, away from the LFT at node 13 to

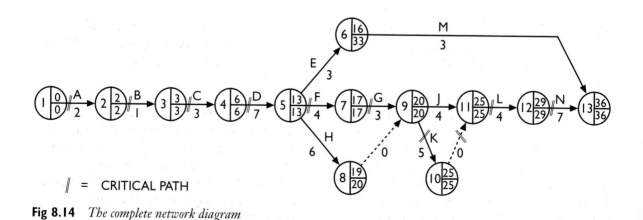

║ = CRITICAL PATH

Fig 8.14   *The complete network diagram*

get the figure of 29 (36 − 7) for the LFT at node 12. This process is carried on from right to left. Node 9 is an example of what happens when two activity arrows go back into the same node. The arrow from node 11, representing activity J, gives an LFT value of 21 (25 − 4). The arrow from node 10, representing activity K, gives an LFT value of 20 (25 − 5). As we said earlier, the lower value is taken and so the LFT at node 9 is 20. The same process takes place at node 5.

Once all of the LFTs have been calculated, it is possible to identify the critical activities, and thus the critical path. In this case, the critical activities are A–B–C–D–F–G–K–L–N. This is therefore, the critical path. It should be noted that it actually passes through the dummy between nodes 10 and 11. The critical path may also be identified by node numbers and so this would be 1–2–3–4–5–7–9–10–11–12–13. There is a slight problem in identifying the critical path around nodes 9, 10, and 11. Although the ESTs and LFTs are the same for all three nodes, closer inspection shows that activity J actually has some leeway, because it only takes 4 days and the gap between nodes 9 and 11 is 5 days. This means that it cannot be a critical activity.

Once the network has been drawn, all of the figures calculated and the critical path identified, the real use of CPA can be seen. CPA is both a planning tool and a means of monitoring progress. Once the project begins, the network diagram can be used to compare actual and planned progress and then to deal with any problems that might arise.

If, at the outset, it is found that the project is to take too long, then plans can be made to reduce the length of the project. To do this, it will have to be critical activities that are reduced. Also, it must be remembered that reducing the duration of a critical activity might lead to other activities in the network becoming critical. Thus, in Fig 8.14, we can see that reducing the length of critical activity D, build the outer shell, by three days would reduce the length of the whole project by three days. However, if the length of critical activity K was reduced by three days, this would not have the same effect, since activity J would become critical and only one day would be saved.

The leeway, or lack of it, for all activities can be calculated and is known as the 'float'. There are two types of float that are calculated.

1 **Total float** This is the amount of time that an activity can be delayed before it extends the duration of the whole project. Critical activities will always have total floats of 0. The total float for any activity is calculated by the formula:

$$\textbf{Total float} = \textbf{LFT at end of}$$
$$\textbf{activity} - \textbf{duration of activity} - \textbf{EST at}$$
$$\textbf{start of activity}$$

Thus, for example, the total float of activity M in our example would be $36 - 3 - 16 = 17$ days.

2 **Free float** This is the amount of time that an activity can be delayed before it extends the earliest start time of the next activity. Critical activities will always have free floats of 0. The free float for an activity is calculated by the formula:

$$\textbf{Free float} = \textbf{EST at end of}$$
$$\textbf{activity} - \textbf{duration of activity} - \textbf{EST at}$$
$$\textbf{start of activity}$$

Thus, for example, the free float of activity J in our example would be $25 - 4 - 20 = 1$ day. It is worth remembering that the total float on any activity will always be equal to, or greater than, the free float. If you calculate the free float to be larger than the total float for any activity, then the calculation must be wrong!

The floats for the whole example are shown below.

Activity letter	Total float (LFT − duration − EST)	Free float (EST − duration − EST)
A	0	0
B	0	0
C	0	0
D	0	0
E	17	0
F	0	0
G	0	0
H	1	0
J	1	1
K	0	0
L	0	0
M	17	17
N	0	0

We can see that most of the activities are critical. However, if problems arise, there might be a chance to delay activities E and M and to move workforce to the critical activities that have a problem.

In more complicated networks, the concepts of earliest finish time (EFT) and latest start time (LST) are also introduced. The earliest finish time is simply the earliest that an activity can be finished and is calculated by the EST + duration for the activity. The latest start time is the latest that an activity can be started without going beyond the LFT and so is LFT − the duration for the activity.

The following table shows the EST, EFT, LST and LFT for each activity in our example.

Activity	EST	EFT	LST	LFT
A	0	2	0	2
B	2	3	2	3
C	3	6	3	6
D	6	13	6	13
E	13	16	30	33
F	13	17	13	17
G	17	20	17	20
H	13	19	14	20
J	20	24	21	25
K	20	25	20	25
L	25	29	25	29
M	16	19	33	36
N	29	36	29	36

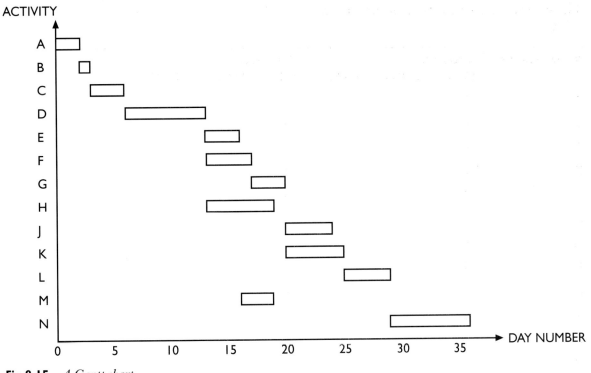

Fig 8.15 *A Gantt chart*

Gantt charts

Henry L. Gantt (1861–1919) worked with F.W. Taylor for a time. He was an advocate of implementing effective methods of planning and control and his chart is probably his best-known contribution.

The Gantt chart is a form of horizontal bar chart, where each activity is shown as a bar and the time scale for the project is on the horizontal axis. The activities are shown in the right order and also reflect the dependencies between them. In this way, it is possible to plan the project and then, most importantly, to compare actual progress with planned progress and thus control the project.

Figure 18.15 shows how a Gantt chart can be used to give an alternative visual representation of a network analysis. In this case, the chart shows the example that was used in the previous section.

MARKS & SPENCER DECIDE ON STORE LOCATION

Marks & Spencer is one of the world's most successful retail chains, merchandising clothing, household furnishings and food. Within its stores, Marks & Spencer aim to offer their consumers high quality products, in a comfortable, attractive environment. The location, design and layout of their stores has to be absolutely right in order to achieve this. The company has to consider all these aspects when it is opening new stores and also when it is redeveloping existing stores. The key factors Marks & Spencer needs to take into account when it is opening new stores are as follows.

1 **Number of potential consumers**   A store should be located so that it is easily accessible to as many consumers as possible.
2 **Selling space**   The site has to offer a sufficiently large selling space that matches the potential number of customers who will visit the store.
3 **Cost**   The cost of buying and developing the site has to be at a level that the potential profit generated by the store over time can support.
4 **Frontage**   The store's frontage must be wide and attractive to reflect the products that are on sale inside.
5 **Access for deliveries**   The store must be accessible so that it can easily take deliveries of products.

During the 1980s more and more retailers, including Marks & Spencer, sought to develop sites 'out of town' on greenfield sites. These major shopping developments, including the Metro Centre in Gateshead, Meadowhall in Sheffield and Lakeside in London, have offered Marks & Spencer the types of site that fulfil the factors outlined above.

QUESTIONS

1 a Discuss two other factors, apart from the ones discussed above, that you think Marks & Spencer should take into account when locating its stores. [10]
  b Analyse the factors that would determine the cost of developing a particular site. [10]

  c Analyse the locational factors that would determine the potential revenue that could be earned by a store. [10]

2 Discuss the advantages and disadvantages of Marks & Spencer relocating a high street store to an out of town site. [10]

Total [40]

ALLIED BAKERIES – BREAD PRODUCTION

Allied Bakeries is part of one of the world's largest food producers, Associated British Foods. Allied Bakeries produce a number of well known brand names, including Sunblest, Allinson and Hi bran. The company produces its products from a number of large bakeries located throughout the country. Each bakery produces bread that is supplied directly to local retailers through an extremely extensive distribution network. The retailers Allied supplies range from small, independent grocer shops, to large, multiple retailers. Indeed, Allied supply many major supermarket chains, such as Marks & Spencer, with their own label bread.

The production process

The bread produced by Allied begins its life as raw ingredients, many of which are bought in from a sister company in the Associated British Food group, called Allied Mills. Before production is started, the amount of each brand of bread that needs to be produced that day has to be decided. The quantities of each product to be produced are called production runs.

Production begins with the mixing of ingredients. This is tightly controlled through guidelines set by the company on specific weights of each ingredient used in a given quantity of bread that is going to be produced. Once the bread dough has been mixed it is put into individual bread tins. This is a completely automated process which is carried out by releasing a set quantity of dough into each tin.

When the dough is in the tin it passes into large ovens to be baked. The bread moves through the large ovens for a set period of time. When it has passed through the ovens, the bread is automatically removed from its tin by machine. The bread then passes through a cooling process. After it is cooled, the bread is put through automatic slicing machines, and then bagging machines. The bagged bread is then packed into bread trays and finally moved into the distribution department.

The diagram below illustrates the production process.

Throughout the process the quality of the bread is checked, so that the quality of the final output meets set minimum standards.

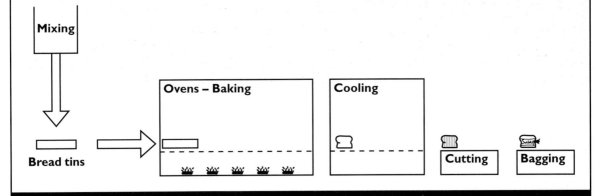

QUESTIONS

1 a Briefly describe each of the following types of production: job, batch, and flow. [10]

b What type of production does Allied Bakeries use to produce bread? [2]

c Explain why this type of production has to be used in the production of bread by Allied Bakeries. [6]

d In what circumstances would bread be produced using another type of production, other than the production method used by Allied Bakeries? [7]

2 a What do you understand by the term 'production efficiency'? [5]

b In the case of Allied Bakeries, how could you go about measuring production efficiency at one of their bakeries? [8]

c Explain what you understand by the term 'lean production'. [5]

d How could Allied Bakeries apply just-in-time techniques to improve their production efficiency? [7]

3 a What do you understand by the term 'quality control'? [5]

b For each stage of the production process for bread, outline how quality control could be implemented. [10]

c Outline a strategy Allied Bakeries could use to improve the quality of the products it produces. [15]

Total [80]

ACD VIDEO LTD ORGANISE A MAJOR CONTRACT

ACD Video Ltd is the market leader in the design and installation of close circuit television. The company has achieved a huge increase in turnover and profits over the last four years. Much of this increase is due to an increase in demand from security companies, who use CCTV extensively. ACD Video has recently won a major contract to design, assemble and install a security camera system in a city centre. The activities required to complete the project are shown in the table opposite. Each activity's duration, cost per week and interrelationships are also set out in the table.

ACD's managing director, Amrish Sharma, has looked carefully at the plans for this project because he is keen to make sure the project is completed on time. There is a penalty clause built into the contract of £1,000 per week for each week the project runs over maximum time for its completion of 50 weeks. Amrish believes that time could be saved if ACD carried stocks of camera components and housing materials, rather than having to order them for each project individually. However, the company's production director believes this is not technically possible.

Activity	Preceded by	Description	Duration (weeks)	Cost of reducing one week (£)
A		Design camera	9	5,000
B		Design camera housing	5	1,000
C	A	Order camera components	6	2,000
D	A	Acquire patents	5	2,000
E	B	Order housing materials	3	1,000
F	C	Camera prototype	10	3,000
G	D	Health and safety audit	9	4,000
H	E	Camera housing prototype	8	1,000
I	G, F	Assemble cameras	7	6,000
J	G, H	Manufacture housing	10	6,000
K	I, J	Assemble final product	6	8,000
L	K	Locate on sites	8	8,000

QUESTIONS

1 a Draw a network diagram for the project. [7]
 b Calculate the earliest starting time (EST) for each task and the minimum time for the whole project. [7]
 c Calculate the latest finishing time (LFT) for each task. [7]
 d Determine the critical path. [5]
 e Calculate total floats for each activity. [7]
 f What would be the penalty cost of a five week delay in the delivery of camera components? [7]

2 a The project manager would like to reduce the duration of the project by five weeks. No single activity may be reduced by more than two weeks. Showing full working, calculate the cheapest method of achieving this reduction. [8]
 b Does the critical path remain the same after the reduction of five weeks? Identify any new critical path. [7]

3 a Explain carefully what you understand by stock-holding costs and stockout costs. [10]
 b How could ACD try to establish its optimum stock level? [10]
 c What problems would ACD face in trying to do this? [7]
 d Suggest why ACD's project director believes it is not possible to reduce the duration of the CCTV installation for the city centre by holding stocks of camera accessories and housing materials. [8]

Total [90]

BADEN AND CLARKE DEVELOP A NEW PRODUCTION SITE

Baden and Clarke PLC manufacture burglar alarm systems. They are an established company in the market with a turnover of £38 million. Most of the systems they produce are for the domestic household market, although they have recently decided to develop a new production site to manufacture alarms for the commercial market. Alan White, the company's production director, has recently been on a tour of factories in Japan, where he has been looking at a number of production techniques they use, in the hope of employing them in their new factory. Alan was particularly interested in the application of total quality management (TQM) and just-in-time (JIT).

In planning the proposed production site and setting up production, the company's Alan White and his team have broken down each stage of the project into the following tasks.

Task letter	Task	Must be preceded by	Duration (weeks)
A	Clear the site	–	2
B	Order and take delivery of building materials	–	3
C	Order and take delivery of machinery	–	16
D	Dig the foundations	A	3
E	Build the shell	B, D	5
F	Put on the roof	E	2
G	Install gas and electricity	F	2
H	Install plumbing	F	3
I	Install the machinery	C, G	3
J	Decorate the building	I, H	2
K	Appoint the workforce	J	5

QUESTIONS

1 a What do you understand by the just-in-time approach to stock management? [5]

b What benefits do you think Baden and Clarke PLC might derive from using just-in-time stock management? [8]

c Discuss the problems Baden and Clarke PLC might face when trying to apply just-in-time stock management. [7]

2 a Explain what you understand by total quality management. [5]

b What benefits do you think Baden and Clarke PLC might derive from using total quality management? [8]

c Discuss the problems Baden and Clarke PLC might face when trying to apply total quality management. [7]

3 a Draw a network diagram for the project. [7]

b Calculate the earliest starting time (EST) for each task and the minimum time for the whole project. [7]

c Calculate the latest finishing time (LFT) for each task. [7]

d Determine the critical path. [5]

e Calculate total floats for each activity. [7]

4 a Draw a Gantt chart to represent each activity within the project. [7]

b Evaluate the usefulness of Gantt charts and network analysis for business decision making. [10]

Total [90]

SUMMARY

1 A market exists where buyers and sellers come together in order to trade a good or service.

2 Market growth usually measures the percentage increase in the sales turnover of the whole market. Market share is the percentage of market sales that are accounted for by an individual firm in that market. Market segmentation takes place where the market is split up into a number of segments, either geographically, demographically or psychographically.

3 Marketing is finding out what consumers want and then supplying it.

4 Marketing research covers research into every aspect of the marketing process. Market research is a sub-set of marketing research.

5 The marketing mix consists of four, or five, variables – product, price, promotion, place and packaging.

6 Effective products should be a mixture of functionally sound, aesthetically sound and capable of economic production.

7 Pricing may be demand-based, cost-based, or competition-based. Different pricing approaches might be adopted for new products.

8 The promotional mix is a combination of advertising, sales promotion, personal selling and publicity.

9 Distribution covers three main areas, physical distribution, distribution channels and customer service.

10 Marketing planning is essential and should include analysis of the present situation, a SWOT analysis, the making of assumptions and the setting of marketing objectives, the devising of a strategy and the measurement of results.

A market exists where buyers and sellers come together in order to trade a good or service. The market may not have a physical existence, since the deals may take place over the telephone or by post, but the concept of a market is still of great importance. If a market is identified, then firms can aim their products at that market or at a specific part of that market.

THE MARKET AND MARKETING

Market growth and market share

The size of a market can be measured in a number of ways, but the most common method is to measure the aggregated sales turnover of all the firms involved. By measuring the market size over time, it is possible to measure market growth. Market growth usually measures the percentage increase in the sales turnover of the whole market. Markets exist within the economy as a whole and so, if the economy is not growing, market growth can only take place in one market at the expense of another market. This highlights the competitive nature of business.

Market share is usually measured as the percentage of market sales that are accounted for by an individual firm in that market. If the market is static, then it is only possible for a firm to increase its market share at the expense of another firm. This again highlights the competitive nature of business.

Figure 9.1 shows the concepts of market growth and market share. Obviously, the best situation would be for a firm to be gaining market share in a market that is experiencing market growth, in an economy that is also growing. The drive for market share is an essential element of the importance of marketing.

Market aggregation and market segmentation

Market aggregation simply refers to the whole market for a good or service. If a firm was to adopt an aggregated approach to its marketing, then the firm would treat the whole market as being the same and adopt a single marketing strategy for the whole market. This marketing approach is sometimes known as the 'shotgun' approach. This approach only tends to be effective in markets where the products are basic and where there are minimal geographic, demographic and psychographic differences in the purchasers. It is difficult these days to find this sort of market. Perhaps the market for safety matches might come close to being an example?

Market segmentation takes place where the market is split up into a number of segments.

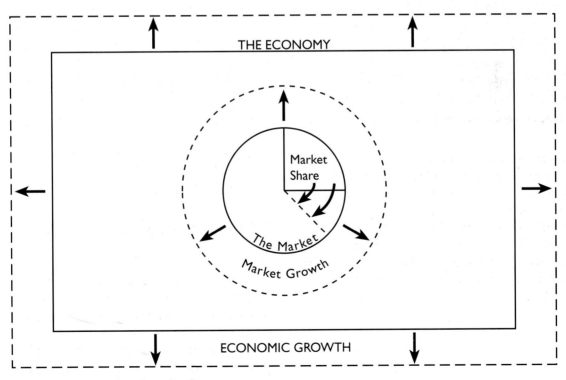

Fig 9.1 *Market growth and market share*

Once this has been done, firms may choose to simply concentrate upon one segment. However, the firm may alternatively choose to operate in more than one segment, but to adopt a different marketing strategy in each of the segments chosen. This approach is sometimes known as the 'rifle' approach. Products are aimed at specific market niches and an attempt is made to give them a unique position within that niche, in terms of the features of the product. The main aim is to discover a unique selling proposition (USP) which is a feature that clearly distinguishes a product from the rest of those available.

Market segmentation may be carried out in three main ways.

1 **Geographic**   Firms may feel that tastes vary in different geographic regions and so they may split their total market into different areas and then market each area in a specific manner. In this way, a national brewing company might split the country into different regions and offer alternative brands to each region, highlighting regional differences in tastes and attitudes. Smaller firms may just concentrate upon one geographic region.

2 **Demographic**   Here, the market is segmented by factors relating to the population, such as age, sex, income and ethnic background. It is the most common basis for segmentation. If adopting this approach, the national brewing company might promote a beer as being best suited to younger people, such as alco-pops, or they might promote a beer directed primarily at women.

3 **Psychographic**   This provides three common bases for segmentation: social class structure, personality characteristics and lifestyles. The brewing market mentioned earlier might be segmented on a social class basis, with different beers being aimed at different perceived social classes.

The advantages of segmentation are many.

Firms are able to allocate their resources, especially those involved in marketing, more efficiently. They can gain a good understanding of their market, because they are dealing with a smaller, more specific area and, because of this, they are able to respond quickly to changes in market trends.

The advantages of segmentation are large and so there are only a few situations where segmentation is not worthwhile. The first is where the total market is so small, and worth relatively so little, that there is no economic sense in splitting it into smaller markets. The second is where the main users of the product account for such a high proportion of total sales that it is not worth targeting other users. The final situation is where the major product accounts for such a high proportion of total sales that, again, it is not worth targeting other areas.

What is marketing?

Marketing might be looked upon as the link between production and consumption. Efficient marketing ensures that a firm supplies its market with the goods or services that the would-be consumers in the market wish to purchase. Kotler described marketing as '. . . a human activity directed at satisfying needs and wants through exchange processes'. Put more simply, it has been said that marketing is finding out what customers want and then supplying it.

Marketing research and market research

As was said in Unit 4, there seems to be a great deal of confusion between the terms marketing research and market research. However, in reality, the difference is easy to understand. Market research is simply a sub-set of marketing research.

Marketing research covers research into every aspect of the marketing process. The

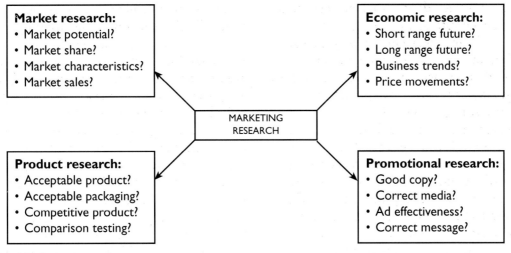

Market research:
• Market potential?
• Market share?
• Market characteristics?
• Market sales?

Economic research:
• Short range future?
• Long range future?
• Business trends?
• Price movements?

MARKETING
RESEARCH

Product research:
• Acceptable product?
• Acceptable packaging?
• Competitive product?
• Comparison testing?

Promotional research:
• Good copy?
• Correct media?
• Ad effectiveness?
• Correct message?

Fig 9.2 *Marketing research*

main areas covered under marketing research are shown in Fig 9.2.

Market research is the analysis of the actual, or potential, market for a good or service. Marketing research includes additional research into the product, the promotional vehicles, and the economic and business environment.

Market research has been looked at in detail in Unit 4, including the difference between data and information, research methods and sampling methods.

THE MARKETING MIX

The marketing mix is normally said to consist of the four variables, product, price, promotion and place, which make up a marketing strategy. These variables are often called the four Ps. However, whilst it has been the custom to include packaging under the heading of promotion, a number of writers on marketing are now talking of five Ps and treating packaging as a variable in its own right.

Product

A product is something that is able to fulfil a consumer's need or want. Many would argue that the product is the most important element of the marketing mix, because if the product does not give the customer what he or she wants, then it will not be purchased.

The product will usually evolve from a combination of factors. Market research will tell the producers what the customers want and then whether the proposed product satisfies their wishes. Research and development will eventually create the product and operations management will then produce it. The usual sequence of events in the generation of a new product is shown in Fig 9.3.

Product ideas are developed and then a choice is made as to which ones should be considered. The market is then researched in order to find if there is a potential market for the product. If there appears to be a market for the product, the firm will then attempt to build a prototype. This will identify any potential production problems and give some idea of costs. If economic production is possible, then the product will often be tried

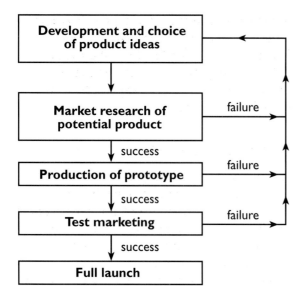

Fig 9.3   *The development sequence of a new product*

out in a test market; a small geographical area that is, hopefully, representative of the whole potential market. If this is a success, then a full launch, to the whole market, will normally occur. It is clear from Fig 9.3 that there are many points at which the development of a product can fail and this explains, to some extent, why new products have such a high failure rate. As a general rule of thumb, fewer than a third of new products that actually make the market place survive for more than two years.

Products usually need to fulfil three basic requirements, if they are to be considered as worthwhile.

1   **They must be functionally sound**   Products must be fit for the purpose that they have been bought to satisfy. If a product does not fulfil its purpose, then it is unlikely that it will be purchased more than once. A waterproof jacket that lets water in, or a depth-resistant watch that fails to operate, would soon be discarded and not replaced.

2   **They must be aesthetically sound**   Products need to be visually appealing, although the importance of this will very much depend upon the type of product and its cost. People do not expect a cheap pen to be too attractive, they simply want it to work efficiently. On the other hand, expensive clothing will only be purchased if it is aesthetically pleasing.

3   **They must be capable of economic production**   As we have said, products must be capable of being produced at a cost that will mean that a profit margin can be added and customers will be prepared to pay the resultant price. If this is not the case, the product can be the best in the world, but it will not sell and so it will not be produced.

The Boston matrix

The Boston matrix was devised by the Boston Consulting Group in the USA. It is a visual means of showing the possible routes that a new product might take through its life, in terms of market growth and market share. The diagram is shown in Fig 9.4.

New products usually begin in the problem child (wildcat) segment of the diagram. They

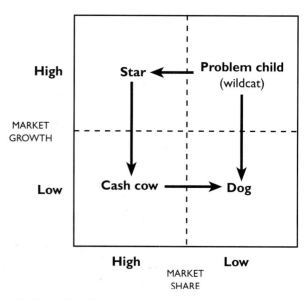

Fig 9.4   *The Boston matrix*

have a relatively low market share in a high-growth market. The hope is that, with relevant investment, the product will move on to be a star and then a cash cow. Sadly, as we know, the great majority of new products move straight from this segment to being dogs. Dogs are products that hold a low market share in low-growth markets. They have little future and, unless they are a necessary part of the product mix of the company, perhaps an essential complementary product for a very profitable item, they will be discontinued very quickly.

If a problem child product becomes successful, in the short run, it moves into the star quadrant. Here, the product is gaining a high market share in a market that also has high growth. The product generates high levels of cash but, because the market is fast growing, it is necessary to invest high levels of cash in order to maintain or increase the product's market share. Thus, although turnover is high, profits are not necessarily the same.

As the star market growth begins to slow down, the product moves into the final quadrant, the cash cow. Here, the market is mature, with low growth, and the product has a high market share. Little investment is necessary to maintain the market share and large cashflows are generated, so the product becomes very profitable. Part of these profits will, hopefully, be used to generate new products, some of which might achieve the same level of success.

The product life cycle

Another way of depicting the life of a product over its existence is the product life cycle. This breaks down the life of a normal product into six development stages. It shows the development in terms of profits, or sales revenue, over time. Figure 9.5 shows a product life cycle expressed in terms of profit over time.

The first stage is development, where there is no income and so losses are made. Thus, the profit line is below zero. In the second stage, the product is being introduced to the market, either in a partial sense, through a test market, or fully. Profits are slow to develop, because promotional expenditure is high. Many products do not get beyond this stage and fail. However, if they do so, then the next stage is growth. Here, both market share and market growth are high and profits begin to rise. Eventually, the market growth slows and

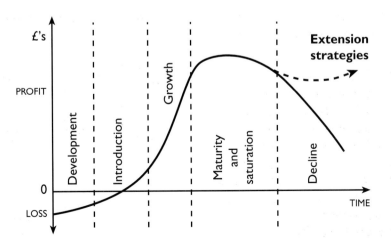

Fig 9.5 *The product life cycle*

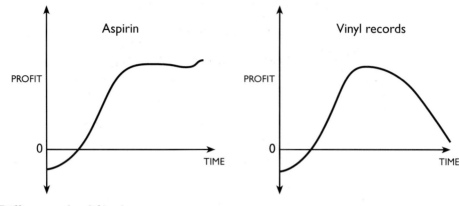

Fig 9.6   *Different product life cycles*

the maturity and saturation stages are reached. High levels of cashflow and, hopefully, profits are achieved here as the product enjoys a high market share in a stable market. Eventually, although not always, the demand for the product will begin to decline. This point may be delayed if successful extension strategies can be devised. These may take the form of redesigning the product or the packaging, searching for new markets, searching for new uses for the product or developing add-on products.

The actual shape of the product life cycle curve will vary for every product, as will the length of each of the stages. The main factors will be the arrival of new products, changes in technology, changes in tastes and changes in consumer income and expenditure. For example, the product life cycles for aspirin and vinyl records might appear as they do in Fig 9.6.

It is interesting, and informative, to attempt to combine the Boston matrix and the product life cycle. If this is done, then the outcome will resemble Fig 9.7.

The problem child segment of the matrix coincides with the development and introduction stages of the product life cycle. As introduction takes place, we would expect the firm to keep high stocks, to avoid stockouts, and we would expect promotion to

be informative, attempting to create awareness. The pricing strategy may be either high or low. If the product is unique, then a high price may be set to 'skim' the market. Otherwise, a low price may be set in an attempt to build market share rapidly. In the growth segment, coinciding with star, promotion should be moving towards being persuasive, building brand loyalty, and prices should level out. Maturity and saturation stages coincide with cash cows, where promotion becomes defensive, non-price competition becomes common, and extension strategies are considered. The decline stage, if extension strategies do not work, coincides with the dog. Products may, of course, come straight here from the problem child segments. Firms should be aware that products will rarely sell forever, so they should endeavour to create a sensible product portfolio. This is sometimes also known as the product mix. The product portfolio is the total range of products and/or brands that are produced by a single firm. In an attempt to spread risk, firms will have a balanced portfolio in which, ideally, there would be products that related to different markets and to different stages of the product life cycle or Boston matrix. In this way, a slump in one market can be balanced by a surge in another one, and products in their mature stages can

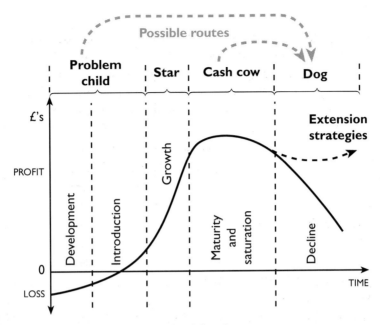

Fig 9.7   *The Boston matrix combined with the product life cycle*

be used to fund the emergence of new, and hopefully successful, stars.

Price

Price is the amount of money that a consumer is prepared to pay in order to take possession of a good, service, asset or resource. Price is an important element in the marketing mix and the price set for a product can lead to its success or ruin. There are four basic approaches to pricing and we shall look at each of them in turn.

Demand-based pricing

In this case, the price charged is the one which it is thought the market will bear. However, this is not necessarily an easy thing to evaluate. In many cases, a middle price is chosen and sales revenue is lost because the best price would have been lower, or indeed, higher. The relationship between price and quantity demanded is usually inverse. In most

cases, as price rises demand falls and as price falls, demand rises. This is shown by a demand curve, which usually slopes downwards, from left to right. An example of a demand curve is shown in Fig 9.8.

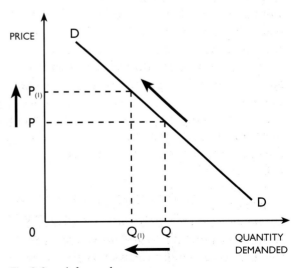

Fig 9.8   *A demand curve*

Remember that whilst price is a determinant of demand, demand is not a determinant of price. This means that although a rise in price leads to a fall in demand, it does not follow that a fall in demand should lead to a rise in price. The relationship is not two way.

Price elasticity of demand

The relationship between demand and price can be measured, albeit with difficulty, via the concept of price elasticity of demand (PED). This uses the simple formula below.

Price elasticity of demand (PED) =

Percentage change in quantity demanded
Percentage change in price

If a firm were to raise the price of its good from 20p to 25p and discover that the demand for the product fell from 20,000 units to 18,000 units, then the price elasticity of demand could be calculated as:

$$PED = \frac{-10\%}{+25\%} = -0.4$$

The value of PED is usually negative, because of the inverse relationship between price and quantity demanded. The example gives a PED of −0.4, which means that the demand for the good changes by a smaller percentage than the price. A one percent change in price will only lead to a 0.4 percent change in quantity demanded. The lower the value of price elasticity, the less responsive demand will be to changes in price.

If a good has a PED value between 0 and 1, then the demand is said to be inelastic. This means that demand is not very responsive to changes in price. If this is the case, then the sales revenue can be increased by raising price. In our example above, where demand is inelastic, the sales revenue rises from £4,000 (20p × 20,000) to £4,500 (25p × 18,000), when the price is raised. However, it should be remembered that the price cannot be raised indefinitely, because PED becomes more elastic as price rises.

If a good has a PED value between 1 and infinity, then the demand is said to be elastic. This means that demand is very responsive to changes in price. If this is the case, then the sales revenue can only be increased by lowering price. If we take a PED value of 2 as an example, this means that a one percent fall in price will lead to a two percent increase in demand and thus an increase in sales revenue. An increase in price would lead to a reduction in sales revenue. It must be remembered that sales revenue is not the same as profit and that PED only indicates the probable effect on sales revenue.

If a good has a PED value equal to 1, then the demand is said to be unitary. This means that demand changes by the same, but opposite, percentage as price. If this is the case, then the sales revenue will be constant when price is altered, because any change in price is countered by the equal and opposite resultant change in quantity demanded.

Other factors influencing price

The demand for a good can be influenced by a number of factors other than price. The price of other goods, both complements and substitutes, will affect the demand for a good. For example, let us consider the case of beef and assume that chicken is a substitute for it and that horseradish sauce is a complement. It is then easy to see that a fall in the price of chicken might well lead to a fall in the demand for beef and vice versa. Thus, we can conclude that changes in the price of a substitute will affect the demand for a good. In the same way, a fall in the price of horseradish sauce might lead to an increase in the demand for it and, therefore, an increase in demand for beef which is a complement. However, the effect would not be too great because beef is much the more expensive member of the relationship. It would be sensible to conclude that changes in the price of beef would have a greater effect upon the demand for horseradish sauce than the other way around.

Another determinant of demand is consumer income. For most goods, as income rises, so will demand. There are some exceptions. Necessity goods, such as salt or bread, tend to have limits to consumption and so repeated rises in income do not lead to increases in demand above a certain level of income. Inferior goods usually suffer a fall in demand as income rises. They tend to be purchased by people on low incomes and, when their income rises, they respond by switching their demand to goods that they consider to be superior.

Consumer tastes also determine demand and these can be influenced by successful promotion, which is why firms spend so much on their promotional budgets. Further factors influencing demand are the size of the population and the changing age structure within it, government policy on such things as interest and tax rates, and seasonal factors.

The major weakness of demand-based pricing is the fact that a demand curve is so hard to draw, in reality. The other weakness is that the price takes no account of the cost of producing the good or supplying the service.

Cost-based pricing

There are a number of methods of cost-based pricing, but all of them seem to involve the calculation of a unit price and then the addition of a mark-up. The problem revolves around the calculation of the unit price.

One method, known as full cost pricing, or absorption cost pricing, attempts to allocate all costs, both direct and indirect, to individual units. The indirect, or fixed, costs are allocated on a logical basis, such as factory space occupied, and then the agreed profit margin is added. The main weakness of this method is that it assumes that all units are going to be sold and it takes no notice of the

actual price that the market is prepared to pay. It is also true that the price will vary with the method by which the fixed costs are allocated.

Another method is contribution cost pricing, which is also known as marginal cost pricing. In this case, only the variable unit cost is calculated and then a price is set that should cover the variable cost and make a contribution to the fixed costs. If enough units are sold, then the total contributions should cover the fixed costs and, after that, any extra units are providing profit instead of contribution. Again, the weakness is the fact that no notice is taken of the price that the market is prepared to pay.

Competition-based pricing

In many markets, it is normal for the basic level of price to be set by the largest producer. This process is known as price leadership. If firms produce similar products, then it follows that they must be aware of what their competitors are charging and react when price changes are made.

Competitive pricing is also said to take place when tendering, or sealed bidding, occurs. This is where firms are asked to offer a price to do a job, such as build a bridge, in secret. The would-be customer then chooses from the bids that have been entered.

Another form of competition-based pricing occurs where firms group together to make price agreements. These groups are known as cartels. In most countries, the formation of price cartels is against the law, but no-one would deny that it still takes place on an unofficial basis. Governments place themselves above such laws and take part in international cartels for the pricing of, for example, oil and air fares.

New product pricing

Different pricing strategies may be used when a new product is being launched. Penetration pricing is where a low price is set, and strong promotion is undertaken, in order to generate high volume demand and thus a high market share. The firm will then benefit from all of the advantages associated with high volumes, such as economies of scale and brand loyalty.

Market skimming describes the situation in which a firm does not expect to have the lead in a market for a long period of time and so sets out to make high, short-term profits by setting a relatively high price in the period before competitors enter the market. The best example of this is the pharmaceutical industry, where firms are given a seven year monopoly on new products under the provisions of the Sainsbury Committee rules. The firms have high development costs, which have to be recouped, and they would not be able to do so without the seven year monopoly. They tend to set high prices for the first five or six years and then to drop their prices just before the entry of competing firms into the market.

In new product markets, and indeed in all markets, psychological pricing is often employed as an addition to another pricing method. Here, the price is set just below a whole number, so that it will appear to be cheaper. For example, a car priced at £9,999 seems to be a lot cheaper than one priced at £10,000.

Promotion

Promotion forms an important part of the marketing mix and should not be overlooked. There is a tendency to think of promotion as being solely advertising, but it is in fact much more than that. There are many ways that company and product information can be communicated, some of which are controllable and some of which are not. Non-controllable communication tends to occur in two main ways. The first is word-of-mouth communication and personal recommendation. Opinions and recommendations passed from person to person can be very influential in affecting

consumer choice. Once a firm has managed to gain the respect and trust of its customers, it can benefit greatly from their opinions, as they pass them on to other people. However, the opposite is also true and a loss of customer confidence can be very damaging. The second main form of non-controllable communication is through independent and objective publicity and journalism. An example of this would be a magazine such as *Which?*. This magazine investigates all sorts of products, ranging from stereo stacks to motor cars, passes opinions upon them and chooses the best buys. Television and investigative reporting in newspapers can also be very influential. The health scare regarding the mineral water Perrier, which was reported in the newspapers, had an extremely damaging effect upon sales.

Controllable methods of promotion are obviously of great importance to firms and can be placed under the general headings of advertising, sales promotion, personal selling and publicity. The promotional mix of a firm is the combination of these methods that it adopts. Often, the funds available will limit the form of the promotional mix. It is best if we look at each of the elements in turn.

Advertising

The term 'advertising' is one that is used very loosely by students and it is important that we begin by giving a precise definition. Advertising is purchased, non-personal communication using mass media, such as television and newspapers. It should not be confused with sales promotion. It is also known as above-the-line promotion. Advertising usually involves three parties. There is the firm that is paying for the advertising, the agency that produces the advertising plan and the media that is used as a vehicle for the advertisement.

There are three main forms of advertising.

Institutional advertising

The first is institutional advertising, where the firm gives information about its activities or tries to improve or create its public image. This advertising does not have the objective of selling a specific product. The advertising might simply be general information about the business, such as opening hour changes or changes in payment methods, and it is known as patronage advertising. The creation of public image is known as public service advertising.

Product advertising

The second main form of advertising is product advertising, where a firm tries to inform the market about a specific product or service. There are a number of different forms of product advertising. Competitive advertising is where an attempt is made to push the sales of one product at the expense of another; in simpler words, to increase market share. This tends to happen in well established markets, such as the cola market, where Coke and Pepsi are in direct competition. Another form of product advertising is direct-action advertising, where the firm is looking for a quick response from its advertising. This might be an advertisement with a free sample coupon attached. A third form of product advertising is indirect-action advertising, where the firm is attempting to stimulate demand over a longer period of time. Customers are informed that the product exists and it is hoped that, when they do come to buy such a product, then they will buy this one.

Primary advertising

The third main form of advertising is primary advertising. This is an attempt to generate demand for a general category of a product, e.g. meat. It tends to be carried out by trade associations. These are groups sponsored by firms in the same industry, to represent that industry. Thus, the Tea Council produces advertisements that attempt to encourage people to drink more tea, rather than to promote a specific brand of tea.

Obviously, because of its use of mass media, advertising is a very expensive form of promotion and so it is only really available to large organisations.

Sales promotion

This is also known as below-the-line promotion and it is basically the offer of incentives to purchase and/or the creation of features that will lead to consumer interest and brand loyalty. There are many forms of sales promotion, but the most common are immediate and delayed consumer incentives.

Immediate consumer incentives

Immediate consumer incentives are techniques that give an immediate return to the consumer. Examples of these might be price reductions marked on the pack, bonus packs that contain extra quantity for the same price, free samples, multi-pack offers of the 'buy one and get one free' type, the giving of free gifts, money-off coupons and competitions where the consumer can win a prize on the spot, once the purchase has taken place. All of these can be seen in a local supermarket at some point in the year.

Delayed consumer incentives

Delayed consumer incentives are techniques that offer an eventual return to the consumer. Examples of these might be trading stamps which can be exchanged for gifts from a catalogue, tokens which are collected and then sent away for a free gift, refunds which are returned by post after proof of purchase, competitions which require entry and do not have an immediate return and charity offers where the purchase by the consumer leads to a donation to a charity.

Other forms of sales promotions

There are a number of other forms of sales promotion that should be considered. The first of these is point-of-sale (POS) display.

There are many psychological concepts that can be employed at the point-of-sale, such as putting impulse-buy items near to cash tills in garages, where people will have their credit cards in their hands, and putting children's items close to the checkout desks in supermarkets. A second form is branding, where the firm attempts to create a favourable brand image that will lead to brand loyalty from the consumers. If this can be achieved, then the firm may even be able to charge a slightly higher price for the product, known as a premium. Packaging can also be a form of sales promotion and frequent changes may keep customer interest and, again, lead to brand loyalty. Other forms of sales promotion are the offering of credit, exhibitions and sponsorship.

Personal selling

Personal selling involves face to face contact between the customer and the salesperson. This means that the customer has the opportunity to ask questions and to seek advice and the salespeople can alter their sales approach to suit the particular needs of each customer. It is for this reason that firms who are selling industrial goods and services, which are only sold to a small number of professional buyers, concentrate their promotion in personal selling. The modern salesperson plays a very important role in marketing.

There are three main types of personal selling.

Product delivery
The first is product delivery. In this case, the salesperson delivers the good in question, the best example being daily milk deliveries.

Inside-order taking
The second type is known as inside-order taking. This is where the salesperson operates at the selling point, such as in a shop or a car salesroom. The importance of this role has

been recognised a great deal of late and firms are investing large amounts in the training of point-of-sale employees.

Outside-order taking
The third type is outside-order taking. Here, the salespeople go out of the firm to sell the goods and services. The sales representatives have an important, and varied, role to play. They seek out new customers, help with ordering, give advice, supply technical and product knowledge, provide feedback on the products and, above all, build long-term relationships, which create goodwill.

Publicity

This is any promotional message about an organisation and its products, where the message is not paid for by the organisation. It is often thought that publicity must be a good thing, but it is often uncontrollable by the organisation and, if negative, can be very harmful. The effects of the BSE scare on the sales of UK beef are a classic example. Publicity usually takes the form of either a promotional 'plug' made by an individual in a speech or interview, or a news story in some form of mass media. Firms might attempt to gain publicity in a number of ways. First, the firm might release a press statement or a feature article to the mass media in the hope that they will take it up and use it. Second, a representative of the firm might give a presentation to a group audience. This could take the form of a speech, a press conference or a tour of the firm's plant. The third method is where a public figure or celebrity endorses the firm's products.

Promotional strategies
A promotional strategy is an important part of any firm's planning. Promotion should always be coordinated. There are many strategies that could be adopted, but all of them should include the setting of promotional objectives, consideration of the available budget, the

choice of media, the creation of a promotional campaign and an after-campaign evaluation to assess the success or otherwise of the strategy.

The promotional strategy adopted will be influenced by the nature of the product, the stage that it has reached in its product life cycle and the budget available.

Many campaigns work on the simple basis of AIDA (Attention-Interest-Desire-Action). The promotion is organised in such a way as to go through four stages. The first stage is to capture the Attention of the would-be consumer and to make them aware of the product. After this, it is necessary to stimulate Interest and, eventually, a Desire to purchase. In the end, this desire should lead to the Action of making a purchase. AIDA tends to apply itself well to campaigns designed to sell expensive products that are only bought occasionally, such as cars or holidays abroad, but it does not really apply to everyday purchases, such as bread or newspapers. These are known as low-involvement products. Here, once a particular brand of product has been purchased, then further purchases tend to be made out of habit.

Place

The place element of the marketing mix refers to distribution. This is the process of getting goods from the producers to the consumers, in the right quantities and at the right time. Distribution costs account for approximately 20 percent of unit costs and so they are of great importance. Distribution actually covers three main areas: physical distribution, distribution channels and customer service. We shall look at each of these in turn.

Physical distribution

This relates to the physical movement of products from the producers to their eventual destinations. Physical distribution costs are made up of the costs of distribution facilities, such as warehouses, stock and stock-holding costs, transport costs and communication costs.

Distribution channels

These are the routes that a product might follow on its journey from producer to customer. There are three main categories of routes: direct supply routes, short-channel routes and long-channel routes. Different possibilities are shown in Fig 9.9.

Direct supply routes exist where the producer sells direct to the consumer. Although this has always been common in industrial goods markets, it is interesting to note that it is now becoming more common in consumer goods markets as well. The most common method is through mail-order, where goods are advertised in mass media and catalogues. Another method is direct-mail advertising, where leaflets are sent to houses by post or are included in other publications, such as newspapers. A growing form of direct supply is the use of factory shops (or outlets), where the producers set up a shop at the factory and sell direct to customers. The products are able to be sold more cheaply than in retail outlets, because there are not distribution costs attached. Many firms, such as Timberlands and Cristal d'Arques, have adopted this method of distribution.

Short-channel routes tend to involve just the producer, the retailer and the customer. This is probably the most common form of distribution route.

Long-channel routes tend to involve the use of intermediaries between the producer and the retailer. There are two main types of intermediary: wholesalers and agents. Wholesalers perform the function of breaking bulk and holding stock. Many retailers are too small to buy in bulk from producers and so wholesalers do this and then sell in smaller quantities, with a mark-up, to the small retailers. This especially applies to

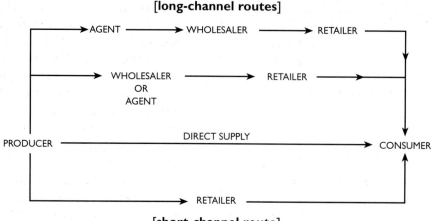

Fig 9.9   *Various distribution channels*

independent high street shops. Agents are people with the authority to enter into a contract on behalf of the producers that they represent. The agent manages relations between customers and the manufacturer, but does not take legal title to the products. They usually operate for a fee or commission. Firms often employ agents in foreign markets, where they do not have outlets or retailers of their own.

Customer service

The main components of customer service are consistency of order cycle time, effective communication between the producer and the consumer, and the level of availability. Basically, the right product must be with the consumer at the right time. Customer service is the service given to a consumer from the time that an order is made, through to the time that the product is delivered.

Choice of distribution channel

The eventual choice of distribution channel selected will depend upon a number of factors. First is the type of market. If it is a widely spread, perhaps national, market, then there will be a need for a great deal of

wholesaling activities and the use of a lot of retailers. The type of product is the second factor. For example, perishable products, such as agricultural goods, will require direct channels to ensure that they reach the marketplace as soon as possible. A third factor will be the size of the producer. Large firms are more likely to be able to carry out their own distribution, as is the case with Coca Cola, who have the largest distribution fleet in the world. The final factor will be, quite simply, cost. The benefits of different distribution channels must be balanced against the costs of using those channels.

◼ MARKETING PLANNING

There are many examples of firms that have failed to develop any sort of marketing strategy and have simply promoted themselves in a haphazard manner. Efficient planning of marketing can do many things for a firm, giving them understanding, identity, purpose and success. There is much more to marketing than simply applying a mix of the four Ps and a suitable guide to the steps

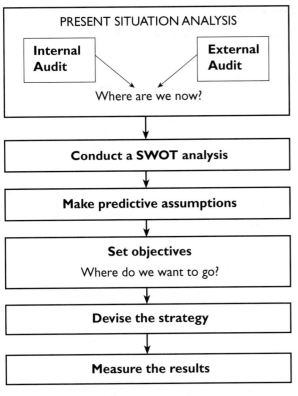

Fig 9.10 *The steps involved in developing a marketing strategy*

involved in devising a marketing strategy is shown in Fig 9.10

The steps are simple.

1 **Analyse the present situation**   In doing this, the firm is asking the question, 'Where are we now?'. The firm needs to carry out two sets of research. It is necessary to conduct an internal audit in order to find out what are the resources and strong points of the firm and also to discover what the firm is capable of achieving. It is also necessary to conduct an external audit, which should show external, possibly uncontrollable, factors in the market and the economy that might affect the performance of the firm.

2 **Conduct a SWOT analysis**   After the present situation has been analysed, a great deal of data, much of it irrelevant, will have been collected. A SWOT analysis should enable the firm to discover the information that is most pertinent to the present situation and, also, the future. SWOT analysis is an analysis of Strengths, Weaknesses, Opportunities and Threats, thus the acronym SWOT. SWOT analysis tends to separate into internal and external factors. The strengths and weaknesses part of the analysis highlights the internal strengths and weaknesses of the firm. These would be factors such as market share, financial performance, quality of products, quality of distribution, effectiveness of pricing strategies and so on. The opportunities and threats part of the analysis highlights the external opportunities and threats that face the firm. These would be factors such as the economic climate, the performance of the competition and the situation in the whole market.

3 **Make predictive assumptions**   Once the analysis has been carried out, it would be wrong to suppose that the situation that has been discovered will prevail into the future. By definition, the analysis has been one of the present situation. The firm should now attempt to look at the internal and external factors that it feels might alter over the future period in which the marketing strategy is going to be conducted. This is one of the most difficult parts of the process. Internal changes should be able to be predicted fairly accurately. However, alterations in external factors, such as changes in inflation rates, interest rates and exchange rates, are much harder to predict. If these are not taken into account, and do occur, then they can completely negate a seemingly good marketing strategy.

4 **Set objectives**   Once all of the research and assumptions have been completed, it is time for the firm to set objectives. The

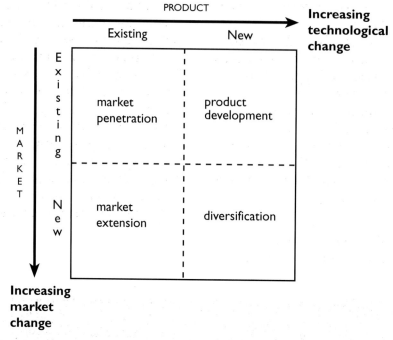

Fig 9.11 *Ansoff's matrix*

question to be posed is, 'Where do we want to go?'. There are only a limited number of directions and possibly the best way to summarise them is by using the concept of Ansoff's matrix, which is shown in Fig 9.11.

Igor Ansoff felt that firms had four choices of direction. First, they could stay in their present market, with the present product, and attempt to increase market share. Second, they could take their present product and attempt to introduce it to a new market. Third, they could develop a new product for their present market and, fourth, they could attempt to develop a new product in a new market. Obviously, the more that a firm moves away from its present product and market, the greater the risk that is being taken. The choice of direction at this stage will very much influence the form of the marketing strategy that should be adopted.

5 **Devise the strategy**   Once objectives have been set and the firm is aware of the

direction to pursue, they must then decide upon a strategy that will take them there. The strategy will be a combination of changes to elements of the marketing mix and it will very much depend upon the direction chosen.

If the firm has opted to stay in the same market, with the same product, then the emphasis of the strategy will revolve around promotion and, to a lesser extent, pricing and distribution. If the decision is to place their existing product in a new market, then market research and penetration promotion strategies will be paramount, along with distribution.

If the decision is to develop new products for the existing market, then product development must take the lead and, after that, pricing, promotion and distribution must all be considered. If the highest-risk option is chosen, a new product in a new market, then all elements of the marketing mix must be considered, but product development and market research will be of ultimate importance.

6 **Measure the results** Once the strategy has been decided upon and implemented, it should not just be left to happen. Too often, the importance of monitoring performance is overlooked. Predicted performance and actual performance should be compared and, where necessary, changes should be made to the marketing strategy when the predicted performance is not matched by the actual.

A marketing strategy should not be contradictory. Many students suggest improving the product, which would raise costs, reducing the price, which might reduce revenue, increasing promotion, which might well also increase cost, and improving distribution, which might also increase costs. The outcome of all this would almost inevitably be a fall in profits. It is much easier to take a more simple approach and to concentrate on just two or three variables. For example, an improvement in product quality, whilst expensive, might lead to the chance to charge a slightly higher price, in a market where demand is relatively inelastic, and so lead to an increase in revenue and, hopefully, profit.

QUALITY INNS TEST THE MARKET

Quality Inns has 50 hotels spread throughout the UK. Their target market segment is the business market, serving company executives who are travelling on business. The hotels provide conference and leisure facilities. The company wishes to move into banqueting, offering large scale dinners for companies, parties, weddings and social club functions. To do this a major market research survey was carried out, and the organisation's Manchester hotel is being used as a test market. The following table outlines the costs of putting on a function for 500.

When setting a price for a ticket the company uses a 200 percent mark-up on variable costs. The company is also deciding on a policy of discounts for dinner tickets. If it sells 400 tickets and feels it will not sell the

Variable costs:	£ per head served
Food	4.00
Drink	2.90
Napkins, serviettes	0.60
Fixed costs:	
Staff	£200
Capital	£1,000

remaining 100, it is prepared to offer a discount on these tickets.

As part of its entire marketing strategy for the banqueting project the marketing department are also looking closely at the type of promotion they will use. As a major company in the industry, a substantial amount of funds have been made available.

QUESTIONS

1 Explain what you understand by the following terms contained in the text: **a** market segment; **b** mark-up; **c** variable costs; **d** marketing strategy. [20]

2 Calculate, using the above figures:
   a the price per head for the banquet; [5]
   b the break-even number of people needed to attend; [8]
   c the maximum profit the hotel would make from the evening. [7]

3 The company is considering a discount scheme using marginal cost pricing.
   a On the basis of marginal cost, state and explain clearly the minimum price you would advise Quality Inns to set for the discounted tickets. [5]
   b Discuss the other factors, apart from cost, that Quality Inns would need to consider before it sets the discounted prices. [10]

4 Quality Inns want to produce a survey of the type of food and drink they would need to offer. Write a brief report on how you would survey the market. Include the following in your report.
   a An explanation of the type of sampling you would use.
   b An explanation of the questions you might include in a questionnaire. [20]

5 **a** Explain what you understand by the term 'promotional mix'. [5]
   b What type of promotional mix would you advise Quality Inns to use to successfully launch banqueting? [10]

Total [90]

YOUTH APPEAL – MOTORING: WHY ROVER TRANSFORMED THE METRO

For some years the Metro has been one of the best superminis around in terms of ride, refinement and handling. Yet, surveys revealed that the car lacked sales appeal because of its angular, early-1980s styling. Potential buyers, Rover discovered, were put off by the middle-aged appearance of the car.

In 1995 Rover set about transforming the image, appearance and the name of its supermini. It now sells as the Rover 100, which is what it has been called for several years on mainland Europe – where 'metro' means an 'underground railway'. The car enjoys a sleeker design, intended to make it more attractive to the younger end of the market. The Rover 100 has been enhanced further by safety and security improvements, including a driver's air-bag option, combined alarm and immobiliser, and standard side intrusion beams in the doors. In addition to Rover's own K-series 1.1-litre and 1.4-litre petrol engines, the 100 may be had with a Peugeot Citroen 1.5-litre diesel. Prices start at £6,495.

The results of a survey carried out are illustrated below. Both existing and potential customers were interviewed at Rover dealerships across the UK.

▶▶

Socio-economic grouping

Socio-economic group	% of responses
AB	38%
C1	43%
C2	15%
DE	4%

Note: Socio-economic groups:

A Upper/upper middle class – higher managerial, administrative, professional

B Middle Class – intermediate managerial, administrative, professional

C1 Lower middle class – supervisory, junior managerial, clerical

C2 Skilled working class – skilled manual

D Working class – semi-skilled, unskilled

E Lowest level of subsistence – long-term unemployed, casual workers

Salary levels of individuals in the sample

£0–15,000	£15,001–20,000	£20,001–25,000	£25,001–30,000	£30,001–35,000
250	450	500	550	250

QUESTIONS

1 a What is the difference between open and closed questions in a questionnaire? [3]

   b Outline the advantages of using closed questions in a questionnaire. [5]

   c Explain why Rover might have used open rather than closed questions to find out about driver attitudes to the Metro. [7]

2 a What do you understand by the term 'socio-economic grouping'? [5]

   b Explain why Rover would find it useful to divide up a market into socio-economic groups. [10]

3 Consider the table above, which relates to the salaries of individuals in the sample.
   a Give the modal salary. [3]
   b Why would a knowledge of the average salary of people in the sample be useful to Rover when marketing its new cars? [7]

4 Discuss the importance of the different elements of product design that Rover needs to consider when it is producing its cars. [10]

Total [50]

NIKE OUTSPRINTS ITS RIVALS

Running shoes were invented over 100 years ago, but it took another 80 years for the industry to get out of its starting blocks. Today about 300 million pairs of 'trainers' are sold around the world each year. As each pair only lasts approximately 500 miles and the youngsters that wear them are so responsive to changing fashions, 'trainers' represent a marketeer's dream. The market is tied together with mega-buck advertising, linking fashion and fitness with the personalities who use this type of footwear professionally.

Most of the growth in the $10.7 billion global sports-shoe market is expected to come from emerging markets. This has not yet bothered Nike, which has emerged as the market leader. On 18th September 1995 Nike announced a 55 percent increase in operating profits (to $640 million) on sales up 38 percent (to $3.2 billion) compared with the same period in the previous year.

Nike's success stems, in part, from their bold advertising campaign which linked high-profile sports stars, such as Eric Cantona, Pete Sampras, Monica Seles and Andre Agassi with their product – a clear attempt to equate success with the Nike name. Nike persisted with this strategy during the early 1990s despite a temporary decline in demand for their product as Doctor Martens and similar types of 'grunge' footwear became *de rigueur*. Now fashion has swung back its way. Nike is reaping the reward.

After early success in developing a new market for shoes for women, Reebok has trailed in Nike's wake. Even their American basketball idol, the mighty Shaquille O'Neal (who wears size 22 Reebok basketball boots) has failed to revive their flagging share of the market. Of greater threat to Nike is the recently revived Adidas. After a disastrous period in the hands of Bernard Tapie (a businessman better known for his football match-rigging convictions), the firm was bought in 1993 by the French businessman Robert Louis-Dreyfus (with a proven record in reviving flagging businesses – a notable success had been the ailing Saatchi and Saatchi group). Mr Louis-Dreyfus set about reducing costs by transferring all but three percent of production from Germany to Asia and cutting the workforce down from 14,300 to 5,500. He is also responsible for producing shoes that are technically more advanced and more fashionable. Adidas also enjoys another in-built advantage: it manufactures a wide range of sports clothes in addition to sports shoes, whereas three-quarters of Nike's and Reebok's sales are from shoes. Analysts believe the future of sports clothing sales are rosier than that of the shoe market. This is borne out by Adidas's operating profits which, for 1995, doubled to the equivalent of $222 million.

Adidas's next target is America where its aim is to double its traditionally low market share. The Olympics, held in Atlanta in 1996, were used as an advertising arena for their sportswear as many track and field athletes sported the Adidas label.

However, it is widely believed that the future profits of the sports-shoe business lie not in America or Europe but in Asia, for that is where the feet are . . .

QUESTIONS

1 a Distinguish between the terms: market share and market growth. [5]

b Describe what has happened to Nike's world market share in the training shoe market. [3]

c Calculate Nike's market share of the sports-shoe market. [3]

d Where in the world is most of the market growth in the training shoe market coming from? [2]

e Discuss the marketing difficulties Nike will encounter as it continues to expand into the markets of developing countries. [12]

2 a Explain the Boston Matrix and the Product Life Cycle. [7]

b How would an understanding of these two models help a company like Nike to manage its product portfolio most effectively? [8]

c Produce a strategy that Nike could use to extend the life cycle of a product that had entered the declining phase of its life cycle. [10]

3 a Explain what you understand by SWOT analysis. [5]

b Produce a SWOT analysis for Nike as it tries to increase its sales in developing countries. [10]

c Use your SWOT analysis to produce a marketing strategy for Nike as it tries to introduce a new brand of training shoe into developing countries such as China. [15]

Total [80]

SPONSORSHIP BY COCA COLA

The image associated with the product that the consumer buys is an absolutely critical factor in the consumer's buying decision. Fundamentally, this is because people are concerned with the way the product they are consuming fits in with their own image, and the perceived image they believe they have amongst other people. If someone is questioned about why they have purchased a Ralph Lauren Polo shirt they would say that it was because of the quality, style and design of the garment, but the image associated with that brand name is just as important in the buying decision as its quality. The Ralph Lauren name reflects an opulent, sporty, upwardly mobile image that consumers of the product want to be associated with, which is why Ralph Lauren Polo shirts carry the polo player logo clearly on the garment.

The influence of image is also important when someone is buying a soft drink, like Coca Cola. A cold, soft drink carries with it basic thirst quenching benefits, as well as the satisfying taste consumers expect to benefit from. However, the image the product puts forward is just as critical in persuading people to buy the product. The Coca Cola company has tried to build its image by tying the product and the company closely to sports. The company has focused its attention on four major sports:

1 **The Olympic Games**   Coca Cola began its involvement with the Olympics in 1928 when a freighter arrived with the US team and 1,000 cases of Coca Cola. This involvement has continued in a variety of forms including the provision of facilities, the setting up of an Olympic Museum and the organisation of the Olympic Torch Relay for the Barcelona games.

2 **Football**   Coca Cola supports soccer at all levels from junior soccer to professional club football and the World Cup. Coca Cola had a major involvement with Euro '96 held in the UK. The company has its own cup competition in the UK, and it has also organised a huge junior soccer coaching programme.

3 **Tennis**   In 1996 diet Coca Cola announced a partnership with the Wimbledon Lawn Tennis Championships.

4 **Special Olympics**   Since 1985, Coca Cola has sponsored the Special Olympics for people with learning difficulties. This has helped the company become associated with the concept of 'sport for all'.

QUESTIONS

1 a What do you understand by the terms 'above-' and 'below-the-line promotion'? [5]

   b Explain why sponsorship is considered to be below-the-line promotion. [5]

   c Outline two below-the-line methods of promotion Coca Cola could use to promote its products. [7]

2 a Analyse how the association with sport has enhanced Coca Cola's brand image. [7]

   b Explain how Coca Cola's sponsorship of sport has increased its profitability. [8]

   c Explain why you think Coca Cola has chosen to sponsor each of the sports outlined in the case example. [8]

Total [40]

The Business Environment – Section A: The market

SUMMARY

1 Economics is used to study the way that the market environment, in which businesses have to operate, behaves.
2 Demand from consumers has critical importance on the sales of organisations.
3 Demand is determined by a variety of factors, including the price of the product, price of related products, income and consumer taste.
4 Elasticity of demand is used to measure the response of demand to changes in the factors that determine it.

5 Supply from producers is the second critical element that affects markets.
6 The interaction of demand and supply determines the price and output set in markets. Changes in demand and supply factors, will alter the market price and output.
7 The social environment is affected by demography and culture. Changes in the social environment have a major impact on the behaviour of markets.

The business environment is the setting where all stakeholders of organisations have to make decisions. It may be a decision where the impact of the business environment will influence the outcome, or the environment itself may initiate the decision. For example, many companies have had to react positively to growing environmentalism in the last twenty years. Stakeholders either have to make decisions to exploit the opportunities made available by the environment, or make decisions to react to the threats it poses them. For this reason, it is vital that stakeholders have a clear understanding of the business environment within which their organisation operates.

All organisations have to trade within a market. This is the place where businesses sell their goods and services to consumers. This could be firms selling to final consumers, or businesses selling to other businesses. It could also be a market where people sell their services to businesses as workers. Economics is the social science that studies the behaviour of markets. The economist's understanding of the way the market operates also allows organisations to understand the market environment.

■ WHAT IS ECONOMICS?

All organisations have to exist and react to changes in the economic environment within which they operate. Economics can be defined as 'the study of how the global society allocates scarce resources to satisfy human wants.'

Scarce resources

There are four resources available in society that can be used to produce goods and services and these are limited in supply.

1 **Land**　The natural resource that provides the raw materials that businesses process into products, such as oil, water, soil and so on.
2 **Labour**　The workforce used by organisations to produce final products. This can be unskilled workers in manufacturing, or skilled workers in service-based industries or managers of large multinational corporations.
3 **Capital**　These are the tools and machines used by organisations, ranging from the pencils used by graphic designers, to the nuclear reactors used by the electricity industry.
4 **Entrepreneurship**　This is the group of people in society who respond to a profit-making opportunity by organising land, labour and capital to produce a final product for the consumer. People such as Rupert Murdoch, Bill Gates III and Alan Sugar, are well known for the opportunities they have seized by identifying consumer wants and producing a product to satisfy those wants.

Allocation

The allocation of resources relates to the use of resources to produce different goods and services. The process that guides this movement of resources takes place via the market. For example, the production of compact discs occurs because entrepreneurs spot the demand for this product through the market, and organise resources to produce a product that satisfies the consumers' demand for it. The product is then traded in the market and is purchased by consumers. If consumers wish to buy more of the product, demand for it increases and firms will produce more to try and satisfy this demand.

Thus, economists seek to analyse and understand how societies allocate resources and produce products for consumers. By doing this, economists are able to forecast what might happen to the economy in the future, given their understanding of how consumers and producers behave. This understanding of how the economy works is important for business because it tells business why their fortunes have changed due to the behaviour of the economic environment, and how their fortunes might change in the future as the economic environment changes.

Micro and macroeconomics

Microeconomics

Microeconomics involves looking at resource allocation and its impact at a localised level within society. If you consider the market for footwear, or ice cream, then we are considering the microeconomy, because we are looking at individual units that make up the whole economy.

Macroeconomics

This looks at the economy as a whole, and how changes in aggregates affect the whole economy. Aggregates are totals, such as demand of all consumers, and the supply of all producers. Economic problems such as inflation and unemployment are considered to be macroeconomic because they affect the economy as a whole.

Organisations will be influenced by economic changes at both the micro and macro levels. An organisation, such as Marks & Spencer, will be influenced by micro changes, like a decline in demand for two-piece suits. At a macro level, they will be affected by a fall in overall consumer demand as a result of an economic recession.

THE MARKET MECHANISM

A market is a notional place where consumers and producers interact, and where the price and output of that market is determined. When people talk about markets they often refer to particular industries where certain types of products are produced, such as the car industry. Within a market or industry there are segments. For example, the total car market is made up of a large number of individual segments, ranging from sports cars to four-wheel drive landcruisers.

The market's mechanism is the process of interaction between buyers and sellers that determines how much of a product is produced and at what price the product is sold. Thus, the key determinants of the behaviour of a market is buyer activity represented by consumer demand, and seller activity represented by producer supply.

Market demand

Definition

Effective consumer demand is defined as 'the willingness and ability of a consumer to pay a sum of money for a good or service at a particular point in time'. It is not just desire to purchase a good on the consumer's part, it is ability actually to pay for the good as well. The demand for products changes as the factors which affect demand, or the determinants of demand, change.

Determinants of demand

The demand for a good is determined by the following factors.

Price

There is an inverse relationship between the price the consumer is prepared to pay for a good and the quantity they will buy. At higher

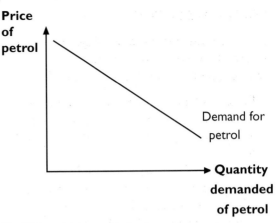

Fig 10.1   *An example of a demand curve*

prices consumers will demand less of a good because they are less able to afford it, and because other substitute goods become relatively better value. If the price of petrol rises the quantity demanded of it falls because people can afford less of it, and public transport becomes a relatively cheaper option.

This relationship is summarised by Fig 10.1, which is called a demand curve. As the price of petrol rises and falls the quantity demanded can be established by moving along the demand curve to read off the quantity demanded.

Consumer income

The amount of income consumers have obviously influences the amount they will buy of certain goods. If incomes rise, the demand for consumer durables, such as clothing, will increase. These goods are called normal goods. However, the demand for certain goods such as bread, milk and eggs will change very little, and these goods are called necessities. The demand for certain goods may even fall as incomes rise, as would be the case with nylon clothing, and cheap, own-label food products. These are known as inferior goods.

Unlike a change in price, a change in consumer income causes the demand curve to shift. An organisation like Tesco would see

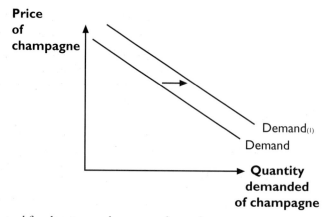

Fig 10.2 *A rise in demand for champagne shown on a demand curve*

the demand for certain goods change dramatically as incomes rise. Demand would increase for products such as champagne and smoked salmon, whereas the demand for bread and eggs would stay the same and the demand for basic range, Tesco own-label products may well fall. This will have a major impact on the revenue they receive from those products, the levels of stock they will require and the amount they need to order.

Related goods

Goods can be related to each other as either substitutes or complements. A substitute product for a good is an alternative product that the consumer could buy. This could be an alternative brand, or an alternative product altogether. For example, British Telecom has to compete against Mercury Communications as a substitute for its telephone services, and it also has to compete against the Post Office in the general communications market. If the price of a substitute for a good rises, then the demand for that product will go up as consumers switch towards it as an alternative product. Similarly, if a substitute for a good falls in price, the demand for the good will fall as consumers switch towards the substitute. In the communications market the fall in the cost of using e-mail has led to a fall in demand for fax machines.

In a complementary relationship, a rise in the price of a complement for a good will lead to a fall in the demand for that good, as people buy less of the complement after the price rise. The demand for petrol and cars is seen as a complementary one. If the price of petrol rises the demand for cars will fall. In the same way, a fall in the price of a complement for a good will lead to a rise in the demand for that good: a fall in the price of car insurance will lead to a rise in the demand for cars.

Organisations often sell ranges of products which may be substitutes or complements for one another. For example, if Kellogg's reduces the price of one breakfast cereal, it will sell less of substitute brands of the cereals it sells. If Canon reduces the price of its cameras, it will sell more lenses and tripods as complementary products. Businesses can develop strategies on promotion, stock management and pricing to maximise the benefits from selling related products. Organisations will also have to react to change in the price of substitutes and complements sold by other businesses.

Consumer taste

The demand for a product will change if the consumer's taste changes. Products go into and out of fashion; the recent BSE crisis has seen a fall in the demand for beef as consumers, who are wary of the health

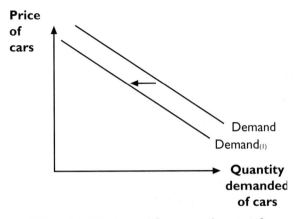

Price of cars

Quantity demanded of cars

Demand

Demand(1)

Fig 10.3 *A fall in demand for cars as the price of petrol rises*

concerns associated with beef, buy other products such as chicken and pork. Organisations can manipulate consumer tastes through marketing; the demand for Levi 501 jeans increased dramatically as a result of their 1980s advertising campaign.

Future price expectations

If consumers believe that prices are likely to rise in the future then they are likely to move their consumption decision forwards and buy in the present. This situation particularly applies to assets, like houses and shares, where the buyer can make a capital gain if they buy now and prices rise. House builders, such as Wimpey and Barratt's, will experience a rise in the demand for their houses if there is house price inflation and the consumer expects future prices to increase.

Population and demography

A rise in population increases the number of potential consumers and demand. This is important to organisations that market their products in developing countries where population is rising. Many companies expand into international markets where there are more people to increase the potential demand for their products. As the structure of population changes, companies will

experience a change in demand for their products. Most developed nations are now experiencing an ageing population which has increased the demand for a whole range of products, from retirement homes to private health care.

Interest rates and credit facilities

Many major household purchases, from houses and cars to furniture and home entertainment take place on credit. The demand for these products has risen as a result of the increase in credit facilities offered by finance houses and banks in the UK over the last 15 years. If the interest charged on the credit used to buy products changes, then the demand for these products changes. A rise in interest rates reduces demand because the cost of buying goods on credit increases. Most people buy their house using a mortgage which, because of the size of the loan, normally accounts for between 25 and 30 percent of household income. Any change in interest rates has a major impact on household income, altering demand for products in the same way that a change in income would do.

Consumer confidence

An individual's decision to buy is often based on their financial circumstances, and what they believe will happen to these circumstances in the future. If they feel uncertain and lose confidence because rising unemployment makes them worried about their own employment prospects, then they are less likely to make major purchases, and demand will fall. If, however, they feel confident about the future they will spend more and demand will rise. Products that represent major items of expenditure, such as cars and furniture, tend to be most affected by changes in consumer confidence.

Wealth

Wealth is accumulated income that households own in the form of property, cash in bank accounts and shares. If the value of this wealth rises, consumers are more likely to spend because they feel more confident about their financial circumstances, and the rise in wealth may provide them with funds for spending. If, for example, house prices increase then peoples' wealth will rise and there will be a rise in demand for certain products. On the other hand, the slump in house prices in the early 1990s saw household wealth fall and the demand for products fell.

Elasticity of demand

Elasticity is the reaction of consumer demand to changes in one of the variables that affects demand.

Price elasticity of demand

Definition of price elasticity
The strength of the relationship between changes in price and changes in consumer demand can be measured by the price elasticity of demand (PED). Price elasticity measures the responsiveness of consumer demand to a change in price.

Measuring price elasticity of demand
The equation

$$\frac{\text{\% change in quantity demanded}}{\text{\% change in price}}$$

gives a value that indicates how responsive the consumer is to a price change. For example, if after a 10 percent fall in the price of petrol the quantity demanded rises by 7 percent, then the value of PED would be calculated as:

$$\frac{+7}{-10} = -0.7$$

Because price and quantity demanded is a negative relationship the value of PED will always be negative. The value −0.7 means that for every one percent change in price, quantity demanded changes by 0.7 percent.

The higher the value is, the more responsive the relationship between price and quantity demanded is. When the value of PED for a product is less than one, it is described as price inelastic. If the value of PED is above one it is considered price elastic, and if the value is equal to one PED it is considered to be unity.

Applying PED
An understanding of price elasticity of demand is useful to businesses because it gives managers some insight into how sales are going to respond when prices are changed. In fact, by having a value for PED it is possible for firms to predict whether sales revenue will rise or fall when price is changed.

When the PED of a good is above one there is an inverse relationship between price changes and sales revenue. If a business increases its price, sales revenue will fall and when it reduces its price, sales revenue will rise. On the other hand, if PED is less than one, and considered inelastic, a rise in price would lead to a rise in sales revenue and a reduction in price would see sales revenue fall.

For example, a small airline is running flights to Paris. Its standard fare is £100 and it normally sells 200 seats on a Friday when PED is inelastic, with a value of −0.5. The sales revenue of

$$200 \times £100 = £20,000$$

could be increased by increasing the price to £120, a 20 percent increase in price. Remember, with a PED of −0.5, for every one percent increase in price, quantity demanded falls by 0.5 percent, so quantity demanded falls by (20 × 0.5) 10 percent.

The new revenue is calculated as:

$$200 \times 0.9 \times 120 = £21,600$$

An increase of £1,600. (200 × 0.9 is calculated to work out the 10% fall in sales. This is then multiplied by the new price £120 to give the new sales revenue.)

On Saturdays, the airline normally sells 150 seats at a price of £100, and demand is considered to be price elastic with a PED of −1.6. The current sales revenue is therefore:

£100 × 150 = £15,000

This revenue could be increased by reducing the price to £70, a 30 percent reduction. Remember, with a PED of −1.6, for every one percent reduction in price, quantity demanded increases by 1.6 percent, so quantity demanded rises by (30 × 1.6) 48 percent.

The new revenue is calculated as:

1.48 × 150 × £70 = £15,540

Revenue is increased by £540.

This example shows how businesses can use an understanding of price elasticity to raise their sales revenue. The example also shows how certain businesses, like airlines, experience differing PED values for the product they sell. In this case, the differing value is based on the time of travel. At weekends, demand here may well be price elastic because people buy holiday flights on Saturdays. PED is determined by the degree to which a product is a luxury or necessity. Holiday travel is a relative luxury so demand is price elastic. On Fridays, travel is more of a necessity because business people, to whom the service is a necessity, will be using it. This example illustrates a pricing strategy called price discrimination where a firm charges different prices for the same product that is sold in different markets. The different markets are based on the time people travel, and the elasticities vary because at different times the elasticity varies. Price discrimination is used in a variety of different markets, including rail and bus services, cinemas and hotels.

Assessing elasticity

There are two ways businesses can assess the PED of the products they sell.

1 **Product characteristics**   If a product has many close substitutes it will be more price elastic because consumers will switch towards it from competing products if price falls, and against it if prices rise. If a product is a luxury or necessity its PED can be assessed. A relatively luxurious good tends to have a higher PED because people will forego the product if its price rises, because they do not need to buy it.

2 **Past information**   By looking at information on how the demand for a product has changed in the past when the price of it has been changed, it is possible to have a figure to predict what will happen to demand when price is changed in the future.

Income elasticity of demand

Definition of income elasticity of demand
Income elasticity of demand (YED) seeks to measure the response of consumer demand to changes in their income. As people experience a rise or fall in their income the demand for products will change, but the extent of that change will vary from product to product.

Measuring income elasticity of demand
YED is measured by the equation:

$$\frac{\textbf{\% change in quantity demanded}}{\textbf{\% change in income}}$$

In our airline example, demand increased by seven percent last year as the economy grew and consumer incomes increased by three percent. This is a YED of:

$$\frac{+7\%}{+3\%} = 2.33$$

The YED tells us that for every one percent rise in consumer incomes, demand increases by 2.33 percent. The answer is positive, so the air tickets sold would be considered a normal good. Indeed, because the value is relatively high they would even be described as a luxury good because demand rises significantly if incomes rise. If, on the other hand, the value of YED was negative, the product would be described as an inferior good. This means that demand falls as consumer incomes rise. Bus travel would be an example of an inferior good. A YED that is at or around zero indicates that the demand for the product does not change when incomes change. Necessity goods, such as basic foodstuffs, fall into this category.

Applying income elasticity of demand

An understanding of YED is useful to organisations in that it allows them to plan and develop strategies to deal with changes in incomes. In our example, an airline is likely to see a rise in demand for its flights as consumer incomes rise. If the European economy is growing strongly, incomes are likely to rise and the demand for business flights will increase. Managers may well respond to this by increasing the number of services they run.

Cross elasticity of demand

Definition of cross elasticity of demand

Cross elasticity of demand (CED), measures the responsiveness of quantity demanded for one good when the price of a related good changes. The opening of the channel tunnel rail link has substantially reduced the cost of travelling by train between London and Paris. This has increased the competition for air travel, which means that our airline will experience a fall in demand for its flights.

Measuring cross elasticity of demand

The degree of fall would be measured by the equation:

$$\frac{\% \text{ change in quantity demanded of good A}}{\% \text{ change in the price of good B}}$$

A 30 percent fall in rail fares has led to a 10 percent fall in airline ticket demand in our example. The elasticity is calculated as:

$$\frac{-10\%}{-30\%} = +0.33$$

This means that for every one percent fall in the price of train fares the demand for air tickets, in this case, falls by 0.33 percent. The value of the CED is positive which indicates that the two goods are substitutes. If the two goods were complements, for example the demand for air tickets and hotel prices in Paris, then the value would be negative because a fall in hotel prices leads to a rise in the demand for flights. Our airline could use the complementary relationship to raise its revenue; by buying up cheap hotel space in Paris, which it would then sell at a discount to customers who used their flights, it is likely to sell more flights. Some businesses will at times sell the related complementary at a loss to sell more of the main product. This pricing strategy is called loss leadership.

Elasticity	Equation	Interpretation
PED	$\dfrac{\% \Delta qd}{\% \Delta p}$	>1 elastic =1 unitary <1 inelastic
YED	$\dfrac{\% \Delta qd}{\% \Delta y}$	+ve normal 0 necessity −ve inferior
CED	$\dfrac{\% \Delta qdy}{\% \Delta px}$	+ve substitutes 0 unrelated −ve complements

Fig 10.4   *The various ways of interpreting the different elasticities of demand*

Market supply

Supply is the organisation's willingness and ability to produce a product to meet consumer demand. The producer organises resources to produce a product that will earn them a profit in return for the risk taken in setting up production. This could be a sole trader setting up a small retail outlet, or a major corporation

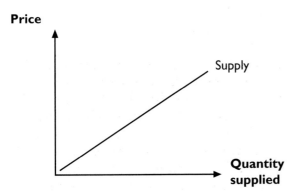

Fig 10.5   *An illustration of a supply curve*

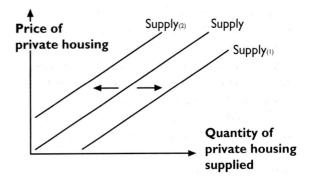

Fig 10.6   *An illustration of the movement in the supply of private housing*

launching a new branded product. Like demand, supply changes because the factors that determine the level of supply change.

Determinants of supply

Price

There is a positive relationship between the quantity supplied by a firm, and the price they receive from selling the product. As prices increase, a producer is willing to supply greater amounts onto the market. The relationship is illustrated by a supply curve or schedule, which is shown in Fig 10.5. The quantity that producers are willing to supply increases with price, because the producer earns a greater profit margin from a higher price which acts as an incentive to increase production.

This is not a straightforward relationship because the ability of producers to increase supply in response to a price change will depend on how easily they can increase output. A company that is running at capacity will find it impossible to increase their output immediately, so there will be a time lag as the firm has to alter the scale of production before more can be produced to be sold in the market. Where the production process is particularly technical, say in the chemical industry, this time lag could be considerable as specialised capital and labour may prove

difficult for the firm to find and hire.

Price of other products the organisation could produce

Many businesses produce a mix of products that they sell to different market segments. Each product they sell occupies a certain amount of their available resources. If the price they receive from one of their markets increases, the firm will look to supply more to that market, which means increasing output, and taking available resources away from the production of other products. Thus the supply for these other products falls. Figure 10.6 illustrates a fall in supply, showing the supply curve moving to the left.

Changes in non-price determinants of supply, which are discussed below, cause the supply curve to shift. A construction company, like Wimpey, see an increase in the price of commercial property that causes them to divert resources into this area away from housing, leading to a fall in the supply of housing. The supply curve for private housing shifts to the left in response to the change in the price of commercial property. The opposite would occur if commercial property fell in price and Wimpey decided to concentrate more resources on the supply of private housing. Figure 10.6 shows the supply curve of private housing shifting to the right as supply increases.

Costs of production

Changes in the cost of labour and capital alter the profit that producers can earn from a market and subsequently the amount they supply to that market. If banking workers negotiate higher wages, then the costs of banking services increases, and banks will reduce supply and the supply curve will shift to the left. If wages fall, firms increase output, and the supply curve shifts to the right.

Technology

Over time, improvements in technology allow firms to increase output from a given resource input, reducing their costs of production, allowing them to obtain a greater profit margin, and, as a result of this, they increase supply. The introduction of fibre optic cable in telecommunications has increased the efficiency of the industry, reduced the unit cost of production and led to an increase in the supply of telecommunication services.

Organisation objectives

An assumption in microeconomics is that firms are profit maximisers, and that they base all their supply decisions on achieving as much profit as possible. Whilst profit is a key objective, other objectives are always under consideration. If an organisation decides that it wants to maximise sales to try and obtain greater market share, then supply will increase. On the other hand, an organisation may feel that they would like to reduce the output of a product to make it more exclusive.

Tax and subsidy

If a government imposes an indirect tax, such as VAT, on a product, then this adds to the cost of supplying the product and leads to a fall in supply. A reduction in tax will reduce costs and lead to an increase in supply. In contrast, a subsidy put on a product will reduce the costs of supply, causing the supply of a product to increase.

Number of producers

The more producers there are in a market the

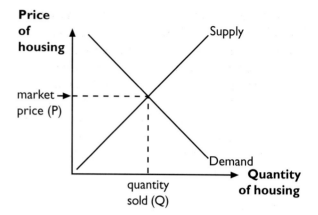

Fig 10.7 *An illustration of an equilibrium price in the market for housing*

greater supply will be. Over time, organisations enter and leave markets as the profitability of those markets changes. The 1980s saw an increase in the profitability of the housing market that attracted more construction firms into housing, increasing its supply. The recession of the early 1990s saw profits fall along with the number of producers, causing supply to fall.

Market price and output

It is the forces of demand and supply that determine both the market price, and the amount sold in a market. In Fig 10.7, the intersection of the demand and supply curves represents the equilibrium point where market demand equals market supply, and this sets the market price and the quantity sold. As demand and supply conditions change the market price and quantity sold changes. If, for example, the demand for housing increases as a result of rising incomes then, assuming all other factors remain constant, the demand curve will shift to the right and the price of new housing will rise. Should the costs of labour fall in the construction industry then the costs of producing houses will fall, the supply of houses will increase and price will fall as output increases.

It is the interaction of demand and supply conditions that explains how resources are allocated between different markets. In information technology, for example, more resources have been allocated to the area because of improvements in technology that have increased supply. At the same time there has been an increase in demand for all the products associated with the information technology industry.

Limitations of the model

There is no doubting the power of the market mechanism in the way it explains how price and output change in different industries. However, the operation of the mechanism is much more complicated than just simple shifts in demand and supply curves.

A dynamic market

When an analysis is made of changes in a market, factors that lead to a change such as a shift in demand tend to be looked at in isolation. In reality, demand and supply factors are all changing at the same time, and it is misleading to just consider one factor on its own. The slump in house prices at the

beginning of the 1980s was caused by a whole range of demand and supply factors, from falling consumer incomes, to expectations of a fall in prices.

Price and output setting

In theory, markets are seen as highly competitive with firms setting price on the basis of the equilibrium set in the market. In practice, organisations exert a good deal more control than this. A company like Microsoft is the sole producer of its own software, so it sets the price for its products by balancing out its own cost and demand based factors. Many firms also choose not to compete on price because continuous reductions in a price war simply reduce all their profit margins. A number of firms opt to fix a price at a certain level, and then they all follow this price.

Monopoly

A monopoly exists when a single producer accounts for a large proportion of the industry's output. For example, the Post Office has a monopoly over the postal service. In this situation, the single producer controls supply, and does not allow the supply in the market to operate in the way market theory

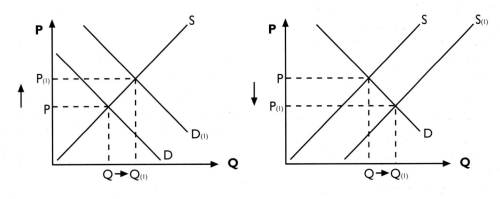

The impact on the housing market of a rise in the demand for houses as incomes increase.

The impact on the housing market as the supply of houses increases as labour costs fall.

Fig 10.8 *An illustration of the interaction between demand and supply*

predicts. By controlling supply, the monopolist can increase price to raise profits.

IMPLICATIONS OF THE MARKET FOR ORGANISATIONS

Organisations are affected by markets either as a seller of their product, or as a buyer of resources used to produce their products. The effect of the market on organisations is a crucial external influence on their decision making. By understanding how markets behave, companies can plan more precisely how they will market new and existing products in the future. This in turn improves their budgeting and long-term planning. Organisations can also analyse markets retrospectively to see why the outcomes of their decisions went well or badly. For example, which determinant of demand was most important in causing the fall in sales of a product.

The impact of the social environment on the market

The social environment within which organisations operate is based on the attitudes, ethics, cultures and beliefs of the people who make it up. These constituents will vary geographically depending on the region or country in question, demographically between age groups, and psychographically depending on social class. The social environment will also change over time. The environmental revolution that has changed the way many people across the world think about life has changed the way multinational companies produce and market their products. The green forecourt design of BP's service stations is a good example of this reaction.

It is important to consider in detail the factors that shape the social environment.

Demography

Demography is the study of the human population including its size, age and sex.

Size

The size of the population in a region or country is dependent on its birth rate, death rate and rate of migration. In most developed countries the size of the population is fairly static at country level, although changes are taking place at a regional level. Companies in the Southeast of England have had to react to an increasing population in the last 25 years. At a simple level, there are more consumers so the potential demand for products is higher. This will vary from products such as houses, to schools and healthcare. Building companies such as Barratt, Wimpey and Fairclough will have had to build more houses in this region in response to higher demand, but will also have had to pay more for the fixed amount of land available.

In developing countries such as those in South America, Africa and Asia, total population growth is more prevalent. These changes have not just led to marketing opportunities for domestic producers, they have also attracted foreign multinationals in search of expanding markets.

Age

Most developed countries are experiencing an ageing population, where the average age of the population is rising. Falling birth and death rates have lead to a growing proportion of older people in society. In the UK between 1971 and 1991, the number of people of pensionable age increased by 16 percent, and it is forecast to rise by a further 38 percent by 2031. These changes are likely to have a dramatic effect on markets. Older people require more healthcare, so any organisation associated with this industry is going to experience a rise in demand for its products. A drugs company, such as Glaxo-Welcome will experience a general rise in demand for its products as a whole, but also for products like arthritis treatments that are specifically targeted at the elderly.

Sex
The gender balance in most societies only really changes during times of war. However, many countries have seen the growing independence of women. A major factor here is the growing numbers who not only work, but have careers and become the dominant bread winners in families. Leisure organisations, such as professional soccer clubs, have reacted to this by altering their product mix by improving the facilities they offer at stadiums.

Culture
Culture is the beliefs, attitudes, values and ethics of the people in society. Culture is important in establishing a peoples' behaviour and this then influences markets as it affects the way individuals buy products and offer their services as employees. Individuals in society are 'socialised' (conditioned) into the prevailing culture. As the culture changes, individuals are 'socialised' into the new culture.

In the 1980s the traditional thriftiness that was present in the UK began to be eroded as borrowing became an accepted way of paying for everyday goods, not just houses. This change heralded an explosion in consumer credit at that time. Major retailers, like Marks & Spencer and Dixons, responded by offering 'storecards' that allowed customers to buy products easily on credit. The use of credit cards is now one of the most common forms of payment for all types of products, including food.

Sub-cultures
The dominant culture runs through society, but there are also sub-cultures that are clustered around different age, geographic, social and ethnic groups. It is these sub-cultures that organisations frequently segment to market their products. Barclays Bank has promoted its products to the young by using tactics that will appeal to the youth culture.

The impact of consumer demand on the market

The social environment has a strong influence on the buying decisions of consumers within society. The group of existing and potential consumers, the consumer base, on which all organisations rely is shaped by the changes in the social environment over time or between regions and nations. In order to consider this we need to look at the factors that affect consumer behaviour and thus demand. The culture of society has a major influence over consumer needs, which are a vital factor in determining the buying decision.

Impact on supply – the labour force

In order to produce goods to supply the market, businesses enter the labour market to hire workers in every type of function, whether it be part time cleaning staff or a sales director. The social environment has a major impact on the available workers and the salaries that need to be paid to them. This in turn affects the supply of goods produced by those workers and supplied to the market. The primary determinant of the number of workers available is population. More precisely, this is the number of people of working age that are able and prepared to offer their services to organisations. As wages change the cost of production facing businesses changes, which in turn determines the amount the business produces and the prices it charges. The higher wages are, the higher the costs of production are, which means that organisations either have to increase their prices or accept lower profit margins.

As the social environment changes this will change the labour market that faces organisations. In the UK one in three school leavers now stays on to go into higher education, compared to one in eight in 1980. A more educated labour force improves the quality of labour available to firms and also means it can be hired at a reasonable cost. Many of the new graduates will be in arts and social science based courses which will help the rising number of organisations in the service sector. However, many employers still identify a deficiency of education amongst the labour force.

How do organisations react to the market?

As a seller – Sony camcorders

Changes in market demand have had a major impact on the way Sony has tried to exploit this rapidly growing market. As part of its planning, Sony had to forecast the potential cashflow the project would generate over a period of years. By understanding how demand based factors might change over the period, the company could more accurately forecast potential revenues.

Sony would have looked to see how:

- Rising consumer incomes tend to increase the demand for camcorders because they tend to be highly responsive to income changes
- The price being charged by their competitors would affect demand
- A fall in the price of video cassettes and players as complementary products would raise demand
- A general shift in fashion towards camcorder ownership which would increase demand
- Technological improvements associated with the production of camcorders would lead to a fall in their price and raise quantity demanded

Fig 10.9   *A camcorder – competing in a rapidly growing market*

- The market price of the product is likely to change over the budgeted period

As a buyer – Nestlé coffee

Nestlé produce the leading brand of instant coffee, Nescafé. In order to produce the product they need to buy coffee beans, whose price is determined by the world demand and supply for coffee. The current price of coffee is very much supply determined, and this in turn is dependent on the year's crop. In 1989, poor weather conditions spoiled the coffee crop, reducing supply. Given the current level of demand, this led to a dramatic rise in the market price of coffee beans, increasing the cost of producing Nescafé and reducing the profit margin earned by the product. By understanding this, Nestlé could more accurately assess the performance of its instant coffee brand, and consider its financial performance in the light of this.

THE CLASSICAL MUSIC BUSINESS

FANFARE FOR THE COMPACT DISC: THIS IS A GREAT TIME TO BE A LOVER OF CLASSICAL MUSIC

In the last few years the catalogue of recordings has expanded dramatically. Never before has so much music been available to so many. Can it last? The classical music department of any big record store offers today's listeners such a wide range of products that their counterparts of, say, 30 years ago would have been astonished. As never before they can choose from an enormous variety of titles, many available in numerous different recordings. The works of many composers, stretching back over centuries, are available for the first time.

Why has this occurred? Especially in the past decade, the classical music market has increased dramatically. Between 1980 and 1992 sales of recorded music in the five largest markets (America, Britain, Japan, France and Germany) increased from $9 billion to $20 billion, a rise of more than 40 percent in volume terms. Classical recordings still account for only a minute part of that total, but as the market for recorded music expands, they benefit too, often increasing their share. In America's growing market, the share of classical recordings went up from three percent in 1980 to 4.4 percent in 1992.

A number of factors have driven the expansion in the market for recorded music in general, and for classical music in particular. The launch of the compact disc (CD) was critical. The CD format beats the vinyl record on most criteria. Longer playing times suit classical pieces, which vary in length more than rock music and frequently run to more than the vinyl record's limit of 20 to 25 minutes a side. As vinyl LPs become obsolete and collections are rebuilt in the new format, a thriving replacement market bolsters sales of new material. Classical music has acquired a more popular appeal due to musicians with looks and personality as well as talent. Luciano Pavarotti (arguably stronger on personality than looks), is probably the best known. Instrumentalist, Nigel Kennedy attracted an impressive following for his unorthodox attitudes and amusing haircut (though for the moment this British violinist has faded from view). Especially remarkable was the success of a PolyGram Group recording of the 'Three Tenors' (Mr Pavarotti together with Placido Domingo and Jose Carreras). Released in 1990, it sold 11 million units (CDs, LPs and cassettes combined) up to the end of 1993 alone. Remembering that the average annual sale of a classical recording from the big companies is rather less than 10,000 units, the effect of this success on record company bosses is easy to see. Even if it could not be repeated, it showed that the potential market for classical music was bigger than people suspected. Hundreds of

▶ ▶

thousands of new buyers, at the least, had entered the market and some of them might be persuaded to stay. In all the main markets, populations are getting older. This demographic shift has also helped sales of classical music, according to many in the industry. Younger buyers may be attracted by the image of a Nigel Kennedy, an adventurous repertoire such as that of America's Kronos Quartet, or an occasional collaboration between a pop star and a chamber group (the Brodsky Quartet recently made a recording with Elvis Costello). But classical music is still preferred by people of 30 or older. The new buyers of classical music have split the market into two areas. The first is the hard core of enthusiasts: passionate about the music, they buy regularly and look for recordings by lesser-known or downright obscure composers and artists. The other comprises occasional customers, whose likes and dislikes are often influenced by the music used on television or in films. This group is much larger, but more difficult to reach and is unpredictable. Nobody knows if or when there will be another success like the 'Three Tenors'. This split in the market, however, has created new opportunities for the record companies.

On the supply side, like consumers, the record companies divide into two groups – majors and independents. The majors are PolyGram (including the Decca, Philips and Deutsche Grammophon labels); EMI (the HMV label); Sony (owner of CBS and the Columbia label); Warner Bros; and BMG (owner of RCA). The most popular artists, and the big money, are to be found at the majors. Big hits, however, do not always follow. The investment in a single recording can be very large, and the payback slow. Why do they bother? The answer for the big record companies is that most of their revenue comes from their back-catalogues – recordings made in earlier years. These represent the major part of sales each year (around 70 percent, in the case of the EMI international classical division). With skill and investment, a small number of recordings each year may be good enough to become precious items in the back-catalogue. If they do, they will sell for years, earning high profits for their producers. But nobody knows for sure which recordings will do this. In the effort to find some, the majors keep rolling out new titles.

One of the greatest successes of recent years is the ultra-low-price label, Naxos. It is run by Klaus Heymann, a distributor of electronic hardware based in Hong Kong, who decided in 1987 to introduce a series of standard repertoire recordings on CD, but at LP prices. The idea was to use little-known musicians (no union rates to pay) but make high-quality recordings. The success of Naxos has been astonishing: the firm sold eight million units worldwide in 1993. Some competitors and retailers complain about poor performances by underpaid musicians – as they would. Mr Heymann says it is better to attract new customers than to discourage potential ones with high prices and elitist marketing. Once hooked they can be persuaded to trade up. The major producers recognise the lack of really exciting musical talent to replace the money-spinning giants who have reached the end of their careers, such as Dietrich Fischer-Dieskau or the late Leonard Bernstein and Herbert von Karajan. To continue attracting new customers, they

▶ ▶

must change things. As the independent budget labels have taken a bigger share of the classical market, forcing British full-price album sales down, so major record companies have responded by launching their own budget labels, such as the 'Mad About . . .' series from the PolyGram Group.

A great deal of the growth in the market for classical music has been due to the enterprise of the independent record labels in finding new pieces to record. Could they run out? Hardly. The *Grove Encyclopaedia of Music* runs to 20 volumes with details of nearly 10,000 composers, most of them still unrecorded. Even the works of the most celebrated composers are by no means exhausted. New pieces are often discovered, for example, a work by Berlioz was performed and recorded for the first time in 1993. Meanwhile, living composers are producing works which can be surprisingly successful, such as the Third Symphony of Gorecki, a Polish composer and recent best-seller worldwide. Could the 1990s be the decade of the living composer? This is unlikely, as Beethoven is still selling more than all of them put together. But relationships between composers and record companies appear to be growing closer. Nonesuch, an American label owned by Warner Bros, has signed up John Adams. And PolyGram has signed up Michael Torke, a young American composer, and Graham Fitkin from Britain. Sales of their records are still small, 'but they'll be famous in ten years' is the company's claim. Keep listening.

QUESTIONS

1 a Outline the factors which influence the demand for a product. [5]

  b Using a diagram, illustrate what has happened to the demand for classical music recordings. [3]

  c Account for the change in demand for classical music recordings. [7]

2 a What is a supply curve or supply schedule? [4]

  b Account for the shape of the supply curve. [5]

  c Explain what has happened to the supply curve of classical recording in recent years. [6]

3 As the manager of a small chain of record shops that is considering whether to start stocking classical records, suggest what type of classical records they should stock. [5]

4 A record company that specialises in popular music is considering whether they should start to market classical records. What are the advantages and disadvantages of moving into this new market? [15]

Total [50]

COFFEE FROST DAMAGE PUT AT 40%

When Brazil issued a frost damage estimate to their coffee crop in 1994 which was far higher than most analysts were expecting, the impact on the London Commodity Exchange was immediate. The initial response was a $177 jump in the September delivery price for coffee, resulting in a trading price of $3,650 a tonne. This reflected the Brazilian industry and commerce ministry's revised estimate of 15.7 million bags (60 kg each). That was about 11 million bags down on the 26.5 million bags initially forecasted before frosts struck. The immediate response was, in actual fact, trimmed back a little but the overwhelming trend of large increases in price remained.

It emerged later, however, that most analysts' damage forecasts settled into a 6–9 million bag range, leading the September price at the L.C.E. to sag to $3,662 a tonne. In contrast, Mr Robalinho, the Brazilian trade minister said, "The situation is really dramatic. We had a loss of approximately 11 million bags. These numbers are preliminary, but ... they will only change a little." He made his estimates following a meeting of representatives from nine states, climatologists and government coffee experts.

QUESTIONS

1 Using a demand and supply diagram, illustrate and explain what has happened to coffee prices on the London Commodity Exchange. [5]

2 As a producer of instant coffee:
  a explain what impact this change in coffee prices might have on each aspect of your business; [10]
  b suggest a strategy you could develop to deal with the problems created by this change in coffee prices. [15]

  Total [30]

The Business Environment – Section B: The macroeconomy

SUMMARY

1. All businesses have to trade in the macroeconomy which is the national economic environment.
2. Economic growth is the rise in the output of the whole economy over time. It is measured by the rise in GDP.
3. Economic growth normally makes the trading conditions for business favourable.
4. Economic recession makes the trading conditions for business unfavourable.

5. Inflation is the continuous rise in the general level of prices in the economy. Businesses need to allow for this change in prices when they are trading.
6. Unemployment is people within the macroeconomy who do not have work. Organisations have to trade in the poor demand conditions that exist with high unemployment.

Macroeconomics is concerned with the study of the whole economy. It aggregates the activities of consumers, firms and other countries to see how they behave in national terms. Whereas in microeconomics we would consider the sales revenue of an individual firm to measure its output, in macroeconomics we would look at the total sales revenue of all firms to obtain a national value for the whole country's output. Much of government economic policy is concerned with macroeconomy, and how it can be manipulated to benefit the nation's citizens. Organisations have to react and make decisions in the prevailing macroeconomic climate, and respond to changes in it.

ECONOMIC GROWTH

Economic activity

Economic activity takes place when a business combines resources to produce goods and services, which are then sold to consumers. The total value of this activity, which comes in the form of output produced by all the businesses in society in one year, is called the national income.

Measuring national income

The national income measured by the value of output produced by resources within the domestic economy is called the gross domestic product or GDP. There are three ways of measuring the GDP.

GDP

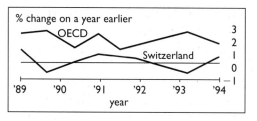

Balance of payments

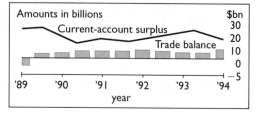

Consumer prices

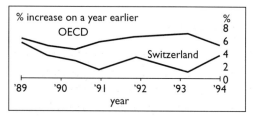

Unemployment

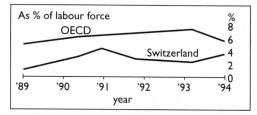

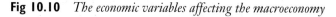

Fig 10.10   *The economic variables affecting the macroeconomy*

1 **Output approach**   This involves taking the value of the output produced by each business organisation in the economy, and taking the total of this for one year.
2 **Income approach**   Because the value of output produced is paid to the resources used in production (wages are paid to workers, and dividends to shareholders) the value of income earned by individuals will be equal to the value of output produced.
3 **Expenditure approach**   The amount spent on all the goods and services produced by businesses will be equal to the value of output produced, which gives us the expenditure method of measuring national income.

Economists also use the gross national product or GNP to measure the national income. The gross national income is GDP plus the value of income earned from assets owned overseas, such as dividends and interest; outflows of income earned on foreign assets owned within the domestic economy are subtracted.

Measuring economic growth

Economic growth is the rise in the national income measured by either GDP or GNP over time. It is measured by the percentage change in GDP or GNP year on year. The table below shows the growth rates of major industrialised countries in 1997. An allowance is made for inflation over time, so that growth is expressed in real terms, or constant prices.

Country	Growth rate 1997 (%)
Canada	1.2
France	1.2
Germany	2.4
Italy	0.5
Japan	3.2
Spain	1.9
USA	2.2
UK	2.3

If this did not happen, the fact that money falls in value with inflation would give a false picture of the rise in national income over time.

Causes of economic growth

The output of an economy will rise either if more resources are employed, or if the productivity (the amount of output produced from each unit of resources) goes up. By looking at each resource in turn we can see the potential causes of economic growth.

Labour

If the population available to work rises then there are more workers to raise output. With high levels of unemployment in most countries, rising population is not seen as particularly critical, whereas the skills of available workers is. A more educated and trained labour force is more productive, and is an important factor in contributing to economic growth. Indeed, a shortage of skilled labour is a critical factor that hinders growth.

Capital

The accumulation of capital (increase in the number of machines) is called investment. The level of investment is seen as a vitally important factor in contributing to growth, since machines improve the productivity of labour. However, it is the technological advance of capital that has been the most important factor enhancing growth over time. The break-throughs in microchip technology and the development of computers over the last 20 years has, and will continue to have, critical importance in growing economies. The source of funds from capital markets is very important in allowing investment, and the development of new technology.

Land

The exploration and discovery of the natural resources, oil and gas, has contributed significantly to UK economic growth since they first came online in the 1970s. More recently, the exploitation of wind and solar power has also added to output. However, improving the productivity of raw materials, and developing new natural resources such as wind and solar energy, is dependent on the development technology in capital.

Entrepreneurship

The desire of individuals to set up production is the final factor contributing to growth. Many economists have identified the entrepreneurial spirit present in South East Asian economies as being important in the rapid growth they have achieved in the last 15 years.

The consequences of growth

As economic growth occurs, the output of the economy rises, which means individuals receive, assuming the population remains constant, higher incomes, and they buy more goods and services. As people earn more they also pay more tax, giving the government more funds to spend on public expenditure items, like education and health. In material terms, the country's population should experience a rise in living standards. These conditions lead to rising consumer and business confidence, where consumers and businesses generally feel better about their prospects, and make decisions in the light of this. However, whilst material living standards may well rise, growth often results in environmental pollution, and greater stress on individuals, which makes it difficult to assess the effect growth has on the overall wellbeing of the population.

Organisations are affected by economic growth in a number of ways.

Fig 10.11   *The impact of growth on organisations*

1 As incomes rise, along with higher consumer confidence, demand tends to rise, particularly for consumer goods that are responsive to changes in consumer income, such as cars, holidays and clothing. Thus businesses in these sectors can expect to experience rising sales, which means increasing production, hiring more staff, building up stocks, and perhaps looking to expand production.

2 Higher sales may well increase profits.

3 As most firms will experience rising sales, there will generally be more cash flowing from consumers and between businesses, resulting in better cashflow for organisations.

4 Most businesses will be looking to expand output, which means buying in more stock, hiring more workers, and acquiring new capital. This means that the markets for all these inputs will experience rising demand, which in turn increases their price. As a result, organisations will have to pay more for their resource inputs, which increases their costs.

5 Greater consumer demand makes it easier for companies to increase their prices to achieve greater profit margins. This, combined with an upward pressure on costs, tends to cause generally rising prices in markets and inflation.

The article which follows shows how economic growth benefits business when the economy recovers from a recession. Growing demand improves business conditions and reduces the number of businesses that fail.

ECONOMIC RECOVERY PROMPTS DRAMATIC FALL IN BUSINESS FAILURES

In December 1994, Dun & Bradstreet, the business information group, reported that the economic recovery had led to a sharp fall in the number of business failures, both large and small.

Its 1994 tally of business liquidations and bankruptcies recorded that the number of failures in England and Wales had dropped 16.3 percent to 40,255 following a figure of 48,066 in 1993. Mainland Britain, including Scotland, showed an even more prominent drop of 21.8 percent to 43,598 from 55,733 in 1993. This was due in part to the 56.4 percent drop in business failures which Scotland enjoyed after changes were made in their bankruptcy regulations, reducing the financial incentive of bankruptcy for companies. Anthony Nelson, Treasury minister, was confident that these overall figures would boost confidence in the job market. He predicted a prosperous new year for the many small businesses that had provided recent growth in employment. Mr

Philip Mellor, a senior analyst at Dun & Bradstreet, commented that such a dramatic fall in the number of business failures had not occurred since before the recession in 1987. The number of failing companies at that time, however, was a great deal smaller: less than 20,000 in England and Wales. The fact that the figures indicated that small businesses were participating in the recovery was, in Mr Mellor's words, 'the most encouraging part'.

Dun & Bradstreet saw the bankruptcy figures as a good proxy for small-company failures, whereas larger companies go into liquidation. In 1994 England and Wales, excluding Scotland, saw a 15 percent drop in bankruptcies to 24,505 down from 28,846 in 1993. This was only marginally behind the 18 percent fall in liquidations to 15,750 from 19,220.

Recession

The official definition of a recession is two consecutive quarters of negative economic growth. In other words, the output of the economy is falling. In reality, periods of low growth also give the characteristics of a recession which are: rising unemployment, low or falling demand for goods, low inflation and little investment. Both business and consumer confidence tend to fall as these groups feel less certain about the future in a recession.

A recession will have the following consequences for businesses.

1 Falling incomes and low consumer confidence will lead to low or falling demand which will reduce an organisation's sales and profits, particularly in those industries that are responsive to changes in consumer incomes, such as cars and household goods.

Fig 10.12   *The consequences of recession for businesses*

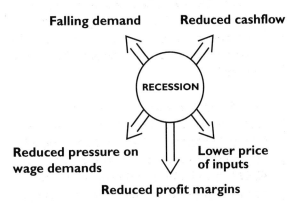

Fig 10.13   *The impact of recession on an organisation*

2 Generally, lower demand from firms for resource inputs will lead to slow growth or even falling prices, that in turn reduce a business's costs.

3 Falling sales will reduce the amount of cash entering businesses, which slows down the rate at which businesses pay each other, and this has an adverse effect on the individual firm's cashflow.

4 Lower demand in the market for goods means firms may have to reduce prices to maintain sales, which reduces their profit margins.

The business cycle

The business cycle is the pattern of upturns and downturns in economic growth that occur over time. Figure 10.14 shows the phases of the business cycle, as periods of rapid growth or booms are followed by periods of falling growth or recessions. The UK economy has followed this pattern of economic activity for the last 150 years, with the pattern repeating itself every five years or so. The explanation of the business cycle is not fully understood, but history shows that it is so predictable that businesses must be aware of it in their planning and decision making. For example, a business carrying out an investment appraisal will need to build changes in the business cycle into their cashflow forecasts.

■ MACROECONOMIC ISSUES

As the economy moves through the business cycle, inflation and unemployment are the two main macroeconomic problems it faces. Organisations have to come to terms with the consequences of these problems when they are making decisions.

Inflation

Inflation is the continuous and sustained rise in the general level of prices in the economy.

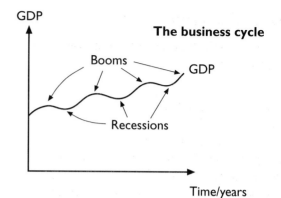

Fig 10.14   *The path of GDP as the economy moves through the business cycle*

Prices across all markets tend to increase over time due to inflation, and this should be distinguished from price changes as they occur at the micro level due to demand and supply shifts.

Inflation is measured using a price index, which, in the UK, is called the retail price index. This takes the average price of a representative basket of goods bought by households. The percentage change in this average price year on year is the inflation rate. The following table shows the inflation rates of major industrialised nations over the last five years.

Country	1997 % rate of inflation
Canada	1.8
France	1.8
Germany	1.5
Italy	2.6
Japan	0.5
Spain	3.5
USA	3.0
UK	2.7

Causes of inflation

The causes of inflation are broken down into two distinct types.

Demand pull inflation

Demand pull inflation occurs when total or aggregate demand from consumers rises during periods of rapid economic growth. Organisations who run short of supply, or see the opportunity to increase profit margins, raise prices. In addition, rising demand for resources from firms trying to increase output pulls up resource costs and forces firms to increase prices.

For example, as the demand for houses rises, the demand for building workers increases, which in turn leads to a rise in their wages. Building firms that face a higher wage bill subsequently put up their prices.

Cost push inflation

Cost push inflation occurs when there is a rise in resource costs, and organisations pass on these higher costs in the form of higher prices. This happens if workers, through their trade union, bid up wages, or a raw material price increases.

The following article illustrates the importance of input costs in causing inflation.

RAW MATERIAL PRICE RISES INCREASE FEARS ABOUT INFLATION

Raw material costs increased significantly in 1994 following a surge in world commodity prices. This pushed up the price of imported materials. The rise fuelled fears that there could be price pressures in the pipeline which could increase the UK's low inflation rate at the time.

The price of goods leaving factory gates rose at a relatively subdued rate, suggesting that many companies were still being forced to absorb the rising costs. Government sources said that the price of goods purchased by the manufacturing industry had risen by a seasonally adjusted 0.7 percent in September 1994 and by 5.7 percent in the 12 months to September. The increase was larger than the City had expected. In August 1994 the annual growth rate was 3.9 percent. The cost of goods leaving factory gates rose by 0.2 percent in September that year, however.

Measured without the volatile elements of food, beverages, tobacco and petroleum, output price inflation grew by a seasonally adjusted 0.4 percent in September 1994 and by 2.1 percent over the 12 months. The cost of imported materials, particularly commodities such as rubber and copper, rose very sharply. The sharpest price increases were reported in manufacturing sectors which have the greatest exposure to world commodity price changes, such as the pulp and paper, metals, rubbers and chemicals sectors. In October 1994, the Government said that the underlying trends remained relatively subdued. 'This is a sharp price increase, but it is from a pretty low level,' it said. It should also be remembered that any rise in material costs should be partly offset by the fact that unit wage costs – the key component of business costs – had fallen slightly.

Consequences of inflation for organisations

The severity of inflation's consequences for organisations will depend on how high inflation is, and its volatility. If inflation is relatively stable below five percent, then its consequences will be relatively minor. However, if inflation rises above 10 percent and is unpredictable, then its effects will be much more marked. At the extreme, where hyperinflation exists, such as in Brazil in the early 1990s where inflation peaked at around 3,000 percent, trading conditions for organisations become extremely difficult.

Changing prices

During periods of relatively high inflation businesses have constantly to reset prices. This means taking time to set prices and reprint price lists. This becomes a time consuming exercise that adds to costs. Businesses can, however, use inflation as a way of adding to their profit margins because they can hide profit-making price increases under the guise of inflation. For example, an off-licence that buys in beer at £12 a case and sells it for £18 earns a contribution of £6. The cost to off-licences of buying the beer increases by 10 percent to £13.20, and the off-licence adds 10 percent to its price to £19.80, which increases the margin by 10 percent to £6.60.

Altering accounts

Inflation alters the true values of costs, revenues, assets and liabilities. The high inflation of the 1970s forced firms to develop a new system of accounting which took into account the inflation of that time. This increased administration costs, and made accounts more difficult to interpret.

Borrowing and lending

Inflation reduces the value of money over time, which means that the real value of debts repaid after a certain time period falls. For example, if a business borrows £100,000 to buy a new piece of machinery, and repays this after two years with inflation at an annual rate of five percent, then the real value of the £100,000 repaid will be lower than at the start of the period. In this case, the lending organisation is seen to lose and the borrower gain. However, lenders compensate themselves for inflation by raising the interest rate they charge on loans. Because lenders may also be worried that inflation could suddenly rise and catch them out, as it may do with high, unpredictable inflation rates, they will add an interest premium to the rate they charge. So with inflation at five percent, banks may charge a 10 percent rate of interest. This interest premium makes the cost of borrowing even more expensive for organisations. Higher interest rates add to a business's finance costs, and makes the cost of new investment more expensive.

Rising costs

During periods of inflation, firms experience a rise in costs as all resources tend to go up in price. Workers will demand larger wage increases to maintain their standard of living, and suppliers will pass on their own higher costs by raising the price of raw materials and components.

Government macroeconomic policy

Governments will step in to deal with the problem of inflation by contracting aggregate demand using higher interest rates. The fall in consumption resulting from higher interest rates reduces the sales of firms, particularly those which sell consumer durables. Higher interest rates also push up the borrowing costs of organisations, and this adversely affects their profitability.

International competitiveness

When there is inflation in the domestic economy that is higher than the inflation rates of the country's main international competitors, domestic producers will be at a competitive disadvantage. Domestic firms will see their costs rising faster than their competitors, which means they either have to settle for lower profit margins or increase their prices. This loss of competitiveness on behalf of domestic producers will put pressure on their market shares, sales and profitability.

Unemployment

Unemployment occurs when people who are willing and able to work cannot find jobs. Unemployment is either measured as an absolute number, or as a percentage of the workforce. The figure is quoted each month, and is seasonally adjusted to take into account the natural rise and fall in unemployment that takes place at certain times of the year, such as the fall that takes place in the summer as people are taken on in tourism. Since the early 1980s, the level of unemployment has risen to historically high levels in most major industrialised countries. The following table summarises the levels of unemployment in OECD countries in 1997.

Types of unemployment

Unemployment is categorised into four different types.

1 **Frictional unemployment**   This type of unemployment occurs when people leave

Country	1997 % rate of unemployment
Canada	10.0
France	12.6
Germany	10.7
Italy	12.2
Japan	3.4
Spain	21.9
USA	5.2
UK	7.2

one job to get another as part of the everyday turnover in the labour market. People decide to leave a job in search of a better one, or they get sacked. It then takes them time to find another job. This is a short-term type of unemployment that is present whatever stage in the business cycle the economy is in.

2 **Structural unemployment**   Structural unemployment occurs when there is a mismatch of skills between those who are unemployed and available job vacancies. Workers may be made redundant because their work can now be done by machines, or the markets for the products they produce are competed away by cheaper foreign competition. This type of unemployment has affected many of the older heavy industries, such as ship-building and coal mining, where cheap foreign competition, along with the use of new technology have caused these industries to decline.

3 **Demand deficient unemployment**   This type of unemployment occurs when the economy experiences a downturn in the business cycle, and is in recession. Consumer demand falls, which leads to a reduction in output by most firms, who in turn make workers redundant. In a recession, there is a spiral effect where workers who are made redundant no longer spend as much, and employed workers cut their own spending for fear of unemployment. This causes businesses to reduce output, shedding labour in the process.

4 **Real wage unemployment**   When wage levels are pushed up to a level beyond that which organisations can afford, they will look to make workers redundant. This could occur because of the negotiating power of trade unions, or because a government imposes a minimum wage to protect workers. At present, a minimum wage does not operate in the UK but it

does in Europe, and is considered to be a factor in contributing to the high level of unemployment in France and Spain.

Consequences of unemployment to organisations

As with inflation, it is the level of unemployment that has the critical impact on business decision making. It is difficult to be exact when identifying the point where unemployment becomes critical, but when the economy is in recession, and the rate rises above 10 percent, as it has in much of Europe in 1997, then it has a significant impact on decision making. This is also important for firms in certain regions when high levels of unemployment become concentrated there.

The consequences can be looked at in the following ways.

1 **Sales and profits** At the bottom of the business cycle, organisations will see the demand for their products fall as unemployed workers spend less, and workers in employment, who are frightened of being made redundant, reduce their spending. Companies that produce goods that are responsive to changes in income, such as those in household furnishing, video and TV, and holidays will be particularly hard hit. Companies producing at the cheap end of the market, or in the food sector, will not

be as affected. As sales fall, profits will also fall; because revenue is reduced, firms struggle to maintain profit margins in a depressed market.

2 **Recruitment** With a high level of unemployment the pool of available workers increases for organisations to choose from, which means that firms will find it easier to find the staff they want.

3 **Wage rates** The surplus supply of labour that exists with high unemployment tends to put downward pressure on wage rates. Organisations do not have to pay as much to tempt workers to their businesses, and workers are less likely to push for higher wages when they are frightened of losing their jobs.

4 **Staff turnover** Whilst business may well be forced to make workers redundant, which obviously adds to the numbers who leave organisations, workers are far less likely to change jobs when they feel uncertain about getting a new job, and fewer firms are taking on new employees.

5 **Motivation** The motivation of workers can be looked on in two ways: workers who are frightened about losing their jobs will work harder to keep it, and are more likely to do what management demands. However, the added stress which the fear of unemployment brings may well reduce the morale of workers, adversely affecting their performance at work.

THE CHINA COMPANY LTD ATTEMPT TO MAINTAIN MARGINS

The China Company Ltd produce a range of quality china products for the domestic market. They are a family run business who have been in existence for over 150 years. The accounting department are in the process of producing a budgeted profit and loss account for 1998. The profit and loss account for the year ending 1997 is set out below.

	£000s
Sales	1,800
Direct costs	700
Gross profit	1,100
Overheads	400
Net profit	700

The domestic economy is expected to grow by three percent in the coming year, with particularly strong growth in the household goods sector. The finance director believes sales will increase by eight percent in the coming year if their selling price is left the same. However, he is worried by the increase in labour costs which he forecasts will raise direct costs by 15 percent, reducing profit margins. Overheads are expected to fall by two percent because of lower energy prices, and falling communications costs. The China Company could increase prices to maintain margins, but there are concerns about the impact this might have, because the demand for the company's products is price elastic.

QUESTIONS

1 a What do you understand by the term 'economic growth'? [5]
  b Explain the impact economic growth is expected to have on the demand for The China Company's products. [5]
  c Why do you think the rise in demand for The China Company's products is much greater than the rise in economic growth? [5]

2 Produce a budgeted profit and loss account for The China Company for the year ending 31 December, 1998. [10]

3 a Suggest reasons why direct costs are expected to increase so dramatically in the coming year. [7]
  b Discuss how The China Company might try to hold down the rise in direct labour costs. [8]

4 Discuss the problems which The China Company will face if it tries to maintain profit margins by either increasing prices or reducing costs. [20]

Total [60]

CONSTRUCTION INDUSTRY STEEPED IN GLOOM

The slump in the British building industry deepened in 1992. Even the annual building show, Interbuild, held in Birmingham at the N.E.C. could not find enough exhibitors. Two halls remained completely unused and many of the rest had huge, empty areas partitioned off. Many big company names like Tarmac and Marley were absent. Others were staying away to save money.

During the week there was even more bad news for the trade. On November 25th the National Council of Building Materials Producers in its forecast anticipated a decline of 8.5 percent in total construction output in 1991, with the heaviest falls in office and home building. No sustained revival was expected before 1993. The gloom deepened when, on the same day, Sir Clifford Chetwood, the chairman of Wimpey, forecasted a loss of 250,000 jobs in the construction industry by summer 1993. This pessimism was felt keenly in the City where the building-materials sector hit a 15-year low in a slump on a similar scale to that experienced in the 1974–76 downturn when construction fell by 16 percent.

Those who did attend the 1992 building trade show were able to communicate the pessimistic mood of the industry. Procter and Lavender, a Midlands brick distributor, claimed that their monthly turnover had fallen 30 percent on the same period for the previous year. They were receiving a few enquiries for sales in the south-east, but in the north things were getting worse. To further problems, margins were being squeezed by a price war in the brick market. Continental brick producers who had shipped finished bricks during the boom of the 1980s were eagerly waiting on the sidelines to take over struggling firms and set themselves up as local producers. As a result of these pressures, Procter and Lavender had to cut its workforce by a third.

A similar message was conveyed by Ideal-Standard, a sanitary-ware maker. Sales during this period fell by 30 percent and money for reinvestment was extremely limited. As it is owned by an American parent company with other subsidiaries on the continent, pursuing exports within the EC was no solution to the domestic recession.

In fact the building industry in general appeared to be under threat from continental rivals who were evident at the Birmingham trade fair. The more vulnerable businesses were seen as easy prey for the predatory continental firms searching to enter the British market disguised as local firms.

There was one upbeat exhibitor at the trade fair. Yale, a well-known ironmongers, claimed that rising crime had been responsible for a surge in the locks and home security-business.

QUESTIONS

1 a What are the characteristics of an economic recession? [5]

b Why do you think the building industry is affected by recession more than other industries such as food and energy? [10]

2 Using demand and supply analysis, explain what has happened to the price of bricks. [10]

3 Aspect Carpets is a regional chain of carpet retailers. The recession in the building industry outlined in the article above has had a dramatic effect on their business.

a Analyse the impact of the recession in the building industry on Aspect Carpets. [10]

b Suggest a strategy Aspect Carpets could use to deal with the problems of an economic recession. [15]

Total [50]

The Business Environment – Section C: International business

SUMMARY

1 The global economy is an increasing challenge to all organisations.
2 Trade between countries is recorded in the balance of payments. If exports are greater than imports, the balance of payments is in surplus.
3 Trading in international markets offers opportunities, such as greater sales, and threats such as more competition.

4 The exchange of currencies that needs to take place when businesses trade internationally adds to the complexity of trading.
5 Changes in the exchange rates alter the prices that businesses set in international markets, and change the costs of goods they buy in from abroad.

The international business environment represents a wider economic arena within which organisations have to operate. There is no doubt that the global economy affects firms more now than it has ever done before as the volume of international trade between countries increases. It does not just affect organisations that export, but any business that competes with foreign imports on the domestic market, or that relies on imported inputs in production. Therefore, the international market has an impact on almost all businesses, although obviously those firms that compete directly in the global market place will experience the greatest impact.

RECORDING TRADE – BALANCE OF PAYMENTS

The balance of payments records the value of trade that takes place between the domestic economy and overseas. It does this by recording the inflow and outflow of funds between the domestic economy and other countries. The balance of payments is frequently used by economists to measure an economy's success when trading abroad. The account is broken down into three sections.

1 **Current account** This section of the account records trade in goods (visible trade), and services (invisible trade). A good produced within the UK, and sold to a foreign buyer is an export; it is an inflow of funds into the UK economy. If a UK buyer purchases a good produced abroad, then this is an import into the UK and causes an outflow of funds from the UK. It is the money value recorded on this account that is used in the media to report a country's trading position. The table opposite shows the current account position of major developed economies.

Country	Balance of payments (Bn $)
Canada	−2.2
France	+28.8
Germany	−12.4
Italy	+42.2
Japan	+74.0
USA	−166.3
UK	+3.6

2 **Capital account** This section of the balance of payments records the inflow and outflow of funds as a result of the buying and selling of assets. If a UK investor buys shares abroad or makes a loan to a foreign company, then this is an outflow on the capital account. If a foreign investor buys shares in UK companies or makes a loan to a UK company, then this causes an inflow of funds.

3 **Official financing** When the current and capital accounts are combined there will either be an overall deficit or surplus. An overall deficit has to be financed by the economy's monetary system through the central bank which uses reserves of gold and foreign currency. A net surplus means that reserves of gold and foreign currency can be built up by the central bank.

Current account surpluses and deficits

The current account is focused on by economists and business people, because it reflects the trading strength of the economy. When the current account is in surplus, the value of exports is greater than the value of imports and there is a net inflow of funds into the UK. When imports are greater than exports, the current account is said to be in deficit, and there is a net outflow of funds from the UK. If the UK economy is performing well and its industries are competitive against foreign producers, then the current account is more likely to be in surplus, and the economy on the whole is in a strong trading position. A deficit, on the other hand, is a weak trading position because UK industry has failed to compete effectively in foreign markets. Governments set a current account surplus as one of their macroeconomic policy objectives.

■ TRADING IN FOREIGN MARKETS

When organisations enter foreign markets, either as buyers or sellers, they come across a whole series of opportunities and threats.

Export opportunities

Export markets represent a number of major opportunities for business.

1 **Greater sales** Businesses that move into overseas markets increase their potential sales because they are targeting a much larger group of consumers. Multinational corporations like Coca Cola, IBM and Shell, have, over time, moved well beyond their saturated home markets in search of greater sales.

2 **Economies of scale** As sales rise, the scale of production increases and organisations benefit from economies of scale. Ford, for example, is able to expand production onto larger scale machinery, buy components in bulk and allow its personnel to specialise, all of which improves its efficiency and allows it to reduce unit costs.

3 **Risk spreading** By diversifying into a number of countries, an organisation spreads the risk associated with

concentrating on one market, should that market go into a recession. An organisation like Toyota sells its cars on every continent, so if sales fall in a depressed North American market, they can still sell in Europe and Asia.

4 **Business development**   Trading in foreign markets means that an organisation will come across a whole new set of business ideas as it is forced to compete and cooperate with foreign organisations. Computer manufacturers are able to learn from technical developments in foreign markets. Many multinationals have embarked on joint ventures with foreign partners, such as Honda and Rover, to develop new, better products.

Exporting threats

However, there are also threats that businesses need to be aware of as they seek to develop overseas markets.

1 **Language and cultural differences**   Firms will come up against a completely different set of challenges when they look to expand into another country; challenges that will affect their entire marketing mix. When Proctor and Gamble markets products on European markets it has to change the name of products to take into account language differences.

2 **Competition**   As world trade increases, the amount of global competition facing organisations goes up, which means that firms have to react continuously to more competition. The rapid growth of South East Asian economies, such as South Korea, Taiwan, and China, has introduced a great deal of low cost competition in a whole variety of goods from cars to computers.

3 **Trade barriers**   When a business looks to export a product to a new foreign market it may well come across trade barriers set up by the foreign country's government, who

are trying to restrict the volume of imports. Barriers can be official in the form of tariffs where a tax is levied on products as they enter the country, increasing the price of the import, and reducing the demand for them. Restrictions can also be unofficial, where governments use red tape and bureaucracy to make it more difficult for companies to sell exports in their market. The Japanese have always required prohibitively high safety standards from imported cars as a way of restricting the supply of imported cars.

4 **The exchange rate**   The impact of the exchange rate is discussed in greater depth later in this section. Because different countries use different currencies, currencies have to be converted when trade takes place. This process complicates buying and selling, and increases its cost.

Importing opportunities

Businesses import products for the following reasons.

1 **Raw materials and components**   Many organisations buy imported raw materials and components, either because domestic supplies are not available, or because imported components offer better value for money. A number of service based industries, such as banks, have transferred some of their administrative operations overseas to reduce costs. This process is called out-sourcing. Cheap, highly skilled labour in India is used by UK banks to carry out work on computers that can be transferred via the internet back to the UK.

2 **Final products**   Retailers, agents, and dealers import products because they improve the product mix they can offer to their consumers. Supermarket chains, such as Tesco and Sainsbury's, broaden their range of grocery products considerably by importing.

Importing threats

Importing, like exporting, does introduce certain threats to organisations.

1 **The exchange rate** This is particularly important here because any change in it can alter the price at which importers buy foreign products.
2 **Transport costs** The physical distances between the importer and their foreign supplier can increase costs.

3 **Communication** There may also be communication difficulties between the importer and the foreign supplier because of language and cultural differences.

The article below illustrates how organisations can develop the opportunities presented to them by the international marketplace.

OPERATING IN GLOBAL MARKETS – ALLIED DOMECQ

Allied Domecq is a company whose activities are focused on spirits, wine and retailing. In recent times the emphasis of the group has been on turning the organisation into a world-class competitor in the wine and spirits industry. At the end of 1994 Allied Domecq owned 13 top spirit brands, including Beefeater, Courvoisier and Canadian Club. These brands would be used by the organisation to grow market share in Europe, the Americas, Pacific Rim, Asia, Eastern Europe and Africa. Whilst the developed economies of North America and Europe have provided stable, core markets, it is the newly industrialising markets of Asia and Eastern Europe which will provide the new mass markets of the future. Asia is seen as particularly important because it has over half the world's population.

Because of the diverse nature of the new global market place in terms of culture, race, religion and social characteristics, it is vital that Allied Domecq develops a product portfolio that is equally diverse to accommodate differing tastes in different markets. Evidence from China has already shown that there is a substantial demand for cognac and whisky.

Part of the strategy for developing new international markets is to use the expertise that already exists in these markets. Allied Domecq has done this by setting up joint ventures with local producers who help them become established. Joint ventures give Allied the benefits of:

- Better local knowledge of markets
- The provision of expertise and an established distribution network
- Greater speed in setting up operations
- Being seen as a local company
- Developing favourable links with the country's government

Thus by using joint ventures Allied Domecq takes the risk associated with moving into new markets and cements local relationships.

THE EXCHANGE RATE

Countries use different currencies within their economies. When trade takes place the currencies between the buyer and seller of goods traded needs to be exchanged. For example, when a UK car dealership goes to Germany to import BMW cars it has to pay in

Deutchmarks, which means buying Deutchmarks from the bank. Banks get their Deutchmarks from the foreign exchange markets, where currencies are bought and sold.

How an exchange rate works

The exchange rate is the price of one currency in terms of another. If the exchange rate between pounds sterling and the dollar is £1 : $1.50 then the price of one pound sterling is $1.50 to an American buyer.

The example below illustrates how the exchange rate of £1 : $1.50 affects the cost of imported and exported products in the USA and UK.

- US buyer of a UK suit at £1 : $1.50
- Price in sterling £120   Price in dollars $180 (£120 × $1.50)

- UK buyer of a US car at £1 : $1.50
- Price in dollars $15,000   Price in sterling £10,000 ($15,000/$1.50)

Changes in the exchange rate

The exchange rate changes like any other price, when the demand and supply for the currency changes. This occurs on the foreign exchange markets where exchange dealers buy and sell currencies. The following factors will lead to a change in the exchange rate between pounds sterling and the dollar.

1 **Demand for UK goods**   If the demand for UK goods increases in the US, then the demand for sterling will rise which causes its value to rise against the dollar. The opposite occurs if the demand for UK goods falls in the US, causing the demand for sterling to fall.
2 **Demand for UK investments**   Much of the demand for foreign currencies is based on investors looking to make a return from moving funds between assets, such as shares and bonds, on international markets. Bonds

are like debentures; they are loans made to governments and businesses that earn a rate of interest. Because of this, the demand for currencies is affected by changes in the rate of interest. If interest rates rise in the UK, investors looking to increase returns on their investments will move funds into UK bonds, which increases the demand for sterling, and causes the value of the pound to rise. The opposite occurs if interest rates fall, and investors move their funds out of sterling into other currencies.
3 **Speculation**   Because of the volatile nature of exchange rates, which change continuously on the exchange markets, speculators can make capital gains from buying currencies at one price and selling them at another. If speculators look to buy pounds, then the demand for the pounds will increase, and its exchange rate value will rise. Again, the opposite will occur if speculators sell a currency. Speculators tend to cause the major fluctuations in currencies that can occur.

Following the example we considered above, we can examine the effects of a change in the exchange rate.

A rise in the value of sterling

The value of sterling rises or appreciates against another currency when £1 can buy more of the foreign currency. In the example below, the pound has appreciated in value against the dollar, rising from £1 : $1.50 to £1 : $1.75.

- US buyer of a UK suit at £1 : $1.75
- Price in sterling £120   Price in dollars $210 (£120 × $1.75)

- UK buyer of a US car at £1 : $1.75
- Price in dollars $15,000   Price in sterling £8,571 ($15,000/$1.75)

If the value of sterling rises from £1 : $1.50 to £1 : $1.75 then the cost of UK goods to US buyers increases from $180 to $210, as we can see from the example. This makes the UK suit more expensive to American buyers who are likely not to buy as many, which means that the sales revenue of UK businesses may fall, although this depends on the response of the buyer to the price increase. If demand for the goods sold is price inelastic because of strong brand loyalty, then demand will remain relatively strong, whereas if demand is price elastic it will fall more markedly.

The rise in the value of sterling causes the price of the American car to UK buyers to fall, because they now have to pay less for the dollars with the higher exchange rate for pounds. The UK company which imports the cars now has to pay less for them, which means they can either reduce the price to final customers and increase sales, or leave their final price the same and increase profit margins.

A fall in the value of sterling

Sterling is said to fall in value or depreciate against another currency, when each pound can now buy less of the foreign currency. In our example, the pound has depreciated from £1 : $1.50 to £1 : $1.25.

- US buyer of a UK suit at £1 : $1.25
- Price in sterling £120   Price in dollars $150 (£120 × $1.25)

- UK buyer of a US car at £1 : $1.25
- Price in dollars $15,000   Price in sterling £12,000 ($15,000/$1.25)

The fall in the value of sterling has reduced the price of the UK suit to the US buyer, who may well buy more as a result, which could increase revenue to the UK supplier. As with a rise in the exchange rate, the resulting effect on demand depends on the elasticity. If demand is price elastic in the US then the sales revenue earned in the US may well rise, as demand rises by a large amount. However, if demand is inelastic, sales will only increase

marginally as prices fall. As the pound depreciates, the British buyer of the American car will have to pay more for it because the cost of dollars has increased. The UK buyer can either increase the price to the final consumer, or accept a lower profit margin.

The consequences of the exchange rate for business

Trading internationally has the added complication of the exchange rate that is not present in domestic trading. The extent to which businesses are affected often depends on changes in the exchange rate, and the relative size of any change. Currencies can become very over or under valued at different times. In the last 20 years the pound at different times has been as low as $1.10 and as high as $2.00. This volatility can have quite dramatic consequences for firms that trade internationally. The exchange rate has the following consequences for organisations that either buy or sell on foreign markets.

1 **Setting prices**   The exchange rate can have a marked effect on the price of a good in another country. The example above illustrates how changes in the exchange rate cause the price of exported goods to change. This makes price setting a more complicated task, and may mean that firms often have to change prices as the exchange rate changes.

2 **Managing costs**   If an organisation relies heavily on imported raw materials and components, changes in the exchange rate can alter costs dramatically. If the exchange rate falls, the cost of imported inputs increases, which either forces price increases or causes a fall in margins.

3 **Planning and budgeting**   Changes in the exchange rate can upset forecasted revenues and costs, which can then throw out budgeted values. Organisations can overcome this by using the futures market,

where the price of a currency can be set in the future, and goods can be bought at a price set at some point in the future. For example, a contract can be set up allowing a UK company to buy in an American car at the exchange rate of £1 : $1.50 for delivery in six months time. However, the UK buyer will have to pay a commission for doing this.

4 **Commission**   Banks fulfil the function of changing currencies, and businesses have to buy their foreign currency from the banks. To do this banks charge a commission. For example, if the exchange rate is $1.50 the bank will sell dollars to UK buyers at $1.47 for each £1, and when companies try to change dollars back into pounds they will have to pay $1.53 for each £1. This is an additional cost trading internationally.

Monetary union

In 1999 there is a plan that the different national currencies that exist in each of the member countries of the European Union, will be replaced by a common single currency called the Euro. This means that firms will no

Fig 10.15   *The logo of the European Union*

longer have to exchange currency before trading with countries that have become part of the European Monetary Union (EMU). This means that all the trading problems associated with exchange rate, pricing, costs, budgeting and commission, will all be removed. However, the introduction of monetary union does raise the prospect of the huge conversion costs of changing to a new currency. Prices need to be reset, the accounting system changed, new cash introduced, along with wages and other costs that need to be reset.

CASPER AND SONS IN EUROPE?

Casper and Sons manufacture high quality toys that it has, up to now, sold solely in the UK market. It is a small family-run business that has been established for over 80 years in the Casper family name. Its main product is toy soldiers and war games sets. Whilst some of its market is made up of children aged between 8 and 16, most of its buyers are adult enthusiasts. Its products are sold through 50 outlets in the UK, and it also distributes through mail-order. Anthony

Casper, the company's MD, has attended a number of European toy fairs with a view to expanding into the European market, beginning by selling through specialist retailers in Paris, Berlin and Milan. Other members of the family who make up the board of directors are suspicious of such a move, although the company has done a limited amount of international business through their mail-order section.

QUESTIONS

1 Write a report to Casper and Sons' board of directors outlining the advantages and disadvantages of marketing their product in Europe. [20]

2 Produce a marketing strategy to sell the product in Europe successfully. [20]

Total [40]

CLOCKWISE LTD DEAL WITH EXCHANGE RATES

The Aston Group is a multinational holding company based in the UK. It owns a number of different businesses in a variety of markets ranging from financial services to leisure wear. It has recently bought a UK-based company called Clockwise Ltd that markets watches sold mainly in Europe. Clockwise used to manufacture their watches in the UK, but since 1990 all production has been out-sourced to a manufacturer in China and the watches are imported into the UK. The unit costs of producing the watches, along with their selling price, are set out in the following table. The unit direct costs are based on 14 Chinese yen to £1.

France is one of Clockwise's major markets. In 1997 the firm sold 500,000 units to French buyers at an exchange rate of 9FF to £1. Clockwise is preparing its budget for 1998 in

	£
Selling price	14.99
Unit direct cost	2.00
Unit contribution	12.99
Overheads	2.50
Promotion	1.50
Transport	1.40
Net profit	7.49

the knowledge that the pound is expected to rise to 15 Chinese yen to the pound and to 10 French francs to the pound. With the rise of the value of the pound against the franc, French sales are expected to fall to 450,000 units.

QUESTIONS

1 a Explain why you think Clockwise chose to move production from the UK to China. [3]

b Discuss the problems Clockwise might encounter when moving production to an out-sourced producer in China. [7]

2 a How much does Clockwise pay for the watches in Chinese yen? [3]

b Calculate the budgeted unit contribution for 1998 after the expected change in the value of the pound against the Chinese yen. [7]

3 a Calculate the revenue Clockwise earned from its French sales in French francs. Use the exchange rate of £1:9FF. [5]

b Calculate the 1998 budgeted revenue from the French market after the rise in the value of the pound to £1:10FF. [5]

4 Write a report to the directors of Clockwise on a strategy for dealing with the problems caused by a rise in the value of the pound. [20]

Total [50]

GLOBAL COMPETITION

Will fiercer competition from low-wage developing countries destroy jobs and lower living standards in rich economies?

Developing countries are enjoying increasing economic power. Together with the countries of the former Soviet Union and Eastern Europe, these countries are now responsible for 46 percent of world output. More important, from the point of view of jobs in the rich world, is that developing countries have three times as many people of working age as do OECD countries. Significantly, they are willing to work for considerably lower wages. In the past 30 years only a few developing economies, notably South Korea and Taiwan have emerged as truly industrialised nations. However, if over the next decade economic liberalisation is sustained, dozens of these so-called tigers will join the ranks of the newly industrialised, including huge ones such as China. Rising imports from the newly industrialising countries are often blamed for causing unemployment in America and Europe. Some people consider competition from low-wage countries 'unfair' because workers accept low wages and poor working conditions (no holidays and low safety standards). Pessimistic forecasters have expressed concern that continued 'social

▶ ▶

▶ ▶

dumping' will result in developed countries having to force third-world working conditions or high unemployment upon its labour force.

Labour costs in manufacturing vary greatly between countries. In Germany it costs a mighty $24.90 per hour to hire a worker; American and Japanese workers are cheaper at $16–17 per hour. In contrast, labour costs are only $4.90 and $2.40 per hour in South Korea and Mexico respectively. In China these fall further to less than $1 per hour. There is an obvious incentive for labour-intensive industries to relocate in cheaper countries. The North American Free-Trade Agreement (NAFTA) with Mexico, Canada and the USA was heavily opposed by those in the United States who predicted that if trade barriers between the two countries were scrapped, there would be a huge movement of jobs across the border to Mexico. It is important to note that the productivity of the average American worker is higher than that of the Mexican. That means that labour costs per unit of output vary by much less than pay differentials alone would suggest. So

long as American workers possess better skills and use better technology, they can compete despite enjoying higher wages.

Worries about cheap foreign labour pushing workers out of their jobs also rest upon the incorrect notion that the world's output is fixed, so any increase in Mexico's output must come at the expense of American output and jobs. In fact the opposite may be true. As developing countries grow through rising export earnings they acquire the wealth to purchase products produced by developed countries. As Mexicans experience a rise in earnings they become a market for products produced by the United States. Markets in the Far East and Eastern Europe have become extremely profitable new opportunities for European businesses.

The growth of industrial power in the newly developing economies could provide a threat to traditional business organisations. However, they also provide considerable opportunities to those who are dynamic enough to respond to the challenges their new competitors throw at them.

QUESTIONS

1 Describe the production advantages which industries in the developing world have over those in the developed world. [7]

2 How will economic growth in developing economies provide marketing opportunities for UK firms? [8]

3 Outline a strategy for a computer manufacturer who is looking to reduce the threat posed by competition from developing countries, and trying to maximise the opportunities they offer. [15]

Total [30]

The Business Environment – Section D: The influence of government

SUMMARY

1 Government economic policy has a major impact on the macroeconomy, and the trading environment within which business has to operate.
2 Government sets economic policy to achieve: stable prices, low unemployment and economic growth.
3 Government can apply three types of economic policy; fiscal, monetary and supply side. Each policy, in its own way, affects the business environment within

which organisations have to trade.
4 Fiscal policy is the manipulation of tax and expenditure by governments to achieve economic objectives.
5 Monetary policy is the adjustment of interest rates to achieve economic objectives.
6 Supply side policy involves manipulating the production sector of the economy to achieve economic objectives.

Government has a very important role in shaping the business environment within which organisations operate. Every piece of legislation it passes will have an impact on the decision making of at least a few organisations, and many of the laws passed will have an impact on all organisations. The impact of the government in legal terms is looked at in greater depth in the next section of the business environment. In this chapter we shall concentrate on the government's influence on the economy, and the effect that has on the environment within which businesses trade.

OBJECTIVES OF GOVERNMENT ECONOMIC POLICY

Governments in all countries have a critical impact on the way economies behave, not just because they control so many key economic institutions, such as central banks, but because the level of economic activity by governments accounts for around 40 percent of most developed economies' gross domestic products. Because governments have such a key impact on the macroeconomy, their policies will have a major impact on the operations of businesses within the economy.

Ultimately, governments attempt to manage the economy to achieve the highest living standards possible for the citizens of the country. To do this, a government will try to achieve the following macroeconomic objectives:

- Stable economic growth
- Low unemployment
- Low inflation
- Balance of payments surplus

The achievement of these objectives simultaneously is difficult because in trying to attain them there are conflicts. Economic growth, for example, will mean rising demand in the economy, leading to the build-up of inflationary pressures. In trying to reduce inflation, the government would look to cut aggregate demand, but this would have the effect of reducing economic growth, causing unemployment to rise. However, many economists now feel that these objectives can be achieved in the long term if they are tackled in the right way. They feel that by achieving low inflation, the efficiency of the economy is increased, and this, in the long term, will give the economy stable growth, falling unemployment, and a balance of payments surplus.

Government tools of economic control

To try and achieve its economic objectives, the government has the following policy options:

- Fiscal policy
- Monetary policy
- Supply side policy

▮ FISCAL POLICY

Fiscal policy can be defined as the manipulation of tax and government expenditure to achieve economic objectives. The UK Government sets fiscal policy through its finance department, which is

called the Treasury. Each year the Chancellor of the Exchequer, the UK Government's finance minister, sets out the Government's fiscal policy through the Budget. There are two tools that governments can use under the heading fiscal policy.

Taxation

Tax can be broken down into two types.

1 **Direct tax**   This is tax imposed directly on individuals and organisations. Individuals pay income tax and businesses pay corporation tax on their profits.
2 **Indirect tax**   Indirect or expenditure tax is levied on goods, and is paid by the individuals that buy the goods. VAT, along with duties on beer, wine and cigarettes are examples of indirect tax.

Taxation has the effect of dampening demand in the economy because the income of individuals is reduced by direct tax, and indirect tax increases the price of goods.

Government expenditure

There are three types of government expenditure.

1 **Current expenditure**   This is government expenditure on running the public sector and public services, like education and health. It includes spending on wages, administration and overheads.
2 **Transfer expenditure**   This is spending on welfare payments, such as unemployment benefit, child benefit and state pensions.
3 **Capital expenditure**   This is when governments spend funds on capital projects, such as building schools, hospitals, bridges and motorways.

Government spending accounts for a large proportion of economic activity within the economy; in most developed economies it accounts for around 40 percent of GDP. For this reason, any changes in government expenditure will have a major impact on the economic environment within which businesses have to operate.

Government borrowing

The government raises money through taxation to pay for public spending. However, the amount of tax raised in each year is normally never enough to cover total government spending. In order to meet their spending commitments, when there is a shortfall from taxation, governments are forced to borrow. This is done by selling bonds to the country's population. A bond, like the debentures issued by firms, is a unit of debt sold by the government, which offers a rate of interest to the people that buy them. The government sells a mixture of short-term bonds called Treasury Bills, and long-term bonds called Gilts throughout the year. The total borrowing in any one year by the government is called the budget deficit, which in the UK is called The Public Sector Borrowing Requirement (PSBR).

Expansionary fiscal policy

When the government wants to stimulate economic activity in an attempt to encourage economic growth and reduce unemployment, it will use an expansionary fiscal policy. This means reducing taxation, and/or raising government expenditure. The reduction in taxation encourages consumers to raise spending because they now have a greater disposable income. The rise in public spending naturally increases demand as the state, for example, builds new roads and hospitals. This type of policy tends to increase the budget deficit as the government receives less income from taxation and spends more. As demand rises from the expansionary fiscal policy, output from firms increases, leading to a rise in economic growth and lower unemployment.

An expansionary fiscal policy has the following consequences for businesses.

1 **Sales**   Greater demand for their products as consumption rises. This will be particularly marked in areas likely to benefit directly from higher government spending, such as construction. Firms that produce products that are responsive to changes in demand, like cars and housing, are also likely to benefit. As sales increase, organisations will also see a rise in their profits.
2 **Efficiency**   Reduced taxation offers workers higher after tax incomes. This may well result in greater motivation from workers who earn better rewards from their efforts. Workers may also reduce their wage demands if they take home more pay. In both cases, organisations could benefit from increased efficiency and reduced pressure on wages to rise.
3 **Profits**   If corporation tax is reduced, then firms get to keep more of their profits. Higher profits can provide more funds for investment, and also a greater dividend to shareholders.
4 **Prices**   If indirect tax is reduced, then the price of the final product will be reduced to consumers, which will increase sales. The pattern of indirect taxation, however, has been for increases in the last 20 years.

Tightening fiscal policy

Governments may wish to operate a tight fiscal policy to reduce aggregate demand as they try to reduce inflation. They could also be forced to tighten fiscal policy to try and reduce a budget deficit. By increasing taxation, and/or cutting public expenditure, the level of aggregate demand is reduced. Consumers who are paying more tax will consume less, and public sector demand for goods, in say construction, healthcare, and education, will be reduced. Lower aggregate demand will reduce the demand pull inflationary pressures. The consequences for businesses will be as follows.

1 **Sales**   Sales will fall as consumption falls, and public sector demand goes down. As sales fall, profits are also likely to fall. This will be particularly marked in areas likely to be directly affected by lower government spending, such as construction. Firms that produce products that are responsive to changes in demand, like cars and housing, are also likely to see sales fall.

2 **Efficiency**   Increased taxation offers workers less income after tax. This may well result in lower motivation from workers who earn less from their efforts. Workers may also increase their wage demands if they take home a lower wage. In both cases, organisations could be adversely affected by a fall in efficiency and increased pressure on wages.

3 **Profits**   If corporation tax is increased, then firms see their after tax profits fall. Higher tax, which leads to a fall in sales, will also reduce profits. Lower profits reduce the funds for investment, and the dividend to shareholders.

4 **Prices**   If indirect tax is increased, then the price of the final product to consumers will increase, which will reduce sales. Governments tend to choose products whose demand is price inelastic, like petrol and alcohol, if they raise indirect taxation. Obviously businesses in these sectors will be affected more than other sectors.

■ MONETARY POLICY

Monetary policy is the manipulation of the supply of money using interest rates and credit controls to achieve economic objectives. The government imposes its financial control over the economy through the central bank, which in the UK is called the Bank of England. The Bank of England is a state-owned institution that fulfils a number of functions including: the setting of interest rates, issuing of currency, administration of the banking system, the management of foreign exchange and the administration of monetary policy. The operation of monetary policy was changed in 1997 when the Labour party replaced the Conservatives in government. The Chancellor of the Exchequer, Gordon Brown, gave the Bank of England freedom to set interest rates itself with the objective of achieving a certain inflation target, which, in the first instance, was 2.5 percent. Thus the Bank has the responsibility for setting interest rates to achieve this target.

There are two ways that monetary policy can be applied. Firstly, through credit controls, which are limits put on bank lending by the Bank of England and, secondly, through interest rates. The former method was applied extensively in the 1970s, but it was removed in the 1980s, and interest rates became the main tool of monetary control.

Interest rates

Interest rates represent the price of money borrowed or lent over time. The borrower has to pay interest on the funds they borrow for the time they borrow them, and the lender receives an interest payment as a reward for lending their funds for a set time period. All interest rates are based on the base rate set by the Bank of England. The base rate is the rate charged by the Bank of England when it lends money to UK commercial banks. The commercial banks set their own rates based on this. For example, if base rates are increased by the Bank of England, the commercial banks are forced to pay more interest on the funds they borrow, which in turn means they charge more to their own borrowers, and pay more to their depositors. Other financial institutions are then forced to follow suit, otherwise depositors will take their money from them, and deposit it with the commercial bank. Thus any change in base rates heralds a general change in interest rates throughout the economy.

Within the economy there are a variety of different interest rates paid to lenders and charged to borrowers. These rates depend on the following factors.

1 **Risk**   The higher the risk associated with funds borrowed, the higher the rate of interest charged. This is because lenders require a higher return for money they lend if there is a risk that they may not get it back. This is one of the reasons the rates charged on credit cards are so high.
2 **Secured loans**   If a loan is secured, it means that an asset can be taken by the lender if the borrower defaults on payment. This obviously reduces the risk of non-payment and reduces the rate of interest charged. Mortgages, where a loan is secured against the borrower's property, have lower interest rates than unsecured loans.
3 **Size of the loan**   The more money borrowed by a firm or an individual the lower the rate of interest charged because the administrative cost of the funds lent is spread across a larger sum, which means that the administrative cost per pound borrowed is reduced. In the same way, a larger amount deposited receives a larger interest rate because the administrative cost of managing the account is spread over a larger amount.

Expansionary monetary policy

This is where monetary policy is used to stimulate economic activity, as the government strives for faster economic growth if there is a recession, which in turn should reduce unemployment. If interest rates are reduced, the cost of borrowing falls. This makes the cost of borrowing to finance

spending on cars, houses and consumer durables cheaper. It also means that the interest expense of existing borrowing is reduced; this is particularly important where individuals have bought their own house, and mortgage interest payments account for a large proportion of their disposable income. These two factors combined with the lower returns earned on savings, account for a rise in consumption as interest rates fall. In addition to this, organisations see the cost of borrowing to finance new investment go down, which increases the demand for capital equipment. This rise in investment spending has a major impact on industrial output because investment spending takes place in such huge sums of money. The combination of a rise in consumption and higher investment can lead to a surge in economic growth.

Impact on business

Lower interest rates have the following effects on business.

1 **Sales**   As the economy grows, the sales made by firms, particularly in the housing and car markets where a great deal of consumption is financed through borrowing, expand quickly. The sales of companies that sell consumer durables also increase because credit is cheaper, and more disposable income is freed up by lower mortgage payments. The sales of businesses in the capital goods market rises as investment spending by industrial buyers goes up.
2 **Costs**   Business costs go down with lower interest payments on borrowed funds. This is particularly important for highly geared companies, who have a large proportion of long-term finance in the form of borrowing.
3 **Profits**   The combination of higher sales and lower costs increases profits for business.

4 **Investment projects**   Lower interest rates mean that the opportunity cost of funding new investment projects goes down. Firms are, as a result, more likely to expand into new technology and new products.

5 **Importing and exporting**   When UK interest rates fall, investors see the return on their funds held in UK banks drop; this causes them to sell pounds as they move their funds abroad, which in turn causes the value of the pound to go down. The lower value of the pound makes UK goods cheaper on foreign markets, which increases the sales of exporters. However, the falling pound does make imported raw materials and components more expensive, forcing up costs to certain industries.

A tight monetary policy

When the Bank of England sees inflation as a problem it will raise interest rates to try and reduce aggregate demand and constrain demand pull inflationary pressures. This has been a tactic used by many countries' governments since the early 1980s and 90s. As base interest rates are increased, the cost of borrowing goes up, making the cost of buying houses, cars, and any other items bought on credit, more expensive. The cost of existing borrowing goes up, particularly on mortgages; this reduces consumer disposable incomes, and spending on goods that are closely related to this. Investment spending by firms also falls as the cost of borrowing to finance capital projects goes up. The fall in consumption and investment spending reduces aggregate demand in the economy, which reduces demand pull pressures on inflation.

Impact on business

1 **Sales**   Lower consumption spending will reduce the sales of firms, particularly where consumers often borrow to finance their purchases, as in the case of houses and cars. Sales made by capital good producers will also fall as investment demand goes down.

2 **Costs**   Interest expenses rise with higher interest rates, which increases costs to industry, particularly where organisations have a high proportion of borrowed finance.

3 **Profits**   Lower sales and higher interest expenses reduce company profits.

4 **Importing and exporting**   Higher interest rates increase the exchange rate as foreign investors buy pounds to take advantage of higher returns in UK banks. As the exchange rate rises, the cost of UK goods abroad becomes more expensive, and this may well reduce sales. The higher exchange rate will, however, reduce the cost of imported raw materials and components.

SUPPLY SIDE POLICIES

The supply side of the economy is the production sector made up of business organisations that produce goods and services. Whereas demand side monetary and fiscal policies targeted consumers, supply side policies target producers. During the 1980s and 90s supply side economic policies are now seen as the key to governments achieving their long-term goal of stable growth in real terms. Economists increasingly believe that the total amount that can be produced by the economy depends on the productive capacity of the organisations within the economy. If demand increases too quickly the economy cannot meet the rise in demand, so prices simply go up and there is inflation. However, if the capacity of the economy can be increased, businesses are able to raise their potential output, leading to sustained long-term economic growth.

The aim of the government is to try and make the supply side operate more efficiently through its policies. By considering the resources that make up the supply side it is possible to see the forms the policy can take.

Labour market

In order to improve the efficiency of the labour market, governments would either want to raise the skill level of employees and/or improve their motivation. Both of these factors would increase labour's productivity, which is the amount of output produced by each worker employed. The government would also want to encourage more workers to take jobs because this would reduce unemployment and again increase output. These are the policy options the government has to try and do this.

Income tax

There is a great deal of debate between people in business regarding the importance of money, or more precisely wages, as a motivator. However, there is no doubt that an employee's salary does have some impact on how motivated they are when doing their job. If income tax is reduced people keep more of their income, increasing their returns from working, and they are likely to be more motivated. This could be in the form of people being prepared to do overtime, take on more work in their existing working time, and even just generally push themselves harder at work. The marginal tax rate, the rate at which tax increases as people earn more, is seen as important because if the rate increases too dramatically people will not want to put the extra effort in to raise their salary beyond a certain level. In the UK, the marginal rate of tax increases from 23 percent to 40 percent once people start to earn more than around £30,000. In the 1980s the marginal rate was much higher than this with workers having to pay rates as high as 60 percent when their incomes rose beyond a certain level. The

Conservative Government reduced the rate to its current level to try and increase worker incentives.

National Insurance Contribution is another tax on income in the UK. It is paid by both the employer and the employee, and as such acts as a tax on employment; any reductions in this tax may well encourage more employees to take jobs and more employers to take on workers.

Income and motivation is a complicated argument, with factors such as the nature of the task and other non-monetary factors also influencing motivation, but there is some evidence to suggest that productivity can be increased by reducing direct taxation. However, any reduction in tax has to be financed. Governments either do this through borrowing, reducing spending or by increasing indirect taxation. During the 1980s and 90s, when income tax has been cut from 33 percent to 23 percent, the Conservative Government has increased the amount of tax raised through indirect means. VAT, for example, has increased from 8 percent to 17.5 percent.

Welfare benefits

Welfare payments are made to people for a variety of different reasons, from unemployment to housing benefit. They are paid to give the less well off a minimum standard of living. Many supply side economists feel that benefits hinder the labour market because they prevent people from taking low-paid jobs because they can receive more income on benefit. Thus a policy of reducing benefits and changing the way it is paid encourages people to take jobs, reducing unemployment and raising economic output. The UK Government has introduced the Job Seekers Allowance where people are only paid benefit if they are looking for a job and will take a job offered, and also Family Credit where people are paid benefits if they are working in low-paid jobs. When benefit reductions are combined with tax cuts on low paid workers their impact on employment is even stronger.

Education and training

Improving the skills of new and existing workers will increase their potential productivity. This can be done by the government setting up schemes, such as the UK's Youth Training Scheme, or by allowing firms tax incentives on funds they spend on training schemes. The government can also try and improve the quality of school and further education. In the UK, the growth of the numbers in universities can be seen as evidence of this.

The impact of these labour supply side policies has considerable benefits for businesses. A more motivated and skilled labour force should improve efficiency and reduce costs, and also make business more competitive, which may well increase sales.

Trade unions

Many business people feel that the operation of powerful trade unions contributes to inefficiency in the labour market. In the past unions have operated closed shops where only union members can be accepted to do a particular job. Through collective bargaining they have also been able to force wages to levels above the true market wage for a job. Using supply side policies, the UK Government has reduced the power of trade unions, so that managers can do their job more effectively, and labour markets can operate more efficiently.

Labour market laws

Through supply side policies the UK Government has tried to reduce the amount of regulation that exists in the labour market, to make it easier for organisations to hire

workers and shed workers. Ironically, it is the ease with which businesses can shed workers which seems to be a key factor in their willingness to take on new workers. If a business can hire workers on short-term contracts, and knows it can make these workers redundant if demand for their products falls, then they are more likely to take them on than if they know they will have to make redundancy payments.

The reduction in the power of trade unions, along with reduced regulation in the labour market, has made it easier for managers to run their businesses more effectively. A business's management now does not have to be as concerned over conflict with trade unions and labour laws that reduce its flexibility. Both of these advantages reduce costs, although they have contributed to greater uncertainty for the workforce which may have a detrimental effect on staff motivation. They have also allowed unscrupulous employers to exploit their workers.

■ INDUSTRIAL STRUCTURE

The market framework within which businesses operate is important to the efficiency of those businesses. Many economists have identified the level of competition as being the vital factor that pushes businesses into becoming more efficient as they strive to keep up with their rivals in the same business. For example, speed of service in many UK supermarkets has improved with the introduction of scanning at service points. As one company developed the technology others had quickly to follow suit or lose market share to the stores that could serve their customers more quickly. In order to enhance this level of competition, the UK Government has operated a policy that seeks to encourage competition. It does this in the following ways.

Office of the Director General of Fair Trading

This office was set up by the 1973 Fair Trading Act which sought to oversee competition policy in the UK on behalf of the Government. As an organisation, its brief is to encourage competition throughout industry to ensure that business practice is in the public interest. Anti-competitive practices, such as predatory pricing where an organisation reduces its prices to levels below cost in the hope of forcing competitors out of the market, are outlawed. Price fixing agreements where a number of competitors in the same market agree not to compete on prices that would reduce their profit margins, are similarly treated.

Monopolies and Mergers Commission

A monopoly is a market situation where a single firm accounts for a very high proportion of a particular market. British Telecom, for example, commands a large proportion of the domestic telephone market. Monopolies, once established, are able to prevent new firms entering markets to increase competition because no new entrants to the market are able to match the low costs enjoyed by the monopoly. The Monopolies and Mergers Commission steps in when the merger of two firms, or the take-over of one firm by another, leads to a monopoly. It may also step in when existing businesses start acting as a monopoly.

Impact on business

Competition policy makes the business environment more competitive. New firms can enter a market and compete with existing businesses, which means that incumbent businesses in a market need to be continuously on their guard to react to new challenges. Companies also need to ensure that their trading behaviour does not contravene the rules set down by the Office of Fair Trading.

The ownership of industry

Up until the early 1980s in the UK, a large proportion of industrial output was accounted for by public sector or state owned organisations called Nationalised Industries. British Gas, British Telecom and British Rail were all state-owned and run by a board of directors appointed by the Government. However, the last 15 years has seen these industries sold to the private sector, as shares have been sold in these organisations; a process called privatisation. The privatised businesses are now run in the same way as other large corporations that are answerable to their shareholders. The profit motive, along with the competitive pressures now faced by these formerly state-owned organisations, should, it is hoped, force these businesses to become more competitive and efficient, enhancing the effectiveness of the supply side of the economy.

The advantages associated with the privatisation of formerly nationalised industries come in a number of forms.

1 Privatised firms are not subject to the political interference that the old nationalised industries were. In the 1970s the UK Government would use nationalised industries to carry out economic policies, such as overmanning them to prevent a rise in unemployment.
2 The introduction of competition into many of the markets where privatisation has taken place has forced the privatised industries to become efficient. In the telecommunications market, the entry of Mercury and Orange has brought more competition to British Telecom.
3 Privatised industries now have to earn a rate of return for their shareholders which

Fig 10.16 *Two companies in privatised industries*

is a stronger motivator than the targets set by the UK Government when the industry was state-owned.

4 Privatised industries now have access to private funds which increases the money they have available for investment.

However, there have been a number of problems associated with privatisation.

1 Unprofitable services, such as the provision of rail services in rural areas, may not be provided by private companies striving for higher profits.

2 Private shareholders looking for short-term returns may not be interested in providing the funds for the major long-term projects needed in many of the privatised industries.

3 Many of the old nationalised industries were monopolies, which, when allowed to operate in the private sector, could exploit their market power to increase profits at the expense of higher prices to the consumer.

The article below shows the process by which British Rail was privatised.

THE PRIVATISATION OF BRITISH RAIL

In 1993 the Railways Act received Royal Assent, opening up the process of the privatisation of the railway industry in the UK. The main objective of this policy by the Government was to improve the quality and efficiency of rail services. The process should take place in three ways:

• To introduce competition to the rail market
• To encourage private sector investment
• To allocate the subsidy to the railways clearly to both consumer and producers

British Rail comprises a large range of diverse operations. Through privatisation, these activities have been transformed into independent businesses designed to compete with other forms of travel in the marketplace. The Railways Act (1993) has introduced fundamental changes to the railway industry to bring about this new structure.

• It has separated ownership and control of the infrastructure (track, stations and signals) from the provision of train services (locomotives, ticket sales, and catering). The company, Railtrack PLC, now controls

▶▶

►► all the fixed asset infrastructure, which sells contracts to train operators to allow them access to the track network and stations. It has also sold contracts with specialist engineering organisations for maintenance and repair of the infrastructure.

- The remaining operating and support functions of British Rail have been sold off or franchised. In 1993 a franchise director was appointed to franchise services and to determine the levels of service and payments of Government subsidies. A franchise is an agreement between the franchising director and a chosen company to run a particular group of rail services for a defined period of time, around seven years, to set standards. All the passenger rolling stock, locomotives, carriages and multiple unit trains used for domestic passenger services which are due to be franchised, have been transferred to new leasing companies who lease the assets to franchise operators.

Passenger Train Services

Passenger train services have been divided up into 25 train operating units (TOUs) which will become vested as train operating companies (TOCs). These companies will be franchised to companies who will operate the services to a standard specified by the franchising director. The franchises will earn revenue by selling tickets, and receive a subsidy from the Government to support unprofitable services that they have to provide. The franchises will have to pay for all the normal expenses of running a business, along with a franchise fee to Railtrack for using the track and stations and a leasing cost to the company that owns the trains.

Safeguards

Two new statutory officers have been appointed to oversee the operation of the newly privatised service. These are (i) the franchising director, whose role is to oversee the successful operation of companies that take up the franchises, and (ii) the rail regulator. The regulator has the specific function under the 1993 Railways Act to protect the interests of all rail users. The regulator has the power to revoke the licences of operators considered not to be operating in rail users' interests.

Impact on business

Privatisation has had a huge impact on the industries that have been involved in it. Indeed, privatisation has brought forward major opportunities because the markets have been opened up to new entrants.

1 **New business opportunities** Stage Coach was initially set up in the 1980s to take advantage of the bus industry. It is now taking up the opportunity to get involved in the privatisation of the railways by buying the franchise rail services now on offer to the private sector. As the telecommunications industry has grown, many companies have been able to supply a number of the new companies set up.

2 **Lower costs** Privatisation has certainly reduced the costs of many of the vital services that businesses depend on, such as telecommunications, gas and electricity. The privatised industries in the new competitive environment have reduced prices to many of their business users.

3 **More competition** Privatised industries have not only increased the competition in their own markets, but also between markets. For example, the privatisation of British Rail will increase the competition for domestic flights within the UK.

The capital market

Access to funds to finance new investment and technology is crucial in creating the conditions for greater capacity on the supply side. These funds are created because people in the economy save money. The savings provide the funds for banks to lend to business to invest. In the 1980s the UK Government had a number of initiatives to try and increase the funds available to industry.

1 **Wider share ownership** The UK Government actively sought to increase the number of people who owned shares, because if more people bought shares, firms would find it easier to finance investment through Stock Market flotation. Personal equity plans (PEPs), were launched by the UK Government to offer people a tax allowance against money they invested in shares. The flotation of privatised industries, such as British Gas, was also designed to increase share ownership.

2 **Greater saving** The introduction of TESSAs (tax free saving bonds) by the UK Government in the 1980s, was designed to increase the volume of savings, providing more funds for investment.

3 **Deregulation of financial markets** During the 1980s the UK Government deregulated the financial markets so that it became easier for industry to borrow money from a variety of sources. For example, it became possible for banks to broaden their activities to offer mortgages. The result of this was a large increase in borrowing as financial institutions, keen to make loans, competed for borrowers.

The deregulation of the financial markets with greater access to funds for investment has helped many organisations raise money. With greater competition amongst lending institutions, businesses are able to obtain cheaper loans, which reduces their existing borrowing costs and makes funding new investment cheaper.

DIFFICULT TRADING CONDITIONS FOR HEA LTD

HEA Ltd is a clothing retailer based in the South of England. It has a chain of nine outlets located in major towns and cities in the South, from Bristol to Canterbury, with their biggest store in London's West End. The company specialises in high quality casual clothing and leisure wear, selling designer names such as Ralph Lauren, Lacoste, Yves St Laurent and Timberland. The chain of stores was started ten years ago by two brothers who wanted to offer quality clothing at reasonable prices. Because the company has expanded so quickly, after its original store was opened in Canterbury, it has had to raise a great deal of long-term finance through borrowing. One of its great successes has been the proportion of sales it has made to tourists; this has particularly been the case in its Canterbury and London stores.

The last 12 months have brought about more difficult trading conditions for HEA, who have started to experience difficulties as a result of government macroeconomic policies. Rising economic growth and consumer spending has increased inflationary pressures. To combat this, the Bank of England has increased interest rates and increased taxes.

QUESTIONS

1 a Explain what you understand by:
  • Fiscal policy
  • Monetary policy [8]
  b How does a tightening of fiscal and monetary policy reduce the prospect of future inflation? [7]

2 a Analyse in detail the impact of the tightening of fiscal and monetary policy on HEA. [15]

b Explain why the stores in Canterbury and London are likely to be the hardest hit of HEA's stores by the Government's economic policy. [10]

3 Write a report to the directors of HEA explaining how they should deal with problems caused by the tightening of monetary and fiscal policy. [20]

Total [60]

THE GOVERNMENT BUDGET AFFECTS HEALSTROME LTD

Healstrome Ltd manufacture picture frames. They are a mass producer, who sell low cost frames to a whole variety of major high street retailers, such as WH Smith and Athena. The company are currently producing their budgets for 1999. The budgeted profit and loss account for 1999 is set out below.

Healstrome Ltd budgeted Profit and Loss Account year ending 31 December, 1989	£m
Sales	22.5
Cost of goods sold	8.2
Gross Profit	**14.3**
Operating expenses	3.1
Net Profit	**11.2**
Interest expense	1.2
Profit before Tax	**10.0**
Tax 30%	2.7
Profit after Tax	**7.3**
Dividends	3.2
Retained Profit	**4.1**

However, the most recent budget set by the Government will, the accounts department believe, alter the figures they have set. The budget set in October 1998 is forecast to affect Healstrome in the following ways.

1 A reduction in income tax to 22p at the basic rate is forecast to increase sales revenue by three percent.
2 A reduction in the employer's contribution to National Insurance is forecast to reduce direct costs by two percent.
3 A rise in corporation tax from 30 percent to 32 percent will reduce after tax profits.

At the same time as the budget was announced, a 0.5 percent cut in interest rates was announced and it is forecast that a further fall of 0.75 percent will take place during 1998. If this takes place, sales revenue will rise by another four percent. The interest expense forecast by Healstrome will fall to £1 million as a result of this.

QUESTIONS

1 a Explain why Healstrome has forecast that their sales revenue should rise as a result of the budgetary decisions taken by the Government, along with the interest rate reduction made by the Bank of England. [10]

b Why do you think direct costs are forecast to fall after the reduction in National Insurance made in the budget? [5]

2 Produce a revised budgeted profit and loss account for Healstrome for 1999. [15]

3 Analyse the short-term and long-term benefits Healstrome might derive from a reduction in corporation tax. [10]

Total [40]

UNIT 10

The Business Environment – Section E: The impact of the law

SUMMARY

1 The legal framework set up by the state has a critical impact on all aspects of business decision making.
2 Employment law, through the contract of employment, sets up a legal relationship between employers and employees that both parties have to adhere to.
3 Health and safety legislation regulates the conditions of work which organisations must provide to their employees in the workplace.
4 Wage protection law sets out the regulations business must follow when setting wages.
5 Employers must follow set statutory procedures when terminating the employment of their employees.
6 Equal opportunities legislation is set up to make sure that all employees are treated in the same way by firms.
7 Contract law sets out to protect both buyers and sellers when trading.

EMPLOYMENT AND THE LAW

A considerable amount of legislation has been passed over the years to ensure that the rights of workers are protected. Without these laws employees can be exploited by unscrupulous employers. The main areas that are covered by legislation are as follows.

Contract of employment

This is the legal document that sets out the terms and conditions that govern an individual's rights in a job. By signing a contract the employer and the employee have a legally binding agreement that they are both legally obliged to follow. Any transgression of this agreement by either party breaks the contract and makes the transgressor liable in a court of law. If an employee is dismissed for not completing a task, and this task is not included in the contract of employment, then the employee could take the employer to court for unfair dismissal.

The contract is extremely useful from both the employer's and employee's perspective, in terms of their expectations in relation to the job. The employer can set out precisely what they want from their workers in terms of duties, hours of work and responsibility. Employees, on the other hand, are clear about what is required from them, and what benefits they will receive for doing their job successfully.

The contract of employment should lay down regulations relating to the following areas.

1 **Job title**   This is the employee's official job title, for example direct sales manager.
2 **Job role**   This sets out the areas of responsibility the employee has to undertake when doing the job. A direct sales manager would be responsible for overseeing the work of six sales representatives, and negotiating key multiple accounts.
3 **Pay**   The level of pay for the job and method of payment – for instance a sales manager earns a basic salary of £30,000 per year, paid monthly, with a bonus of 10 percent on basic salary for on-target sales, paid annually.
4 **Hours**   Normal hours of work, including breaks.
5 **Holidays and holiday pay**.
6 **Pension rights**   Such rights would include whether the employee received a non-contributory pension or had to make all the contribution themselves.
7 **Disciplinary rules and grievance procedures**   This covers situations when the employer and employee are in dispute.
8 **Length of notice given on resignation or termination**   This is the amount of time the employee has to work for after they have resigned or been dismissed.

Health and safety

Health and safety at work is of vital importance to both the employee and the organisation. The employee enjoys better working conditions from health and safety regulation, such as the control of noise and regulation of temperature in a factory. Whilst this may well increase costs for the organisation in the short term, in the long term it is likely to enhance the motivation of the employee, and benefit the organisation with higher productivity. Fredrick Hertzberg saw these conditions as hygiene factors and produced evidence that workers would become dissatisfied, and de-motivated, if working conditions were unsatisfactory.

Employer's duties

Employers have a legal obligation, as set out in the Health and Safety at Work Act (1974), 'to ensure that they safeguard all their employees' health, safety, and welfare at work'. The Act covers areas such as the provision and maintenance of safety equipment and clothing, maintenance of workplace temperatures, provision of breaks and protection against dangerous substances. Organisations have to ensure their employees' health and safety as 'far as it is reasonably practicable'. This interpretation, when a case is brought in law, will depend on whether the court believes the business has taken action that is 'reasonably practicable'. The court's view will depend to a large extent on the inherent risks associated with the particular business. Organisations such as those involved in the production of chemicals will have to take greater care to protect their employees' health and safety than those in a service sector organisation, like a law firm.

Health and safety legislation also applies to those who are visiting a business's premises, as well as people who live near by and are affected by the organisation's activities. For example, a business can be held liable in law for the toxic fumes that might adversely affect the local population near its factory.

Employee's duties

The Health and Safety at Work Act (1974) made the point that safety at work cannot be achieved without the active interest and support of employees. It is the employees' responsibility to act in a manner which takes reasonable care of their own and other people's safety. Employees must act responsibly and follow all health and safety guidelines.

The Health and Safety Executive

The Health and Safety at Work Act is backed up by the Health and Safety Executive, which has the responsibility of ensuring that the Act is carried out, and for improving health and safety practices in businesses. This is done by inspectors who are employed by the commission.

Vicarious liability

When an employee is carrying out their work for an organisation, situations may arise in which the employee commits a wrongful act (a tort). When this happens, the injured party can seek redress from the employer as well as any employee involved. This obviously has significant legal implications for all organisations. Vicarious liability could arise when one employee, for example, injures another employee while they are acting in the course of their employment. The injured employee can sue the organisation for the act of the other employee. The principle exists in law because it is felt that the employer should take responsibility for the work carried out by its employees, work which benefits the organisation. Secondly, it is felt the employer will be better able to pay compensation than the employee.

The implication for business of vicarious liability is that the legal costs have to be covered by the business which ultimately affects the profits paid to its owners, or forces up the final price paid by its customers.

Wage protection

Wages are defined as any sum paid by an employer to an employee as a reward for doing work for the employer. The Wages Act (1986) sets out conditions for payment to workers and deductions from wages. It covers bonuses, commission and sick pay, as well as the basic pay associated with the job. Deductions include: Income tax, National Insurance, and pension contributions. The contract of employment sets out the wage the

employer must pay along with any deduction they have to take from this wage. For example, employers frequently make deductions as a pension contribution.

Minimum wages

A minimum wage is a rate of pay set by the Government that employers must pay as a legal minimum to their employees. If the wage is set at £3.50, then no employer can legally pay less than this.

Up until 1993 in the UK, minimum wages were set by wages councils in certain industries, such as retailing. However, these agreements were dismantled by the Government in 1993. There is now considerable political debate surrounding the implementation of a national minimum wage, like those set in France, Germany and USA.

Any minimum wage set has considerable implications for the costs of all organisations, and particularly those that pay wages below the minimum wage level. If a minimum wage was applied there would be a rise in costs for any firms who had originally set wages below the minimum wage. If the wages of the lowest paid workers were increased this would mean the differences between their wages and the wages of more highly paid employees (wage differentials) would be reduced. This fall in differentials could lead to a rise in the wage demands of the more highly paid workers, who seek to maintain differentials. It could also lead to industrial conflict, as more highly paid workers resent the erosion of their differentials. The rise in labour costs brought about by a minimum wage could lead to firms shedding labour, resulting in unemployment.

The counter argument to this is that minimum wages prevent unscrupulous employers reducing wages to very low levels, which means they gain a cost advantage over employers who pay a fair wage. This cost advantage may then force the better employers to reduce wages as well, or they will be forced out of business.

Employment protection

The law seeks to protect the jobs of workers from unscrupulous employers and to create a wider stability in the labour market.

Dismissal

A worker can be dismissed (sacked) over a failure to comply with their contract of employment. This could be due to incompetence, or a breach of discipline. The Employment Protection Act (1978) ensures that every employee who has been with an employer for more than two years has the right to claim for unfair dismissal.

Unfair dismissal

If an employee feels they have been dismissed unfairly, for example a worker was dismissed for trying to join a trade union, then this would be grounds for unfair dismissal.

The employee then has the right to take their case to an industrial tribunal within three months of their dismissal, provided they have worked for their employer for at least two years. An industrial tribunal is far simpler, quicker and cheaper than an ordinary court of law. The chairperson of the tribunal will listen to the case put by both the employer and the employee and will reach a legally binding decision based on this evidence. The decision could be to find in favour of the sacked employee and have him reinstated, or it could find for the employer and uphold the dismissal.

Redundancy

Redundancy occurs when a job function of an employee is no longer required, and the employee subsequently loses their job. Redundancy can be voluntary, where workers

apply to take redundancy and the payments that go with it. The law states that employers have to make the following minimum payments to workers made redundant.

Age of employee	Payment per year of service
18–21 years	Half a week's pay
22–41 years	One week's pay
Over 41 years	One and a half week's pay

The terms only apply to those employed for more than 16 hours per week and with over two years of continuous employment.

Short-term contracts

A short-term contract is one agreed for a set period of time. This could be a matter of months to a few years. When the contract is finished, the employer and employee are both free to renegotiate another contract or sever their relationship. The growth of short-term contracts has tended to be employer led because it gives organisations the flexibility to increase and reduce their workforce on the basis of the demand for their products. If sales are rising, employers are more likely to increase their workforce, and reduce it when sales fall. This means that workers find it easier to gain employment because employers are more willing to take on workers in the knowledge that they can shed them easily when business is in recession. However, short-term contracts have led to greater uncertainty amongst the workforce, as well as a fall in loyalty to the organisation.

Equal opportunities

Equal opportunities describes a situation where employees have an equal chance of being employed or promoted, whatever their sex, race, colour, religion or disability. The Sex Discrimination Act (1975), Race Relations Act (1976) and Equal Pay Act (1970) have all been passed to ensure that equality of opportunity is carried out in the workplace.

Discrimination

The legislation was designed to combat racial and sexual discrimination that had existed in certain businesses. For example, the number of women in senior positions in organisations is far fewer than men, and women's pay tends to be lower than that of men, despite the fact that many women have skills and qualifications at least as good as their male counterparts.

The Equal Opportunities Commission

This organisation was set up in 1975 to eliminate discrimination in all organisations, and was backed by the Race and Sex Discrimination Acts (1975). This was legislation that the Government had put into place to enhance equal opportunities.

Many organisations now employ an equal opportunities officer to promote and monitor its practice in organisations, and to ensure that discrimination is not taking place.

Recruitment

Equal opportunities play an extremely important part in the regulations governing the recruitment of workers. No job advertisement should have a religious, an ethnic or a gender bias. The same rules apply when candidates are interviewed and ultimately offered a job. This can raise considerable problems for organisations who wish to recruit a specific type of employee, say a woman for a management position to balance up the sexes in a management team; recruitment cannot take place simply on this basis. If a man applied for the job who, at least on paper, was better qualified, and the job was given to a woman then the man rejected could have a case in law.

LAW OF CONTRACT

What is a contract?

A contract is an agreement between parties which is enforceable by the courts. For a contract to be made the agreement has to be a bargain for both parties. Each side must give something of value to the other side for the contract to be enforceable. When a customer enters a supermarket and buys some groceries then the shop receives cash and the customer receives the goods, and a contract is formed.

What makes a valid contract?

There are three essential features of a valid contract.

1 **The agreement**   This consists of one party making an offer which is accepted by the other. The offer can be made specifically or be implied. For example, a vending machine is an implied offer to a customer to purchase confectionery. Once the offer is firmly accepted, and this is accepted by the offeree, then an enforceable agreement is made.
2 **The bargain**   A contract is a bargain when both parties benefit from the exchange; each side must receive something of value. Paying cash for goods received at the supermarket is an example of this.
3 **The intention to create legal relations**   For a bargain to be legally binding between parties, they must have intended their bargain to be legally binding. This intention is implied in every commercial agreement. However, parties to an agreement can insert a clause into it, stating that the agreement is not legally binding in law.

Why is the law of contract important?

The law of contract can be seen as an enabler for business in that it facilitates trading. Both buyers and sellers know they are entering into a contract which is designed to protect them. The buyer of a car is more likely to make the purchase if they know that the agreement made with the dealer can be enforced in the courts. The seller, in this case the car dealer, is more likely to make the sale if they know that their right to payment is protected in law. Thus the law encourages business to take place.

However, the law does also act as a constraint and increases costs. The regulations surrounding a contract obviously have to be fulfilled by both parties. Organisations will need to employ lawyers to make sure these regulations are followed, and this increases the complexity of trading and its cost.

SALE OF GOODS

The Sale of Goods Act (1979) provides the foundations for the protection of the consumer in a trading situation. The Act sets out the conditions for the goods when they are bought from someone who sells in the course of business. Goods must be:

- Of satisfactory quality – new goods must not be broken or damaged and must work properly

- Fit for their purpose – goods must correspond to their description, and do what they are supposed to

If goods do not meet these two conditions then the buyer has the right to return the goods and receive the purchase price back. The buyer of faulty goods can also claim damages for other losses, such as property and personal injury. The Sale of Goods Act is important to businesses from the practical point of view of ensuring that the goods sold are in saleable condition, a responsibility that falls on production and quality control. When goods are marketed, any claims made by the firm about the good, through advertising or on packaging, must accurately reflect what the product can do. These conditions will be a constraint because ensuring they are met will force up costs. However, they are also an enabler because they prevent organisations from claiming that their products do things that they do not, which may well adversely affect the sales of all firms in the industry.

Trade descriptions

Under the Trade Descriptions Act (1968) it is a criminal offence for traders to describe goods inaccurately, or to make false statements about services, if they know the information is false, or do not care whether the statements are true or false. The Act also covers pricing, making it an offence to cross out the price on a good, and substitute it for a lower price unless the goods have been sold at the higher price for at least 28 consecutive days in the last six months.

PLAYRIGHT TOYS MAKES REDUNDANCIES

Playright Toys Ltd manufactures toys for the UK and European markets. It employs 200 staff at its main production site in the East Midlands. The business is expanding and the nature of production is also changing. The introduction of new technology means that 20 staff are going to be made redundant. The company wants to hire five new employees, who will need to have experience in the computer technology used with the new capital employed. These workers will be employed on short-term contracts. The trade union which represents many of the shop floor workers at Playright are unhappy about the redundancies, the introduction of short-term contracts, and the employment of part time workers. Colin Edwards, the company's personnel director, has been given the responsibility of introducing the change and is concerned to ensure that it goes smoothly.

QUESTIONS

1 What legal factors would Colin Edwards need to take into account when making the redundancies necessary? [7]

2 a Explain what you understand by the term 'contract of employment'. [5]
  b Outline the main differences between a short-term contract and a normal contract of employment. [5]

c What are the advantages and disadvantages of employing workers on short-term contracts? [8]

3 Advise Colin Edwards on the ways he could present the employment changes to the trade union, to ensure they accept the proposal. [15]

Total [40]

PIZZA VILLAGE BURNS AN EMPLOYEE

Pizza Village is a wholly owned subsidiary of a multinational food corporation. It has a chain of 70 shops throughout the UK. The Evesham shop employs seven full time and 12 part time staff. The restaurants serve pizza, pasta, desserts and drinks from a limited menu and at low prices. They have a takeaway, as well as an eat-in section. Caroline Wallis is the outlet's manager. On the 24 November a part time worker picked up a deep fat frying pan without any gloves on and burnt his hands. As a result, he dropped the pan of hot oil which splashed onto another employee who was burnt quite badly and had to go to hospital. This hospitalised employee is planning to sue Pizza Village. Caroline Wallis had to discipline the worker who dropped the fryer for not wearing gloves, and said that he would be liable to pay damages to the injured worker. In response, the worker wrote a letter of complaint to Pizza Village's head office. The letter made the following points:

- He had not been told to wear gloves and there were not enough gloves provided
- He had received no training on the use of the fryer
- Someone had told him that the firm was legally responsible to pay damages to the injured employee

The worker who wrote the letter had also felt aggrieved in the past because he had been passed over for promotion. On two occasions women had been appointed ahead of him, despite the fact he had more experience and better qualifications.

QUESTIONS

1 a Explain the piece of legislation that is designed to protect workers in case of accidents like the one at Pizza Village. [8]

 b To what extent do you think Pizza Village might not have followed this legislation? [7]

2 a Explain what principle of law would protect the worker who spilled the fat from being sued by the injured worker. [5]

 b Discuss the implications of this legal principle to organisations like Pizza Village. [10]

 c What actions do you think Pizza Village could take to guard against the negative consequences of this legal principle? [5]

3 Outline the legislation that is in place to protect workers from being discriminated against, as the worker who was passed over for promotion feels he has been by Pizza Village. [10]

4 Pizza Village has to follow a whole number of employment laws. Discuss the advantages and disadvantages of the existence of these employment laws to Pizza Village. [15]

Total [60]

Employer–Employee Relations

SUMMARY

1 The quality of relationship that exists between employers and employees is critical to the success of the organisation.
2 There is formal machinery to aid the relationship between employers and employees: joint consultative committees, quality circles and worker-directors.
3 There are a number of different groups that represent employers and employees. These include: trade unions, employers' associations and staff associations.
4 Trade unions are the most influential group that represents the interests of employees.
5 Trade unions aim to represent the interests of their members when they are dealing with management on issues that affect their members.

6 Trade unions have a number of different methods of industrial action to protect their members' interests.
7 Whilst most industrial disputes are resolved through negotiations between workers and management, industrial tribunals, along with the conciliation service ACAS, are bodies set up by the Government to try and resolve conflict.
8 Trade unions can help management when they work with them in the decision making process.
9 Trade unions have, for a variety of reasons, declined in importance in recent years.

The effectiveness of the people employed by an organisation is absolutely critical for that organisation's success. Countless studies have shown that the human resources employed by the organisation are their most valuable resource and that effective human resource management is needed for an organisation to achieve its objectives. For good human resource management to take place it is important that the relationship between employers and employees is a harmonious one. The key to harmonious relationships is the quality of communication and consultation which exists between the organisation and its workforce.

EMPLOYEE REPRESENTATION AND CONSULTATION

Many businesses have set up specific machinery to enhance communication and consultation within the organisation.

Joint consultative committees

These are meetings set up between management and workers to discuss issues that specifically affect the labour force. The committees meet regularly and often involve discussions relating to working conditions, pay and industrial relations, along with the organisation's long-term strategy. The meeting is normally a forum where management invite the views of the workforce.

The committees can be in the form of:

- An advisory body
- A consultative body
- A negotiating body

If the committee is of the final type, its recommendations are binding on the organisation.

Quality circles

This is a discussion group that meets regularly to identify quality problems, look at possible solutions, and make recommendations to management. They normally involve workers drawn from all parts of the workforce from sales to production so that the perspective of the whole organisation is represented. The method was first devised by the Toyota Motor Company in the 1950s, and is now used increasingly by companies in the West.

Worker-directors

These are representatives from the workforce that sit on the business's board of directors. They are common in Europe, particularly in Germany, although they are rare in the UK. By introducing workers to the board of directors the organisation provides the workforce with considerable influence on decision making. The scheme is unpopular in the UK because managers fear it will slow down the decision making process.

By setting up specific machinery to encourage employee participation, organisations have encouraged the workforce to feel closer to the organisation and to work more cohesively towards its success. Industrial conflict is reduced and the business has access to a greater pool of ideas which look at issues from a different perspective.

Representative groups in organisations

The relationship between employers and employees is heavily influenced by the bodies that represent groups of employees and employers. This can be within individual organisations, or on a more national scale.

Trade unions

Trade unions are probably the best known type of representative group, and arguably the most influential from management's point of view. They are discussed in greater detail later in this section.

Employers' associations

Employers' associations are organisations set up by groups of businesses to represent the collective interests of their members as employers. Examples include the Newspaper Society and the Engineering Employers' Association. It considers issues from the employer's view point in the same way that a trade union considers issues from the employee's view point. However, whilst trade unions are primarily concerned with industrial relations, their objectives are much broader than this. They provide advice on product design, joint research and development projects, and the standardisation of products.

Employers' Associations often provide the representative team of negotiators used to deal with trade unions over pay and conditions. In this context they are very useful to small firms negotiating with large powerful trade unions.

The Confederation of British Industry (CBI), is the Employers' Association counterpart to the TUC. Like the TUC it has a national structure of full time staff working on a variety of issues relating to the interests of employers. The Director General of the CBI heads the organisation. At a national level, the CBI is an extremely influential institution, lobbying the Government from an industrial perspective. CBI surveys on business confidence, employment prospects, business investment intentions, etc., are reported extensively in the press.

Staff associations

Staff associations, like trade unions, represent the interests of workers in an organisation, but are not formally set up as trade unions. They tend to represent workers in a particular organisation, like, for example, the Sun Life Staff Association. Their functions include providing information on issues such as pensions, liaising with management on decisions taken that affect employees and organising social events.

Professional associations

Professional associations are again similar to trade unions but they are not registered as trade unions. They represent workers in professions such as the Police Federation, the British Medical Association (BMA), and the Law Society. These institutions wield a fair amount of power over their respective professions, and their influence is something management has to be concerned about when decisions are taken that affect their members. For example, the introduction of changes to the National Health Service by the Government has met with strong resistance from the BMA.

◼ TRADE UNIONS

A trade union is an organisation representing the interests and needs of the workers it represents. Whilst legislation put into place

Fig 11.1   *Trade unions have existed in the UK for around 200 years*

during the 1980s in the UK has restricted the operation of trade unions, they still have an important influence over UK industry. Trade unions have existed in the UK for around 200 years; the earliest ones were formed by groups of workers with the same skills. These are sometimes called craft unions.

Types of trade union

Trade unions can be categorised into a number of distinct types.

1 **Craft unions**   These are groups of skilled workers who are joined together on the basis of their skill. Equity, the union that represents actors, or the National Union of Journalists, are present day examples of craft unions.

2 **Industrial unions** These are unions formed to represent workers in particular industries. The National Union Of Mine Workers represents workers of different skills in the mining industry.

3 **General unions** These are the largest trade unions that represent workers of different skills in different industries. The Transport and General Workers Union is one of the largest trade unions that represents workers from a variety of different industries.

4 **Occupational or non-manual unions** These unions are concerned with organising technical, clerical, professional, supervisory and managerial staff. They are sometimes called white collar unions, and their significance has increased in recent years as manufacturing employment has fallen, and the number of people employed in services has increased. The Banking Insurance and Finance Union (BIFU) is an example of a trade union that represents workers in these areas.

The structure of trade unions

Trade unions are financed through funds collected by their membership. These funds are used to employ a full time staff that works from official headquarters. An executive committee runs the union and is in charge of setting policy, although the membership has the right to vote on policy at the union's annual general conference, or through postal ballots. The general secretary is the person in charge of the union. The headquarters have professional staff who serve the membership with services such as legal advice, welfare and social services. There are also professional negotiators who take part in national level negotiations with employers. Delegates are elected by union members at local branch level, and they represent the members' interests on general issues that do not require

the votes of the whole membership. Larger unions also have regional offices, which are run by full time branch officials. At local level there are branches that operate at individual places of work. Branches are manned by voluntary officials, drawn from the union's membership. At the workplace level, shop stewards represent the union's members. The shop steward has the following responsibilities.

1 Shop stewards provide a daily point of contact for union members on issues that concern them.

2 The shop steward deals with management on a day to day basis about issues relating to the union's members.

3 Shop stewards provide information to union members on policy issues that are being considered by the union.

Trade Union Congress

The Trade Union Congress or TUC is the collective voice of the trade union movement. It represents the interests of trade unions and their members at a national level. It particularly tries to lobby the Government when it is putting forward legislation that will affect union interests. An example of the legislation it would lobby for would be on the setting of a national minimum wage. The TUC meets annually to debate resolutions that are put forward by delegates that represent individual unions.

The aims of trade unions

Trade unions seek to maintain and improve the working conditions of their members. They do this by concentrating on a variety of aspects of their members' interests.

Pay

The process of collective bargaining governs the way that unions represent their members in negotiations over pay. The trade union will negotiate with management on behalf of a whole group of employees. By representing a group of workers in this way the union has the power derived from collective action which would diminish if each worker negotiated their pay individually. Whilst the employer faces a more powerful force in the negotiating process, it does have the advantage of simplifying wage setting that is organised for all workers at one point in the year.

Working conditions

This involves the union in negotiating for their members on arrangements for holidays, working hours, breaks, overtime payments, staffing levels, fringe benefits, etc. These would, like pay, be settled through collective bargaining. Employers would often look to grant a pay increase on the basis of an agreement to increase productivity. For example, a five percent wage rise for car workers would perhaps mean the workforce increasing the amount they produce by five percent. The workforce may need to work longer hours to achieve this.

Employment protection

Trade unions try to protect the jobs of their members. This has been a very important task for many unions over the last 20 years as organisations have sought to replace workers with capital, out-source elements of production to cheaper foreign producers, and generally reduce the numbers of people they employ (downsizing). In the past trade unions have used closed shops as a way of doing this. A closed shop exists when a trade union forces a 100 percent union membership on a workplace, or job function. Closed shops dominated the newspaper printing industry up until the early 1980s where closed shops called 'chapels' meant that only union members could be printers. The closed shop protected jobs because it limited the

employer's ability to recruit new workers if union members were sacked. Closed shops were outlawed by the Employment Act (1988).

General employee support

Trade unions provide their members with general support in a variety of different areas. This could involve representing the worker in a claim for unfair dismissal or providing funds to support any legal action involving workers. Trade unions also provide services such as insurance schemes, pensions, education courses, etc.

National employee representation

The Trade Union Congress (TUC) is the national body that represents all trade unions. As a body it looks to put across the interests of union members to government. The TUC would look to influence government policy on issues such as employment law, industrial policy and overall macroeconomic policy.

Industrial conflict

Trade unions have a variety of different sanctions at their disposal to add weight to their bargaining position when they are negotiating with employees. These include the following.

1 **Strikes**   Workers have the right to withdraw their labour if this course of action is agreed in a full secret ballot conducted amongst its members. Strikes can take place over a continuous period, or as a series of one day strikes.
2 **Picketing**   This occurs during a strike when those on strike try to persuade non-strikers to join the dispute. The mass picketing associated with disputes in the 1970s and early 1980s is now illegal, and only six pickets are allowed to stand at each workplace.

3 **Secondary action** This occurs when employees from another organisation are persuaded to join the dispute even though they are not in dispute with their own employers. For example, car workers may be on strike, and ask lorry drivers who deliver parts to the car manufacturer who employs the car workers not to cross picket lines and deliver the parts that the car manufacturer needs.

4 **Work to rule** In a work to rule, the union sets down a specific set of procedures that their members must adhere to during an industrial dispute. By doing this the employer finds that the efficiency of the workforce falls as they effectively withdraw the cooperation necessary to do a particular job. The union will set out procedures on manning levels, overtime, and job descriptions. If a manager asks the worker to do a task that does not fit the procedures set down they will refuse to do it.

5 **Sit in** A sit in occurs when workers occupy a workplace for a given period of time, preventing any production from taking place.

The industrial action facing JW Arrowsmith illustrates the variety of different types of industrial action that trade unions can resort to. It also shows what type of management decision often leads to industrial disputes.

PRINT UNION CALLS OFF 18-MONTH STRIKE

Industrial action by the Bristol printing company JW Arrowsmith was called off on 19th October 1994 after 18 months of picketing. It had been the longest dispute in the city's history.

Arrowsmith made 120 employees redundant in April 1993 after they voted to take industrial action in pursuit of a national pay claim. At the same time it derecognised their union, the GPMU. In spite of an official picket the family-owned business continued to trade and the GPMU failed to make it negotiate. But the company became smaller and hoped to sell its site in south Bristol and move to smaller premises. Mr John Monks, general secretary of the Trades Union Congress, said that the sacked workers' dispute had inspired trade unionists across the country. He said the struggle 'should serve to show other employers that such shortsighted, unjust and anti-union management is no way to build a successful business'. Arrowsmith, which began trading in the mid-nineteenth century and specialises in technical typesetting, sacked the staff for breach of contract. The company, which had made a loss the previous year, said it had lost orders because of an overtime ban and could not afford the claim for £6.50 a week and an extra day's holiday. It offered to re-employ staff on personal contracts and with a pay freeze, but only a handful came back to work.

The consequences of industrial action for organisations

1 **Loss of sales** If a strike prevents production taking place then the reduction in output will lead to a fall in sales. A week long strike at a car plant may well lead to a multi-million pound reduction in sales revenue.

2 **Loss of customers** The initial loss in sales may have more serious implications

for sales in the longer term as customers, who have been let down by the organisation, seek alternative supply. Any industrial action is also generally damaging to a business's reputation, so the dispute could put off potential customers.

3 **Loss of morale**　Industrial disputes are extremely damaging to the relationship between employees and managers. The resulting loss of morale that often occurs during a dispute will have serious implications for managers' effectiveness in the future, as well as the quality of the individual employee's work.

4 **Loss of finance**　Most organisations rely heavily on external sources of finance, either in the form of loans, or share issues. An industrial dispute that damages a business's reputation may find that investors are less willing to risk their funds with the organisation. This loss of potential finance, along with the loss of cash generated by falling sales, could have serious implications for cashflow.

A poor record of industrial relations for any organisation will obviously have an adverse effect on their profits and cashflow, and in serious cases industrial disputes can push an organisation out of business. However, there are a number of disputes where management have taken on trade unions and won their way through a dispute to achieve long-term success for the organisation. In the early 1980s Rupert Murdoch's News International took on the print unions to force through changes in technology that completely revolutionised the way newspapers were produced.

Resolving industrial conflict

Ultimately, the method by which organisations can resolve industrial conflict lies in the negotiating process that brings employers and employees together. If there is a good working relationship between the two,

and both parties understand the position of each other, then conflict is more likely to be avoided. However, if the two parties cannot reach agreement on dispute there is a mechanism in place to help resolve the situation.

The Advisory Conciliation and Arbitration Service (ACAS)

Set up in 1975 by the Employment Protection Act (1975), ACAS was designed to facilitate the smooth working of industrial relations through an extension of collective bargaining. It is an independent body that exists to supplement existing negotiating procedures rather than replace them.

ACAS will intervene if it is invited by one or more parties involved in the dispute, but its involvement must be agreed by all parties in the dispute. If the dispute goes to arbitration, where it is settled by an independent party, then the settlement is binding on both parties. ACAS will also involve itself in disputes on unfair dismissal, race and sex discrimination, and equal pay.

ACAS is not solely concerned with industrial disputes; in addition to this, it fulfils an advisory role, not just to trade unions but also to employers, on matters such as employment procedures, manpower, planning and recruitment.

Industrial tribunals

Employees can take their disputes to industrial tribunals. These are bodies set up to settle disputes between employers and employees or trade unions relating to the statutory terms and conditions of employment. A tribunal would hear complaints made about equal pay, unfair dismissal, redundancy, etc. Tribunals can also hear complaints made by union members relating to disciplinary action taken against them by their union. The tribunal has the power to award compensation, or order the reinstatement of a dismissed employee.

The impact of trade unions on organisations

A general view of many outside observers of the impact of trade unions on businesses is a negative one. It is certainly true that powerful unions can impede the smooth operation of the decision making process, particularly when major changes take place that have an impact on employees. The introduction of new technology in all industries has in many cases led to redundancies, and, as a result, trade unions have stepped in to resist this process. As we have already seen, industrial disputes can be extremely costly to business, and even threaten their existence. Collective bargaining can force up costs beyond the levels that would otherwise exist, which in turn forces up prices or reduces profit margins. However, trade unions can also have a positive influence on organisations.

1 **Effective groups**   There is a lot of evidence to suggest that workers who form close group relationships at work are more effective in their jobs. The Hawthorne Effect, which was reported on by Elton Mayo in the 1930s, showed that greater group cohesion at work enhanced the effectiveness of individual workers. Trade unions can provide this cohesion.
2 **Effective negotiation**   Because a trade union represents a group of workers, in some cases a very large group, it makes the process of negotiating over pay and conditions a much simpler arrangement for management than if each worker is negotiated with separately.
3 **Effective communication**   A trade union provides an important focal point for workers to express their views about the job they do. This collective bank of information can then be passed on to management by the union. This gives management a broader picture of views than would be the case if workers expressed their ideas in a more fragmented way, as would be the case if they were not represented by a union.
4 **Effective information**   The workforce often has a completely different perspective on issues relating to the business compared to managers. Often workers who are directly on the production line, or who are face to face with customers hold invaluable information about decisions made by management. The union can hold much of this information, and can relay it to management to improve their decision making. For example, the union that represents banking employees can relay to the banks how customers are feeling about new procedures on paying in cheques.

The effectiveness of unions

The ability of unions to fulfil their functions has been reduced substantially over the last 20 years. A number of factors have probably accounted for this.

1 New employment laws have greatly restricted the ability of unions to impose their will on employers.
2 The growth of part time and short-term contract work has weakened the bargaining power of employees whose employment rights are limited, so workers are not in a position to support union action.
3 The level of unemployment is higher now than it was in the 1960s and 70s. As a result of this, workers have become less militant for fear of losing their jobs, which means that workers are not as willing to support union action.
4 The demise of the old heavy industry which had been the roots of trade unionism, along with the general fall in union membership, has weakened the influence of unions at a national level.
5 Some people believe that new, innovative management techniques have improved industrial relations, reducing the workforce's willingness to take on management.

YARROW WORKERS VOTE FOR ACTION OVER 2% PAY OFFER

Workers at Yarrow Shipbuilders on the Clyde voted in 1995, by a substantial majority, for industrial action in response to a two percent pay offer. Of even greater significance was that this offer was linked to the introduction of performance-related pay.

All the trade unions represented at Yarrow met together to discuss the next move. Action was initially expected to be confined to overtime bans, one-day strikes and a general work to rule. However, the all-out stoppage was a possibility. John Dolan, the GMB general union's chief convener at the yard described the pay offer as 'shocking'. Their expectations were for a 'substantial increase'. As many as 80 percent of those voting among the 3,400 workforce backed the use of industrial action and an all-out strike if necessary.

The company proposed that the two percent increase would be conditional on sweeping changes in working practices. Reforms included the introduction of Friday afternoon working at overtime rates that would increase the basic week from 36 to 42 hours, the end of a 10-minute tea break, plus, and most controversially, the introduction of performance-related pay for all manual workers. The unions feared this would produce inequalities among workers and also saw it as a threat to their traditional method of obtaining pay increases by collective bargaining.

At this time Yarrow Shipbuilders was in a strong commercial position with a full order book until 1997 and contracts with both the Royal Navy and the Malaysian Navy to build at least five frigates.

In order to avoid a repetition of the 1994 strike by workers that lasted a full month, during which time the white-collar staff worked as usual, union officials pursued a strategy of gradual escalation, thus giving the company an opportunity to improve its offer, whilst avoiding the consequences of an extended stoppage.

QUESTIONS

1 Explain what you understand by 'industrial conflict'. [5]

2 a Explain the process of collective bargaining. [5]
  b Analyse the advantages and disadvantages to Yarrow Shipbuilders of the use of collective bargaining in negotiations. [10]

3 a What do you understand by 'performance-related pay'? [5]
  b Why do you think the GMB are so concerned about the introduction of performance-related pay? [10]

4 a Discuss the problems Yarrow Shipbuilders will face if the dispute leads to a sustained period of industrial conflict. [10]
  b Discuss the problems the union will face as a result of a sustained period of industrial conflict. [10]

5 Write a report to Yarrow Shipbuilders outlining a management strategy to reduce the likelihood of industrial action. [15]

Total [70]

A SHOCK FOR JAGUAR

Jaguar car workers reject 7.5% pay package

Jaguar car workers rejected, by an overwhelming majority, a two-year pay deal worth 7.5 percent. This came as a shock to both the company and the trade unions that negotiated the agreement.

The decision aroused worries that discontent might spread to other parts of the UK car industry as economic recovery, which the country was undergoing, increases the demand for cars and strengthens employees' bargaining position. The rejection was concerning to the unions covering 28,000 employees at the Rover group as they were preparing to announce the results of a workplace ballot on a 7.7 percent two-year

pay deal. Nissan and Peugeot Talbot were due to negotiate in the near future.

The unions and management at Jaguar were expected to meet to try to change the offer. A strike was likely to be called for by the unions if no improvement could be secured. The original offer had been rejected by six to four. The Transport and General Workers Union said it believed that the pay element of the negotiated offer had been accepted, which brought their basic pay up by 3.5 percent. The following year the company would pay a further 4 percent. However, the unions and the company believed that employees disliked working compulsory overtime on top of their basic 37-hour week. Under the proposed deal, workers would have been expected to work overtime

▶ ▶

► ►

'should it become necessary to meet operational needs and/or maximise efficiency'. Both sides were keen to avoid dispute. Jaguar said it believed there was still room for negotiation. A senior TGWU official added that the union believed that a settlement could be reached that the workforce would find acceptable. The offer guaranteed that there would be no compulsory redundancies provided the workforce continued to back efficiencies, and gave greater security of earnings where workers had to be laid off.

QUESTIONS

1 a What type of trade union is TGWU? [5]

   b Explain the advantages and disadvantages to Jaguar of negotiating through the TGWU, as opposed to dealing directly with the workforce. [10]

2 a Why have the Jaguar workforce rejected the management pay offer? [5]

   b Evaluate the consequences of the breakdown of pay negotiations for both the company and the workforce. [15]

3 Explain how ACAS could have been used to resolve this potential dispute. [5]

4 What rules will the union have to follow if it wants to call a strike? [5]

5 Applying the work of different human resource theorists, produce a report on how the management of Jaguar could introduce the proposals and avoid an industrial dispute. [15]

Total [60]

LOW MORALE IN HOSPITAL

The Queen Mary II is an NHS Trust hospital. Located in the Midlands it is a large busy hospital that employs over 1,000 full time staff and 700 part time staff. It is an institution that has gone through considerable change over the last ten years, changes that have seen the relationship between workers and management deteriorate. Doctors have become increasingly overworked both in terms of the performance targets on waiting lists they have to achieve, and also on the growing amount of paper work they have to complete. The nursing staff also have very low morale. They feel underpaid for the job they do, particularly given the increased workload that has resulted from the hospital becoming an NHS Trust. This is made worse by a constant shortage of staff due to recruitment problems. As if this is not enough, ancillary staff such as porters, kitchen staff and secretaries are threatening industrial action over pay and conditions.

The Government has told the hospital management that it will increase its annual operating budget in line with inflation, which is currently running at two percent. However, the costs of materials such as drugs, have increased by five percent, which means that staff will have to be made redundant if the Trust is to operate within its budget. The Government, which is concerned to recruit the best managers for the NHS, has just agreed to increase senior management salaries at NHS Trusts by 15 percent when doctors and nurses are due to receive less than four percent.

QUESTIONS

1 a Outline the role of the BMA. [5]
   b In what ways do you think the operation of the BMA might both help and hinder the management of the Queen Mary II NHS Trust? [5]

2 If the ancillary staff at the hospital resort to industrial action:
   a What form might that action take? [5]
   b How might the management try to resolve the dispute? [5]

3 a Discuss the key motivational problems facing the Queen Mary II. [10]
   b Produce a report outlining a strategy for dealing with these problems. [15]

4 As an NHS manager, argue the case for and against the management of the Queen Mary II hospital accepting the 15 percent pay offer. [15]

Total [60]

Index